$2.95X

Romanticism and Realism

Edmund Kean as Richard III. 19th-century engraving.
Harvard Theatre Collection

MASTERWORKS OF WORLD DRAMA

ROMANTICISM
AND
REALISM

Anthony Caputi

CORNELL UNIVERSITY

D. C. HEATH AND COMPANY

Copyright © 1968 by Raytheon Education Company

All rights reserved. No part of this publication may be reproduced or transmitted in any form or by any means, electronic or mechanical, including photocopy, recording, or any information storage or retrieval system, without permission in writing from the publisher. Printed in the United States of America.

Library of Congress Catalog Card number 68-15400

CONTENTS

THE DRAMA OF *Romanticism and Realism*
introductory essay   ix

Heinrich von Kleist
PRINCE FRIEDRICH OF HOMBURG   3
translated by James Kirkup

Georg Büchner
DANTON'S DEATH   64
translated by Stephen Spender and Goronwy Rees

Percy Bysshe Shelley
THE CENCI   117

Nicolai Gogol
THE INSPECTOR GENERAL   182
translated by B. G. Guerney

Ivan Turgenev
A MONTH IN THE COUNTRY   247
translated by George Rapall Noyes

Acknowledgments

DANTON's DEATH by Georg Büchner. © 1938 by Stephen Spender. Translated by Stephen Spender and Goronwy Rees. Published 1938 by Faber & Faber, Ltd., London. Reprinted by permission of the Harold Matson Company, Inc.

THE INSPECTOR GENERAL by Nicolai Gogol. Translated and copyright 1943, 1968 by Bernard Guilbert Guerney. In its present publication *Inspector General* is intended solely for the reading public, all rights of dramatic presentation, in any medium or media whatsoever, being reserved by the Translator, care of the Publisher.

A MONTH IN THE COUNTRY by Ivan Turgenev and translated by George Rapall Noyes. Reprinted by permission of Harvard University.

PRINCE FRIEDRICH OF HOMBURG by Heinrich von Kleist and translated by James Kirkup. Reprinted by permission of Curtis Brown Ltd., London.

Grateful acknowledgment is made for indispensable help in obtaining illustrations
—to MISS HELEN D. WILLARD, *Curator of the Harvard Theatre Collection, and her staff.*
—to PROFESSOR A. M. NAGLER *of Yale University, who made available pictures from his own collection and from his book,* A Source Book in Theatrical History.

Romanticism and Realism

The Drury Lane Theater in 1813.
The second, enlarged theater
had been destroyed by fire in 1809;
the third Drury Lane, shown
in this contemporary print,
was patterned after
the theater at Bordeaux
(Vol. V, pp. 214–215).
Harvard Theatre Collection

THE DRAMA OF *Romanticism and Realism*

THE DIFFUSION OF ROMANTIC DRAMA   The eighteenth century had witnessed the slow emergence of Romanticism, a cultural movement that had begun discreetly, then crossed national borders to swell by the end of the century to an international revolution in sensibility and values. As part of this movement, a kind of cross-fertilization between dramatic literatures had developed which led, gradually, to the merger of distinct traditions in a broad tradition. Although each drama retained its national idiosyncracies, national differences were progressively blurred and the growing commonalty of orientation and direction was accentuated. By the first decade of the nineteenth century, Romantic drama was an international institution.

In theater architecture and dramatic production Romanticism gave new impetus to many of the reforms introduced but not realized in the eighteenth century. Because the theater continued to flourish as a popular entertainment, the number of theaters continued to increase. The new theaters, however, became progressively smaller in size in response to Romantic esthetic theories. In general, these theories sought to base theater practice on the premise that theatrical art was a species of magic—poetical, musical, in its most perfect realizations, ineffable. In practice the theory typically produced a paradoxical blend of verse, bravura, and rather fanciful attempts at authenticity. In scene-design, for example, a passion for accuracy developed with the new vogue for historical drama. August Wilhelm Iffland (1759–1814) produced Schiller with huge casts and extravagant sets; Francois-Joseph Talma (1763–1826) attempted realistic treatments of antiquity in France; and Charles Kean (1811–1868) became famous for his elaborate stagings of Shakespeare. Actually much of this work was highly confused and inconsistent —fancifully realistic rather than authentic—but it focussed attention on sets and backgrounds as it had rarely been focussed before, and it made of the craft of painting detailed panoramic scenes a fine art.

The limitless possibilities of carefully designed sets, and particularly of so-called realistic settings, were not fully imagined, much less realized, however, until the discovery and exploitation of controlled light in the theater. Of course covered theaters had been lighted in some way or other from earliest times, at first by candles, and then by oil lamps. But it was not until the introduction of gaslight in 1817 in London that light could be easily located in any part of the theater and be easily controlled. This innovation, coupled with the gradual introduction of the limelight and arclight, both of which provided brilliant spotlights, immensely increased the director's power to control the stage picture and, accordingly, greatly enhanced interest in that picture. It is scarcely surprising, then, that with the gradual perfection of controlled light came the interest in realistic stage backgrounds that finally replaced the wing-and-backdrop scheme with the box set. The box set, with its real walls and moldings, its operative doors, and its ample and appropriate furniture, announced a new era in stagecraft and the ascendancy of a new dramatic idiom. First seen at the Court Theater of Mannheim as early as 1804, in France as early as 1811, where Goethe had criticized it, then in England in 1832 in the work of Mme. Julia Vestris (1797–1856), a pioneer in Realist theater, the box set was firmly established in Mme. Vestris' famous production in 1841 of Dion Boucicault's *London Assurance.*

Much the same interest in authenticity can be traced in the arts of costuming and acting in the early nineteenth century. Despite the pioneer efforts at historical costuming made in the eighteenth century, serious study of the subject did not get underway until the Romantic period, with actor-directors like Charles Macready (1793–1873), Mme. Vestris, and Talma leading the way. A key name here was that of James Robinson Planché (1796–1880); his influence with directors like Mme. Vestris and Charles Kean and his scholarship in *The History of British Costume* (1844) were crucial during the years in which costuming was emerging as one of the arts of the theater. In acting, meantime, the same interest in life-like effects was to be seen in the increased popularity of a natural style. Among the Romantics, it is true, the new style was temporarily eclipsed by the extravagant and frequently brilliant bravura manner of players like Edmund Kean (1789–1833) and Talma. But the interest in a naturalness persisted even through the most flamboyant years of Romantic drama to emerge with the box set and other evidences of the new Realist idiom toward mid-century.

By the mid-nineteenth century the picture of theatrical art in Europe was much the same everywhere, but the same in that everywhere several modes of production, several acting styles, and several distinct dramatic idioms existed side by side. Neoclassicism survived in its classics and as a mode of production in the acting style that had been transmitted with them; Romanticism persisted in the continued popularity of the historical play, as a mode of production in the use of extravagant settings, and as an acting style in the continuing supremacy of certain instinctive actors; Realism achieved a secure footing as drama was gradually produced to take advantage of the new discoveries in stagecraft. In England and Germany, indeed, there were even pioneer attempts to revive the stage and the method of Shakespearean production. The future belonged to Realism, but only after the confusion of many decades of eclecticism, and then with no guarantee of permanence.

Emanating from Germany, where it had already achieved definition and distinction, the Romantic drama spread during the first few decades of the nineteenth century to provoke theatrical revolts all over Europe. In Germany, too, the impetus of the movement continued strong. A new generation of writers appeared, less catholic in their outlook than the first, more chauvanistic in their commitment to patriotic themes, more fervid in their inquiry into the vagaries and abnormalities of human character, and more sensational in their attachment to the grotesque and the gothic, but no less productive and impressive as playwrights.

The most important figure at the turn of the century was Heinrich von Kleist (1777–1811), a rather neglected writer in his time, but one whose tormented and isolated life led him to anticipate brilliantly the subjective emphasis of the next few decades. Always preoccupied with the conflict between the individual will and society, Kleist handled it with most success, perhaps, in *The Prince of Homburg* (1810), an historical tragedy on the model provided by Schiller, and in comedies like *The Broken Jug* (1805), which ultimately became one of his most popular plays. Yet it was his influential studies of wild, almost paranoic extremes of character in plays like *Penthesilea* (1808) which first opened up the vein of psychological study that his successors were to work with increasing frequency. A solid craftsman and a painstakingly careful writer—despite his chaotic life—Kleist stands as an intermediate figure between the generation of Schiller and the young dramatists who, though scarcely acknowledging him, were often to follow his lead.

Among these young writers, Karl Ferdinand Gutzkow (1811–1878) is readily associated with the political emphasis of much of late Romanticism in Germany. One of the leaders of the political movement known as the Young Germany, he produced a dramatization of its ideology in *King Saul* (*c*.1839), though he also wrote bourgeois drama, comedies, and dramatic satires, as well as other historical plays. The Austrian Franz Grillparzer (1791–1872), on the other hand, reflected all the interests of the Romantics while accommodating them to a theatrical tradition which, in Vienna, had always remained distinctly popular. His early plays, including *The Ancestress* (1817) and *The Golden Fleece Trilogy* (1818–1821), are skillful dramatizations of what Grillparzer understood to be the torments and anxieties of his age; *King Ottocar's Fortune and End* (1823) treats the contemporary political scene in terms of historical analogue; and *The Jewess of Toledo* (published posthumously) is a powerful psychological study in the manner of Kleist. Perhaps because he was constrained to bend his creative impulses to meet practical theatrical needs more frequently than his contemporaries, the best of Grillparzer's plays are among the few from this period that still hold the stage. Probably the best playwright of this group, however, was the short-lived genius Georg Büchner (1813–1837). A friend of Gutzkow's, but so much more radical in his political opinions that he has been called an early Marxist, Büchner wrote only three plays, in each of which he went so far beyond either the Romantic or the budding Realist drama of his time that he is extremely difficult to classify historically. The satirical-romance *Leonce and Lena* (1836) may somehow owe a technical debt to Alfred de Musset's fantasies, but its bitter comedy has no parallel in the early or mid-nineteenth century. In *Danton's Death* (1835) and the fragment *Woyzeck* (published posthumously) Büchner took history as his point of departure in the manner typical of many Romantic historical dramatists. Yet he treated it from a critical, deterministic point of view suggestive rather of the present century than of the last, and, in *Woyzeck* at least, ordered his materials by a dramatic method that has frequently been described as early Expressionism. Like his contemporaries, Büchner was revolutionary; but while his dissatisfaction with contemporary revolutionary programs led him into political and intellectual isolation, his impatience with contemporary dramatic forms prompted him to develop a loose, chronicle structure that caused him to be all but entirely neglected in his time. Although he has frequently been associated with the Realists who were shortly to follow him, his deeper kinship with much later developments is witnessed by the fact that he has won a following only in the present century.

By mid-century, in any event, the important work in German Romantic drama was complete. Büchner was dead, and Grillparzer had passed his prime. By the 1840's, moreover, Friederich Hebbel (1813–1863) had appeared and introduced the new point of view and dramatic method soon to be known as Realism. Reared in an atmosphere of poverty and hardship, Hebbel turned his intimate knowledge of the grayness and grubbiness of German middle-class and working-class life to account in plays that unite carefully rendered, realistic surfaces with new standards of seriousness. Throughout his career as a playwright he pursued a passionate study of the historical process, both for the evolutionary tendencies implicit in it and for the tragic conflicts which it produced in individuals. This philosophical purpose is perhaps most evident in such conspicuous attempts to interpret German history as we find in the trilogy *The Nibelungs* (1861), though it had its widest influence when applied to contemporary problems and backgrounds, as in his masterpiece *Maria Magdalena* (1844). With Hebbel German drama entered a new phase, bringing to a conclusion a record in Romantic drama which no other country was to equal and to which all were to look.

In England, where by the end of the eighteenth century the Romantic Revolt was already in full career, the response to the Romantic achievement in Germany was quick and ambitious. By this time English theater had largely degenerated to melodramas, farces, and water ballets; the most serious work consisted of rather wooden translations of plays by Kotzebue; good, new plays by English playwrights were unknown. Among the voices of protest against this mediocrity, none were more vociferous than those of the Romantics, and no group applied itself more seriously to the task of creating a new, vital drama. It is one of the ironies of dramatic history that, though all the English Romantic poets wrote plays, despite their energy and talent the movement was stillborn in England.

Yet explanations for its failure are not difficult to find. To begin with, despite the genius of Wordsworth, Coleridge, Byron, and Keats, they were poets and not playwrights. Turning as they did to the rather awesome and sometimes ponderous example of Schiller and Goethe and, more remotely, to the Elizabethan tradition for their models, they produced for the most part interesting dramatic poems–long, historical, and often distinguished by superior lyrical passages–but poems deficient in the qualities that make a play a play. With very few exceptions, the plays of this movement are so little adapted to the exigencies of the theater that they were never produced and, even today, comprise a special body of closet drama. Of the poets, in fact, only Percy Bysshe Shelley (1792–1822) succeeded in writing a stageworthy play in his powerful historical tragedy *The Cenci* (*c.*1819), and even it was not performed until late in the nineteenth century because of its treatment of incest. Probably the most successful playwright of those to carry forward the reform in England was Edward Bulwer-Lytton (1803–1873), whose *Lady of Lyons* (1838) and *Richelieu* (1839) won considerable success. By the time of Bulwer-Lytton, however, the Realists had proposed their solution to the problem of decay; Bulwer-Lytton's *Money* (1841), produced in the year that saw the establishment of the box set, is an early English example of the Realist method.

In France, meantime, despite its crucial contributions to international Romanticism, the Romantic movement in letters, and especially in the drama, was retarded by successive decades of internal confusion, war, and the lingering influence of tradition. During the early years of the nineteenth century Guilbert de Pixerécourt (1773–1844), a popular writer of melodramas, prepared for the Romantic playwrights with his emphasis on lavish spectacle. But these writers did not appear until late in the third decade, when the movement was already in its last phase in Germany and England. Then, however, French Romantic drama arrived attended by all the clamor and passion of a new declaration of the rights of man.

Victor Hugo (1802–1885) set forth the manifesto for the new drama in his "Preface" to *Cromwell* (1827), a play designed to illustrate the new principles, but, as even Hugo admitted, too long and confused to be produced. Rigorously anti-Neoclassical, Hugo called for a new discovery of the world, a new dedication to the high calling of depicting man and his condition as they are–complex, grotesque, confused, mysterious–and all this without the constraints and artificialities of rigid verse forms, long *tirades,* and the unities. The central structural aim, he argued, should be to achieve a unity of impression. Having failed to exemplify these principles for the public in *Cromwell* or in *Marion Delorme* (which was prevented by the censors), he finally launched the program with the riotous opening of *Hernani* in 1830. As a play, unfortunately, *Hernani* suffers from the faults that mar most of Hugo's plays and much French Romantic drama. A long, flamboyant historical play in verse, it contains many fine lyrical passages and occasionally a stunning theatrical moment, but, lacking a disciplined structure, it is sprawling and confused. Hugo tried repeatedly, in the luridly grotesque *The King at Play* (1832), in *Lucrèce Borgia* (1833), and in *Marie Tudor* (1833). His best play, probably because it is his best controlled, is *Ruy Blas* (1838), a flaming romance laid in Renaissance Spain; his last, *The Burgraves* (1843), is his most incoherent. .

The novelist Alexandre Dumas (1803–1870) was a better craftsman than Hugo, if one similarly addicted to excess in everything. Actually, it was Dumas who inaugurated the Romantic drama in France before the noisy first-night of *Hernani* with his *Henry III and His Court* (1829). Thereafter, he wrote a great many plays in the historical form, never achieving distinction, but usually sustaining a level of professional competence. His best work appears in *Stockholm, Fontainbleau, Rome* (1830), which has many powerful moments, and *Antony* (1831), a searching study of a Byronic hero which recalls the psychological dramas of Kleist.

Easily the best dramatist of this explosive, shortlived movement, however, was the poet Alfred de Musset (1810–1857). After an initial fiasco that so disappointed him that he rarely had his plays produced, de Musset sufficiently disengaged himself from the tradition taking shape around him to be relatively free of the extravagances that defeat so much of his contemporaries' work. Of his historical tragedies, his *Lorenzaccio* (*c.*1834) is perhaps the best French play of the type from this period, but it was written more with the model of his idol Shakespeare before him than that of Hugo. De Musset's artistic isolation in his time also had the advantage of enabling him to cultivate dramatic forms and a dramatic style atypical of the movement. Perhaps his most memorable work, though it was practically unknown in his time, comprises the series of comedy-romances that includes *Don't Trifle With Love* (*c.*1834) and *Fantasio* (1833); in them and in the somewhat darker *The Caprices of Marianne* (*c.*1834) he combined a delicacy of sentiment and subtlety of perception with an elegance of language and style not seen since Marivaux.

Altogether, in France too the Romantic drama had only limited success. Despite the excitement of its brief vogue and the promise of its illustrious partisans, by 1845 it had already given way to a re-charged version of Neoclassicism and the new Realist idiom. Even during Romantic drama's most productive years, in fact, the most successful French playwright had been its archenemy, the immensely prolific pioneer in the Realist mode, Eugène Scribe (1791–1861). In the course of a career during which he wrote more than 400 plays and attempted practically every known dramatic type—except the five-act drama in verse—Scribe gradually modified every dramatic type he touched. He won tremendous success with an upgraded version of vaudeville-comedy; he devised a tightened and simplified form of historical drama in which, in plays like *The Glass of Water* (1840), he did some of his best work. But undoubtedly his most important achievement was the ingeniously constructed version of bourgeois drama that came to be known as "the well-made play." Typically focussed on a single social question, such modest studies of contemporary manners and morals as

Marriage For Money (1827) were so cleverly designed that it has been said that their plots solve themselves. Yet whatever their faults—they are frequently marred by sentimentality and the defects of Scribe's haste and facility—they gave currency in their time to a new structural formula and a new conception of dramatic seriousness. In the mid-decades of the nineteenth century Scribe was not merely the most popular international playwright, but also the most widely imitated.

THE EMERGENCE OF RUSSIAN DRAMA Russia was the last major European country to develop a national drama and, accordingly, the last to enter and impress itself on the increasingly international theatrical scene of the nineteenth century. Cut off by geography and tradition from the history that had always sustained some form of theatrical activity in western European countries, Russia developed virtually no theater until the middle of the seventeenth century. To that point entertainments at court had consisted largely of performing bears, boxing, and the drolleries of the court jester; and the Eastern Church, in which the liturgies were epic or narrative rather than dramatic, had produced no religious drama. In the mid-seventeenth century, however, mystery plays from Poland were introduced that awakened an interest both in dramatic achievements elsewhere and in native potentialities. Called Polish jests, these plays were first taken up by scholarly communities like the Roman Catholic Ecclesiastical Academy at Kiev where they were performed by students, and in time, despite the resistance of the Orthodox Church, they stimulated a modest production among such learned Russian writers as Dmitri Tuptalo of Rostov (1651–1709). As these plays made their way into courtly circles, Russian drama took its first halting steps.

Thereafter, the history of theatrical developments in Russia was for a considerable period the expression of the tastes and cultural ambitions of successive Czars and members of the imperial families. A key figure, Czar Alexei Mikhailovitch (r.1645–1676), first brought the mystery plays to court and organized a court theater. When the Russian actors proved too primitive, he imported a German troupe and in 1672 had a wooden theater built for them. Although we know almost nothing about this theater except that it did not long survive, it is clear that through the Germans' influence the mystery plays gradually gave way to *Hauptsaktionen* and Hanswurst farces and that for more than fifty years they comprised the fare presented in the royal apartments and elsewhere. After Czar Alexei, his daughter Sophia Alexeyevna carried on his work by organizing performances and by herself writing at least one miracle play in verse and translating plays from German and French. Under her auspices the Russian court had its first view of French drama in a tremendously influential production of Molière's *The Doctor In Spite of Himself*. Under the leadership of Peter the Great (r.1689–1725), finally, the westernizing tendency in all cultural matters became political principle. He imported a German company for which he built a theater in 1702; he instituted the training of Russian actors by German masters; he ordered the schools to give performances of mystery plays; and, when his court moved to St. Petersburg, he ordered that a new theater be one of the first buildings erected. Performances at the Imperial Theater in St. Petersburg began in 1724.

After Peter's death German influence waned as, under the leadership of Empress Anna Ivanovna (r.1730–1740), Italian and French companies were brought to the capital. In 1735 she imported an Italian company led by Francesco Araja, who introduced opera and ballet into Russia; during her reign, too, the Imperial Ballet School and the first Russian chorus were founded. A few years later, under the Empress Elizabeth (r.1741–1762), the first stone theater was built for the French company then in residence. With German, Dutch, English, Italian, and French companies making frequent appearances by mid-eighteenth century, theatrical activity in Russia was, for the limited audiences that witnessed it, reasonably intense and, to judge from the touring companies, of relatively high quality. But it was almost entirely foreign, and, as the century wore on, increasingly French.

Yet important strides were taken during the reign of the Empress Elizabeth toward the establishment of a national drama and theater. Toward mid-century the first serious dramatists in Russian appeared in the persons of M. V. Lomonosov (1715–1765) and Alexander Sumarokov (1717–1777). The more important of the two, Sumarokov wrote tragedies and comedies on French Neoclassical models and achieved a great success with his tragedy on a Russian subject, *Khorev* (1747), which was produced at court in 1749 with the participation of a corps of cadets. An immensely versatile, if a rather difficult man, Sumarokov also wrote a theoretical work on tragedy and directed the Court Theater after 1756, until his many quarrels caused him to be dismissed. During these decades, too, the first opera in Russian was produced and the first provincial theaters were established. Very important in the latter achievement was Feodor Volkov (1729–1763), the son of a wealthy middle-class family in Yaroslav, who, having seen the Italians in St. Petersburg, first gave amateur performances in his father's leather factory and then, with the support of local nobles and merchants, founded a local public theater in 1755. Volkov did everything in this project: he designed the building, directed the plays, acted in them, and even translated the texts. When his fame reached St. Petersburg, he was summoned to the court, where a theater was built for him; ultimately he was sent to Moscow to found a theater there.

During the last four decades of the eighteenth century these tendencies continued: an awareness of theater spread as further theaters were built and ever larger numbers of Russians participated in it; yet the actual circle of its influence was limited largely to the imperial household and noble families, and the plays performed were still dominantly French. During the reign of Catherine II (r.1762–1796) a people's theater was established in St. Petersburg and Moscow, and the first permanent dramatic school was founded in 1779; Catherine herself, in fact, translated many plays. Denis Ivanovitch Fonvizin (1745–1792) was the most important playwright of the period; a disciple of Voltaire and Rousseau, he introduced the posture of reform and a new naturalness of expression into Russian drama with *The Brigadier* (c.1767). Under Alexander I (r.1801–1825), still further theaters were built, repertories were enlarged to include most of the European classics, and Romanticism gained a foothold by way of the new pathetic tragedies and productions of Schiller. The leading playwright of this generation was Vladislav Alexandrovitch Ozerov (1769–1816), who, among other plays, wrote the very successful *Dmitri Donskoi* (1807), a Russian historical play that bears clear traces of the new sentimentalism.

But the principal evidence of the spread of theater at the end of the eighteenth century comes from the rise of the so-called Nobles' Theaters. As the Russian nobility achieved privilege and status comparable to those enjoyed by their counterparts in western nations, they gradually took a more important role in theatrical affairs. In the cities they sponsored productions of opera and organized troupes for performances in private theaters; at the end of the century there were fifteen such troupes in Moscow alone. In the provinces they established what were known as Serfs Theaters, or troupes consisting of serfs who were trained to entertain the local nobility when they were in the country. All this activity served, of course, to spread a knowledge of theater and to broaden the base of Russian participation in it. But it did not change so much as anticipate changes in the basic situation: the theater at the beginning of the nineteenth century was still the plaything of the privileged classes; Russian talent, even that of the few peasants who rose to prominence by way of the Serfs Theater, was still constrained by foreign models; Russian drama, what there was of it, was largely imitative. By the first decade of the nineteenth century Russian theater still had very little vital connection with the life of the nation; it was for the most part a dilettante's theater.

The flowering of a national literature and a national drama in Russia did not occur until well into the first quarter of the nineteenth century. By this time literature had come under the influence of a mixed class consisting of certain members of the lesser nobility, the liberal intellectuals, and the educated bourgeoisie, a group that attuned itself eagerly to the liberal idealism of Romanticism. This class was stimulated not only by the accomplishments of Romanticism elsewhere, but also by a new sense of national importance following the victory over Napoleon, and it produced the first generation of great Russian writers in men like Lermontov, Pushkin, and Gogol. Guided by members of this group, Russian drama abruptly took a new direction by focusing on Russian history, the Russian social scene, and Russian problems. Although many of the important new plays were not immediately performed, the best work was done in historical tragedy, dramas of social protest, and dramatic satire.

Even the earliest of these developments reflects the speed with which Russian playwrights, once they had cultivated a taste for protest and criticism, were to move through Romanticism to Realism. Primarily a poet, Alexander Pushkin (1799–1837) always remained rather detached from the theatrical scene, but he contributed to the sudden improvement in the quality of dramatic writing and to the break with the derivative past with a small group of plays. His best, *Boris Godunov* (1825), was a historical tragedy based on a Russian subject and cast in the loose, quasi-Shakespearean form of a dramatic chronicle; it was unpublished until 1830, and was not performed until late in the century. Closer to the theatrical world than Pushkin, and far more influential within it, was Alexander Griboedov (1795–1829), a writer of Romantic dramas of protest and one of the most cultivated men of his time. Although Griboedov wrote only a few plays, the most important of them, a bold study of manners and morals entitled *Wit*

Works Woe (1823), contained so scathing an attack on the government and society that it was long known only by way of circulating manuscripts. It became in its time a *cause célèbre,* and so influential that it provided a major stimulus to the vogue for social criticism that in the next few decades carried the new writers ever closer to Realism.

But the masterpiece of this first explosion of native dramatic talent was to come from yet another writer who is better known for his non-dramatic works, Nicolai Gogol (1809–1852). Gogol had tried to enter the theater as an actor, had failed, and had turned to journalism, teaching, and fiction. Then, in 1836, he crowned the young movement in national drama with *The Inspector General,* his most ambitious dramatic effort. This play, a brilliant satirical comedy on provincial society and officialdom, all but sealed the future of dramatic Realism in Russia. Performed at court before Nicholas I (*r.*1825–1855) in 1836, the play produced an effect even more electrifying than that of *Wit Works Woe:* Nicholas was outraged, but the literary and theatrical world immediately saw in the play a masterpiece and in its pungent, hard-hitting critical manner the promise of the future. Although melodrama and Romantic tragedies continued for some time to be the principal fare in the theaters, especially under the conservative Nicholas I, and although Romantic tragedies continued to be written well into the last quarter of the century, even by mid-century the best Russian plays invariably owed an essential debt to *The Inspector General.*

By mid-century, too, related efforts in acting and production methods were making certain, if slow headway in Russia, though the leaders in the movement continued to be playwrights. Less gifted than Gogol but immensely successful and influential in his time, Alexander Ostrovsky (1823–1886) wrote more than fifty plays and excelled in a variety of dramatic types. His most effective work is to be found in his witty, shrewdly observed studies of the bourgeoisie, including *Never Sit in a Stranger's Sleigh* (1853) and *Poverty is No Crime* (1854). Less popular in his time but a better dramatist, Ivan Turgenev (1818–1883) gave only ten years of his literary life to dramatic composition and experimented with a variety of forms before discovering the vein in which he was to do his best work. In *The Parasite* (1848) and *The Single Man* (1849) he produced the earliest of the tragi-comic studies of manners that later were to bulk so large in Russian dramatic literature. With *A Month in the Country* (1850), a play of the same type, but richer for its moving and searching treatment of character, he wrote his dramatic masterpiece and the first play to reveal the profound possibilities of the new idiom.

By mid-century, then, Russia had not only established a national drama and theater, it was already developing playwrights who were to lead the dramatic movement to which all Europe was turning. Once dramatic Realism was secure, Russian genius flourished on it in much the same way German genius had on Romanticism and French genius on Neoclassicism. In 1850, however, Realism as a cultural and artistic movement was still in its first phase in Russia and elsewhere; what was still the beginning for Russia was by the mysterious chemistry of cultural history yet another beginning for European drama.

Bibliography

English and French Drama, 1800–1850:

Arvin, Neil S., *Eugène Scribe and the French Theater, 1815–1860,* Cambridge, Mass., 1924.

Disher, Maurice, *Blood and Thunder; Mid-Victorian Melodrama and Its Origins,* London, 1949.

Downer, Alan S., "Players and the Painted Stage: Nineteenth Century Acting," *PMLA,* LXI (1946), 522–76.

George, A. J., *The Development of French Romanticism,* Syracuse, N.Y., 1955.

Lacey, Alexander, *Pixerécourt and the French Romantic Drama,* Toronto, 1928.

Matthews, Brander, *French Dramatists of the Nineteenth Century,* 5th ed., New York, 1914.

Melcher, Edith, *Stage Realism in France From Diderot to Antoine,* Bryn Mawr, Pa., 1928.

Nicoll, Allardyce, *A History of Early Nineteenth Century Drama, 1800–1850,* 2 vols., Cambridge, 1930.

Rowell, George, *The Victorian Theater,* London, 1956.

Watson, Ernest B., *Sheridan To Robertson: A Study of the Nineteenth Century London Stage,* Cambridge, Mass., 1926.

German Drama, 1800–1850:

Kaufmann, F. W., *German Dramatists of the Nineteenth Century,* Los Angeles, 1940.

Klenze, Camillo von, *From Goethe to Hauptmann, Studies in a Changing Culture,* New York, 1926.

Rees, George Brychan, *Friedrich Hebbel as a Dramatic Artist,* London, 1930.

Walzel, Oskar F., *German Romanticism,* New York, 1932.

Willoughby, Leonard A., *The Romantic Movement in Germany,* New York, 1930.

Witkowski, Georg, *German Drama of the Nineteenth Century,* trans. L. E. Horning, London, 1909.

Russian Drama to 1850:

Baring, Maurice, *Outline of Russian Literature,* London, 1915.

Coleman, Arthur P., *Humour in the Russian Comedy From Catherine to Gogol,* New York, 1925.

Derzhavin, Konstantin N., *Century of the State Dramatic Theatre, 1832–1932,* trans. L. Shillingovsky, Leningrad, 1932.

Fülöp-Miller, René, and Joseph Gregor, *Russian Theatre: Its Character and History,* trans. Paul England, Philadelphia, 1930.

Hare, Richard, *Russian Literature From Pushkin to the Present Day,* London, 1947.

Lavrin, Janko, *From Pushkin to Mayakovsky,* London, 1948.

Macleod, Joseph T. G., *Actors Across the Volga,* London, 1946.

Sayler, Oliver M., *The Russian Theatre,* New York, 1922.

Slonim, Marc, *Russian Theater From the Empire to the Soviets,* New York, 1962.

Spector, Ivar, *Golden Age of Russian Literature,* rev. ed., Caldwell, Idaho, 1952.

Varneke, D. V., *History of the Russian Theatre, Seventeenth Through Nineteenth Century,* trans. Boris Brasol, New York, 1951.

Heinrich von Kleist

Heinrich von Kleist (1777–1811) was the most important playwright of the second generation of German Romantic writers. Neglected and tormented during his lifetime, Kleist tried most of the dramatic forms popular among his contemporaries, including comedy with a national setting and subject in THE BROKEN JUG, *widely considered one of the finest plays of its kind in German, and historical tragedy featuring an idealistic hero in* THE PRINCE OF HOMBURG. *Perhaps even more important to the Romantic movement and to subsequent drama, however, were plays like* PENTHESILEA, *in which he demonstrated the artistic value of psychological studies of morbid, deranged characters; it was in this vein that subsequent playwrights were most often to follow his lead. An ardent patriot, Kleist also served as a public official at various posts and wrote history in support of the cause of German nationalism.*

Chronology

1777 Born at Frankfort-on-Oder.

1792 Entered the Prussian army as an ensign.

1796 Served in the Rhine campaign.

1799 Retired from the service with the rank of lieutenant. He entered the University of Frankfort-on-Oder to study law and philosophy.

1800 Entered the Ministry of Finance in Berlin.

1801 Travelled to Paris and Switzerland, where he settled at Lake Thun. He met Heinrich Zschokke and Ludwig Wieland.

1802 Returned to Germany and visited Goethe, Schiller, and Wieland.

1803 Wrote the tragedy *The Schroffenstein Family* and began *Robert Guiscard*. He travelled to Leipzig, Dresden, and Paris.

1804 Returned to Berlin where he took a post in the Department for the Administration of Crown Lands.

c.1805 Wrote the comedy *The Broken Jug*.

1807 Arrested by the French in Dresden as a spy and imprisoned at Châlons-sur-Marne. Released, he returned to Berlin.

1808 Returned again to Dresden, where with Heinrich Müller he published the journal *Phoebus*. He wrote *Käthchen of Heilbronn* and *Penthesilea*. *The Broken Jug* was performed at Weimar under Goethe's auspices and was a failure.

1809 Travelled to Prague, then to Berlin.

1810–11 Edited the *Berliner Abendblätter,* an evening paper, and wrote *Prince Friedrich of Homburg*.

1811 On November 21, shot himself near Potsdam.

Selected Bibliography

Blankenagel, John Carl, *The Dramas of Heinrich von Kleist,* Chapel Hill, N.C., 1931.

March, Richard, *Heinrich von Kleist,* Cambridge, 1954.

Silz, Walter, *Early German Romanticism, Its Founders and Heinrich von Kleist,* Cambridge, Mass., 1929.

————, *Heinrich von Kleist, Studies in His Work and Literary Character,* Philadelphia, 1962.

————, *Heinrich von Kleist's Conception of the Tragic,* Baltimore, 1923.

Stahl, E. L., *Heinrich von Kleist's Dramas,* Oxford, 1948.

PRINCE FRIEDRICH

OF

HOMBURG

by Heinrich von Kleist

English Version by James Kirkup

Characters

FRIEDRICH WILHELM, *Elector of Brandenburg*
HIS WIFE
PRINCESS NATALIA OF ORANGE, *his niece, colonel-in-chief of a regiment of dragoons*
FIELD-MARSHAL DÖRFLING
PRINCE FRIEDRICH ARTHUR OF HOMBURG, *colonel of cavalry*
COLONEL KOTTWITZ, *of the regiment of the Princess of Orange*
HENNINGS *and* TRUCHSS, *colonels in the infantry*
COUNT HOHENZOLLERN, *of the Elector's suite*
GOLTZ; COUNT GEORG VON SPARREN; STRANZ; SIEGFRIED VON MÖRNER;
and COUNT REUSS, *captains of the horse*
AN OFFICER OF THE GUARD
*Officers. Corporals and Cavalrymen. Courtiers. Ladies of the Court. Pages.
Guards. Servants. Townspeople*

The year is 1675

Act One

Scene 1

*Fehrbellin: a garden in the old French style. In the background, a castle with a
balustraded slope leading down from it. It is night. Early summer.*
(*The* PRINCE OF HOMBURG *is lying on a garden seat, his shirt open at the neck,
half-waking, half-sleeping; the seat is under an oak tree. He is plaiting himself
a wreath.*
The ELECTOR, HIS WIFE, *the* PRINCESS NATALIA OF ORANGE, *the* COUNT
OF HOHENZOLLERN, GOLTZ, *captain of the horse, and others steal quietly out
of the castle and look down upon the* PRINCE *from the balustrade. There are*
PAGES *carrying lighted torches*)

HOHENZOLLERN   There he lies, our brave cousin, the noble Prince of
                                                                Homburg!

Here to our headquarters at Fehrbellin* he has returned at last.
For the past three days, leading his troops of horse,
He has most keenly harried the routed Swedish* squadrons.   5
You, sire, gave orders that he was to pause no more
Than three hours here, time for him to get his breath again
And for his men to provide themselves with fresh supplies.
Then he was to take up his position on the heights of Hackelberg,
And launch a brisk attack upon the Swedish general Wrangel   10
Who now is attempting to make a stand along the Rhyn.

ELECTOR* That is so.

HOHENZOLLERN Well, sire, the Prince has let it be known to his commanders
That on the stroke of ten, according to our plan,
They will set out from here;   15
He himself was to snatch brief rest for his weary limbs
In order to prepare himself for the encounter ·
That is to start as soon as it is light.

ELECTOR So I was given to understand. Well, then——?

HOHENZOLLERN The hour has struck. The cavalry   20
Are in the saddle, and their horses
Paw the ground below the ramparts.
They are all ready, all but one. And that
Is their leader, the noble Prince of Homburg!
We have sought for him with lights and lanterns,   25
And where do we find him? (*He takes a torch from a* PAGE)
Here, as dreamy
As a sleep-walker.
Though you, sire, would never countenance
Our warnings on this subject,   30
The summer moonlight has bewitched him,
And led him to this secluded garden-seat,
Where, as if he were dreaming, he weaves himself
The imagined symbol of his own immortal fame:
The glorious wreath of triumph and renown!   35

ELECTOR What? No!

HOHENZOLLERN These are the facts. Look,
You can see him lying there!

ELECTOR Is he asleep? It can't be!

HOHENZOLLERN Fast asleep. You need only call his name,   40
And you will see him suddenly collapse! (*A silence*)

---

³ A town 75 miles northwest of Berlin, Fehrbellin controlled an important pass for crossing the muddy flats
of the river Rhyn.

⁵ The Swedes were invading Brandenburg in a campaign of the Second French War with the Netherlands
(1672–1679), during which Sweden and France were arrayed against Brandenburg, Holland, Austria, and
Spain.

¹² The Elector of Brandenburg was an independent prince whose title derived from the fact that he had
formerly been called an Elector of the Holy Roman Empire. Brandenburg was a principality in northeast
Germany.

ELECTOR'S WIFE The young man is not well, I'm sure.

NATALIA He needs a doctor.

ELECTOR'S WIFE He needs our compassion.

(*To* HOHENZOLLERN) This is no time for easy jests. 45

HOHENZOLLERN (*Handing back the torch*) Have no fear, ladies.
He is in perfect health, or I'm a dead man!
The Swedes will feel the power of his arm
To-morrow in the field!
Believe me, ladies, what you see is nothing more 50
Than a passing abstraction of the mind.

ELECTOR Indeed! I thought we were living in a fairy-tale!
Come, friends, follow me,
And let us observe a little closer
This strange indisposition. (*They proceed down the slope*) 55

COURTIER (*To* PAGES) Hold back there with the torches!

HOHENZOLLERN No, let them come too!
The whole town could go up in flames,
And his mind would have no more heed of it
Than of the diamond that sparkles on his finger. 60

(*They gather round the* PRINCE: *torches flare*)

ELECTOR (*Bending over him*) What kind of wreath is he making?
A wreath of willow leaves?*

HOHENZOLLERN Hah! A wreath of willow? No, my lord,
It is a laurel wreath* he winds, 65
Such as he has seen in the portraits of the heroes
That hang in the Armoury in Berlin.

ELECTOR Where did he find a laurel bush,
Here in the sandy soil of Brandenburg?

HOHENZOLLERN The gods alone can tell us that! 70

COURTIER Sir, the gardeners here
Cultivate in the French gardens
Some queer foreign plants.

ELECTOR By heaven, how strange it is! And yet,
I think I understand 75
The fire that slumbers in this young fool's breast.

HOHENZOLLERN The fire of to-morrow's battle, I'll be bound, sire.
He's dreaming now of heaven-gazing astronomers
Who weave to-night's great stars for him
Into a victor's crown. (*The* PRINCE *gazes on the wreath*) 80

COURTIER Look, now he's finished it.

HOHENZOLLERN Oh, what a thousand pities
That there's no mirror here!
Then he would go to it, as vain as any girl,
And try his wreath on this way, that way, 85

---

[63] Symbol of grief.
[65] Symbol of victory.

As if it were a new hat covered with flowers.

ELECTOR   By Jupiter, but I must see
How far he'll go in this bedevilment. (*The* ELECTOR *takes the wreath from
the* PRINCE, *who looks at him in sudden confusion. The* ELECTOR *twists his
golden chain about the wreath and gives it to* NATALIA. *The* PRINCE *jumps up.*   90
The ELECTOR *steps away and walks slowly backwards, with* NATALIA *holding
the wreath aloft. The* PRINCE, *with outstretched arms, follows after her*)
PRINCE (*Whispering*)   Natalia! My love! My bride!
ELECTOR   Quickly, now! Away!
HOHENZOLLERN   What does the fool say?   95
COURTIER   What was that he whispered to her?
                 (*They all begin ascending the slope*)
PRINCE   Frederick! My lord! My father!
HOHENZOLLERN   What devil's got into him?
ELECTOR (*Still moving backwards*)   Open the door for me!   100
PRINCE   Oh, my mother!
HOHENZOLLERN   Why, he's mad! Mad!
ELECTOR'S WIFE   Whom does he call mother?
PRINCE (*Snatching at the wreath*)   Oh, my dearest one!
Why do you turn away from me? Natalia! (*He seizes the* PRINCESS' *glove*)   105
HOHENZOLLERN   What was that?
COURTIER   The wreath?
NATALIA   No.
HOHENZOLLERN (*Opening the door*)   Quick, come in, sire!
Let the whole scene suddenly vanish from his sight!   110
ELECTOR   Back! Back into the darkness, Frederick, Prince of Homburg!
Back into the dark and nothingness!
If you will grace us with your presence,
We shall meet again upon the field of battle.
Victory cannot be won by dreams! (*They all suddenly go inside. The door*   115
           shuts with a great rattle of chains. A silence)

Scene 2

(*The* PRINCE *stands for a moment dumbfounded outside the door, then, his hand
holding the glove against his forehead, slowly descends the slope. When he reaches
    the bottom, he turns round and gazes at the door again*)

Scene 3

(HOHENZOLLERN *returns through a gate set in the wall under the slope. He is*   120
                 followed by a PAGE)
PAGE (*Softly*)   Sir! My lord! A word! I beg of you, my lord——
HOHENZOLLERN (*Testily*)   Quiet, you little monkey! Well, what is it?
PAGE   I have been sent to you my lord—I——
HOHENZOLLERN   You'll wake him with your chattering. Well, what's the   125
                 matter?

PAGE Sir, I am sent to you by the Elector.
His Highness begs you, when the Prince awakes,
Not to breathe a word about the little trick
He played on him just now.   130
HOHENZOLLERN He might have known I wouldn't do that.
Be off with you now and chatter yourself to sleep
In some convenient tree! Hop! (*The* PAGE *off*)

Scene 4

(*Enter the* PRINCE)
HOHENZOLLERN (*Placing himself some distance behind the* PRINCE, *who is still*   135
gazing up at the door) Arthur! (*The* PRINCE *collapses*)
So! A bullet couldn't have done better
Or hit more truly at the very brain. (*He goes closer to him*)
Now I'm curious to know
What sort of tale he will concoct   140
To explain away his sleeping here. (*He leans over him*)
Arthur! Hey, what the devil's the matter with you?
What do you think you're doing here,
Alone, and in the middle of the night?
PRINCE What is it, my dear?   145
HOHENZOLLERN Well, damn me, I must tell him!
The cavalry that is under *your* command
Departed over an hour ago, and you
Lie here in the garden, sound asleep.
PRINCE What cavalry?   150
HOHENZOLLERN The Mamelukes!* By thunder,
As true as I stand here, he doesn't know
That he's a colonel in the cavalry of Brandenburg!
PRINCE (*Jumping up*) Quick! My helmet! My armour!
HOHENZOLLERN (*Ironical*) Now, where would *they* be?   155
PRINCE Over there, Heinrich, to the right,
There, on the stool!
HOHENZOLLERN Where? What stool?
PRINCE But I'm sure—I *think* I put them there,
On the stool.   160
HOHENZOLLERN Then go and take them off the stool!
PRINCE Whose glove is this? (*He stares at the glove in his hand*)
HOHENZOLLERN How should *I* know?
(*To himself*) Confound it!
He's stolen one of the Princess' gloves;   165
No one noticed it!
(*Suddenly sharper*) Come on now! Let's be off!
What are you waiting for? Come on!

151 A regimental nickname taken from a famous military force, originally made up of slaves, which seized
power in Egypt in about 1250.

PRINCE (*Throwing the glove away*)   Yes, I'm coming!
Hey, Franz, you rascal, where are you?   170
You were supposed to wake me up!
HOHENZOLLERN (*Staring at him*)   He's stark, staring mad!
PRINCE   To tell the truth, dear Heinrich,
I hardly know yet where I am.
HOHENZOLLERN   You're in Fehrbellin, you dreamy dunderhead!   175
In one of the garden walks that lie
At the rear of the castle.
PRINCE   Darkness, cover my confusion!
The moonlight must have bewitched me once again!
(*Pulling himself together*)   Forgive me! Now I know what it was.   180
Yesterday, you remember, it was so hot,
I felt it would be too warm to lie in bed to-night.
Half-dead with weariness, I crept
Into the cool of this great garden.
The night, like an Egyptian bride, all stars,   185
So soft, so warm and heavy with the scent of flowers,
Seemed to be waiting here
For me, her bridegroom,
And slowly drew me down into her arms.
What's the time?   190
HOHENZOLLERN   Half past eleven.
PRINCE   And the squadrons have set out?
HOHENZOLLERN   Upon the stroke of ten, according to plan. By now
The regiment of the Princess Natalia of Orange
Will have led them to the heights of Hackelberg,   195
Where in the morning they are to cover
The infantry's secret advance on Wrangel.
PRINCE   No matter! They have as their leader
Good old Kottwitz, who grasps thoroughly
The purpose of this manoeuvre.   200
In any case, I should have had to come back here
To headquarters, and at two o'clock in the morning, to receive
My final instructions from Field-marshal Dörfling.
So it was better, after all, that I should have stayed on here.
Come, let us go! What does the Elector know of this?   205
HOHENZOLLERN   Huh! He's long since in his bed and fast asleep. (*They are
    about to go. The* PRINCE *stops, turns, and picks up the glove*)
PRINCE   What peculiar dream was it I dreamed?
It seemed to me as if a royal castle,
All glittering with gold and silver, suddenly   210
Opened its doors to me.
And down its marble-balustraded slope
Descended towards me, like a ring of dancers,
All those who are nearest to my heart;

The Elector, and his lady, and—the third one— 215
What was her name?
HOHENZOLLERN Who was it?
PRINCE (*Pensive*) The one I am always thinking of.
There *is* only one.
HOHENZOLLERN Baroness Platen? 220
PRINCE Dear Heinrich, how could you——
HOHENZOLLERN La Ramin?
PRINCE No, friend, that's not——
HOHENZOLLERN Mademoiselle Bork? Or the Winterfeld?
PRINCE No, no! Where are your eyes? 225
You cannot see the pearl for the ring that is only its setting.
HOHENZOLLERN Devil take it! Explain yourself, man!
Which lady do you mean?
PRINCE No matter. No, no matter.
Since I awoke, her name 230
Has slipped my memory.
But—it is no matter, it does not concern——
HOHENZOLLERN Good. Well, go on with the dream.
PRINCE All right, but
You mustn't interrupt me! 235
The Elector, his forehead high as Zeus upon Olympus,
Is holding a wreath of laurel in his hand.
He comes right up to me.
My heart beats faster.
He winds his golden chain about the wreath, 240
And, so that she may lay it on my head,
He hands it to—— Oh, dear one!
HOHENZOLLERN Damn it all, to whom?
PRINCE Oh, my dear friend!
HOHENZOLLERN Well, come on, tell me! 245
PRINCE To—— Oh, it must have been Baroness Platen.
HOHENZOLLERN She's away in Prussia now.
PRINCE Baroness Platen. Really, it *must* have been her.
Or else la Ramin.
HOHENZOLLERN Eugh! La Ramin! That one with the red hair? 250
You're sure it wasn't la Platen, the one
With those sly little violet eyes? Eh?
We know she pleases you.
PRINCE *She* pleases me.
HOHENZOLLERN Well, anyhow, you say she—this woman— 255
Held out the wreath to you?
PRINCE She holds it high, like the goddess of Fame herself,
In perfect hands.
I see her lift the wreath, on which the golden chain is glittering,
As if she desires to lay its crown upon a hero's head. 260

And I, with inexpressible emotion,
Reach out my hands to grasp it:
I feel I should cast myself down before her.
And then, as the scent of flowers hanging in a valley
Is suddenly by fresh winds utterly dispersed,   265
So suddenly the faces round me vanish,
Vanish up the long and marble-balustraded slope,
On which I climb, trying to follow them: the path
Seems to stretch out infinitely to the doors of heaven.
I run from side to side and try to capture   270
One face out of all those loved ones.
But in vain! The castle door is opened wide,
A blaze of lightning flashes out, and then
The door swings to, with a heavy thunder-brattle.
Now all that remains to me of that sweet vision   275
Is a glove torn roughly from her in my dazed pursuit.
And, now I am awake again, O ye almighty gods, it is
A glove I hold here in my hand!

HOHENZOLLERN And now you think this glove belongs to *her*?
PRINCE To whom?   280
HOHENZOLLERN Why, to la Platen.
PRINCE Yes. La Platen. Really. Or—to la Ramin.
HOHENZOLLERN (*Laughing*) You're a great joker, you and your visions!
Who knows? Perhaps this glove is just
The fragrant memory of some   285
Idyllic dalliance with a real shepherdess?
The memory of an hour when
You didn't sleep?
PRINCE What! Me? By my one and only love——
HOHENZOLLERN Get along with you! For all I care,   290
It could be la Platen or la Ramin
Or anyone you care to mention.
On Sunday there is a post to Prussia.
You can write and ask your beauty
If she has lost, by any chance, a glove.   295
Away! It's nearly midnight.
PRINCE (*Dreamily, to himself*) You are right. Let's to bed.
But there is one thing more:
Is the Elector's wife still here,
And is her niece still with her,   300
The charming Princess of Orange,
Who arrived some days ago at Fehrbellin?
HOHENZOLLERN Why do you ask me that?
I really believe, the fool——
PRINCE Why?—— Oh,   305
I was ordered to place at their disposal

An escort of thirty men to lead them
Out of the theatre of war,
And as you know
I was to put Captain Ramin in charge of them.   310
HOHENZOLLERN They must have long since left.
They are surely already on the way; if not, then
On the point of departure.
Ramin waited the entire evening at the gate,
Ready to leave at any moment.   315
But let us be off. It is midnight now,
And before the battle starts
I too should like to rest awhile. (*Midnight striking as they go*)

Scene 5

(*The* ELECTOR'S WIFE *and* PRINCESS NATALIA *in travelling clothes, led by a*
COURTIER, *come in and sit down at the side of the stage.* LADIES OF THE COURT.   320
Then the ELECTOR, FIELD-MARSHAL DÖRFLING, *the* PRINCE OF HOMBURG
with the glove tucked into his collar, HOHENZOLLERN, TRUCHSS, COLONEL
HENNINGS, CAPTAIN GOLTZ, *and several other* GENERALS, COLONELS, *and*
OFFICERS)

ELECTOR What was that firing? Is it Götz?   325
DÖRFLING It is Colonel Götz, sire,
Who left yesterday with the advance party.
He has already sent an officer
To set your mind at rest about the issue of the engagement:
There was a Swedish outpost, sire, a thousand strong,   330
That had stormed the lower slopes of Hackelberg,
But Götz has got the situation in the mountains well in hand,
And tells me that you may consider
His forward position well established.
ELECTOR (*To* OFFICERS) Gentlemen, Field-marshal Dörfling here   335
Is familiar with the plan of battle I have made.
I pray you, write it down upon your tablets. (*The* OFFICERS *gather on the*
other side of the stage round the FIELD-MARSHAL *and prepare to write*)
ELECTOR (*Turning to the* COURTIER) Has Captain Ramin come with the coach?
COURTIER He'll be here in a moment, sire.   340
The horses will soon be harnessed.
ELECTOR (*Sitting on a stool behind* HIS WIFE *and the* PRINCESS) Captain Ramin
shall conduct my dear Elsa,
And thirty stout horsemen shall accompany him.
You are to go to Castle Kalkhuhn, the residence of   345
My chancellor, near Havelberg, beyond the river Havel,
Where no Swede now dare let himself be seen.
ELECTOR'S WIFE Is the ferry running again?
ELECTOR Across the Havel? Everything is under our control.

In any case, it will be daylight when you get there. (*A silence*) 350
Natalia, dear child, why are you so silent?
What is wrong with my girl?
NATALIA   Dear Uncle, I am afraid.
ELECTOR   And yet my little one has nothing to be afraid of.
She was no safer in her mother's arms. (*A silence*) 355
ELECTOR'S WIFE   When, do you think, shall we see each other again?
ELECTOR   When God has sent me victory,
As I do not doubt He will.
Perhaps in the course of the next few days.
(PAGES *come and serve the* LADIES *with refreshments.* DÖRFLING *is busy dictat-* 360
ing. The PRINCE OF HOMBURG, *tablets and pencil in hand, is staring at the*
LADIES)
DÖRFLING   Gentlemen, the plan of battle which His Highness has devised
Aims to separate the retreating Swedish troops
From the bridgehead covering their rear across the Rhyn. 365
Our aim is to destroy them. Utterly destroy them.
Colonel Hennings!
HENNINGS   Here! (*He writes*)
DÖRFLING   Who, according to our leader's plan, commands to-day
The right wing of the infantry battalions, 370
Shall endeavour, creeping through what cover he can find,
To circumvent the enemy's left wing.
Then he shall move in resolutely,
Cutting off the enemy line of retreat towards the bridges,
And, together with Baron Truchss—— 375
Baron Truchss!
TRUCHSS   Here! (*He writes*)
DÖRFLING   Who meanwhile will have taken up positions
With his artillery upon the heights——
TRUCHSS (*Writing*)   "With his artillery upon the heights——" 380
DÖRFLING   Have you got that?
(*He goes on*)   Will seek to drive the Swedish forces
Into the marshy region behind their right-hand wing.
(*Enter a* GUARD)
GUARD   Madame, the coach is waiting. (*The* LADIES *rise*) 385
DÖRFLING   The Prince of Homburg——
ELECTOR   Is Captain Ramin ready?
GUARD   In the saddle, sire, waiting at the main gate.
(*The* ELECTOR, HIS WIFE, *and* NATALIA *take leave of one another*)
TRUCHSS (*Writing*)   "Into the marshy region behind their right wing——" 390
DÖRFLING   The Prince of Homburg—— Where *is* the Prince of Homburg?
HOHENZOLLERN (*Whispering*)   Arthur!
PRINCE (*Starting*)   Here!
HOHENZOLLERN   What's the matter with you?
PRINCE   What are my marshal's orders? (*He is blushing: fiddles with pencil and* 395
parchment and forces himself to write)

DÖRFLING   The Prince of Homburg, to whom
His Highness has once more entrusted,
As at Rathenow, the glorious command of all
The cavalry of Brandenburg——— (*He breaks off*)   400
By which we mean to imply no derogation
To Colonel Kottwitz, who will be at hand
To give advice and his most valuable assistance———
(*Half aloud to* CAPTAIN GOLTZ)   Is the colonel here?
GOLTZ   No, sir, he has sent me in his place   405
To receive his instructions from you.
                (*The* PRINCE *is again looking towards the* LADIES)
DÖRFLING   Will establish his position in the plain
Close by the village of Hackelwitz,
Opposite the enemy's right wing,   410
But out of the range of his cannon.
GOLTZ (*Writing*)   "But out of the range of his cannon———" (*The* ELECTOR'S
WIFE *is tying a scarf round the* PRINCESS' *neck. The* PRINCESS, *about to draw on
a glove, is looking about her, as if seeking for something*)
ELECTOR   What are you looking for, my dear?   415
ELECTOR'S WIFE   Have you lost something?
NATALIA   I don't know, Aunt. My glove——— (*They all look about them*)
ELECTOR (*To the* COURT LADIES)   Dear ladies, would you be so kind,
And give yourselves the trouble of helping us?
ELECTOR'S WIFE   You've got it in your hand, child.   420
NATALIA   That's for the right hand. But where's the other?
ELECTOR   Perhaps you have left it in your apartments?
NATALIA   Dear Bork, *would* you mind———? (COURT LADY *off*)
ELECTOR (*Calling after her*)   Make haste!
PRINCE (*To himself*)   By all the powers above! (*He takes the glove from his collar*) 425
DÖRFLING (*Consulting the parchment in his hand*)   But out of the range of their
                                                              cannon.
        (*Continuing*)   His Highness the Prince shall then———
PRINCE   She's looking for the glove.
                (*He looks at the glove in his hand and at the* PRINCESS)   430
DÖRFLING   In accordance with our commander's express desires———
GOLTZ (*Writing*)   "In accordance with our commander's express desires."
DÖRFLING   However the tide of battle turn, the Prince
Shall remain in the position that has been assigned to him———
PRINCE   Now! I must find out if this is it! (*He lets his handkerchief fall and with* 435
*it the glove: he picks up the handkerchief but leaves the glove lying where everyone
may see it*)
DÖRFLING (*Surprised*)   What is His Highness the Prince of Homburg doing?
HOHENZOLLERN (*Whispering*)   Arthur!
PRINCE   Here!   440
HOHENZOLLERN   This is beyond a joke.
PRINCE   At your service, sir. (*He again takes up pencil and parchment tablet. The
FIELD-MARSHAL looks at him for a moment undecided. There is a silence*)

GOLTZ (*Writing*) "Shall remain in the position that has been assigned to
him——" 445
DÖRFLING (*Continuing*) Until the moment when,
Driven back by Hennings and by Truchss——
PRINCE (*Whispering to* GOLTZ) Who? What?
(*Looking at* GOLTZ' *notes*) My dear Goltz! Who? *Me?*
GOLTZ Yes, you! Who else would it be? 450
PRINCE I shall—remain in the position——
GOLTZ That's right.
DÖRFLING Well, now, are you with us, sir?
PRINCE I shall remain in the position that has been
Assigned to me—— (*He writes*) 455
DÖRFLING Until the moment when,
Driven back by Hennings and by Truchss—— (*He breaks off*)
The enemy's left wing, routed and dispersed,
Is forced upon its right-hand flank,
And all the Swedish battalions in disorder 460
Flounder in the marshes that are riddled
With bogs and pits and ditches. Death-traps.
There, gentlemen, we shall annihilate them.
ELECTOR Pages, ho! Bring lights! Dear ladies,
Take my arm! (*They make to go*) 465
DÖRFLING "Then he shall command his trumpeters to sound their fanfares."
ELECTOR'S WIFE (*As some of the* OFFICERS *salute her*) Gentlemen,
Au revoir. Do not let us disturb you.
(*Here* DÖRFLING *also salutes her and* PRINCESS)
ELECTOR (*Stopping short*) Why, here is the Princess' glove! 470
Quick, pick it up!
COURTIER Where?
ELECTOR Right in front of our dear cousin, the Prince.
PRINCE Right in front of *me?* Why! Is it yours?
(*He picks it up and brings it to* PRINCESS) 475
NATALIA Thank you, noble Prince.
PRINCE (*Bewildered*) Is it—yours?
NATALIA It is mine, indeed, the one I was looking for.
(*She takes it and puts it on*)
ELECTOR'S WIFE (*To* PRINCE, *as she departs*) Farewell! Farewell! 480
Good luck, and God be with you!
Well, then, till we meet again! Let it be soon,
And let it be a joyful meeting! (*The* ELECTOR *leaves with* LADIES, *followed
by* LADIES OF THE COURT, GUARDS, *and* PAGES)
PRINCE (*Stands thunderstruck for a moment, then strides back triumphantly to the* 485
group of OFFICERS) Then he shall command his trumpeters to sound
their fanfares! (*He pretends to be writing*)
DÖRFLING (*Consulting his parchment*) Then he shall command his trumpeters
to sound their fanfares—— But

First, lest some misunderstanding 490
Cause him to attack before the appointed time—— (*He breaks off*)
GOLTZ (*Writing*) "Some misunderstanding cause him to attack
  Before the appointed time——"
PRINCE (*Greatly agitated, whispering to* HOHENZOLLERN) Heinrich!
HOHENZOLLERN Now what is it? What's the matter with you? 495
PRINCE But—— Didn't you *see*?
HOHENZOLLERN I saw nothing. Be quiet, now, or you'll be done for.
DÖRFLING (*Continuing*) The Prince will send him a staff-officer
  Who shall convey to him—now mark this well—
  The express order to attack the enemy. 500
  Until that moment, he shall not
  Command his trumpeters to sound their fanfares.
           (*The* PRINCE *stands dreaming*)
  Have you got that?
GOLTZ (*Writing*) "Until that moment, he shall not 505
  Command his trumpeters to sound their fanfares——"
DÖRFLING (*Raising his voice*) Your Highness,
  Have you noted what I said?
PRINCE Sir?
DÖRFLING Have you got it written down? 510
PRINCE About—the fanfares?
HOHENZOLLERN (*In an irritated whisper*) Fanfares! Fanfares! Devil take you!
  "Until that moment, he shall not——"
GOLTZ (*As* HOHENZOLLERN) "Lest some misunderstanding——"
PRINCE (*Interrupting*) Yes, yes! I've got it! "Until then, he shall not——" 515
  And then, "he shall command his trumpeters to sound their fanfares!"
           (*He writes. A silence*)
DÖRFLING Baron Goltz, please make a note
  That, if it is at all possible, I should like
  To speak personally to Colonel Kottwitz 520
  Before the encounter.
GOLTZ (*Meaningfully*) I shall see to the matter.
  You may depend on me, sir.
           (*A silence. Enter the* ELECTOR)
ELECTOR Well, now, gentlemen, the sky is lightening. 525
  Have you taken good note of everything?
DÖRFLING It is done, Your Highness. The plan of your campaign
  Has been communicated most precisely to your generals.
ELECTOR (*Taking up his hat and gloves and cloak*)
  Prince Frederick of Homburg, sir, 530
  Allow me to recommend to you
  The virtues of calmness, coolness in action.
  You know that you already
  Have thrown away two victories along the Rhine;
  Keep a firm hand on yourself, cousin, 535

And do not deprive me of a third to-day.
For upon the day's victorious issue
Depend my honour, my country, and my title.
(*To* OFFICERS)   Gentlemen, follow me. Hey, Franz!
A SQUIRE   Here, sire!   540
ELECTOR   Quickly now, lead out my battle horse, the white one!
I must be on the field before the rising of the sun!
(*He departs, followed by* GENERALS, COLONELS, *and* OFFICERS)

Scene 6

PRINCE (*Alone, coming forward*)   And now, Fortune,
You whose veils the winds of chance   545
Are filling like a lifted sail,
Come, and move beside me!
This night, dear, terrible goddess,
I felt you lightly touch my brow.
Out of the fullness of the starry night   550
You cast a token of your favours to me,
And I seized it as you wandered smiling by.
To-day I shall seek you out, you daughter of the gods,
And grasp you to my breast upon the field of battle
Till you spill out all your riches round my feet.   555
Yes, Fortune! Though you were bound by chains of iron
To all the triumphal chariots of Sweden,
This day I shall possess you utterly,
Possess you, Fortune, and never let you go! (*He strides swiftly away*)

Act Two

Scene 1

The battlefield at Fehrbellin

(*Enter* KOTTWITZ, HOHENZOLLERN, GOLTZ, *and others leading the cavalry*)
KOTTWITZ (*Off*)   Cavalry, halt here, and dismount!
HOHENZOLLERN AND GOLTZ (*As they are entering*)   Halt, men! Halt!
KOTTWITZ (*Off*)   Somebody help me down!   5
HOHENZOLLERN AND GOLTZ   Hold on! We're coming! (*They go off again*)
KOTTWITZ (*Off*)   I thank you, gentlemen. Ouf! A plague on my old bones!
May you both, when you get to my age,
Be blessed with sons who'll do the same for you!
(*He enters, followed by* HOHENZOLLERN, GOLTZ *and other* OFFICERS)   10
Yes, as long as I'm in the saddle, I'm a boy again.
But when the time comes to dismount,
I feel the soul's being torn out of my body. (*He looks round him*)
Where is His Highness, the Prince, our leader?

HOHENZOLLERN The Prince will be back here soon. 15
KOTTWITZ Where is he?
HOHENZOLLERN He went back to the village that we passed
    Just now, on our left, hidden in trees.
    But he will be returning instantly.
AN OFFICER Is it true that he fell from his horse during 20
    The hours of darkness?
HOHENZOLLERN I believe so, yes.
KOTTWITZ He had a fall?
HOHENZOLLERN (*Turning back to him*) Nothing serious!
    His horse shied at a windmill. 25
OFFICER The black horse?
HOHENZOLLERN Yes. Fortunately, he rolled from the saddle as
    The horse fell down, and got away with a scratch.
    Nothing worth speaking about.
KOTTWITZ (*Ascending a slight eminence*) Ah! What a sweet morning! 30
    A day created by the Lord of life
    For gentler things than fighting!
    The sun's rose opens and shimmers through the clouds,
    And the heart, rejoicing in the freshly scented air,
    Soars up to heaven with the leaping lark! 35
GOLTZ Did you find Field-marshal Dörfling, sir?
KOTTWITZ Er—— No, damn it. What does His Excellency think I am?
    An arrow? An eagle? A flash of thought?
    He's had me running everywhere about the battlefield:
    I've been to the forward party at the top of Hackelberg, 40
    And right to the bottom again to visit the rear.
    I met everybody but the Marshal. So
    I went back to my own men.
GOLTZ He will be very sorry to have missed you. It seems
    He had something of importance to tell you. 45
OFFICER Here comes the Prince.

Scene 2

(*The* PRINCE *enters, a bandage round his temples*)
KOTTWITZ A right hearty welcome to Your Highness! Now
    I want you to see how I've disposed, in your absence,
    Our cavalry in this hollow down below. 50
    I think you will approve what I have done.
PRINCE Good morning, Kottwitz! Good morning, friends! Kottwitz,
    You know I approve of everything you do!
HOHENZOLLERN What were you doing, Arthur, down in the village?
    You're looking so serious! 55
PRINCE I—I went to the chapel
    Whose golden spire glints above the trees.
    They were ringing the bells for prayer as we passed by;

I wanted to go and kneel a moment at the altar.

KOTTWITZ That shows a rare devoutness in a young man and a soldier.   60
A task that is begun with prayer
Will find itself crowned with happiness, success, and victory!

PRINCE There was something I wanted to ask you, Heinrich——
                    (*He draws* HOHENZOLLERN *aside a little*)
What were the instructions Dörfling gave me   65
Last night at the general staff headquarters meeting?

HOHENZOLLERN You weren't paying attention. I could see that.

PRINCE My attention was—divided. I don't know what it was.
Writing to dictation always confuses me.

HOHENZOLLERN This time, fortunately, he didn't tell you   70
Anything of much importance.
Hennings and Truchss, who command the infantry,
Are to lead the attack,
And your assignment is as follows:
You stay here in the valley with the cavalry,   75
Ready to move in the moment you are given
The signal to charge against the enemy.

PRINCE (*After a silence, in which he resumes his reverie*) What a wondrous thing!

HOHENZOLLERN What do you mean, Arthur?
                    (*He looks at the* PRINCE. *Sound of cannon*)   80

KOTTWITZ Ho, there, men! Into your saddles!
That was Hennings! The battle has started! (*They all climb the eminence*)

PRINCE *Who* is it?

HOHENZOLLERN Colonel Hennings, Arthur,
Who has brought his men secretly round to Wrangel's rear.   85
Come up; you can see everything from here.

GOLTZ (*From the top of the hill*) See how vigorously he deploys
His companies along the Rhine!

PRINCE (*Shading his eyes with his hand*) Is that Hennings
Over there, on our right flank?   90

FIRST OFFICER Yes, Your Highness.

PRINCE How the devil has that come about?
Yesterday he was on the left. (*Distant cannon-fire*)

KOTTWITZ By thunder, look! Wrangel is turning
All his twelve cannon upon Hennings' men.   95

FIRST OFFICER The Swedes have good entrenchments,
I will say that for them!

SECOND OFFICER The devil they have! They've got their outworks piled
Nearly as high as the church spire! (*Firing close by*)

GOLTZ That'll be Truchss!   100

PRINCE Truchss?

KOTTWITZ Yes, it'll be Truchss, making a frontal attack
To come to the relief of Hennings.

PRINCE But why is he in the centre? (*Loud firing*)

GOLTZ   Look! I think they've set fire to the village!
THIRD OFFICER   It's burning, now, all right!
FIRST OFFICER   It's burning! It's burning!
   The flames are leaping from the tower!
GOLTZ   Ha! The Swedes are sending out messengers!
SECOND OFFICER   Their lines are breaking! They're on the march!   110
KOTTWITZ   Where?
FIRST OFFICER   On their right flank!
THIRD OFFICER   That's right! The columns are moving. Three regiments.
   They look as if they want to strengthen the left flank.
SECOND OFFICER   Upon my oath! And they're bringing their cavalry forward   115
   To cover the advance of the right flank!
HOHENZOLLERN (*Laughing*)   Ha, ha! They'll soon quit the field again
   When they see us laid in ambush up here! (*Musketry fire*)
KOTTWITZ   Look, men! Look!
SECOND OFFICER   Hark!   120
FIRST OFFICER   Musket fire!
THIRD OFICER   They're fighting now in front of the trenches.
GOLTZ   By God! I've never in all my life
   Heard such thunderous din!
HOHENZOLLERN   Shoot! Shoot! Split the ground wide open!   125
   You'll dig your own grave if you do! (*A silence. Then distant shouts of victory*)
FIRST OFFICER   By the great god of victory!
   Wrangel's turning tail!
HOHENZOLLERN   No, it can't be!
GOLTZ   By heaven, boys! Watch their left flank!   130
   They're pulling out of the trenches,
   And taking their cannon with them!
ALL   We've won! Victory! We've won! Won!
PRINCE (*Striding down from hill*)   Into the saddle, Kottwitz!
   Come on and follow me!   135
KOTTWITZ   Wait, gentlemen, be calm!
PRINCE   To horse! Sound the trumpets! Fanfares! Follow me!
KOTTWITZ   I say, wait!
PRINCE (*Passionately*)   Damnation take you! Hell and damnation!
KOTTWITZ   His Royal Highness the Elector made it clear   140
   That we should wait upon *his* order to attack.
   Goltz, read the instructions to this gentleman.
PRINCE   Wait upon *his* order! Oh, Kottwitz! Is your steed
   Afraid to take the jump? Wait upon *his* order!
   Can't you hear the order sounding here—in the heart?   145
KOTTWITZ   What order?
HOHENZOLLERN (*To* PRINCE)   I beg of you——
KOTTWITZ   In my heart? My *heart*——?
HOHENZOLLERN   Be reasonable, Arthur!
GOLTZ   Listen to me, Colonel——   150

KOTTWITZ (*Indignant*) Oho! So that's the way you want it, my young fellow!
  Let me tell you, sir, I could ride you,
  You and your black beauty, to a standstill!
  Forward, gentlemen, forward! Trumpeters, the fanfares!
GOLTZ (*To* KOTTWITZ) Not that, Colonel! You mustn't! No! No!   155
SECOND OFFICER Hennings hasn't reached the river yet.
FIRST OFFICER Take his sword away!
PRINCE My sword? From me? (*He shoves the* OFFICER *away*)
  You impertinent oaf! Do you not know
  How an officer of Brandenburg behaves?   160
  I'll have *your* sword!
  And the scabbard with it! (*He tears off the* OFFICER'S *sword, scabbard, and belt*)
FIRST OFFICER Your Highness, such an action, by——
PRINCE (*Striding up to him*) Hold your tongue!
HOHENZOLLERN (*To the* OFFICER) Be quiet! Are you out of your mind?   165
PRINCE (*To an* ORDERLY) Orderly! (*He hands over the sword*)
  Take him to headquarters.
  Keep him under close arrest.
  (*To* KOTTWITZ *and the other* OFFICERS) Now, gentlemen, these are *my*
                                                            orders!   170
  Whoever will not follow me
  Is a coward and a traitor!
  Is there anyone here who will not follow me? (*A silence*)
  Speak!
KOTTWITZ You've already heard my answer.   175
  Why do you carry on like this?
HOHENZOLLERN (*Conciliatory*) We just wanted to let you know
  Our own opinion.
KOTTWITZ I'm with you. But upon your own head be it!
PRINCE (*Calmer*) On my own head be it! Follow me, gentlemen! (*Exeunt*)   180

Scene 3

(*A room in a village. A* COURTIER, *booted and spurred, enters. A* PEASANT
            and HIS WIFE *are sitting working at a table*)
COURTIER Greetings, good people! Have you any room for guests?
PEASANT Oh yes, we'll make room.
HIS WIFE Who are they?   185
COURTIER Our illustrious sovereign lady, and no other!
  A wheel came off her carriage just outside the village,
  And, as we have heard that victory has been won,
  We do not need to travel any further.
BOTH (*Rising*) What! Victory! Have we won? Merciful God!   190
COURTIER Did you not know?
  The Swedish forces are well and truly vanquished,
  If not for good, at least for this campaign.
  And Brandenburg is safe from fire and sword once more.
  But look: here comes Her Highness now.   195

Scene 4

(*Enter the* ELECTOR'S WIFE, *pale and distraught.* PRINCESS NATALIA *and several* LADIES OF THE COURT *follow her*)

ELECTOR'S WIFE (*In the doorway*) Mademoiselle Bork! Winterfeld!
  Come, give me your arms!
NATALIA My dearest!   200
COURT LADIES She's so pale! She's faint! (*They support her*)
ELECTOR'S WIFE Lead me to a chair. I must sit down.
  Dead, did he say? Dead?
NATALIA Oh, my dearest, dearest one!
ELECTOR'S WIFE Call the bringer of this tragic news.   205
  I shall speak to him myself.

Scene 5

(*Enter* CAPTAIN VON MÖRNER, *wounded, and led by two* CAVALRYMEN)

ELECTOR'S WIFE What do you bring me,
  Bearer of dread tidings?
  Tell me the worst. What is it?   210
MÖRNER Alas, dear lady, what these two eyes,
  To their eternal sorrow, had never wished to see.
ELECTOR'S WIFE What?
MÖRNER The Elector is—no more.
NATALIA Oh, heaven, what dreadful blow is this you send us?   215
                        (*She covers her face*)
ELECTOR'S WIFE Tell me how he met his death.
  And, as the lightning-stroke that fells the wanderer
  For one last instant illuminates his blazing world,
  So let your message strike my brain.   220
  And when you have spoken,
  Let darkness sweep its final curtains down upon my sinking head!
MÖRNER (*Goes up to her, accompanied by his two* CAVALRYMEN) Madame, the
  Prince of Homburg charged
  On Wrangel in the plain as soon as the enemy,   225
  Beset by Truchss, began to waver and withdraw.
  Already through the first two Swedish lines
  The Prince had cut his way with all his cavalry:
  But then they found themselves attacked
  By so murderous a rain of fire, that their ranks   230
  Were beaten down like corn beneath a tempest.
  The Prince then called a halt within the shelter of
  The hill and tried to reassemble his depleted ranks.
NATALIA My dearest! Be brave!
ELECTOR'S WIFE Leave me alone! Go on!   235
MÖRNER At that moment, we saw emerging from the dust of battle
  Our noble sovereign, riding with the standard-bearers
  Right at the front of Truchss' forces:

How straight and splendidly he rode, the sun
Illuminating him, and the white horse he rode upon   240
As if it were the very path of victory they trod!
At this great spectacle we were perturbed,
And grouped ourselves again, though sore beset,
In the cover of a hill, and from there
Beheld him entering the dreadful furnace of the fight.   245
Then, suddenly, both horse and rider
Fell to the dust. Two standard-bearers
Fell beside him and covered our great leader with
Their spreading flags.
NATALIA   Oh, dear lady!   250
FIRST LADY   O God in heaven!
ELECTOR'S WIFE   Go on! On!
MÖRNER   This terrible sight
Struck anguish to the Prince's heart.
Like the wild bear, goaded by fury and revenge,   255
He urged us after him,
And broke through the last enemy defences.
The trenches and the walls of earth
Are overwhelmed at one fell swoop,
The adversary overthrown and routed,   260
Scattered and destroyed, his cannon, flags,
Wagons, drums, and standards—all are seized—
The Swedes' entire equipment captured.
And if the Rhyn itself
Had not saved some from massacre,   265
Not one of the enemy had been left alive
To sit by his fireside and tell his children:
"I was at Fehrbellin and saw the hero fall."
ELECTOR'S WIFE   Your victory, sir, is bought too dearly.
I do not care for victories at such a cost.   270
I would rather have back
The price you paid to win it. (*She falls into a dead faint*)
FIRST LADY   O God in heaven! Help us! Help our lady!
She has lost her senses. Oh! (NATALIA *is weeping*)

Scene 6

(*Enter the* PRINCE OF HOMBURG)   275
PRINCE   Oh, my dearest Natalia! (*He holds his hand to his heart with emotion*)
NATALIA   So it is true?
PRINCE   If only I might answer "No" to that!
If only, with the blood of this still-faithful heart,
I could restore his own to life again!   280
NATALIA (*Drying her tears*)   Have they found the body?

PRINCE Alas! Until this moment I have been concerned entirely
        With vengeance: how could I undertake the task?
        But I have sent a full detachment of my men
        To seek his body on the field of death: 285
        He will be brought back here by nightfall.
NATALIA Who is there now to stand against the Swedes
        In this unhappy war? Who in the world is there
        To shield us from our enemies
        Who now have robbed us of his fortune and his fame?   290
PRINCE (*Taking her hand*) I, lady, shall defend your cause!
        I shall be the guardian angel with the flaming sword
        Defending the approaches to your desolated throne!
        It was the Elector's dearest wish to see
        That Brandenburg was freed before the year was out: 295
        Allow me, lady,
        To be the executor of that last wish!
NATALIA My dear, devoted cousin! (*She withdraws her hand*)
PRINCE (*Breaking off a moment*) Oh, Natalia, have you thought
        What is to become of you now?   300
NATALIA What is there left for me,
        Now that this thunderstroke has opened up
        A chasm at my feet?
        My beloved mother and my father, lie
        In their vaulted tombs in Amsterdam.   305
        Dordrecht, my inheritance, is devastated,
        Now an ashen ruin.
        Hounded by the armies of the tyrant Spain,
        My cousin Maurits, Prince of Orange,
        Despairs of saving either his own children or   310
        Our royal house. And now
        My last support is taken from me: my fortune,
        Always a fragile plant, must wither utterly and die.
        Now for a second time, I am an orphan.
PRINCE (*Putting an arm round her waist*) Oh, my dear friend!   315
        If this hour of sorrow were not sacred to
        The memory of the dead, then I would say to you:
        Cast your tendrils round the bastion of my soldier's breast,
        And feel the heart that now for years has quickened only
        At the scent that only your sweet flowers breathe!   320
NATALIA My dear, good cousin!
PRINCE Will you? Will you?
NATALIA But what if I should grow,
        Not only on the bark of this great trunk,
        But to its very heart? (*She leans against his breast*)   325
PRINCE If only—— If only——
NATALIA We must go.

PRINCE (*Holding her*) It is the heart that matters,
The heart, Natalia, the inmost heart! (*He kisses her; she tears herself away*)
O God, if only he were here   330
To see this union of our souls!
If only we might look at him and say,
"Father, give us your blessing!"
(*He covers his face with his hands:* NATALIA *returns to the* ELECTOR'S WIFE)

Scene 7

                    (*A* CAVALRY SERGEANT *hurries on*)   335
SERGEANT Your Highness, I hardly dare reveal to you
The rumour that is put about!
The Elector is alive!
PRINCE Alive?
SERGEANT Let heaven be my witness!   340
Count Sparren has this moment brought the news.
NATALIA Oh, lady, have you heard?
                    (*She rushes to* ELECTOR'S WIFE *and embraces her*)
PRINCE Who is the messenger?
SERGEANT Count von Sparren, sir,   345
Who with his own eyes has seen our leader
Safe and sound in Hackelwitz with Truchss' army!
PRINCE Quick! Go and bring him here!

Scene 8

        (*The cavalry* SERGEANT *brings on* COUNT VON SPARREN)
ELECTOR'S WIFE Ah! Let me not be cast down twice in the abyss!   350
NATALIA No, no, you will not be!
ELECTOR'S WIFE Is Frederick alive?
NATALIA (*Raising her and holding her with both hands*) Yes, you can be joyful
                                                    once again!
SERGEANT Here is the officer. (*They come forward*)   355
PRINCE Count von Sparren, sir!
Is it true that you have seen our illustrious leader
Safe and sound with Truchss in Hackelwitz?
SPARREN Yes, Your Highness, in the chapel courtyard,
Where he was giving orders to his staff   360
Concerning the burial of the dead.
COURT LADIES Oh, heaven! Tears of joy! (*They embrace each other*)
ELECTOR'S WIFE Oh, Natalia! Natalia!
NATALIA Oh, such happiness
Is almost too great to bear! (*They embrace*)   365
PRINCE But did I not see, from the forefront of the cavalry,
His white horse, hit by cannon-shot,
Fall with him to the dust?

SPARREN The white horse fell indeed, and its rider too.
    But the rider, Your Highness, was not our leader!   370
PRINCE Not our leader? Then how——
NATALIA Oh, wonderful! Oh! (*She stands beside* ELECTOR'S WIFE)
PRINCE Speak! Each word you utter
    Hangs on my mind as heavily as gold!
SPARREN Then prepare yourselves to listen to   375
    The most moving thing you ever heard!
    Deaf to all warnings for his safety, our sovereign
    Persisted in riding his dazzling white charger, which
    Froben, his equerry, bought for him in England.
    As in every encounter, our Elector once again   380
    Was the target of our enemy's concerted fire.
    The riders who escorted him could barely come
    Within a hundred paces of their master,
    So dense a hail of bullets, deadly shot, and splintering grenades
    Surrounded and swept around him like a fiery flood,   385
    While every soldier left alive unwillingly
    Sought refuge on its stormy banks.
    He alone, like an intrepid swimmer breasting the inferno's blazing tide,
    And boldly waving signs of reassurance to his men,
    Pressed slowly upwards to the very source   390
    From which the cataract of molten fire sprang!
PRINCE Yes, by heaven! It was a terrifying sight!
SPARREN Then Froben, one of the few of all those valiant men
    Who was able to follow closely on his leader, said to me:
    "Cursed be the day when I paid good red gold   395
    For that white horse our brave Elector rides!
    Now would I give twice what I paid that day
    If it could have a grey coat, or a brown!"
    Full of a tremulous concern,
    He rides up to our sovereign and cries: 400
    "Your Highness, your horse is getting out of hand.
    Allow me to take charge of him a while!"
    With these words, he jumps down from his sorrel
    And takes our sovereign's charger by the bridle.
    Our leader then dismounts and smiles, then answers: 405
    "The defect that you have noticed, my old man,
    Is hardly one that could be cured by daylight.
    I beg of you, take him away behind the hill,
    Where our foe will not observe him 'getting out of hand.' "
    Then he mounts the sorrel that Froben rode   410
    And gallops off to where his duty lies.
    But scarcely is Froben in the white horse's saddle,
    Than a murderous rain of shot from a redoubt
    Brings down his charger, and Froben falls,

A sacrifice to his fidelity. 415
He did not rise again. (*A short silence*)
PRINCE   His courage had the best reward.
If I had ten lives to lose,
I could not use them better than his one!
NATALIA   Brave Froben! 420
ELECTOR'S WIFE   What a hero!
NATALIA   A less noble death than his
Would still be worthy of our tears! (*They weep*)
PRINCE   Enough! Now to the matter in hand. Where is
The Elector? Has he set up his headquarters in Hackelwitz? 425
SPARREN   I should have told you and I beg forgiveness.
His Highness has departed for Berlin;
His generals are requested to join him there.
PRINCE   Berlin! Is the campaign at an end?
SPARREN   Really, I am astonished that you do not know of this. 430
Count Horn, the Swedish general,
Presented his proposals for an armistice with Sweden,
Which was signed at our headquarters
Almost immediately afterwards.
In fact, if I have understood aright 435
Field-marshal Dörfling, Sweden has begun negotiations
For a general peace which may soon be a reality.
ELECTOR'S WIFE   Oh, happy day! (*She rises*)
My husband safe, and peace at last!
PRINCE   Come. Let us journey to Berlin without delay 440
And join him there. Madame, may I ask you for a seat
In your conveyance that I may more swiftly reach
The capital?
ELECTOR'S WIFE   You are welcome, and with all my heart,
To ride with us. 445
PRINCE (*Sitting down to write*)   I must send first a note to Kottwitz,
And in a moment I shall be with you. (*He hands the note to the* CAVALRY
SERGEANT. *Then he turns again to the* ELECTOR'S WIFE *and lays his arm
round* NATALIA)
Besides, I should like to take advantage of this journey 450
To make of you, with all due modesty, a personal request——
NATALIA   Bork! Quick, my scarf, if you please!
ELECTOR'S WIFE   A request? From you?
COURT LADY   You have the scarf already round your neck, my lady!
PRINCE   Well? Can you not guess? 455
ELECTOR'S WIFE   No. Nothing!
PRINCE   What? Not the slightest inkling?
ELECTOR'S WIFE   It doesn't matter. To-day there is no one in the world
I would say "No" to, whatever he asked me.
And to you, the victor in battle, least of all. 460
Come! We must away!

PRINCE Madame! Do you realize what you have said?
Am I to understand your answer will be "Yes?"
ELECTOR'S WIFE It's time to go. We can talk further in the coach.
Come, Prince, give me your arm!   465
PRINCE O, great Caesar! Now I climb the ladder
That will lead me to your star! (*He leads the* LADIES *off; the rest follow*)

Scene 9

Berlin. The pleasure-garden of the old palace. In the background stands the
palace chapel, with a flight of steps. Bells ringing. The chapel is brightly lit. We
see FROBEN'S *body borne on and placed on a splendid catafalque.* The* ELECTOR,   470
FIELD-MARSHAL DÖRFLING, COLONEL HENNINGS, COUNT TRUCHSS, *and*
several other COLONELS *and* OFFICERS *enter. A number of* OFFICERS *carrying*
dispatches enter to them. In the church and on the castle square there are people
of all ages and of both sexes.

ELECTOR Whoever it was that led the cavalry charges   475
On the day of the battle and made them advance
Without awaiting my express command,
Compelling the enemy to retreat before
Colonel Hennings could destroy the bridges,
He, I proclaim, is to be put to death!   480
He shall be court-martialled.
So it was not the Prince of Homburg who led the cavalry?
TRUCHSS No, he was not, sire.
ELECTOR Who informs me so?
TRUCHSS The cavalry officers can reassure you on that point.   485
They told me before the engagement had begun
That the Prince had had a fall;
He was gravely wounded in the head and thighs.
They saw his wounds being dressed inside a church.
ELECTOR Well, anyhow, this has been a brilliant victory.   490
To-morrow I shall give thanks to God for it
Before His holy altar. But were this victory
Ten times greater, it would not excuse
Him by whose fault it chanced to come my way.
More battles than just this one I must fight,   495
And I demand obedience to the law.
Whoever led the cavalry into that battle
Will answer for his insubordination with his head!
He shall be court-martialled, sentenced, executed.
Come, gentlemen, let us go and pray.   500

---

470 A draped wooden framework used to support a coffin.

Scene 10

(*Enter the* PRINCE OF HOMBURG, *carrying three Swedish standards,* COLONEL
KOTTWITZ *with two,* COUNT HOHENZOLLERN, GOLTZ, *and* REUSS, *each with
one flag, followed by several other* OFFICERS, CORPORALS, *and* CAVALRYMEN
with flags, drums, and standards)

DÖRFLING (*As soon as he sees the* PRINCE)   The Prince of Homburg!   505
Truchss! What does this mean?

ELECTOR   How did you find your way here, Prince?
Where have you come from?

PRINCE   From Fehrbellin, Your Highness.
I bring you these trophies of victory! (*He lays his three standards before the*   510
ELECTOR: OFFICERS, CORPORALS, *and* CAVALRYMEN *do likewise*)

ELECTOR (*Taken aback*)   You are wounded, so I heard, and gravely too?
Did you not say so, Baron Truchss?

PRINCE (*Gaily*)   Not I!

TRUCHSS   I don't understand!   515

PRINCE   My horse fell with me before the fight began,
But I received only the merest scratch.
The field surgeon bound it up for me,
But it was really nothing.

ELECTOR   So it was you who led the cavalry?   520

PRINCE (*Staring at him*)   Of course! Is it me you ask?
Are these trophies not sufficient proof, sire?

ELECTOR   Take off his sword. He is under arrest.

DÖRFLING (*Shocked*)   What? Who?

ELECTOR (*Walking over the flags*)   Kottwitz, my hearty greetings!   525

TRUCHSS   Damnation!

KOTTWITZ   By heaven, I don't rightly know——

ELECTOR (*Looking keenly at him*)   What do you say?
Look what a harvest our victory has reaped!
This flag belonged to the Swedish guard,   530
Did it not? (*He takes up a flag, holds it out and examines it*)

KOTTWITZ   Sire?

DÖRFLING   Highness?

ELECTOR   To be sure it did! It's from the times
Of King Gustavus Adolphus!*   535
Read me the inscription.

KOTTWITZ   I think it's——

DÖRFLING   *Per aspera ad astra,** it says.

ELECTOR   That could not be said
Of the engagement at Fehrbellin. (*A silence.*)   540

KOTTWITZ (*Embarrassed*)   Your Highness, a word——

---

535 The hero-king of Sweden (r.1611–1632) who led the Swedes to many victories over the Catholic states
of Germany in the Thirty Years' War.
538 "Through rough ways to the stars."

ELECTOR   What is it? Take all these flags
And all these drums and standards
And hang them from the pillars of the chapel:
They will look well to-morrow   545
At our victory thanksgiving. (*The* ELECTOR *turns to his* COURTIERS, *takes
the dispatches, opens, and reads them*)
KOTTWITZ (*Aside*)   By thunder, he's going a bit too far! (*After some hesitation,
he takes up his two flags; the others follow suit. Finally, when only the Prince's
three flags are left,* KOTTWITZ *takes these also, so that he is carrying five flags*)   550
AN OFFICER (*Going up to the* PRINCE)   Prince, your sword, if you please!
HOHENZOLLERN (*With a flag, going to* PRINCE'S *side*)   Arthur! Keep calm!
PRINCE   Is this a dream? Do I wake or sleep?
Is this me? Am I still in my right mind?
GOLTZ   Prince, I advise you to give him your sword.   555
And keep silent.
PRINCE   A prisoner?
HOHENZOLLERN   That is so.
GOLTZ   Under close arrest.
PRINCE   May one ask why?   560
HOHENZOLLERN (*Firmly*)   Not now.
We warned you. You engaged the enemy too soon.
The order was, not to move from your position
Until the signal.
PRINCE   Help me, friends! Help me! I'm going mad!   565
GOLTZ   Be quiet!
PRINCE   Well? Was it the troops of Brandenburg
That were defeated? Was it?
HOHENZOLLERN (*Stamping his foot*)   That's nothing to do with it!
Orders are to be obeyed!   570
PRINCE (*Bitterly*)   Ah!
HOHENZOLLERN (*Leaving him*)   Don't worry! You won't lose your head.
GOLTZ (*Likewise*)   He'll probably release you in the morning.
(*The* ELECTOR *folds his dispatches and comes back to join his* OFFICERS)
PRINCE (*After he has unbuckled his sword*)   It seems my cousin Frederick will   575
play the part of Brutus*
And sees himself in some official portrait sitting
In a lofty seat, wearing the imperial toga,
The articles of war held in a magisterial hand,
While in the foreground lie the flags of Sweden.   580
Ha! He will not find in me a faithful son
Who will adore him even as the axe descends!
I am a Brandenburger, heart and soul:
Generosity, forgiveness—these are the virtues I
Was bred to honour.   585

---

576 Marcus Brutus (85–42 B.C.), a high Roman magistrate under Julius Caesar.

And when he comes to me and tries to ape
Some antique Roman with a language
Dead as the ancient history in which his obstinacy lies embalmed,
I feel for him only pity and dismay!
(*He gives the sword to the* OFFICER *and goes*)   590
ELECTOR   Take him to the headquarters at Fehrbellin
And convoke the military court
That will pass judgement on him. (*He goes off into the chapel. He is followed
by the flagbearers. While he is kneeling in prayer with his suite at* FROBEN'S
bier, the flags are hung from the pillars of the chapel. A funeral march)   595

Act Three

Scene 1

The Prince's prison at Fehrbellin. In the background, two CAVALRYMEN
mounting guard over the PRINCE
(*Enter* HOHENZOLLERN)

PRINCE   Is it you, Heinrich? Welcome!
I am free at last?   5
HOHENZOLLERN (*Astonished*)   God be praised!
PRINCE   What do you say?
HOHENZOLLERN   Free? Has he sent you back your sword?
PRINCE   No.
HOHENZOLLERN   Nothing?   10
PRINCE   No.
HOHENZOLLERN   Then how can you be free? (*A silence*)
PRINCE   I thought you had brought me—my release.
It doesn't matter.
HOHENZOLLERN   I don't know anything.
PRINCE   Oh, it doesn't matter! It doesn't matter, do you hear?   15
He'll be sending someone else. (*He carries two chairs forward*)
Sit down! Now, tell me, what's the news?
Has the Elector returned from Berlin?
HOHENZOLLERN (*Absent-mindedly*)   He has. Yesterday evening.   20
PRINCE   And I suppose the victory thanksgiving ceremony
Was performed in the desired way?
Was the Elector present in the chapel?
HOHENZOLLERN   Yes, with his wife and Natalia.
The chapel was most gloriously illuminated.   25
During the *Te Deum* we could hear
Prodigious salvos being fired on the castle square.
The Swedish flags and standards
Hung swaying like solemn trophies from all the pillars.
And on our sovereign's express command   30
Your name was given from the pulpit as
That of the victor of Fehrbellin.

PRINCE So I have heard. Now, what else? What's on your mind?
Your countenance, dear friend, is far from gay!
HOHENZOLLERN Have you spoken to anyone?   35
PRINCE To Goltz. Not here, but at the castle,
Where I was subjected to interrogation. (*A silence*)
HOHENZOLLERN (*Anxiously*) Arthur, what do you think of your position,
After this sudden change of fortune?
PRINCE What do I think? I think the same as you and Goltz;   40
The same as the military court.
The Elector has performed his duty, as required.
Now he will listen to the promptings of his heart.
Oh, he'll put a serious visage on and say:
"You disobeyed me!" Perhaps let fall a word or two   45
Like execution, death, imprisonment.
"But now I give you back your freedom!" he will say,
And round the scabbard that contained the sword of victory
Perhaps he'll tie the ribbon of an order,
Or some decoration—— Though if he doesn't, well,   50
No matter. I don't deserve all that.
HOHENZOLLERN Oh, Arthur! (*He stops short*)
PRINCE Well?
HOHENZOLLERN Are you so sure still of all this?
PRINCE I should think so! He is fond of me, I know,   55
As if I were his son: since my earliest days
He has given me a thousand proofs of it.
Why do you look so doubtful?
Did he not seem always to rejoice,
Almost as much as I did, at my growing fame?   60
Do I not owe everything to him?
And now, after having raised me with his own
Devoted hands, you think he'll trample down into the dust
So ruthlessly his favourite plant
Merely because it put out rather too   65
Abundantly and hastily its buds and flowers?
His greatest foe could not convince me of it;
Much less can you, who know and cherish him.
HOHENZOLLERN (*Grave*) You have stood court-martial, Arthur,
And you still believe all this?   70
PRINCE Yes! Because I have stood court-martial
I still believe! By heaven!
No tribunal goes as far as they have gone
Unless their intention is to pardon me!
It was precisely there, at the bar of justice,   75
That I regained my confidence again.
Was it, after all, such a terrible offence?
One punishable by—death? Was it?
To advance two minutes earlier than I should have,

In order to make the Swedish forces bite the dust? 80
What other criminal offence have I committed?
I have nothing on my conscience.
How could he possibly have set me up before
That court of heartless judges, that like owls
Sat there and hooted their funereal notes at me? 85
How could he do it, if he did not intend
To step among them, like a god from the machine,
At the last moment and reprieve me with a joking word?
No, friend, he piles upon my head these clouds and midnight shadows
Only to be able to disperse their darkness for me like a rising sun: 90
It's a caprice, a royal one. I do not grudge him that!

HOHENZOLLERN All the same, your sentence has been passed.

PRINCE So I hear: the death sentence, I believe.

HOHENZOLLERN (*Astounded*) You knew?

PRINCE Goltz, who was present at the verdict of the court, 95
Acquainted me with their decision.

HOHENZOLLERN But, heavens above, man! Aren't you—— Don't you——

PRINCE Not in the slightest.

HOHENZOLLERN But you're mad!
On what do you base this calm assurance? 100

PRINCE On—a feeling I have about him. (*He stands up*)
I beg of you, leave me alone!
Why should I plague myself with useless doubts?
            (*He reflects a moment, then sits down again. A silence*)
The court-martial *had* to pass a sentence of death: 105
That was according to the laws by which it acts.
But rather than let such a judgement be fulfilled,
Rather than let a faithful and devoted servant
Be delivered up to execution, Frederick would tear
His own heart from his breast and pour out 110
His life-blood drop by drop upon the ground.

HOHENZOLLERN Arthur, I'm telling you that——

PRINCE (*Moodily*) Oh, not again, dear Heinrich!

HOHENZOLLERN The Field-marshal——

PRINCE No! Don't tell me! 115

HOHENZOLLERN Just one word, Arthur!
If this means nothing to you,
Then I'll say no more.

PRINCE (*Turns back to him*) Didn't you hear me say
I know it all? Oh, well, what is it? 120

HOHENZOLLERN Field-marshal Dörfling has just taken
The death-warrant to the castle;
The Elector, instead of exercising the prerogative of mercy,
Wished to append his signature.

PRINCE Well, what of that? 125

HOHENZOLLERN (*Aghast*) What of that?

PRINCE His signature, did you say?

HOHENZOLLERN I can assure you, on my word of honour.

PRINCE On the death-warrant?—— No! Perhaps on some report——

HOHENZOLLERN It was the death-warrant.   130

PRINCE Who told you this?

HOHENZOLLERN Field-marshal Dörfling himself.

PRINCE When?

HOHENZOLLERN Just now.

PRINCE When he came back from seeing the Elector?   135

HOHENZOLLERN As he was coming down the stairway from
    The Elector's private rooms.
    He must have seen my thunderstruck expression,
    For he added: "Everything is not yet lost.
    There's still another day——"   140
    But his grim white lips belied his words,
    Which should have been: "There is no hope."

PRINCE (*Jumping up*) He couldn't—— No! He couldn't dream
    Of imposing such a monstrous penalty!
    Would he, because of the almost undetectable   145
    Flaw in the diamond of victory that I presented to him,
    Would he tread the victor in the dust?
    That would be a deed so infamous,
    The worst excesses of the Dey of Tunis would appear
    As harmless as a children's game beside it.   150
    The luxurious monster Sardanapalus*
    Would seem like a rosy cherub borne on silvery wings;
    Oh, such a deed would set
    The whole tyrannous troop of Roman emperors,
    Like innocent babes expired at their mothers' breasts,   155
    At God's right hand!

HOHENZOLLERN (*Also jumping up*) Arthur, you must realize——

PRINCE And the Field-marshal held his tongue?

HOHENZOLLERN What could he say?

PRINCE Oh, God, I was so full of hope!   160

HOHENZOLLERN Could you perhaps, unconsciously or not,
    Have committed some folly that offended him?

PRINCE Never!

HOHENZOLLERN Try to remember.

PRINCE Never, I tell you!   165
    The very shadow that he cast was sacred to me.

HOHENZOLLERN Arthur, do not be angry with me, if I doubt your words.
    It is said that the Swedish envoy, Count Horn,
    Has come to negotiate the marriage of

---

151 One of the most dissolute of Assyrian rulers.

Princess Natalia of Orange with his master,   170
King Carolus Gustavus,
And that the Elector has been bitterly offended
By something that his wife revealed to him:
The Princess has already set her heart on someone.
Have you had anything to do with this?   175
PRINCE   Why?
HOHENZOLLERN   Have you?
PRINCE   My friend, I have. Now all is clear to me.
The proposal sets the seal upon my luckless fate.
It is I who am the cause of her refusal,   180
For she is betrothed to me.
HOHENZOLLERN   You idiot! What were you thinking of?
How often have I warned you?
PRINCE   Oh, friend, help me, save me!
I am lost! I am lost!   185
HOHENZOLLERN   How can we get you out of this?
Would you like to speak to the Elector's wife?
PRINCE   Guard!
GUARD   Sir!
PRINCE   Bring me your captain. (*He hastily takes a cloak from the wall and puts*   190
on a feathered hat which is lying on the table)
HOHENZOLLERN (*Helping him*)   With a little ingenuity,
This interview can save your life.
If the Elector can make a suitable
Peace-settlement with the King of Sweden,   195
His heart, I am certain, will be reconciled to you,
And in another hour or two you will be free.

Scene 2

(*The* CAPTAIN *comes on*)
PRINCE (*To the* CAPTAIN)   Stranz, you are the captain of the guard.
Will you allow me to absent myself from here awhile?   200
It is an urgent, personal affair.
STRANZ   Your Highness, I have no authority over you.
You are free to go wherever you please.
Those are the orders I was given.
PRINCE   Strange! So I am not a prisoner?   205
STRANZ   You are a prisoner upon parole.
Your word, Prince, is security enough.
PRINCE (*Going*)   I see! Very well. It doesn't matter. Come! Farewell!
HOHENZOLLERN   The fetters follow in the prince's trail.
PRINCE   I am going only to the castle   210
And will very shortly be returned. (*Exeunt omnes*)

Scene 3

The apartments of the Elector's Wife
(She comes in with NATALIA)

ELECTOR'S WIFE Come, Natalia. Now is your chance.
Count Horn and the Swedish delegation 215
Have just left the castle.
I can see a light burning in your uncle's rooms.
Go and see him, speak to him,
And try to save your prince. (*They are about to go*)

Scene 4

(*A* COURT LADY *enters*) 220

LADY Your Highness, the Prince of Homburg waits outside!
I could hardly believe my eyes!
ELECTOR'S WIFE It can't be!
NATALIA The Prince himself?
ELECTOR'S WIFE He's still under arrest? 225
LADY He's waiting. He seems perplexed. He hasn't even
Taken off his cloak and hat. He says he must
Speak to you.
ELECTOR'S WIFE (*Displeased*) How thoughtless! To betray his word!
NATALIA Perhaps he has an explanation——— 230
ELECTOR'S WIFE (*After reflection*) Let him come in. (*She sits down*)

Scene 5

(*Enter the* PRINCE OF HOMBURG)

PRINCE Oh, my lady! (*He falls on his knees before her*)
ELECTOR'S WIFE Prince, what are you doing here?
PRINCE Oh, let me lie here at your feet! 235
ELECTOR'S WIFE (*With controlled emotion*)
You are a prisoner, sir,
And yet you break your word and come to me!
Why do you add another error to the first?
PRINCE (*Insistently*) Do you realize what has happened to me? 240
ELECTOR'S WIFE Indeed, I know it all.
But what can I, a powerless woman, do for you?
PRINCE Oh, lady, you would not speak to me like this
If you could feel the cold of death
I carry round me everywhere! 245
To me, these ladies here around you,
The Princess, you yourself, and all still left alive
Appear endowed with saving grace from heaven,
And with heaven's strength!
The most lowly mortal is to me 250

A god! Oh! I could hang myself upon the neck
Of your most humble stableman,
Imploring him to save me. Save me!
On the whole of God's wide earth,
Only I am helpless, abandoned, and can do   255
Nothing, nothing.

ELECTOR'S WIFE   You are not yourself. What has happened?

PRINCE   Ah! I have seen my grave, my dark hole in the cold ground!
As I was coming here, I saw it in the torch-light,
The tomb that to-morrow morning shall receive   260
This body. Look, lady, these eyes:
They want to cover them with heavy darkness;
This breast: they want to shatter it with lead!
Upon the market square, the windows are already taken
That will look down upon my sandy stage   265
And on my final scene.
And I, who now, from life's most lofty peak,
Still gaze upon the future, as if it were a legendary land,
Shall lie to-morrow rotting between two narrow boards,
With at my head a stone, to tell you who I—*was!* (*The* PRINCESS, *who* 270
until now has been standing, leaning on the shoulders of her COURT LADIES,
collapses with her head upon a table and weeps)

ELECTOR'S WIFE   My son! If such is the will of heaven,
You must face your destiny with courage and with calm!

PRINCE   Oh, God's earth, dear mother, is so fair!   275
I implore you, do not go before the fatal hour strikes
And leave me all alone to enter those black shades!
If I have been in error, let him punish me,
But must it be the bullets of a firing-squad?
Let him reduce me to the ranks, dismiss me from the army,   280
And take my honours all away, if such must be the law!
Oh, God in heaven,
Since I have seen my grave, I only want to live,
And honour and dishonour are alike to me!

ELECTOR'S WIFE   Stand up, my son, stand up! Why do you talk like this? 285
You are distracted. Compose yourself!

PRINCE   No, lady, until you swear to me
That you will cast yourself before him
And beg him for my life!
Your childhood friend, my mother, when she was dying,   290
Gave me into your care and said:
"Love him like a son when I shall be no more!"
And you knelt by her bed and wept
And kissed her hand and said:
"It shall be as if I had myself conceived   295
And borne him."

Now I remind you of that promise.
Go, as if you had yourself conceived
And borne me, and say to him:
"I beg for mercy, mercy for my son! Let him go free!"   300
And then come back to me and tell me: "You are free!"
ELECTOR'S WIFE (*Weeping*) My dear son, I have already done so.
I pleaded with him, but in vain.
PRINCE Every claim to happiness I now abjure!
Don't forget to tell him also   305
That I no longer wish to take Natalia in marriage!
Every spark of feeling for her now has vanished from my heart.
She is free again, free as the wild deer in the heathered hills,
Utterly free, as if I never had existed.
Now she is free to marry whom she will or whom she must.   310
And if it be the King of Sweden, Carolus Gustavus,
She has my warm felicitations.
I only want to go back to my own estate.
There I shall build, pull down, and build again,
And sow my fields, and reap them till the sweat   315
Pours down my breast, and labour hard,
As if for wife and child: but I shall be alone there.
And when I have reaped, then I shall sow again,
Turning calmly in the year's great circle, that is life's
Until, at close of day, life sinks and dies.   320
ELECTOR'S WIFE Come, my son! Go back to prison.
I shall intercede for you again, but not before
You have returned to prison. (*The* PRINCE *rises. He speaks to* NATALIA)
PRINCE My poor child, you are weeping! The sun to-day
Is lighting all your hopes the way to death?   325
I shall always be, I know, your first,
But not, I hope, your only love, although
Your pure face tells me, clear as day,
That you will never give your heart to any other man.
What comfort could I bring you, I, most wretched of all mortal souls? 330
Go, and spend your days within a cloister by the Rhine,
Or find in the mountains a young boy with golden locks
Like mine, and teach him how to call you "Mother."
Then, when he has grown to manhood, you will show him
How they close the eyelids of the dead.   335
That is the only happiness now left to you!
NATALIA (*Bravely, putting her hand in his and rising*)
Go, my hero, return to your prison cell
And, on the way, look calmly, deep into
The grave that has been opened to receive you.   340
It is no more terrible and no wider
Than the grave that always waited for you on the field of battle!

I shall be true to you, even in death,
If death it be. Meanwhile, I shall go and speak
To my uncle and try to find the words to save you: 345
Perhaps I shall be lucky and, if I touch his heart,
I shall deliver you from all your troubles.

PRINCE (*Looking at her enraptured, folding his hands in prayer*)
Lady, if at your shoulders you had two great wings,
I should take you for an angel and this room for heaven!   350
Oh, heaven! Did I hear aright? That *you* will speak for *me*?
Where did you find this quiverful of words,
That now you dare to speak to the Elector?
Can you aim so true, so high, so far?
Ah, how sweet it is, the sudden ray of hope!   355

NATALIA God will put the arrows in my hands,
And, with His grace, they shall reach their mark!
But if the Elector cannot change
The sentence of the court—well, then,
You, the hero, shall submit to death as only heroes can!   360
And you, who in life so often triumphed on the field,
Will triumph even more in this, your final fight!

ELECTOR'S WIFE Away! Time flies, and every moment now is precious!

PRINCE Now may all the saints of paradise protect you.
Farewell! Farewell! And whatever be the outcome,   365
Let me know the answer soon! Oh, let it be—success! (*They all leave*)

Act Four

Scene 1

In the Elector's apartments. The ELECTOR *is standing holding some papers at
a lamplit table.* NATALIA *comes through the centre door and kneels, though at
some distance away from him. A silence*

NATALIA My noble uncle, Frederick of Brandenburg!

ELECTOR (*Laying papers aside*) Natalia! (*He tries to raise her*)   5

NATALIA No! No!

ELECTOR What is it, my child?

NATALIA I cast myself down before you, as is fitting
For a suppliant. I come, sire,
To implore your mercy for our cousin Homburg.   10
Not for my own sake do I wish him to be spared:
No, though I love him and do not conceal my love,
Not for my own sake do I come;
He may take whatever wife he pleases.
What I want, sire, is that he   15
Should simply be allowed to live,
That he should be left to live upon the earth,

Independent, free, and unrestrained,
As I would wish a flower to live,
Whose singularity and beauty pleased me. 20
This I would ask of you, my sovereign and my friend,
And know that you will lend an ear to my request.
ELECTOR (*Raising her*) My little daughter! How could you ask such things?
Do you know what crime it is your cousin Homburg has committed?
NATALIA Oh, my dear uncle! 25
ELECTOR Well? Has he not done wrong?
NATALIA Wrong? Oh, that fault, how innocently he committed it!
Could those clear blue eyes, that pale blond head
Belong to one who willingly would make the least false step?
A little fault it was, that should have been forgiven 30
Even before he had the time to say: "Forgive me!"
You cannot trample this bright flower in the dust!
Rather, for his poor dead mother's sake,
You must press him to your heart and say:
"Come, be sad no more, 35
You are as dear to me as life itself!"
Was it not eagerness to add more glory to your name
That, in the heat of battle, tempted him to break
The letter, not the spirit, of the law?
And, oh! When his youthful rashness fired him to break it, 40
Did he not thrust with manly ardour at the dragon's head?
The reward of victory is not the grave!
To crown the victor, then to execute him!
History does not require such a gesture,
For it would be a gesture so beyond all common use, 45
That it might easily be taken as inhuman, sire.
And heaven knows, there is no gentler man on earth than you.
ELECTOR My sweet Natalia! If I were some fearful tyrant,
Your words—I feel it in my heart—
Would have moved my iron will to fresh compassion. 50
But tell me this: how can my duty allow me to reverse
The verdict that a solemn court has passed?
What would be the consequences of a deed like that?
NATALIA For whom? For you?
ELECTOR No, child, I am not thinking of myself, 55
But of my country.
NATALIA Oh, sire! Is there nothing more? Your country!
Your country is not going to be ruined
Because you showed some human mercy!
You have known only the discipline of camp and battlefield. 60
To countermand the verdict of a military court
Is to you an act of insubordination and disorder.
The rules of war and of a soldier's life

Must be obeyed, I know. How much more
The rules of real, human love must be obeyed! 65
The heart has its rules and reasons too.
The country that you have fought for and created
Stands secure and firm, sire, as a rock.
It would need quite other, wilder tempests now to overthrow it
Than this one small capitulation that I ask of you. 70
I see your country growing to a glorious future,
More splendid and more beautiful each day in your descendants' hands,
With towers and pinnacles and castles rich in legend,
To be the joy of friends and the terror of your enemies.
But such a glittering future will not come 75
From this cold, barren will,
That in my uncle's glowing autumn, now at peace,
Will turn to chilling winter all
The springing summer of our cousin Homburg's blood!

ELECTOR Does our cousin Homburg think as you? 80
NATALIA My cousin?
ELECTOR Does he think that in our land of Brandenburg
It matters little whether law or anarchy is master?
NATALIA Oh, he is young yet——
ELECTOR Well? 85
NATALIA Oh, my dear uncle,
I have no answer but my tears.
ELECTOR (*Moved*) But why, my child? What is the matter?
NATALIA He thinks of only one thing: to be saved!
He only sees the pointing barrels of the firing-team, 90
The rifles laid to their steady shoulders,
So terrible a sight, it drives all thoughts out of his mind
But one: and that is, how to keep alive.
The whole of Brandenburg might be destroyed,
And he would notice nothing. 95
See what you have done to this great hero's heart! (*She turns away, weeping*)
ELECTOR (*Utterly astonished*) No! Natalia! It can't be possible!
Does he—does he beg for mercy?
NATALIA Oh, why did you ever condemn him to——
ELECTOR Answer me! Does he ask for mercy? God in heaven, 100
What has happened to him? Why are you weeping?
Did you speak to him? Tell me! Did you speak to him?
NATALIA (*Leaning on his breast*) Yes, a while ago, in my aunt's apartments,
Where he came to see us under cover of the dusk,
In a dark mantle, with his hat down on his eyes, 105
Embarrassed, furtive, and distracted,
His natural grace and dignity all overthrown,
A lamentable, pitiable sight!
Never should I have dreamed that he,

A man whom history has called a hero, 110
Could have fallen quite so far!
It is only a woman you see here,
One who is frightened by the merest worm:
But if death suddenly appeared before me
Wearing its most terrifying mask, 115
It would not find me so deprived of will,
So weak, so crushed, so utterly unlike a hero!
Oh, how meaningless is human grandeur!

ELECTOR Come, now, dear child! By heaven, courage!
He is free! 120

NATALIA Free, Your Highness?

ELECTOR I have pardoned him! I shall draft at once
The order for his release.

NATALIA Oh, my dearest uncle! Is it really true?

ELECTOR I give my word. 125

NATALIA You've really pardoned him? He will not be executed?

ELECTOR I promise you. How could I resist
The arguments of such a warrior?
You know that in my heart of hearts
I have a great respect for his opinion. 130
If he can show the sentence we have passed on him to be
In any way unjust, I shall reverse it. (*He brings her a chair*)
Sit down here a moment. (*He goes to his table, sits, and writes*)

NATALIA (*Aside*) Heart, why do you beat so hard
Against the walls of this weak house? 135

ELECTOR (*Writing*) Is the Prince still in the castle?

NATALIA No. He returned to the prison. (*The* ELECTOR *finishes and seals the
letter and turns with it in his hand towards the* PRINCESS)

ELECTOR So my little daughter was in tears!
Could I, whose every care it is to make her happy, 140
Cloud the heaven of her candid eyes? (*He puts his arm round her*)
Will you take the letter to him?

NATALIA To the prison?

ELECTOR (*Gives her the letter*) And why not? Ho, guards!
(*Enter* GUARDS) 145
Have the coach brought to the door! The Princess
Is paying a visit to Colonel von Homburg! (*Exeunt* GUARDS)
Then he can thank you for his life. (*He embraces her*)
My dear child! Do you forgive me?

NATALIA (*After a silence*) Sire, what it was that moved your heart to clemency 150
I do not know and do not ask.
One thing I know—I feel it in my soul—
You would not play a trick on me.
Whatever the contents of this letter,
I believe that they may save him 155

And I thank you for your tenderness. (*She kisses his hand*)
ELECTOR Be sure of that, my dear, and set your heart at rest.
Our cousin Homburg's fate
Depends now only on himself. (*They go*)

Scene 2

The Princess Natalia's apartments. NATALIA, *two* COURT LADIES, *and the*   160
COUNT REUSS

NATALIA What is this you bring me, Count Reuss?
Is it from my regiment? Is it important?
Can it not wait until the morning?
REUSS (*Hands her the letter*) It is from Colonel Kottwitz, Your Highness.   165
NATALIA Quick! What does he say? (*She opens it*)
REUSS It is a request, both boldly phrased, as you will see,
And yet respectful, to His Highness the Elector,
Drafted in favour of the Prince of Homburg.
NATALIA (*Reading*) "Humble supplication . . .   170
From the regiment of the Princess of Orange. . . ." (*Pause*)
Who wrote this request?
REUSS As you might guess from that untutored script,
Colonel Kottwitz wrote it.
His noble name stands at the top.   175
NATALIA And what are these thirty or so signatures below it?
REUSS The names of the officers, Your Highness,
In precedence of rank.
NATALIA And why was it to me that the request was sent?
REUSS Your Highness, we would very respectfully ask of you   180
If, as our colonel-in-chief, you would place your name
At the head of all the rest;
A space has been left, as you can see. (*A pause*)
NATALIA Count Reuss, I think this is unnecessary now.
I have just heard that the Prince
Is likely to be pardoned by His Highness.   185
REUSS (*Joyful*) Oh! Is it true?
NATALIA In any case, as this statement, skilfully used,
Will certainly help to turn the scales,
And my uncle may even find it welcome   190
In the last analysis,
I agree to your proposal and will sign my name.
            (*She goes to table, as if to write*)
REUSS We shall be most grateful for your help. (*A pause*)
NATALIA (*Turning back to him*) I can find here only   195
My own regiment, Count!
Where are the Bomsdorf Cuirassiers,
And the Götz and Anhalt-Pless Dragoons?

REUSS   Your Highness, it is not because their hearts
        Are less warmly disposed towards the Prince than ours.   200
        It was rather unfortunate for our petition
        That Kottwitz is encamped at Arnstein,
        Away from all the other regiments
        Which are quartered here at Fehrbellin.
        And there were no facilities   205
        For sending our petition out to every regiment.
NATALIA   All the same, I feel it takes away from
        The value of your intervention.
        Are you quite certain, Count,
        That if you could contact the officers in Fehrbellin   210
        They would lend their support to our petition?
REUSS   I can answer for their undivided loyalty
        To us and to the Prince's cause.
        Not only the cavalry would pledge themselves;
        I'm sure the entire army of Brandenburg   215
        Would gladly sign their names.
NATALIA   (After a silence)   Why do you not send officers
        As delegates to all the regiments in town?
REUSS   The colonel has refused permission.
        He did not wish, he said, to undertake   220
        Anything that might be called sedition.
NATALIA   What a curious hero! Both brave and timorous!
        But fortunately the Elector, I remember now,
        Charged me, as he was so preoccupied,
        With sending orders out to Kottwitz,   225
        Whose present quarters are too cramped,
        To install himself at Fehrbellin.
        I'll do it now. (She sits down and writes)
REUSS   Ah, Your Highness, what an admirable decision!
        Nothing could be more favourable to our cause.   230
NATALIA   (Writing)   Use the occasion to the best advantage, Count! (She seals
                          the letter and stands again)
        Meanwhile—you understand!—this letter
        Will remain in your portfolio; you will not go with it
        To Arnstein to deliver it to Kottwitz   235
        Before I give you my express commission! (She hands the letter to him)
GUARD   (Entering)   Your Highness, at the master's orders
        The coach is waiting for you in the courtyard.
NATALIA   Bring it to the door! I'm coming now. (A pause, during which she
                          goes to the table and thoughtfully draws on her gloves)   240
        Count Reuss, will you accompany me
        On my visit to the Prince of Homburg?
        I wish to speak to him.
        There is a seat for you inside my coach.

REUSS Your Highness, it is a great honour——— (*He offers her his arm*) 245
NATALIA (*To* COURT LADIES) Follow us, my friends.
(*To* REUSS) Perhaps, sir,
This visit will have some bearing on
My instructions for you regarding the letter. (*Exeunt*)

Scene 3

(HOMBURG *in prison. He hangs his hat on the wall and drops dispiritedly on* 250
a cushion on the ground)
PRINCE "Life," says the dervish, "is a journey, and a short one."
How true! The furthest we ever get
Is five or six feet above the earth,
And the same distance underneath it! (*Lying almost full-length*) 255
Well, now I'm halfway between the two! One day
A man can bear his head up proudly on his shoulders;
The next it's hanging low with fear;
And the next day it's laying at his feet.
Ah, well, they say the sun shines up there too 260
And over brighter fields than we have here.
I believe that's true: a pity that the eye should rot
Before it can glimpse those wonders———

Scene 4

(*Enter* PRINCESS NATALIA, *led by* COUNT REUSS, *captain of the horse, and*
followed by COURT LADIES. *An* ATTENDANT *goes before them with a torch*) 265
ATTENDANT Her Royal Highness, the Princess Natalia of Orange!
PRINCE (*Jumps up*) Natalia!
NATALIA (*Whispering to* REUSS) Leave us alone a moment!
(REUSS *and* ATTENDANT *off*)
PRINCE My dearest Princess! 270
NATALIA My dearest cousin!
PRINCE Well, what is the news? How do I stand?
NATALIA Good news, Prince. All is well. As I had guessed,
You have been pardoned, you are free; here is a letter
From the Elector, confirming it. 275
PRINCE It can't be possible! Oh no! It must be a dream———
NATALIA Read the letter. You'll see it's no dream.
PRINCE (*Reading*) "Your Highness, the Prince of Homburg,
When I consigned you, on account of your premature attack,
To prison, I believed I was doing my duty. 280
And I counted on your recognition of this fact.
But if you are of the opinion
That I have done you an injustice,
Then will you kindly send me word—
A single line will do— 285
And at once I shall restore to you

Your sword and your command."
(NATALIA *grows pale. A silence. The* PRINCE *gives her a questioning look*)
NATALIA (*With a look of sudden joy*)   There, you see!
A line, that's all he wants!   290
Oh, my dear friend, you are free! (*She presses his hand*)
PRINCE   My angel!
NATALIA   Oh, happy, happy moment! Look,
Here is the pen. Take it and write!
PRINCE   What signature is this?   295
NATALIA   That is "F," his sign for Frederick.
That is how he always signs himself.
Oh, Bork! You must be happy for me!
You must be happy too!
Oh, I knew his kindness is as infinite as the sea.   300
Bring a chair for His Highness, he must write at once!
PRINCE   He says: If I am of the opinion——
NATALIA (*Interrupting*)   Of course! Hurry, now. Sit down.
I shall dictate your reply to you. (*She sets a chair for him*)
PRINCE   I'll just read the letter over once again.   305
NATALIA (*Snatching the letter from him*)   What good will that do?
Did you not see, in the courtyard of the church,
The grave yawn up to you with open jaws?
Time is short. Sit down and write!
PRINCE (*Smiling*)   Really you're acting now as if the grave   310
Were set to pounce upon me like a panther.
             (*He sits down and takes up the pen. She turns away to weep*)
NATALIA   Now write, if you do not want to make me angry with you!
             (*The* PRINCE *rings for a* SERVANT, *who enters*)
PRINCE   Paper and ink! Some sealing-wax! A seal! (*The* SERVANT, *after having*   315
brought these things, goes off again. The PRINCE *writes. Silence. He tears up the*
             letter he has started and throws it under the table)
A bad beginning. (*He takes another sheet of paper*)
NATALIA (*Picks up the letter*)   Why? What did you say?
But that is very good! That's excellent!   320
PRINCE (*Muttering*)   Pooh! It might have been written by a cobbler,
Not by a Prince. I must turn it more gracefully. (*A silence. He tries to snatch*
             the ELECTOR'S *letter again, which* NATALIA *still holds in her hand*)
What did he really say in the letter?
NATALIA (*Refusing to give it to him*)   Nothing! Nothing at all!   325
PRINCE (*Insisting*)   Give it to me!
NATALIA   But you've read it!
PRINCE (*Tearing it from her grasp*)   What if I have?
I must see what terms to use in my reply.
             (*He opens the letter and reads it again*)   330
NATALIA (*Aside*)   Oh, God! Now all is lost again!
PRINCE (*Perplexed*)   Look here! How very curious!

Did you miss this part?

NATALIA No. Which part?

PRINCE He leaves the decision to myself!   335

NATALIA Oh, that! Yes, he does.

PRINCE How noble of him, and how dignified!
That is the way a great man should behave!

NATALIA Oh, his generosity is boundless!
Now, do as he asks you and write   340
One line in answer! You see,
It is only the outward form that must be
Complied with. As soon as he has just that one line from you,
Then everything will go quite smoothly!

PRINCE (*Putting the letter aside*) No, my dear Natalia,   345
I must think over it until to-morrow.

NATALIA But—— I cannot understand you!
What does it mean, this change?
Why? What is the use of waiting?

PRINCE (*Rising abruptly*) I beg of you, do not ask me.   350
You haven't seen the implications of his letter!
"If I am of the opinion that he has done me an injustice!"
Well, that is one thing I cannot write to him,
And if you force me now to send an answer,
By heaven, it will be: "Your Highness, *you* are in the right!"   355
(*He sits down again by the table and reads the letter*)

NATALIA (*Deathly pale*) You lunatic! What do you say? (*She bends over him*)

PRINCE (*Taking her hand*) One moment! Wait—— I think I've got it!

NATALIA What?

PRINCE I know now how I should reply.   360

NATALIA (*Sadly*) Homburg!

PRINCE (*Taking up the pen*) I'm listening. What is it?

NATALIA My dearest Prince! I can only praise
The generous impulse of your heart.
But let me tell you this: 365
The regiment already has been chosen
Whose firing-team will pay its last respects to you
To-morrow morning. A salvo of musket-shot
Will greet you as you stand upon the mound of earth
That will be shovelled over you when you are lying   370
In the grave it came from.
If your noble conscience now forbids you
To protest against the sentence and to annul it
By writing as his letter asks you to,
Then I can assure you that, as things stand now,   375
He will consider it his duty to be more than human
And to-morrow morning he will have his orders mercilessly carried out!

PRINCE It doesn't matter any more.

NATALIA Doesn't matter——?

PRINCE Let him do as he likes.   380
I know now that I am doing as I should.
NATALIA (*Horror-stricken, approaching him*) You monster!
Have you written it———?
PRINCE "Signed, Homburg. Fehrbellin, the twelfth———"
There! It's finished! (*He puts letter in envelope and seals it*)   385
Ho, there, Franz!
NATALIA Oh, God in heaven!
PRINCE (*Rising, to* FRANZ *who enters*) Take this letter to His Highness, the
Elector. (*Exit* FRANZ)
I will not appear despicable and weak   390
Before a man who treats me with such great nobility!
Guilt lies heavily upon my heart,
And I cannot hide it. If his pardon must depend
Only upon my own impertinent objections,
Then I do not merit and do not want forgiveness!   395
NATALIA (*Embracing him*) Oh, let me kiss you!
And if the bullets were to lay you low
This instant, I should still be unable to contain my love!
I would rejoice as well as weep for you,
And cry, for all to hear, "I love you!"   400
But—if you insist upon the right
To follow the dictates of your heart,
Then I must too!
Count Reuss!
                (ATTENDANT *opens the door: the* COUNT *enters*)   405
REUSS Your Highness!
NATALIA Now go, and take your letter!
Go to Arnstein, and to Colonel Kottwitz!
His Highness the Elector's orders are:
The regiment must come at once to Fehrbellin!   410
I shall wait on its arrival
Here, at midnight! (*They all leave*)

Act Five

Scene 1

(*A room in the castle at Fehrbellin. The* ELECTOR, *in a night robe, comes out
of an adjoining room, followed by* TRUCHSS, HOHENZOLLERN, *and* GOLTZ.
                PAGES *with lighted torches*)
ELECTOR Kottwitz? With the regiment of Princess Natalia?
Here in Fehrbellin?   5
TRUCHSS (*Opening a window*) Yes, your noble Highness!
Look, you can see them there,
Drawn up before the castle!

ELECTOR   Well? Will someone give me an explanation?
  Who gave orders for the regiment to come to Fehrbellin?   10
HOHENZOLLERN   Sire, I do not know.
ELECTOR   The orders I gave them were
  That they take up quarters in the town of Arnstein!
  Go and find Kottwitz! Bring him here!
GOLTZ   Sire, he will presently be here.   15
ELECTOR   Where is he?
GOLTZ   At the Town Hall, so I hear,
  Where the entire general staff is gathered.
ELECTOR   But why?
HOHENZOLLERN   I do not know.   20
TRUCHSS   Sire, would you allow us for a while
  To absent ourselves and join them there?
ELECTOR   In the Town Hall?
HOHENZOLLERN   In the council-chamber of the chiefs of staff.
  We gave our word that we would join them there.   25
ELECTOR   (*After a brief hesitation*)   You may go.
GOLTZ   Come, then, gentlemen! (*The* OFFICERS *depart*)

Scene 2

ELECTOR   Strange! If I were the Dey of Tunis,
  I should sound the alarm at such a mysterious conspiracy.
  The streets would be strewn with the bodies of my janizaries,   30
  And at the doors of my seraglio
  I should deploy a ring of cannon!
  But as it is old Hans Kottwitz I must deal with,
  A native of Preignitz too, who plays the rebel pasha,
  I must handle him as it befits   35
  A Brandenburger and a gentleman:
  I'll take hold of one of those rare silver locks
  He still has on his trusty head
  And lead him by it quietly,
  Together with his twelve great squadrons,   40
  Back to Arnstein, to his headquarters.
  But quietly. Why should I rouse the sleeping town?
  (*He turns again for a moment to the window, then goes back to his table and
            rings. Two* SERVANTS *enter*)
  You, go down into the streets,   45
  Pretend to be a curious stranger,
  And find out all you can!
SERVANT   Yes, Your Highness! (*He goes*)
ELECTOR   (*To the other*)   You, go and find my uniform and wig
  And bring them here! (*The* SERVANT *brings them in. The* ELECTOR *puts*   50
            them on, with his princely regalia)

Scene 3

(*Enter* FIELD-MARSHAL DÖRFLING)

DÖRFLING   Sire! The army has rebelled!

ELECTOR(*Still busy dressing*)   Calm, Dörfling! Keep calm.
You know how I detest it when   55
People enter my apartments unannounced!
What do you want?

DÖRFLING   Forgive me, Your Highness! It is an occurrence
Of particular gravity has brought me here
So unceremoniously.   60
Colonel Kottwitz without authority has brought
His regiment here; about a hundred officers
Are gathered round him in the Hall of the Knights.
They are circulating a petition
That sets your authority in question.   65

ELECTOR   I know already. What else can it be
But an intervention in favour of the Prince
Whom the military court condemned to death?

DÖRFLING   Precisely.

ELECTOR   Well, my heart is with them in their cause.   70

DÖRFLING   But they must be mad! It is said
They want to present their petition to you
In the castle and without delay!
And, should you persevere—Your Highness,
I can hardly say it!—should you persevere   75
In your unrelenting attitude, they plan
To liberate the Prince by force of arms!

ELECTOR   (*Fierce*)   Who told you that?

DÖRFLING   Who? Why, the Countess von Retzoff,
The cousin of my wife, whom you may trust.   80
Last evening she visited her uncle's, the magistrate
Von Retzoff's house, where officers
Were quite openly expressing these ideas.

ELECTOR   If it had been a man who told you that,
I might have believed it.   85
I've only to show myself outside the prison
To scare away those prating heroes from the Prince.

DÖRFLING   Sire, I beseech you, if it is your will
Eventually to free-the Prince and pardon him,
Do it now, before some disagreeable circumstance arises!   90
Every army loves, as you must know, a hero.
Let not this fire that glows in every soldier's breast
Become an unholy and destructive conflagration!
Kottwitz and his supporters still do not know
That I am faithful to you and have warned you of their plans.   95

Send, sire, before it is too late,
His sword back to the Prince, for he has earned it.
History will remember it as a most generous deed
And she will have one sorry deed the less to reckon with!
ELECTOR First I must consult the Prince, His Highness,   100
Who as you know was not imprisoned arbitrarily,
And cannot arbitrarily be freed.
But I shall speak to these gentlemen, when they arrive.
DÖRFLING (*Aside*) Damnation take it!
He is armoured against every attack!   105

Scene 4

(*Two* GUARDS *enter; one is carrying a letter*)
FIRST GUARD Your Highness! Colonels Kottwitz, Hennings,
Truchss, and others respectfully request an audience!
ELECTOR (*To the other* GUARD, *taking the letter from him*) Is it from
The Prince of Homburg?   110
SECOND GUARD Yes, Your Highness.
ELECTOR Who gave it you?
SECOND GUARD The sentinel who guards the outer door,
To whom it was handed by the Prince's orderly. (*The* ELECTOR *sits at the
table and reads; after he has read the letter, he turns and calls a* PAGE) 115
ELECTOR Bring me the Prince's death-warrant!
And also the safe-conduct for Count von Horn,
The Swedish envoy. (PAGE *off*)
(*To the* FIRST GUARD) Bring in Colonel Kottwitz and his followers!

Scene 5

(*Enter* COLONELS KOTTWITZ *and* HENNINGS, COUNTS TRUCHSS, HOHEN-   120
ZOLLERN, *and* SPARREN, COUNT REUSS, CAPTAINS GOLTZ *and* STRANZ
and other COLONELS *and* OFFICERS)
KOTTWITZ (*Presenting the petition*) My noble sovereign, sire,
Allow me to present to you, with all respect,
And in the name of the entire army, this petition.   125
ELECTOR Kottwitz, before I will take it, you must tell me,
Who gave you orders to come to Fehrbellin?
KOTTWITZ (*Surprised*) With the dragoons?
ELECTOR Yes, with the regiment.
I had assigned you to quarters in Arnstein.   130
KOTTWITZ Sire, it was on your orders I came here.
ELECTOR Indeed? Show me the order.
KOTTWITZ Here it is, Your Highness.
ELECTOR (*Reading*) "Natalia. Fehrbellin.
On the orders of my noble uncle,   135
Prince Friedrich Wilhelm,
Elector of Brandenburg——"

KOTTWITZ By thunder, sire, I hope
You knew about this order?

ELECTOR No, no, you see. . . .
Who was it who brought the order to you?

KOTTWITZ Count Reuss!

ELECTOR (*After a short pause*) Well, Kottwitz, you are thrice welcome,
And, after all, your arrival is most opportune.
Colonel Homburg having been condemned to death,
The twelve squadrons under your command are chosen
To pay him the last respects to-morrow, at dawn.

KOTTWITZ (*Horrified*) Sire!

ELECTOR (*Giving back the order*) Is your regiment still standing
In front of the castle, Colonel,
In the cold and foggy air of night?

KOTTWITZ I'm sorry, it was so dark, sire——

ELECTOR Why have you not dismissed them?

KOTTWITZ Your Highness, I *have* dismissed them.
They have been quartered on the town,
As you commanded.

ELECTOR (*Turning towards the window*)
What? A few moments ago——
Well! You've soon found stabling for your horses, Colonel.
That is all to the good! I congratulate you! Now!
What brings you here? What news have you got for me?

KOTTWITZ Sire, this petition from your faithful army.

ELECTOR Give it here!

KOTTWITZ But what you have just said—— Your words
Have overthrown my hopes completely!

ELECTOR What words have cast away can be retrieved by words.
(*Reading*) "Petition to His Highness, the Elector of Brandenburg,
Imploring the supreme favour of mercy for
Our beloved general, now most grievously incarcerated,
Prince Friedrich Arthur von Hessen-Homburg."
(*To the assembled* OFFICERS) Gentlemen, that is a noble name!
It is not unworthy of your universal approbation.
(*He looks at the petition again*) Who is the author of this plea?

KOTTWITZ It is I.

ELECTOR Is the Prince acquainted with the contents?

KOTTWITZ Not in the slightest! It is we alone
Who have conceived and drafted it.

ELECTOR I request your patience for a moment. (*He goes to the table and reads
through the petition. A long pause*)
Hm! Curious!—— So, Kottwitz, you old warrior,
You take the Prince's defence upon your shoulders?
You approve his action in attacking Wrangel
Before the sign was given?

KOTTWITZ Yes, Your Highness. Kottwitz approves his action.

ELECTOR You were of quite a different opinion   185
Upon the field of battle.

KOTTWITZ I had not summed up the situation well enough.
I should have accepted with greater readiness
The Prince's decision, for he is a great tactician.
The Swedes were wavering on their left flank,   190
But their right flank was sending out
Fresh reinforcements. If he had waited, sire,
For your command, they would have captured our redoubts
And victory would never have been ours.

ELECTOR Yes. You like to fancy it was so.   195
But I had despatched Hennings, as you know,
To cut off the retreat to the Swedish bridge-heads
Which covered Wrangel's rear-guard.
If you cavalry officers had respected my orders,
Hennings would successfully have brought off his manoeuvre.   200
In two hours he could have seized the bridges,
Set them on fire, positioned himself along the Rhine,
And Wrangel would have been annihilated, root and branch,
Lost in the marshes and the hidden swamps.

KOTTWITZ Only a bungling novice, sire, not a soldier like yourself,   205
Would want to snatch at Fate's most glorious wreath!
Until to-day, you always took whatever Fate might offer,
However small a triumph it might be.
The dragon that was bleeding Brandenburg to death
Was routed: for one day, was that not enough?   210
What if he lies a week or so and licks his wounds
Until they heal again? We know now how to conquer him,
And are full of eagerness to take him on again!
Let us get hand to hand again with Wrangel,
And by thunder we'll have him pushed back to the Baltic!   215

ELECTOR You old fool, what right have you to hope for that,
When any hot-head takes it upon himself
To jump upon my chariot of war and seize the reins?
Do you believe that disobedience will always be
Crowned with a laurel wreath by smiling Fortune?   220
I do not relish victory that, out of the blue,
Falls into my lap, a sport of chance!
I will uphold the law, the goddess
To whom I owe my life, my throne, my crown,
And who conceived for me a race of triumphs!   225

KOTTWITZ Sire. The supreme, the very highest law
That can govern such a noble heart as yours
Is not a law that can be taken at the letter of your will.
It is your country, and it is your crown.
It is the wearer of that crown—yourself.   230

What does it signify for men like you, a rule
Which says that an enemy cannot be conquered
Unless he lies before you in the dust, with all his flags?
The only and the highest rule is conquest!
Will you brandish in your fist like a living sword   235
The army burning with desire to serve you,
Or let it hang, a lifeless blade,
Upon your golden girdle?
A poor fool it must have been, deprived of sense and feeling,
Who framed those rules! And it is a bad,   240
Short-sighted policy that, because a human instinct
Once proved fatal, determines to forget
The score of times when only instinct,
And obedience to instinct, saved the day!
And on the field of battle, do you think   245
I'd shed my blood for honour or for gold?
God forfend! My blood's too precious for such small rewards!
No! My best, my happiest reward, the one I always hope to win
And work for freely, independently, and owing
No account of it to any man—that is to serve   250
The greater glory and the majesty of Brandenburg, defend
The fame and honour of your own immortal name!
That is the reward for which I sell my heart!
Grant that for this unbidden victory now
You doom the Prince of Homburg,   255
And if I, to-morrow, wandering like a shepherd
Through the woods and mountains with my squadrons,
By chance encounter opportunities for victory,
By God! I should be a miserable coward if
I did not act with vigour, as our Prince once did,   260
And snatch another triumph for the fame of Brandenburg!
If you then came to me, Your Highness,
With your rule-book in your hand, and said:
"Kottwitz, you have forfeited your head!"
Why, then, I'd up and answer: I know, sire;   265
Take it; here it is; for when I swore the oath
That bound me, head and hand to you and to your crown,
My heart and soul were in it, and my head as well,
And I would deny you nothing that belongs to you!
ELECTOR   I cannot hold my own against you,   270
You brave and wonderful old soldier!
Your words have pierced my heart with crafty oratory;
My heart, which, as you know, is full of love for you.
But I must call an advocate, one
Who can plead my cause far better than myself!   275
                (*He rings for a* SERVANT, *who enters*)

The Prince of Homburg! Have him brought here from
The prison! (*The* SERVANT *goes*)
He will teach you, Kottwitz, I assure you,
What obedience and discipline should be!   280
He has, at any rate, sent me a letter here
That reads quite differently from
The subtle disquisitions upon freedom
That you have served up to me here to-day
As if I were a new boy in the bottom class   285
At some pretentious military college!
      (*He returns to his desk and reads the letter*)
KOTTWITZ (*Astounded*) Who? What?
HENNINGS The Prince himself?
TRUCHSS It can't be! (*Rather ill at ease, the* OFFICERS *talk together*)   290
ELECTOR From whom is this other letter?
HOHENZOLLERN From me, sire.
ELECTOR (*Reading*) "Proof that his Highness the Elector
  Was himself responsible for the Prince's act——"
Now, by heaven, that's going a bit too far!   295
Do you mean to say you throw the whole responsibility
For the Prince's error on myself, Hohenzollern?
HOHENZOLLERN I do, sire.
ELECTOR By Jupiter! Will wonders never cease?
One man explains to me he isn't guilty: 300
The other that *I'm* guilty!
I must confess I am curious to see how you will state your case.
HOHENZOLLERN If you will be so good, sire, and recollect that night
In which we found the Prince asleep upon a seat
In the garden underneath an oak, you will remember   305
He was holding in his hand a laurel wreath and seemed
To be dreaming of the victory on the coming day.
You, sire, desiring to sound the deepest motives of his heart,
Removed the garland from his hands and wound
Your golden chain about it. You were smiling.   310
Then you gave the wreath, entwined with gold,
To the lady who is your noble niece.
At such a heavenly sight, the Prince
Rises in confusion, for he longs to take
So dear an object from such lovely hands.   315
But then, you swiftly move away from him,
Drawing the Princess backwards with you;
The door opens to receive you;
The lovely maiden and the gold-hung laurel wreath
Vanish.   320
And he, alone, and bearing in his hand a glove
That comes from he knows not what fair hand,

Remains behind at midnight in the garden
Of the moonlit castle.

ELECTOR What glove? 325

HOHENZOLLERN Sire, let me finish!
The whole thing was just a game; but to him,
I later learnt, it meant much more.
For, when I crept towards him and, as if by chance,
Through one of the garden's lower gates 330
And woke him, and brought him to his senses once again,
The memory caused a flood of joy to fill his being.
You cannot, sire, imagine anything more touching!
He related the whole event, down to the smallest detail,
As if it were a dream that he remembered. 335
And so vividly did he imagine he had dreamed
That the conviction grew in him
That heaven had given him a sign which meant
That everything—the maiden, the wreath, the golden chain—
Would be accorded him by God upon the day of battle. 340

ELECTOR Hm! How strange! But what about the glove?

HOHENZOLLERN This fragment of his dream, the one reality remaining from
his vision,
Both destroys and strengthens his belief.
At first he looks upon it with wide-open eyes. 345
The glove is white: it would appear
It comes from a lady's hand—yet
As he has encountered no one in the moonlit garden
From whom he could have taken it,
He puts it from his mind, forgets what he cannot understand, 350
And tucks it absent-mindedly into the collar of his coat.

ELECTOR Well? What then?

HOHENZOLLERN Then he enters the castle, taking his notebooks
And his pencil, to concentrate most seriously upon
The marshal's orders, which he is to note 355
For reference on the field of battle.
Your own lady, sire, and the Princess, dressed for travelling,
Happen to be waiting also in the hall.
Who can imagine the immeasureable astonishment
That seized him when he saw 360
That the glove out of his dream
Was the one the Princess sought!
Time and again the marshal called him to attention:
"The Prince of Homburg!" "What are your orders, sir?"
Is all he can reply, trying to collect his wits. 365
He was so ringed with wonders,
A thunderbolt could have fallen, and—— (*He stops*)

ELECTOR Was it the Princess' glove?

HOHENZOLLERN He stands like a stone, his pencil frozen in his hand.
And yet he is alive, a living statue!   370
But all feeling is extinguished in him
By so many marvels all at once.
Only in the morning, when
The sound of the cannon brings him to his senses,
He turns to me, and asks: 375
"Heinrich, what was it Marshal Dörfling said to me
Yesterday, concerning the order of battle?"
DÖRFLING Sire, I can vouch for Hohenzollern's words.
The Prince, I recollect,
Paid no attention to whatever I was saying.   380
I'd often known him to be rather cloudy-headed,
But never before that day
Have I seen him in a fit of such intense abstraction.
ELECTOR Well, now, if I have understood you both aright,
This is the crowning proof of Homburg's innocence.   385
If I had not played my little game on this young dreamer,
I should not have anything to reproach him with to-day?
He wouldn't have been distracted at the meeting
Nor disobedient on the field of battle?
Eh? Well? Isn't that your meaning, gentlemen?   390
HOHENZOLLERN Sire, I leave you to draw your own conclusions.
ELECTOR Then you are either an idiot or a silly fool!
If you had not called me down into the garden,
Then, as my curiosity would not have been aroused,
I should not have played my harmless game upon this dreamer.   395
And so I feel quite able to declare
That the one responsible for Homburg's error
Was not me—but you yourself!
Oh! What Delphic oracles I have for officers!
HOHENZOLLERN Sire, I can say no more. But I am sure   400
My words have left their mark within your heart!

Scene 6

(Enter an OFFICER)

OFFICER Your Highness, the Prince of Homburg will presently appear!
ELECTOR Good. Bring him here.
OFFICER Sire, a moment's grace.   405
As he was passing by the chapel
He asked the gatekeeper to admit him to the graveyard.
ELECTOR The graveyard?
OFFICER Yes, Your Highness.
ELECTOR Why?   410
OFFICER To tell you the truth, sire, I hardly know.

It seems, he wanted to see the tomb
To which your sentence has condemned him. (*The* OFFICERS *gather
together and talk*)
ELECTOR Very well! As soon as he comes, let him in. (*He goes back to the* 415
papers on his desk)
TRUCHSS Here he comes now, with the officers of the guard.

Scene 7

(*Enter the* PRINCE OF HOMBURG: OFFICERS *of the guard*)
ELECTOR My dear young Prince,
I have summoned you here to come to my rescue! 420
Colonel Kottwitz has presented me
With this petition in your favour,
Signed by a hundred noble names:
The army, it appears, demands your release
And disapproves the sentence of the court. 425
Read it and see for yourself! (*He gives* HOMBURG *the petition*)
PRINCE (*Gives it a brief glance, then turns to address the circle of* OFFICERS)
Kottwitz, give me your hand, old friend!
What you have done for me is more
Than I deserved from you, 430
Whom I so cavalierly treated in the field!
And now, go back, as swiftly as you came,
To Arnstein and do not grieve for me.
I have thought it over well and have decided
To accept the punishment to which I was condemned. (*He gives the petition* 435
back to KOTTWITZ)
KOTTWITZ No, you can never——
HOHENZOLLERN Does he *want* to die?
TRUCHSS He cannot and he shall not die.
SEVERAL OFFICERS (*Coming towards the* PRINCE) Your Highness! We beg 440
of you! Prince! Listen to us!
PRINCE No. I have made my decision. It is unalterable.
I wish to glorify the sacred laws of war
That I, in view of the entire army, scorned and violated.
It is a freely-given and a willing death. 445
Oh, my brothers-in-arms, what is a victory worth
That I perhaps might gain against the Swedish general
Beside the victory we shall gloriously win to-morrow
Over the most pernicious enemies we know,
The enemies within ourselves: defiance, arrogance? 450
A triumph over Wrangel is a paltry thing.
As for the foreign foes who would subdue us to their yoke,
Whether I live or die, you know they cannot win,
And that the sons of Brandenburg

Will walk in freedom on their native earth. 455
For it is theirs, and all the splendour of its plains
Belongs to them alone!
KOTTWITZ My dear Prince! Friend or son? What shall I call you?
TRUCHSS Dear God in heaven!
KOTTWITZ Let me kiss your hand! (*They all crowd round him*) 460
PRINCE (*Turning away from them to address the* ELECTOR)
My sovereign, you whom I used to call—
For once I had the right, now cast away—
By the gentler name of father, I cast myself
Before you, and my heart 465
Is full to overflowing!
Forgive me, if on the morning of decision
I served you with too-impetuous eagerness:
My death will help to wash away my sin.
My heart now is reconciled and full of ease: 470
It accepts the justice of your will.
But comfort it by saying that your own great heart
Is free from anger too! And let it grant me,
In my hour of death, one more request!
ELECTOR Speak, hero! Tell me your desire. 475
I give you my soldier's word:
Your wish, whatever it is, shall be respected.
PRINCE Sire, do not purchase with your niece's hand
The peace that you must win from Sweden.
Dismiss from your camp the go-between 480
Who made you such an ignominious proposal!
Give him his answer in a round of shot!
ELECTOR (*Kisses* HOMBURG'S *forehead*)
It shall be done, my son. With this last kiss,
I give you my promise. 485
Why should there be another sacrifice
To war's misfortunes?
May every word that you have spoken be the seed
Of new and greater victories for Brandenburg,
And be the death of Sweden! 490
"She is affianced to the Prince of Homburg," I shall tell him.
Victor of Fehrbellin, who gave his life for victory!
His spirit will defend her on the field of battle,
For he is dead but marches on forever with the foremost flags! (*He embraces
    the* PRINCE, *and raises him*) 495
PRINCE Now you have given back my life to me!
I pray that every triumph, every blessing
May now fall upon your hero's head in gay profusion!
Go, my sovereign lord, do battle!
Vanquish the globe itself, if it defy you, 500

For it is your duty and your right!
ELECTOR   Guards, accompany His Highness back to prison!

Scene 8

(NATALIA *and the* ELECTOR'S WIFE *appear at the door, followed by* COURT
LADIES)
NATALIA   No! Do not speak to me of what is fitting: 505
What, in this hour of peril, is
More fitting than my love for him?
Oh, my dear, unhappy friend!
PRINCE (*Brusquely*)   Let me go!
TRUCHSS   Never, Prince! Never! (*Several* OFFICERS *bar his way*)   510
PRINCE   Take me away!
HOHENZOLLERN (*To* ELECTOR)   Your Highness, if your heart——
PRINCE (*Tearing himself away from them*)   You tyrants!
Would you have them drag me to the place of execution
Bound hand and foot with chains?   515
Let me away! I have settled my account with life. (*He goes with* GUARDS)
NATALIA   Oh, Earth, receive me!
Why should I look upon the sun again? (*She weeps on the bosom of her aunt*)

Scene 9

DÖRFLING   God and creation! Must it come to this? (*The* ELECTOR *is speaking
aside to an* OFFICER)   520
KOTTWITZ (*Coldly*)   My lord, after what has happened,
Are we released now from to-morrow's——
ELECTOR   No! I shall discharge you when the time has come. (*He looks at
him a moment. Then he takes the papers that the* PAGE *brought in and turns
away from the table towards the* FIELD-MARSHAL)   525
Here is the safe-conduct for Count Horn!
This would be the Prince's wish, that I am bound to honour:
In three days' time, we declare war again!
        (*A silence. He casts a glance at the death-warrant*)
Gentlemen, I lay the decision in your hands.   530
The Prince of Homburg, during the past year,
Has, through his thoughtlessness and disobedience,
Cost me two of my most brilliant victories.
He also spoilt a third for me.
Now he's a graduate in the school of war,   535
Can you entrust yourselves to him again? A fourth time?
KOTTWITZ *and* TRUCHSS (*Together*)   Your Highness means——
        Do we understand——
ELECTOR   Can you? Can you?
KOTTWITZ   Sire, by the living God,   540
You could be standing in peril of your life

On the very edge of some steep precipice!
He wouldn't lift a finger now to save you
Or ever draw his sword again without your full permission!
ELECTOR (*Tearing up the death-warrant*) Come, then, my friends, 545
Follow me to the garden. (*They all depart*)

Scene 10

The setting is as in Act I. It is night again. The PRINCE *is led, a bandage round his eyes, through the lower garden gate by* CAPTAIN REUSS. OFFICERS OF THE GUARD. *In the distance, the muted drums of a funeral march*
PRINCE Now, Immortality, you are entirely mine! 550
You shine, with the radiance of a thousand suns,
Through my eyes' dark bandages into my very soul!
My arms feel like a pair of slowly spreading wings
That bear my spirit through the quiet lofts of air;
And as a ship whose sail fills with the evening wind 555
Sees the lighted harbour sink along the rising waves,
So, like the happy shore, my dying life
Drowns slowly in the dusk of death:
Now I can distinguish only forms and colours,
And under my weightless feet 560
Drift only clouds and those ethereal vapours
That are the mists of time. (*He sits down on the garden-seat beneath the oak.*
CAPTAIN STRANZ *draws away from him and gazes up
towards the top of the slope*)
PRINCE Ah! How sweet the midnight violet smells! 565
Did you not notice how it smells? (STRANZ *comes back again*)
STRANZ They are gillyflowers and pinks.
PRINCE Gillyflowers? How do they come to be here?
STRANZ I don't know. It seems a maiden
Planted them here. 570
Would you like one?
PRINCE Thank you. When I go home
I'll put it in water.

Scene 11

(*Enter the* ELECTOR, *with the laurel wreath, round which the golden chain is hung;* HIS WIFE, PRINCESS NATALIA, FIELD-MARSHAL DÖRFLING, COLONELS 575
KOTTWITZ, HOHENZOLLERN, GOLTZ, *etc.* LADIES OF THE COURT, OFFICERS *and* PAGES *bearing torches appear on the balustraded slope.* HOHENZOLLERN *comes with a handkerchief, which he waves at* CAPTAIN STRANZ, *who then leaves the* PRINCE *and goes to speak to the* GUARDS *in the background*)
PRINCE Dear Stranz, what is all this light? 580
STRANZ (*Returning to him*) Prince, would you kindly rise?
PRINCE What is it now?

STRANZ   Nothing you need be afraid of!
         I want only to unbind your eyes.
PRINCE   So the hour of my deliverance has come at last?   585
STRANZ   Yes! Look now and live! (*The* ELECTOR *gives the wreath, on which the
         golden chain is shining, to the* PRINCESS, *takes her by the hand, and leads her
         down the slope, followed by all* LADIES *and* GENTLEMEN. *Surrounded by* TORCH-
         BEARERS, *the* PRINCESS *goes up to the* PRINCE, *who stares at her astounded,
         lays the wreath on his head, the chain round his neck, and presses his hand to*   590
         her heart. The PRINCE *falls unconscious*)
NATALIA   Look! His waking has killed him with happiness!
HOHENZOLLERN (*Lifting him up*)   Help me! Help!
ELECTOR   Let the thunder of the royal cannon wake him! (*Cannon are fired.
          A triumphal march. The castle is illuminated in every window*)   595
KOTTWITZ   Hail! Hail to the Prince of Homburg!
OFFICERS   Hail! Hail! Hail!
ALL   Hail to the victor of Fehrbellin! (*A moment's silence*)
PRINCE   Tell me: is this a dream?
KOTTWITZ   A dream: what else?   600
OFFICERS   To horse! Away!
TRUCHSS   Into battle!
DÖRFLING   To victory! To victory!
ALL   Death to all the enemies of Brandenburg!

Interior of the second Covent Garden Theater in 1810.
Shortly after the theater opened in 1809, the introduction of
private boxes and a sixpence rise in the pit admission fee
resulted in the Old Price riots, which lasted more than sixty nights.
From a contemporary print. *Harvard Theatre Collection*

Georg Büchner

Georg Büchner *(1813–1837) was a man in most respects in advance of his time. As a student of history, as a political writer, and as a revolutionary, he anticipated the determinist thought of the twentieth century and, more particularly, certain of the ideas of Marx; this thought is clearly reflected in his most important and best known play, the historical drama* DANTON'S DEATH. *As a playwright, he wrote only two complete plays and a fragment, but his impatience with the forms popular with his contemporaries drove him to experiments that anticipated many of the formal innovations of the twentieth century. In* DANTON'S DEATH *and* WOYZECK, *for example, he used a loose chronicle form and tonal and rhythmic effects suggestive of later Expressionistic drama; in* LEONCE AND LENA, *a satirical romance, he managed a blend of romance and bitter comedy which heralds the dark, ironical comedy of the present. Little else remains of his work except certain fragmentary political writings.*

Chronology

1813 Born at Goddelau, near Darmstadt, the son of an army doctor.

c.1824 Entered the Ludwig Georg Gymnasium in Darmstadt.

c.1832 Entered the Strassbourg Academy to study medicine.

1834 Became involved in the revolutionary movement of the 1830's, publishing a revolutionary pamphlet and founding a radical society.

1835 Wrote *Danton's Death* (first performed in Berlin in 1902).

1836 Wrote *Leonce and Lena,* a romantic comedy (first performed in Munich in 1885). To escape arrest, he fled to Strassbourg, then to Zurich, where he became a lecturer in natural science. He wrote *Woyzeck,* a play which he left unfinished (performed in 1913).

1837 Died of typhoid fever in Zurich.

Selected Bibliography

Baxandall, Lee, "Georg Büchner's *Danton's Death,*" *Tulane Drama Review,* VI (1962), 136–149.

Hardwick, Elizabeth, *"Danton's Death,"* New York Review of Books, V (Nov. 25, 1965), 6–8.

Hauch, Edward F., "The Reviviscence of Georg Büchner," *PMLA,* XLIV (1929), 892–900.

Knight, Arthur H. J., *Georg Büchner,* Oxford, 1951.

Lindenberger, H. S., *Georg Büchner,* Carbondale, Ill., 1964.

DANTON'S DEATH

by Georg Büchner

Translated by Stephen Spender and Goronwy Rees

Characters

GEORGES DANTON
LEGENDRE
CAMILLE DESMOULINS
HÉRAULT-SÉCHELLES
LACROIX   *Deputies**
PHILIPPEAU
FABRE D'EGLANTINE
MERCIER
THOMAS PAYNE

ROBESPIERRE
SAINT-JUST
BARÈRE   *Members of the Committee*
COLLOT D'HERBOIS   *of Public Safety**
BILLAUD-VARENNES

CHAUMETTE, Procureur *of the Paris Commune**
DILLON, *a General*
FOUQUIER-TINVILLE, *Public Prosecutor*
AMAR *and* VOULAND, *Members of the Committee of Security**
HERMAN *and* DUMAS, *Presidents of the Revolutionary Tribunal**
PARIS, *friend to Danton*
SIMON, *a Prompter*
LAFLOTTE
JULIE, *Danton's wife*
LUCILE, *wife of Camille Desmoulins*

ADELAIDE
MARION   *Prostitutes*
ROSALIE
Men and Women of the People, Prostitutes, Executioners, etc.

* *Deputies:* of the National Convention established in 1792. This body, consisting of about 780 members, was the theoretical source of authority during this period, though in fact its internal struggles frequently caused it to lose power to its designated committees. In 1792 its membership divided, roughly, into about 100 Jacobins, supported by the populace and forming the Left, about 180 Girondins, supported by the bourgeoisie and forming the Right, and about 500 members of a group called the Plain, which shifted its

Act One

Scene 1

HÉRAULT-SÉCHELLES, *ladies* (*at a card-table*).

DANTON, JULIE, *a little apart,* DANTON *on a stool at* JULIE'S *feet*

DANTON See the pretty lady, how cleverly she shuffles the cards! Yes, really, she understands! They say she deals hearts to her husband and diamonds to everyone else. She has clumsy legs and she's apt to fall; her husband carries the bumps on his forehead, he thinks they're bumps of humour* and laughs them off. You could make a man fall in love with lies.   5

JULIE Do you believe in me?

DANTON How do I know? We know little of one another. We are thick-skinned, our hands reach out to each other but it's waste of time, leather rubs against leather—we are very lonely.

JULIE You know me, Danton.   10

DANTON Yes, what one calls knowing. You have dark eyes and curly hair and a delicate complexion and always call me "Dear George." But there, there! (*Touching her eyes and her forehead*) What lies behind them? Look, our senses are gross. Know each other! We'd have to break open our skulls and pick out the thoughts from our brain-boxes.   15

A LADY (*To* HÉRAULT) What are you doing with your fingers?

HÉRAULT Nothing.

LADY Don't stick your thumbs in like that, it's unbearable.

HÉRAULT You see, it has a peculiar significance.

DANTON No, Julie, I love you like the grave.   20

JULIE (*Turning away*) Oh!

DANTON No, listen. They say that in the grave there is peace, and that the grave and peace are one. If that is so, then lying in your lap I am already under the earth. Sweet grave, your lips are funeral bells, your voice my death knell, your breast the mound above me, and your heart my coffin.   25

LADY (*To* HÉRAULT) You've lost.

HÉRAULT It was a lover's adventure, that cost money like all the others.

LADY Then you declared your love like a deaf mute—with your fingers.

HÉRAULT And why not? People even say that they are easiest to understand. I had an affair with a queen, my fingers were princes bewitched into spiders,   30 and you, madam, were the fairy; but it went badly, the queen was always

support from one side to the other. At the time of the play the Girondin faction had fallen, leaving the Jacobins supreme.

* *Committee of Public Safety:* established initially to safeguard the separation of executive and legislative functions, this Committee was by this time reduced to nine members and entrusted with the whole of national defense. Meeting in secret, the group rapidly became the supreme power in the Republic.

* *Paris Commune:* the revolutionary council of Paris, immensely powerful because of its location and the intermittent weakness of national governing bodies.

* *Committee of Security:* established to deal with resistance to the Revolution, this group had unlimited powers to effect the discovery and prevention of crime against the state.

* *Revolutionary Tribunal:* established to try all offences against the Revolution without appeal.

4 Refers to the bumps which, according to phrenology, are supposed to indicate character. Danton earlier refers to the horns of a cuckold.

pregnant, and every minute gave birth to a knave. I wouldn't let my daughter play such games; kings and queens lie on top of each other so shamelessly, and the knaves come close behind.

(Enter CAMILLE DESMOULINS and PHILIPPEAU) 35

HÉRAULT What sad eyes, Philippeau! Have you torn a hole in your red cap?* Has St. Jacob* frowned on you? Did it rain during the executions? Or did you get a bad place and see nothing?

CAMILLE You parody Socrates. Do you know what the divine philosopher asked Alcibiades,* when he found him sad and depressed? "Have you lost your 40 shield on the battle-field? Have you been beaten in a race or a duel? Has someone sung better or struck the lyre better than you?" What classical Republicans! Take some of our guillotine romanticism against it!

PHILIPPEAU To-day another twenty victims have fallen. We made a mistake, the Hébertists* were only sent to the guillotine because they weren't 45 systematic enough, and perhaps because the Decemvirs* thought they were lost, if for over a week men existed who were even more feared than they.

HÉRAULT They'd like to send us back to the stone age. Saint-Just wouldn't mind if we crawled on all fours, so that the lawyer from Arras* could give us school-caps and benches and a God Almighty after the mechanism of the 50 Geneva watchmaker.

PHILIPPEAU They wouldn't shrink from hanging on a few noughts to Marat's figures for the proscriptions.* How long must we remain dirty and bloody like new-born children, have coffins for cradles and heads for dolls? We must advance. The Committee of Clemency must be set up, the expelled deputies 55 must be reinstated.

HÉRAULT The Revolution has entered the period of reorganization.—The Revolution must end, and the Republic must begin.—In our Constitution Right must take the place of Duty, happiness the place of virtue, protection the place of punishment. Every individual must count, and be able to 60 assert his own nature. He may be reasonable or unreasonable, educated or uneducated, good or bad—it's no concern of the State's. We are all fools and no one has the right to impose his own particular folly on any one else. —Every one must be allowed to enjoy himself in his own way, so long as he does not enjoy himself at the expense of others and does not interfere 65 with their pleasure. The individuality of the majority must be revealed in the form of the State.

---

36 The cap of the revolutionaries.

37 For the purposes of jest the patron saint of the Jacobins.

40 A handsome Greek aristocrat and friend to Socrates.

45 Followers of the revolutionary leader Jacques Hébert (1755–1794), who especially argued for the destruction of the Church in France.

46 A revolutionary committee named after a comparable group in ancient Rome.

49 Robespierre (1758–1794), soon to become the virtual dictator of the Revolution, was a lawyer from Arras, austere in moral principle (he was called the "Incorruptible"), and a Deist. The reference to God as a watchmaker is to the Deist conception of God.

53 Jean Paul Marat (1743–1793), in his newspaper The Friend of the People, had estimated that 500 heads were ready for the guillotine.

CAMILLE The Constitution should be a transparent veil, clinging closely to the body of the People. It must answer to every throb of their veins, every tension of the muscles, every pulse of desire. The body may be fair or foul, 70 it has the right to be what it is, and we have no right to cut its clothes to our measure.—We will rap over the knuckles those who wish to throw a nun's hood over the naked shoulders of France, loveliest of sinners.—We want naked Gods, Bacchantes,* Olympic games, roses in our hair, sparkling wine, heaving breasts and singing lips; oh, wicked, limb-loosening Love! 75 —We don't want to prevent the Romans from sitting in the corner and cooking roots; but we'll have no more gladiatorial games. The divine Epicurus* and Venus with the lovely buttocks shall be the door-keepers of the Republic, instead of St. Marat and St. Chalier.* Danton, you will make the attack in the Convention! 80

DANTON I shall, thou wilt, he will. If we live till then, as the old women say. After an hour sixty minutes will have passed, isn't that so, my boy?

CAMILLE What do you mean? That goes without saying.

DANTON Oh, it all goes without saying. And who is to put all these fine things into action? 85

PHILIPPEAU We, and all honest men.

DANTON That "and" in between is a long word, it holds us rather far apart; there's a long distance to cover and Honesty will be out of breath before we meet. And when we do!—You can lend money to honest men, you can be godfather to their children and marry them to your daughters, but 90 that's all.

CAMILLE If you know that, why did you begin the struggle?

DANTON Those people annoyed me. I couldn't look at those swaggering Catos,* without giving them a kick. That is my nature. (*Rises*)

JULIE You're going? 95

DANTON (*To* JULIE) I must get out of here, they rub me up the wrong way again with their politics. (*On his way out*) Between the door and the door-post I will prophesy unto you; the Statue of Liberty has not yet been cast, the furnace is glowing, and we can still all burn our fingers. (*Exit* DANTON)

CAMILLE Leave him alone! Do you think he can keep his hands off if it comes 100 to action?

HÉRAULT No, but only to kill time, as one plays chess.

Scene 2

(*A Street. Enter* SIMON *and his* WIFE)

SIMON (*Beats his wife*) You old pimp, you wrinkled pill, you maggotty apple of sin. 105

WIFE Help, help!

---

74 Female revellers and followers of Bacchus, the god of wine.
78 Greek philosopher (c.342–270 B.C.) who posited pleasure as the highest good.
79 A leader of the Jacobins in Lyon who had been executed by groups reacting to his extremism.
93 A Roman statesman and aristocrat (234–149 B.C.); often a model of Roman virtue and integrity.

PEOPLE (*Run in*) Pull them apart, pull them apart!

SIMON Unhand me, Romans! I'll batter these bones to bits! You vestal virgin!

WIFE Me a vestal virgin? I'll say I am.

SIMON Thus from thy shoulders I tear off thy robe,   110
And naked in the sun display thine arse.
You whore's bed, lust breeds in every wrinkle of your body.
(*They are separated*)

FIRST CITIZEN What's the matter?

SIMON Where is the virgin? Speak! No, I can't say virgin. The maiden? No,   115
nor that either. The woman, the wife! Oh, not even that! There's only one
other name; oh, it chokes me! I've no breath to say it.

SECOND CITIZEN Lucky you haven't, or it would stink of brandy.

SIMON Aged Virginius,* veil your hoary head—the raven shame sits upon it
and pecks at your eyes. Give me a knife, Romans! (*He sinks to the ground*)   120

WIFE Ah, usually he's a good man, but he can't carry much drink; brandy gives
him an extra leg.

SECOND CITIZEN Then he must walk on three.

WIFE No, he falls down.

SECOND CITIZEN Quite right, first he walks on three legs, then falls over   125
the third until the third itself falls down again.

SIMON You're the vampire's tongue that sucks my warmest heart's blood.

WIFE Just leave him alone; now's the time he always gets sentimental; it'll soon
be over.

FIRST CITIZEN But what's up?   130

WIFE Well, it was like this, you see. I was sitting on a stone in the sun, warming
myself, you see—we've got no firewood, you see—

SECOND CITIZEN Use your husband's nose—

WIFE —and my daughter had gone down to the corner—she's a fine girl and
supports her parents.   135

SIMON There, she confesses!

WIFE You Judas,* would you have a pair of trousers to put on if the young
gentlemen didn't take theirs off with her? You brandy cask, do you want to
thirst when the fountain ceases to flow?—We work with all our limbs, why
not with that one? Her mother did, when she brought her into the   140
world, and it gave her pain; can't she get something for her mother with
it, eh? And does it give her pain, eh? You idiot!

SIMON Ha, Lucretia! A knife, give me a knife, Romans! Ha, Appius Claudius!

FIRST CITIZEN Yes, a knife, but not for the poor whore! What has she done?
Nothing! Her hunger whores and begs. A knife for the people who buy   145
the flesh of our wives and daughters! Woe to those who whore with the
daughters of the people! Your stomachs are empty, theirs are filled to burst-
ing; you have holes in your coats, they have warm clothes; you have horny
hands, theirs are soft as silk. *Ergo,** you toil and they do nothing; *ergo*, you

---

[119] A Roman plebian who, discovering that his beautiful daughter Virginia was to be prostituted to the
aristocrat Appius Claudius, stabbed her and raised a revolt.

[137] Judas Iscariot, the apostle who betrayed Christ.

[149] "Therefore."

earn your bread and they have stolen it; *ergo,* when you want a few 150
coppers of your stolen property you must whore and beg; *ergo,* they are
thieves, and we must cut off their heads.

THIRD CITIZEN They have no blood in their veins but what they have sucked
out of ours. They told us: kill the aristocrats, they are wolves! We hanged
the aristocrats from the lantern. They said to us: the veto devours your 155
bread. We killed the veto. They said to us: the Girondins are starving you;
we sent the Girondins to the guillotine. But they have taken the dead men's
clothes and we go naked and freeze as before. We will peel the skin from
their bones to make trousers for ourselves, we will melt down their fat and
make soup out of it. Forward! Death to all who have no holes in their 160
clothes!

FIRST CITIZEN Death to all who can read and write!

SECOND CITIZEN Death to all who go abroad!

ALL Death, death! (*A Young Man is dragged on*)

VOICES He's got a handkerchief! An aristocrat! To the lantern! To the 165
lantern!

SECOND CITIZEN What? He doesn't wipe his nose with his fingers? To the
lantern! (*A lantern is let down*)

YOUNG MAN Gentlemen!

SECOND CITIZEN There are no gentlemen here! To the lantern! 170

SOME (*Sing*) Who lie in the earth
Are eaten by worms,
Better hang in the air
Than rot in the grave.

YOUNG MAN Mercy! 175

THIRD CITIZEN Only a game with a hempen noose round your neck! It only
takes a minute, we're kinder-hearted than you. Our life is murder by hard
labour; for sixty years we hang by the rope and struggle, but we'll cut ourselves loose.—To the lantern!

YOUNG MAN I don't care, it won't help you to see any clearer. 180

CROWD Bravo, bravo!

SOME VOICES Let him go! (*He disappears*)

(*Enter* ROBESPIERRE, *followed by Women and Sansculottes**)

ROBESPIERRE What's wrong, citizens?

THIRD CITIZEN What's wrong? The few drops of blood shed in August and 185
September have not made the cheeks of the people red. The guillotine is
too slow. We need a hailstorm.

FIRST CITIZEN Our wives and children cry for bread, we want to feed them
with the flesh of aristocrats. Death to all with no holes in their clothes!

ALL Death, death! 190

ROBESPIERRE In the name of the law!

FIRST CITIZEN What is the law?

ROBESPIERRE The will of the people.

FIRST CITIZEN We are the people, and our will is there should be no law; *ergo,*

---

183 Literally "those without trousers," that is, the poor.

our will is the law, *ergo,* in the name of the law there is no law, *ergo,* 195
death!

VOICES Silence for Aristides!* Silence for the Incorruptible!

A WOMAN Hear the Messiah, who is sent to elect and to judge; he will strike
the wicked with the edge of the sword. His eyes are the eyes of election, his
hands are the hands of judgment.   200

ROBESPIERRE Poor, virtuous People! You do your duty, you sacrifice your
enemies. People, thou art great! In flashes of lightning and in thunder thou
art revealed. But, my people, your blows must not wound your own body;
you murder yourself in your fury. You can fall only through your own
strength; your enemies know it well. Your legislators watch over you, 205
they will guide your hands; their eyes are unerring, your hands are inescapable. Come with me to the Jacobin Club!* Your brothers will open their
arms to you, we will hold a bloody assize on our enemies.

MANY VOICES To the Jacobins! Long live Robespierre! (*All off*)

SIMON Alas, abandoned! (*He tries to rise*)   210

WIFE There! (*Supports him*)

SIMON Ah, my Baucis,* you heap coals of fire on my head.

WIFE Now stand up.

SIMON You turn away? Can you forgive me, Portia?* Did I strike you? It was
not my hand, it was not my arm, my madness did it.   215
    His madness is poor Hamlet's enemy,
    'Twas not Hamlet struck you, Hamlet denies it.*
Where is our daughter, where's my little Susie?

WIFE There, on the corner!

SIMON Let us go to her! Come, my virtuous spouse! (*Exeunt*)   220

Scene 3

The Jacobin Club. A group from the Jacobin faction, including ROBESPIERRE,
LEGENDRE, *and* COLLOT D'HERBOIS.

A CITIZEN FROM LYONS Our brothers in Lyons have sent us to pour out their
bitter anger on your breast. We do not know if the tumbril* that carried
Ronsin* to the guillotine was the hearse of Liberty; but we do know that 225
since that day Chalier's murderers have trod the earth as safely as if no grave
were waiting for them. Have you forgotten that Lyons is a stain upon the
earth of France* which must be covered by the limbs of traitors? Have you
forgotten that this whore of kings has only the waters of the Rhone in
which to wash her scabs? Have you forgotten that the flood tide of the 230

---

[197] An Athenian statesman (530–468 B.C.), renowned for his honesty and fairness.

[207] The leftist political club in Paris which gave its name to the Jacobin faction.

[212] In Greek legend the devoted wife of Philemon.

[214] Steadfast wife of Marcus Brutus (85–42 B.C.).

[217] *Cf. Hamlet,* V, ii, 245–248: "If Hamlet from himself be ta'en away,/And when he's not himself does
wrong Laertes,/Then Hamlet does it not, Hamlet denies it./Who does it, then? His madness."

[224] Two-wheeled cart.

[225] A revolutionary general and follower of Hébert, he was executed by the Committee of Safety.

[228] Because of the brief anti-extremist movement there which had taken Chalier's life.

Revolution must wash Pitt's Mediterranean fleet* aground on the corpses of aristocrats? Your compassion is murdering the Revolution. The breath of an aristocrat is the death rattle of Freedom. Only a coward dies for the Republic; a Jacobin kills for her. I warn you; if we no longer find in you the energy of the men of the 10th of August,* of September,* and the 235 31st of May,* there remains for us, as for the patriot Gaillard, only the dagger of Cato.* (*Applause and confused cries*)

A JACOBIN We will drink the cup of Socrates* with you!

LEGENDRE (*Springs to the tribune*) We have no need to turn our eyes to Lyons. In the last few days the people who wear silken clothes, who ride in 240 carriages, who sit in boxes at the theatre and speak like the dictionary of the Academy* have carried their heads firmly on their shoulders. They are witty and say Marat and Chalier should be given a second martyrdom and be guillotined in effigy.* (*Sensation throughout the assembly*)

SOME VOICES They are dead men, their tongues have guillotined them. 245

LEGENDRE The blood of these saints be upon them! I ask the members of the Committee of Public Safety here present, since when have their ears become so deaf——

COLLOT D'HERBOIS (*Interrupting*) And I ask you, Legendre, whose voice gives breath to such thoughts, so that they come to life and dare to speak? 250 The time has come to tear off the mask. Listen to me! The cause is accusing its effect, the voice its echo, the premise its conclusion. The Committee of Public Safety is more logical than that, Legendre. Be calm! The busts of these saints will remain undisturbed and like heads of Medusa* they will turn the traitors to stone. 255

ROBESPIERRE I demand the tribune!

THE JACOBINS Silence, silence for the Incorruptible!

ROBESPIERRE We waited only for the cries of dissatisfaction which resounded on every side before we spoke. Our eyes were open, we saw the enemy arm and rise, but we did not sound the alarm; we let the people watch over 260 itself, and the people has not slumbered, the people has rushed to arms. We allowed the enemy to come out of hiding, we allowed him to advance; now he stands free and unconcealed in the light of day, and every stroke will find its mark; he is dead as soon as you have seen him.

I have said it to you before; the internal enemies of the Republic have 265

231 William Pitt (1759–1806), at this time Prime Minister of England. The English Mediterranean fleet was blockading French ports.

235 (*a*) August 10, 1792, when the Jacobins stormed the Tuileries and captured the royal family. (*b*) That is, of the September Massacres in 1792, when about 1200 priests, royalists, and aristocrats were murdered in prisons.

236 May 31, 1793, the day the Girondins fell.

237 The dagger of suicide. Like Cato, Gaillard had committed suicide when he heard that Ronsin had been arrested.

238 The cup of poison hemlock.

242 The French Academy supposedly safeguarded the purity of the language by means of its dictionary.

244 There had been talk of destroying the reputations of the "saints" Marat and Chalier, especially by Hébert and his followers.

254 A Gorgon of Greek mythology whose hair was serpents and whose face turned all who saw it to stone.

fallen into two groups,* like two armies. Under different flags and by different ways they march towards the same goal. One of these factions is no more. In its affectation and madness it tried to set aside as worn-out weaklings the most proven patriots, so as to deprive the Republic of its strongest arms. They declared war on God and on Property, to create a diversion 270 in favour of the Kings. They parodied the sublime drama of the Revolution, so as to discredit it by calculated excesses. The triumph of Hébert would have transformed the Republic into chaos, and despotism would have been satisfied. The sword of the law has struck down the traitor. But what do the foreigners care, so long as they have criminals of another brand 275 through whom to achieve the same end? We have accomplished nothing, so long as a second faction remains to be destroyed.

That faction is the opposite of the first. They force us to be weak, their battle-cry is: Mercy! They wish to rob the People of its weapons, and the strength to use these weapons, so as to hand the people over naked and 280 enfeebled to the Kings.

The weapon of the Republic is the Terror, the strength of the Republic is Virtue—Virtue because without it the Terror is pernicious, the Terror because without it Virtue is powerless. The Terror is the consequence of Virtue, the Terror is nothing else than swift, strong, and unswerving 285 Justice. They say that the Terror is an instrument of dictatorship and that our Government therefore resembles a dictatorship. Granted! But only as the sword in the hand of Freedom's heroes resembles the sabre with which the satellites of tyrants are armed. If a tyrant rules his brutish subjects through terror he is, as a tyrant, justified; destroy the enemies of freedom through 290 terror and as the founders of the Republic you are no less justified. The Revolutionary Government is the dictatorship of freedom against tyranny.

Certain people shout "Mercy on the Royalists!" Mercy for criminals? No! Mercy for the innocent, mercy for the weak, mercy for the unfortunate, mercy for Mankind! Only the law-abiding citizen deserves protection by 295 society.

In a republic only republicans are citizens, royalists and foreigners are enemies. To punish the oppressors of mankind is mercy; to pardon them is barbarism. Every display of false sensibility seems to me a sigh that flies to England or to Austria. 300

But they are not content to disarm the People; they even try to poison the purest sources of its strength by Vice. Of all attacks on Freedom, that is the subtlest, the most dangerous, the most loathsome. Only the most hellish Machiavellianism*—but no! I will not say that such a plan could be misbegotten in a human mind! It may not be intentional, but the intention 305 is beside the point, the effect is the same, the danger equally great. Vice is the brand of Cain* on the forehead of Aristocracy. In a republic it is not

266 The Girondins and the Indulgents (Danton's faction).

304 A vague style of political behavior associated with Niccolò Machiavelli and emphasizing treachery, intrigue, and amorality.

307 God's curse on Cain for killing his brother Abel.

merely a moral but a political offence. The libertine is the political opponent of freedom, and is the more dangerous the greater the services he seems to perform. The most dangerous citizen is he who finds it easier to wear ₃₁₀ out a dozen red caps than to do a single good action.

You will find it easy to understand me, if you think of people who once lived in attics and now ride in carriages and fornicate with *ci-devant** countesses and duchesses. We may well ask: have they plundered the People or have they pressed the golden hands of the Kings, when we see the ₃₁₅ People's law-givers parading with all the vices and luxury of the former courtiers, when we see these counts and marquesses of the Revolution marrying rich wives, giving magnificent banquets, gambling, keeping servants, and wearing costly clothes. We may well be astonished when we hear of their wit, their culture, and their good taste. A short time ago one of ₃₂₀ them gave a shameful parody of Tacitus,* I could answer out of Sallust and travesty Catiline; but I imagine there is nothing more for me to add, the portrait is complete.

No compromise, no truce with men who thought only of exploiting the people, who hope to carry out their plans with impunity, to whom the ₃₂₅ Republic is a speculation and the Revolution a trade! Terrified by the mounting tide of examples, they now softly seek to mitigate our justice. One might think that each of them said to himself: "We are not virtuous enough to employ such terror. Philosophic law-givers, have pity on our weakness! I dare not say to you that I am vicious; so I say to you rather: be not ₃₃₀ pitiless!"

Be calm, virtuous People, be calm, you patriots! Tell your comrades in Lyons: the sword of the law does not rust in the hands to which you have entrusted it!—We shall set the Republic a great example. (*General applause*)

MANY VOICES Long live the Republic! Long live Robespierre! ₃₃₅
PRESIDENT The session is closed.

Scene 4
A street.
(*Enter* LACROIX *and* LEGENDRE)

LACROIX What have you done, Legendre? Do you realize whose head you've thrown down with those busts of yours? ₃₄₀
LEGENDRE A few dandies, and some elegant women, that's all.
LACROIX You're a suicide, a shadow who murders his original and with it himself.
LEGENDRE I don't understand.
LACROIX I thought Collot spoke clearly enough. ₃₄₅
LEGENDRE What does that matter? It was as if a champagne bottle burst. He was drunk again.

---

³¹³ "Former."
³²¹ A Roman historian (*c*.55–*c*.117 A.D.), as was Sallust (86–34 B.C.), who wrote about the conspiracy of Cataline (*d*.62 B.C.). All the names are applied to contemporary figures in the Revolution.

LACROIX Fools, babes, and—well?—drunkards tell the truth. Whom do you think Robespierre meant by Catiline?

LEGENDRE Well? 350

LACROIX The thing's simple. The atheists and the extremists have been sent to the guillotine; but the people are no better off, they go barefoot in the streets and want to make shoes out of the skins of aristocrats. The thermometer of the guillotine must not fall; a few degrees lower and the Committee of Public Safety can make its bed on the Place de la Révolution. 355

LEGENDRE What has all this to do with my busts?

LACROIX Still don't you see? You have made the counter-revolution known officially, you've forced the Committee to take energetic measures, you've directed their hands. The people is a Minotaur* that must be fed with corpses every week if it is not to eat the Committee alive. 360

LEGENDRE Where is Danton?

LACROIX How should I know? He's trying to discover the Venus de Medici* piecemeal in all the tarts in the Palais Royal; he's making mosaics, as he says. God knows what limb he's got to now. What a pity that Nature cuts up beauty into so many pieces, like Medea with her brothers,* and 365 deposits it in fragments in people's bodies.—Let's go to the Palais Royal.

(*Exeunt*)

Scene 5

A Room. DANTON *and* MARION.

MARION No, don't touch me! At your feet like this. I'll tell you a story.

DANTON Your lips have better uses. 370

MARION No, let me alone for once.—I came of a good family. My mother was a clever woman and brought me up carefully. She always told me that modesty is a great virtue. When people came to the house and began to speak of certain things she sent me out of the room; if I asked what they meant she said I ought to be ashamed of myself; if she gave me a book 375 to read, there were almost always some pages I had to leave out. But I could read as much as I liked of the Bible; every page of it was holy. There were some things in it I couldn't understand. I couldn't ask any one; I brooded over myself. Then the Spring came, and all around me something was happening, something I had no share in. A strange atmosphere surrounded 380 me; it almost stifled me. I looked at my own body; sometimes I felt as if there were two of me, and then again I melted into one. In those days a young man came to visit us; he was handsome and often said silly things to me; I didn't quite know what they meant, but I couldn't help laughing. My mother made him come often; it suited us both. In the end we 385 couldn't see why we shouldn't just as well lie beside each other between the sheets as sit beside each other on two chairs. It gave me more pleasure

---

359 The mythical beast in the Cretan Labyrinth who every ninth year devoured a sacrifice of young people.

362 A famous statue of Venus.

365 Medea killed and dismembered her brother to prevent her father from pursuing her and Jason.

than his conversation and I didn't see why I should be allowed the smaller and denied the greater. We did it secretly. That went on. But I was like a sea that swallowed everything up and sank deeper and deeper into itself. 390 For me only my opposite existed, all men melted into one body. It was my nature, who can get beyond that? In the end he noticed. One morning he came and kissed me as if he was going to suffocate me; his arms closed tightly round my neck, I was in terrible fear. Then he released me, laughed and said he had nearly done a very stupid thing. He said I need only 395 keep my dress and use it, it would soon wear out by itself; he didn't want to spoil my fun for me too soon, and after all it was the only thing I had. Then he went away; I still didn't know what he meant. In the evening I was sitting at the window; I am very sensitive and my only hold on everything around me is through feeling; I sank into the waves of the sunset. Then 400 a crowd came down the street, children ran ahead, women watched from the windows. I looked down; they carried him past in a basket, the moon shone on his pale forehead, his curls were wet—he had drowned himself. I had to cry. It was the one break in my whole being. Other people have Sundays and weekdays, they work for six days and pray on the seventh, 405 once a year they have a birthday and feel sentimental, and every year they look forward to New Year. All that means nothing to me; for me there are no dates, no changes. I am always one thing only, an unbroken longing and desire, a flame, a stream. My mother died of grief; people point their fingers at me. That is stupid. Only one thing matters, what people enjoy, 410 whether it's the body, or holy images, wine, flowers, or toys; the feeling is the same; those who enjoy most, pray most.

DANTON   Why can't I gather your beauty into myself, embrace it completely?

MARION   Danton, your lips have eyes.

DANTON   I wish I were part of the air, to bathe you in my flood and break 415 myself on every wave of your beautiful body.

(*Enter* LACROIX, ADELAIDE, *and* ROSALIE)

LACROIX (*Remains in the doorway*)   I must laugh, I must laugh.

DANTON (*Suspiciously*)   Well?

LACROIX   I was thinking about the street. 420

DANTON   And?

LACROIX   In the street two dogs—a mastiff and an Italian poodle—were having a go at each other.

DANTON   What does that matter?

LACROIX   It just occurred to me and I couldn't help laughing. It was so 425 edifying. The girls were watching from the windows; people ought to be more careful and not let them sit in the sun. The flies tickle their hands and that puts ideas into their heads.—Legendre and I have visited nearly every cell here, and the nuns of the Revelation through the Flesh* clung to our coat tails and demanded a blessing. Legendre is administering 430 penance to one of them, but he'll have to fast a month for it himself. Here are two priestesses of the body I've brought with me.

429 Prostitutes.

MARION Good day, Mlle Adelaide, good day, Mlle Rosalie.

ROSALIE It's a long time since we had the pleasure.

MARION I was sorry not to see you. 435

ADELAIDE Oh God, we're busy night and day.

DANTON (*To* ROSALIE) What slender hips you've acquired, little one.

ROSALIE Oh, one improves every day.

LACROIX What's the difference between an ancient and a modern Adonis?*

DANTON And Adelaide's become spiritually suggestive; it's a piquant change. 440
Her face looks like a fig leaf which she holds before her whole body. Such
a fig-tree gives a refreshing shade in so crowded a street.

ADELAIDE I'd be a cattle track, if Monsieur——

DANTON I understand; only don't be angry, my girl.

LACROIX Listen! A modern Adonis is torn not by a boar but by sows. He 445
receives his wound not in the thigh but the parts, and from his blood no
roses blossom but buds of mercury* shoot up.

DANTON Mlle Rosalie is a restored torso, of which only the hips and feet are
antique. She's a magnetic needle, and what the pole of the head repels the
pole of the feet attracts; the centre is an equator where every one crossing 450
the line for the first time needs to be ducked in mercury.

LACROIX Two sisters of mercy; each works in a hospital, that is, in her own
body.

ROSALIE Aren't you ashamed of yourselves? Our ears are burning.

ADELAIDE You ought to have more manners! 455

(*Exeunt* ROSALIE *and* ADELAIDE)

DANTON Good night, pretty children.

LACROIX Good night, mercury mines.

DANTON I'm sorry for them, they've lost their supper.

LACROIX Listen, Danton, I've come from the Jacobins. 460

DANTON Is that all?

LACROIX The delegation from Lyons read a proclamation, as if there was nothing
left for them but to wrap themselves in a toga.* Every one made a face as
if to say to his neighbour: "Paetus, it doesn't hurt." Legendre cried that
there were some who wished to destroy the busts of Marat and Chalier. 465
I think he wants to paint himself red again. He's come through the Terror
with a whole skin and the children tug at his coat in the streets.

DANTON And Robespierre?

LACROIX Tapped his fingers on the tribune and said: "Virtue must rule through
Terror." The phrase gives me a pain in the neck. 470

DANTON It saws the planks for the guillotine.

LACROIX And Collot cried as if possessed that the masks must be torn off.

DANTON The faces will come away with them.

(*Enter* PARIS)

---

439 A beautiful youth of Greek legend who was killed by a boar.

447 Used as a cure for venereal disease.

463 That is, to assume the garb of a citizen. The "Paetus" referred to is probably P. Paetus Thrasea, a Roman
senator and philosopher who was condemned for his liberal opinions by Nero and executed.

LACROIX What is it, Fabricius?*

PARIS From the Jacobins I went to Robespierre; I demanded an explanation. He tried to look like Brutus sacrificing his children,* generalized about duty and said that in the defence of freedom he had no scruples and would make every sacrifice—himself, his brothers, his friends.

DANTON That's perfectly clear; one has only to reverse the order and he 480 comes underneath and holds out the ladder for his friends. We ought to thank Legendre, he has made them speak out.

LACROIX The Hébertists aren't dead yet, and the people are starving; that is a terrible lever. The scale of blood must not grow lighter or it will lift the Committee of Public Safety to the lantern. They need ballast, they need 485 one heavy head.

DANTON I know, I know—the Revolution is like Saturn and devours her own children. (*After a pause*) And yet, they will not dare.

LACROIX Danton, you're a dead saint; but the Revolution has no use for relics, it threw the limbs of kings into the gutter and all the holy images out of 490 the churches. Do you think they'd leave you standing as a monument?

DANTON My name! The People!

LACROIX Your name! You're a moderate, and so am I and so are Camille, Philippeau, Hérault. To the people moderation is the same as weakness; they kill every one who lags behind. The tailors in the Section of Red 495 Caps* would feel all Roman history in their needles if the Man of September* had become a moderate compared with them.

DANTON Perfectly true; and besides—the People is a child who smashes everything to see what's inside.

LACROIX And in any case, Danton, as Robespierre says, we are vicious; that 500 is, we enjoy ourselves. The People are virtuous, that is, they do not enjoy themselves, because work dulls their organs of pleasure; they don't drink because they have no money, and they don't go to brothels because their breath stinks of cheese and herrings and the girls are disgusted by it.

DANTON They hate the pleasure-loving, as eunuchs hate men. 505

LACROIX They call us rogues, and (*In* DANTON's *ear*) between ourselves there's something in what they say. Robespierre and the masses will be virtuous, Saint-Just will write a novel, Barère will cut a Carmagnole* and wrap the Convention in a mantle of blood and—I see it all.

DANTON You're dreaming. They had no courage without me, they'll have 510 none against me. The Revolution is not yet ended, they may still need me; they'll hang me up in the Arsenal.

LACROIX We must act.

DANTON A way will be found.

---

475 A Roman hero (*d.c.*270 B.C.), renowned for his honesty and incorruptibility.

477 Lucius Junius Brutus, a Roman consul who ordered the execution of his own sons when it was discovered they were part of a conspiracy to overthrow the government.

496 (*a*) One of the administrative districts of Paris. (*b*) Danton, who was associated with the September Massacres.

508 A short jacket with wide lapels and brass buttons adopted by the revolutionaries as part of their costume; also a revolutionary song and dance.

LACROIX A way will be found when we are lost. 515

MARION (*To* DANTON) Your lips have grown gold, your words have choked your kisses.

DANTON (*To* MARION) So much time wasted! It's not worth the trouble!— (*To* LACROIX) To-morrow I'll go to Robespierre; I'll make him angry, he can't keep his mouth shut then. So to-morrow! Good night, my friends, 520 good night! Many thanks!

LACROIX Get out, my good friends, get out! Good night, Danton! A girl's legs will be your guillotine, the Mound of Venus your Tarpeian Rock.*

(*Exit with* PARIS)

Scene 6

A Room. ROBESPIERRE, DANTON, *and* PARIS 525

ROBESPIERRE I tell you, any one who falls on my arm when I draw the sword is my enemy—his motive's beside the point; a man who hinders me from defending myself kills me just as much as if he attacked me.

DANTON Where self-defence ends, murder begins; I see no reason that forces us to go on killing. 530

ROBESPIERRE The social revolution is not yet ended; to carry out a revolution by halves is to dig your own grave. Aristocracy is not yet dead; the healthy forces of the people must take the place of this completely degenerate class. Vice must be punished, Virtue must rule through the Terror.

DANTON I do not understand the word punishment.—You and your virtue, 535 Robespierre! You have not taken money, you have no debts, you haven't slept with women, you've always worn a respectable suit and have never been drunk. Robespierre, you're appallingly righteous. I'd be ashamed to walk between heaven and earth for thirty years with the same moral expression, merely for the miserable pleasure of finding others less virtuous 540 than myself.—Isn't there something within you which sometimes whispers, softly, secretly: you lie, you lie?

ROBESPIERRE My conscience is clear.

DANTON Conscience is a mirror before which a monkey torments himself; every one gets himself up as best he can and goes out to take his pleasure 545 in his own way. It's not worth the trouble to make a fuss about it. Every one has the right to protect himself if some one else spoils his fun. Have you the right to turn the guillotine into a washtub for other people's dirty linen and use their heads as cakes of soap for washing their dirty clothes, merely because your coat has always been brushed and clean? Yes, you 550 can defend yourself if they spit on it and want to tear it to rags; but so long as they leave you in peace, what business is it of yours? If they don't trouble about the way they carry on, does that give you the right to lock them up in the tomb? Are you God's policeman? And if you're not able to look on, like your good God Himself, then hold your handkerchief before 555 your eyes.

---

523 That is, a woman's underbelly will be the rock from which you will be thrown as traitors were thrown from the Tarpeian Rock in Rome.

ROBESPIERRE You deny Virtue?

DANTON And Vice. All men are hedonists,* some crude and some sensitive; Christ was the most sensitive of all; that is the only difference between men I've been able to discover. Every one acts according to his nature, that is, 560 he does what does him good.—It's a shame, isn't it, Incorruptible, to tread on your corns like this?

ROBESPIERRE Danton, at certain moments Vice is High Treason.

DANTON But you mustn't suppress it, for God's sake don't, it would be ungrateful; you owe it too much, by contrast I mean.—But to speak in your 565 terms, our blows must be of service to the Republic, we mustn't strike innocent and guilty alike.

ROBESPIERRE Who says that an innocent man has been struck?

DANTON Did you hear that, Fabricius? Not one innocent man dead! (*He goes; on his way out, to* PARIS) There's not a moment to lose, we must show 570 ourselves to the people. (*Exeunt* DANTON *and* PARIS)

ROBESPIERRE (*Alone*) Let him go! He wants to halt the wild horses of the Revolution at a brothel, like a coachman with his tame hacks. They'll have enough strength to drag him to the guillotine.

To tread on my corns!—To speak in my terms!—Stop! Stop! Is that it? 575 —They will say his gigantic figure threw me so much into the shade that I had to get him out of the sun.—What if they're right?—Is it so necessary? Yes, yes, the Republic! He must go. It's laughable, how my thoughts suspect each other.—He must go. A man who stands still in a crowd that presses forward is as much of an obstacle as if he opposed it; he'll be trampled 580 under foot.

We will not allow the ship of the Revolution to run aground on the shallow scruples and mudbanks of these people; we must cut off the hand which dares to hold it back—yes, and even if he tries to hang on by his teeth!

Away with a clique that has stolen the clothes of the dead aristocrats 585 and inherited their sores!

No Virtue! Virtue one of my corns! In my terms!—How that always comes back to me!—Why can't I get away from the thought? Always he points a bloody finger there, there! I may wrap as many bandages as I like around it, but the blood still pulses through.—(*After a pause*) I don't 590 know what it is in me that denies the pretence. (*He goes to the window*)

Night snores over the earth and tosses in wild dreams. Thoughts, desires, hardly conscious, confused and formless, that timidly hide away from the light of day, now take form and raiment and steal into the silent house of dreams. They open the doors, look out of the windows, they half 595 become flesh, limbs stretch themselves in sleep, the lips murmur.—And is not our waking a clearer dream? Are we not sleep-walkers? Are not our actions those of our dreams, only more precise, defined and brought to completion? Who will blame us for that? In one hour the mind performs more acts of thought than the sluggish organism of our body can carry 600

---

558 According to hedonism, the pursuit of pleasure is the proper goal of action.

out in years. The sin is in our thoughts. Whether the thought becomes action, whether the body carries it out, is mere chance.

(*Enter* SAINT-JUST)

ROBESPIERRE Help, who's there in the dark? Help, lights, lights!

SAINT-JUST Do you know my voice?   605

ROBESPIERRE Oh, you Saint-Just! (*A maid brings lights*)

SAINT-JUST Were you alone?

ROBESPIERRE Danton had just left.

SAINT-JUST I met him on the way in the Palais Royal. He was making his revolutionary face, speaking in epigrams, and fraternizing with the *sans-* 610 *culottes;* the whores clustered around his legs and the crowd stood still and whispered to each other what he had said.—We shall lose the benefit of the attack. Must you delay any longer? We shall act without you; our minds are made up.

ROBESPIERRE What do you want to do?   615

SAINT-JUST Summon the Legislative Committee, the Committee of Security, and the Committee of Public Safety to a solemn session.

ROBESPIERRE Very formal.

SAINT-JUST We must bury the great corpse decently, like priests, not murderers. It mustn't be torn to pieces, all the limbs must be there.   620

ROBESPIERRE Speak more clearly.

SAINT-JUST We must bury him in full armour, and sacrifice his horses and slaves on the tomb. Lacroix—

ROBESPIERRE An absolute scoundrel, formerly barrister's clerk, now Lieutenant-General of France. Go on.   625

SAINT-JUST Hérault-Séchelles.

ROBESPIERRE A lovely head.

SAINT-JUST He was the finely engraved capital letter of the Constitution;* we've no need of such ornaments any more, he shall be obliterated.—Philippeau.—Camille.   630

ROBESPIERRE Him too?

SAINT-JUST (*Gives him a paper*) I thought as much. Read that.

ROBESPIERRE Oh, *Le Vieux Cordelier.** Is that all? He's a child, he laughs at you.

SAINT-JUST (*Points to a passage*) Read that; read that!   635

ROBESPIERRE (*Reads*) "This bloody Messiah, Robespierre, on his cavalry between the two thieves, Couthon and Collot, to whom he sacrifices and himself is not sacrificed. The holy sisters of the guillotine stand at his feet like Mary and Magdalene. Saint-Just lies in his bosom like John the Beloved Apostle and imparts to the Convention the apocalyptic revelations of the Master; 640 he carries his head like a monstrance."*

SAINT-JUST I'll make him carry his like Saint-Denis.*

---

628 He had drafted the Act of Constitution.

633 The newspaper edited by Camille Desmoulins.

641 That is, like the vessel in which the Holy Sacrament is carried.

642 St. Denis is often represented as carrying his head in his hands.

ROBESPIERRE (*Reads on*) "Must we believe that the Messiah's neat frock coat is France's winding-sheet, that his thin fingers twitching on the tribune are the knives of the guillotine?—And you, Barère—who once said money 645 would be minted on the Place de la Révolution! But enough—I will not delve into that old sack. He is a widow, who already has had six husbands and helped to bury them all. But what can be done? That is his talent—to see death in people's faces, like Hippocrates,* six months before they die. Who wants to sit with corpses and smell their decay?" You too then, 650 Camille?—Away with them! Quickly! Only dead men never return. Have you the indictment ready?

SAINT-JUST It's not difficult. You gave the hints in the Jacobins.

ROBESPIERRE I wanted to frighten them.

SAINT-JUST I need only carry out your threats. Forgers shall give them meat 655 and foreigners drink*—they'll die of their meal, I give you my word.

ROBESPIERRE Quickly then, to-morrow! No long death struggle! I've grown sensitive in the last few days.—Only be quick. (*Exit* SAINT-JUST)

(*Alone*) Yes, a bloody Messiah, who sacrifices and is not sacrificed.—He redeemed men with His blood, and I redeem them with their own. He 660 made them sin against Him and I take the sin upon myself. He had the pleasure of suffering and I have the torments of the hangman. Who denied himself most, He or I?—And yet there's something of folly in that thought Why must we always look towards Him? Truly the Son of Man is crucified in each of us, and we all wrestle in bloody sweat in the Garden of 665 Gethsemane,* but not one of us redeems the others by his wounds.

My Camille!—They are all leaving me—all is waste and empty—I am alone.

Act Two

Scene 1

A Room. DANTON, LACROIX, PHILIPPEAU, PARIS, *and* CAMILLE DESMOULINS

CAMILLE Quickly, Danton, we have no time to lose!

DANTON (*Dressing*) But time loses us. How tedious drawing on the shirt first and then the trousers over it, and evening for bed and then creaking out again in the morning, and always setting one foot in front of the other; 5 there's no prospect at all of its ever being any different. That's very sad, and that millions have already done so, and that millions will do so again, and that over and above all, we consist of two halves which both do the same thing, so that everything happens double—that is very sad.

CAMILLE You speak absolutely like a child.   10

DANTON The dying often become childish.

---

649 Greek physician (*c.*460-*c.*377 B.C.) known as the Father of Medicine.
656 The Committee of Safety often tried to implicate its political enemies with foreign bankers accused of profiteering at the expense of the Republic.
666 The scene of Christ's agony before his arrest.

LACROIX You fall into ruin by your delay and you drag all your friends with you. Inform the cowards that it's time for them to rally round you, summon them from the valleys as well as from the hills; shriek over the tyranny of the Committee, speak of daggers, invoke Brutus, then you'll terrify the 15 spectators and collect round you even those who were threatened as accomplices of Hébert's. You must give yourself over to your anger. At least don't let us die disarmed and thrown in the mud, like the shameful Hébert.

DANTON You have a bad memory, you called me a dead saint. You were more in the right than you yourself thought. I have been to the Sections, they 20 were respectful but like undertakers. I am a relic, and relics are thrown into the gutter; you were right.

LACROIX Why have you let things come to this?

DANTON To this? Yes, indeed, finally it bored me, always going round in the same coat and knitting my brow into the same wrinkles! It's so pitiful! 25 To be such a miserable instrument, on which one string always gives out one note! It's not to be borne. I wanted to make myself comfortable. I've succeeded; the Revolution sets me at rest, but in a different way from what I thought.

What else can one rely on? Our whores might take it up with the nuns 30 of the guillotine. I can think of nothing else. You can figure it all out on your fingers. The Jacobins have declared that virtue is on the agenda; the Cordeliers* call me Hébert's hangman; the Commune does penance. The Convention—that might still have been a way!—But there was a 31st of May, they wouldn't soften willingly. Robespierre is the dogma of the 35 Revolution which can't be struck out. In any case it wouldn't work. We haven't made the Revolution, the Revolution made us.

And even if it worked—I'd rather be guillotined than guillotine. I've had enough of it, why should we men fight with each other? We should sit down side by side and have peace. A mistake was made in the creating of 40 us; something's lacking in us, I don't know the name for it, but we won't be able to burrow it out of each other's entrails, so why break our bodies over it? Enough, we're sick alchemists.

CAMILLE Said with more pathos, it would run: how long will humanity in everlasting hunger devour its own limbs? Or how long shall we shipwrecked 45 beings on a wreck suck the blood from each other's veins in unquenchable thirst? Or how long must we algebraists in flesh, in our search for the unknown, ever-withheld x, write our sums with mutilated limbs?

DANTON You are a powerful echo.

CAMILLE You think so?—A pistol shot resounds just like a thunderclap. So 50 much the better for you, you should have me always by you.

PHILIPPEAU And France remains with her hangmen?

DANTON What of it? The people enjoy themselves just the same. They are unhappy; can a man ask more to make him compassionate, noble, virtuous, witty, or never bored?—Does it matter whether they die on the guillotine 55

---

33 The leftist political club of which Danton had been a member.

or from fever or from old age? The first is even preferable; they tread with supple limbs behind the scenes, and are able to gesticulate prettily as they go off, and hear the spectators clap. It's very proper and suits us who always stand on the stage, even though finally we're stabbed in earnest.

It's quite right that the length of life should be reduced a little; the coat 60 was too long, our limbs couldn't fill it out. Life becomes an epigram, that's good; for who has breath and spirit enough for an epic in fifty or sixty cantos? It's time one started drinking one's little elixir out of tubs not out of liqueur glasses, so long as one still fills one's mouth full; otherwise one could scarcely make the few drops run together in the clumsy vessel. 65

But finally I have to cry out that the effort is too great for me, life is not worth the trouble one takes to hold on to it.

PARIS Then fly, Danton!

DANTON Can you take your country with you on the soles of your shoes? And finally—and that's the chief thing: they won't dare. (*To* CAMILLE) Come, 70 my boy, I tell you, they won't dare. Adieu, adieu!

(*Exeunt* DANTON *and* CAMILLE)

PHILIPPEAU There he goes.

LACROIX And doesn't believe a word of what he said. Nothing but laziness! He'd sooner be guillotined than make a speech. 75

PARIS What's to be done?

LACROIX Go home and like Lucretia study some honest matter.

Scene 2

A Promenade. Enter SIMON, ROSALIE, ADELAIDE, *and passers by*

A CITIZEN My good Jacqueline—I mean to say Korn . . . I meant. . . . Cor. . . .

SIMON Cornelia, citizen, Cornelia. 80

CITIZEN My good Cornelia has blessed me with a little boy.

SIMON Has borne a son to the Republic.

CITIZEN The Republic? That sounds too universal: one might say. . . .

SIMON That's exactly it; the particular and the universal must. . . .

CITIZEN Ah yes, that's what my wife says too. 85

BALLAD-SINGER (*Sings*) What is then, what is then
                    A joy and pleasure for all men?

CITIZEN Ah, but the names; I can't get them right.

SIMON Christen him Pike, Marat!

BALLAD-SINGER In spite of care, in spite of sorrow 90
                    Toil and sweat from early morrow
                    Till the day is past again.

CITIZEN I should like three; there's something about the number three, something useful and something right; now I have it: Plough, Robespierre. And then the third? 95

SIMON Pike.

CITIZEN Thank you, neighbour; Pike, Plough, Robespierre, three pretty names, that sounds well.

SIMON   I tell you, the breast of your Cornelia will, like the udder of the Roman she-wolf—no, that's no good. Romulus* was a tyrant, that's no good. 100
(CITIZEN *and* SIMON *walk aside*)
A BEGGAR (*Sings*) "A handful of earth and a little moss!" Dear sirs, lovely ladies!
FIRST GENTLEMAN   Work, you lout, you look quite well-nourished.
SECOND GENTLEMAN (*Gives him money*) There, he has a hand like silk. 105 Shameless.
BEGGAR   Sir, where did you get your coat from?
SECOND GENTLEMAN   Work, work! You can have the same; I will give you work, come with me, I live. . . .
BEGGAR   Sir, why did you work?   110
SECOND GENTLEMAN   Fool, in order to have the coat.
BEGGAR   You've tortured yourself, in order to have a pleasure; for a coat like that's a pleasure, a tramp does that as well.
SECOND GENTLEMAN   Certainly. It's the only way.
BEGGAR   If only I were a fool then. It cancels itself out. The sun shines warm 115 on the corner, and things go easily. (*He sings*) "A handful of earth and a little moss."
ROSALIE (*To* ADELAIDE) Hurry along, there come the soldiers! We haven't had anything warm in our bodies since yesterday.
BEGGAR   "Is once upon this earth my final lot!" Ladies and Gentlemen!   120
SOLDIER   Halt! Where are you going, my children? (*To* ROSALIE) How old are you?
ROSALIE   Just as old as my little finger.
SOLDIER   You're very sharp.
ROSALIE   And you're very blunt.   125
SOLDIER   Then I'd better sharpen myself on you.
     (*He sings*)   Christina, my Christina,
                         Does the pain hurt you sore,
                         Hurt you sore, hurt you sore, hurt you sore?
ROSALIE (*Sings*) Oh no, Mister Soldier,   130
                         I'd gladly have some more,
                         Have some more, have some more, have some more.
(*Enter* DANTON *and* CAMILLE)
DANTON   Isn't it a merry scene?—I scent something in the atmosphere, it's as though the sun hatched out lechery. Wouldn't one like to spring into the 135 middle of it, tear off one's trousers and take them from behind like dogs in the street? (*Both walk aside*)
YOUNG GENTLEMAN   Ah, Madame, the sound of a bell, the evening light on the trees, the twinkling of a star. . . .
MADAME   The scent of a flower, the natural pleasures, this pure enjoyment 140 of nature! (*To her daughter*) See, Eugénie, only virtue has eyes for this!
EUGÉNIE (*Kisses her mother's hand*) Ah, Mamma, I see only you!
MADAME   Good child.

100 The legendary founder of Rome who, with his brother Remus, was supposedly raised by a she-wolf.

YOUNG GENTLEMAN (*Whispers in* EUGÉNIE'S *ear*) Do you see the pretty lady with the old gentleman over there? 145

EUGÉNIE I know her.

YOUNG GENTLEMAN They say her barber has done her hair *à l'enfant.**

EUGÉNIE (*Laughing*) Naughty gossip!

YOUNG GENTLEMAN The old gentleman walks beside her, he sees the bud swell and carries it into the sun and thinks that he is the thundery shower which 150 has made it grow.

EUGÉNIE How improper! I feel like going red!

YOUNG GENTLEMAN That could make me go white.

DANTON (*To* CAMILLE) Only don't expect me to be serious. I fail to understand why the people don't stand still in the street and laugh in each other's 155 faces. I mean they must laugh up to the windows and out of the graves, and Heaven must burst, and Earth must waltz round with laughter. (*Exeunt* DANTON *and* CAMILLE)

FIRST GENTLEMAN I assure you, an extraordinary discovery. Through it, all the technical arts assume an altogether different physiognomy. Humanity 160 hurries with giant strides towards its high destiny.

SECOND GENTLEMAN Have you seen the new play? A Babylonian tower, a maze of arches, steps, gangways, and all blown up so light and brave into the air. One grows dizzy at every step. A bizarre head! (*He stands thoughtful*)

FIRST GENTLEMAN What is it? 165

SECOND GENTLEMAN Oh nothing! Your hand, sir. The puddles, look! Thank you, thank you, I can hardly get past: that might be very dangerous.

FIRST GENTLEMAN Surely you weren't afraid?

SECOND GENTLEMAN Yes, the earth is a thin crust, I mean I might always fall through where a hole like that is. 170

You must go carefully, you might fall through. But go to the Theatre, I recommend it very strongly.

Scene 3

A room. DANTON, CAMILLE, *and* LUCILE

CAMILLE I tell you, if they don't have wooden copies of everything scattered in theatres, concert halls, and art exhibitions, people have neither eyes nor 175 ears for it. Let some one cut out a marionette, so that you see the string by which it's tugged hanging down, and with its joints cracking out a five-foot blank verse at every step—what a character, what consistency! Let him take a little feeling, a sentence, an idea, and dress it in jacket and trousers, give it hands and feet, paint its face and let the thing moan its way 180 through three acts until finally it's married or shoots itself dead—an ideal! Let him fiddle out an opera which reproduces the floating and sinking of human life as a bird warbler does the nightingale—behold art!

Turn the people out of the theatre on to the street—behold pitiful reality! They forget their Lord God Almighty on account of his bad imitators. 185

---

147 "In the style of a child."

Of creation, the glowing, roaring, lightning, newly born in them each moment, they hear and see nothing. They go into the theatre, read poems and novels, and make grimaces like the faces they find in them, and say to God's creations, "How commonplace!" The Greeks knew what they were saying when they told how Pygmalion's statue* came to life but bore 190 no children.

DANTON   And the artists treat nature like David,* who, when the murdered bodies were thrown out of La Force* on to the streets in September, cold-bloodedly drew them and said: I snatch the last spasms of life from these scoundrels. (*He is called outside*)   195

CAMILLE   What have you to say, Lucile?

LUCILE   Nothing, I so like watching you talk.

CAMILLE   Do you listen as well?

LUCILE   Why, certainly!

CAMILLE   Am I in the right? Did you know what I was saying?   200

LUCILE   No, really not.

(DANTON *comes back*)

CAMILLE   What's the matter?

DANTON   The Committee of Public Safety has decided on my arrest. I've been warned and offered a place where I can take refuge.   205

They want my head; they can have it, for all I care. I'm sick of these vexations. Let them take it, what does it matter? I'll know how to die with courage: it's easier than living.

CAMILLE   Danton, there's still time!

DANTON   Impossible—but I shouldn't have thought . . .   210

CAMILLE   Your laziness!

DANTON   I'm not lazy, but tired; the soles of my feet burn me.

CAMILLE   Where will you go?

DANTON   Yes, who knows where?

CAMILLE   Seriously, where?   215

DANTON   For a walk, my boy, for a walk. (*Exit*)

LUCILE   Camille—

CAMILLE   Quiet, dear child!

LUCILE   When I think that they . . . this head . . . ! Camille, dear, it's nonsense, I'm crazy, aren't I?   220

CAMILLE   Quiet, Danton and I are not one person!

LUCILE   The earth is broad and there are many things on it—then why always this one thing? Who would take it from me? It would be outrageous. And what do they want it for?

CAMILLE   I tell you again: you need not be disturbed! I spoke yesterday with 225 Robespierre: he was friendly. We're a little on edge, that's true; different points of view, nothing else.

190 Pygmalion, a legendary sculptor, fell in love with his statue of Venus, which came to life in answer to his prayers to the goddess.

192 Jacques Louis David (1748–1825), a painter and supporter of Robespierre.

193 A prison.

LUCILE Go to see him.

CAMILLE We sat together on the same school bench. He was always sombre and lonely. I alone sought him out and made him laugh sometimes. He 230 has always shown a great affection for me. I'll go.

LUCILE So swiftly, my friend? Go! Come! Only this (*She kisses him*) and this! Go! Go! (*Exit* CAMILLE)

These are wicked times. Sometimes things happen like that. Who knows the way out? One must restrain oneself.   235

(*Sings*) Oh, parting, parting, parting,
                 Who of parting had thought?

Why does that, of all things, run through my head? It's bad that it should come of its own like that.—When he went out it seemed to me as though he could never come back again and must always go further away from 240 me, ever further.

How empty this room is! The windows are open, as though a corpse had lain in here. I can't stand being up here any longer. (*Exit*)

Scene 4

A field. Enter DANTON

DANTON I can go no further. In this silence, I will make no noise with the 245 chattering of my footsteps and the panting of my breath. (*He sits down. After a pause*) I've been told of an illness which makes one lose one's memory. There is something of that in death. Then sometimes the hope comes to me that it is still more powerful and makes one lose everything.—Oh, if that were so!—Then I'd run like a Christian to rescue an enemy, that is, my 250 memory.—This place should be safe, yes, for my memory but not for me: the grave gives me more safety, it gives me at least forgetting. It would kill my memory. But here my memory lives and kills me. I or it? The answer is easy. (*He gets up and turns round*) I flirt with death, it is very pleasant to make eyes at her through lorgnettes from a distance.   255

Actually, I have to laugh at the whole business. There's a sense of permanence in me which says: to-morrow and the day after to-morrow and so on and on, and everything will be as it is now. This is just a false alarm to frighten me; they'd never dare! (*Exit*)

Scene 5

A room. Night. DANTON *and* JULIE   260

DANTON (*At a window*) Will it never stop? Will the light never cease glowing and the echoes never be up to date? Will it never be still and dark, so that we no longer listen to and watch each other's filthy sins?—September!

JULIE (*Calls from within*) Danton! Danton!

DANTON Eh!   265

JULIE (*Enters*) What did you call out?

DANTON Did I call?

JULIE You spoke of filthy sins and then you groaned: September!

DANTON   I, I? No, I didn't speak, I hardly thought anything—they were only
quite gentle, secret thoughts.   270
JULIE   You are trembling, Danton.
DANTON   And have I no cause for trembling, when the walls chatter so? If my
body is so jarred that my fitful thoughts speak madly with lips of stone?
That's strange.
JULIE   George, my own George.   275
DANTON   Yes, Julie, it's very strange. I'd better not think any more, if my
thoughts immediately speak. Julie, there are thoughts for which there should
be no ears. It's bad that they should cry out like children at their birth;
it's bad.
JULIE   God preserve your reason, George. George, do you recognize me?   280
DANTON   Yes, why not? You're a human being and then a woman and finally
my wife, and the earth has five continents, Europe, Asia, Africa, America,
Australia, and twice two makes four. You see, I'm in my senses. . . . Didn't
I cry out "September"? Didn't you say something of the sort?
JULIE   Yes, Danton, I heard it through all the rooms.   285
DANTON   When I went to the window—(*He looks out*) the town is quiet, all
the lights out.
JULIE   A child is crying near by.
DANTON   When I went to the window—through all the streets it cried out and
shrieked: "September!"   290
JULIE   You were dreaming, Danton: pull yourself together!
DANTON   Dreaming? Yes, I dreamed; but that was different. I'll tell you quickly
what—my poor head is weak—quickly. Good, now I have it. Under me the
globe panted in its rotation; I had laid hold of it like a wild horse, with
giant limbs I clutched into its mane and gripped its flanks, my head bent   295
backwards, my hair streaming over the abyss; so I was dragged along. Then
I called out in terror and I awoke. I sprang to the window—and there I
heard it, Julie.
        What is it that the word wants? Why that of all words? What have I to
do with it? Why does it stretch out its bloody hands to me? I never   300
struck it.—Oh, help me, Julie, my brain is numb. Wasn't it in September,
Julie?
JULIE   The kings were within forty hours of Paris* . . .
DANTON   The fortresses had fallen, the aristocrats were in the city . . .
JULIE   The Republic was lost.   305
DANTON   Yes, lost. We couldn't let our enemies stab us in the back, we should
have been fools, two enemies on a single plank; we or they, the stronger
would push the weaker under, isn't that right?
JULIE   Yes, yes.
DANTON   We killed them, that was no murder, it was civil war.   310
JULIE   You saved the fatherland.
DANTON   Yes, I did, it was self-defence, we did what we had to do. The Man
on the Cross made it so easy for himself: "It must needs be that offences

303 The foreign powers which threatened to invade France.

come; but woe to that man by whom the offence cometh."—It must; that was this must! Who will curse the hand on which the curse of "must" has fallen? Who spoke that "must," who? What is it in us that whores, lies, steals, and murders? 315

We're puppets drawn by unknown powers on wire; nothing, nothing in ourselves—the swords with which spirits fight—only one doesn't see the hands, as in fairy tales.—Now I'm quiet. 320

JULIE Perfectly quiet, dear heart?
DANTON Yes, Julie, come to bed!

Scene 6

A street before DANTON'S *House. Enter* SIMON *and citizens armed as soldiers*
SIMON How late is it in the night?
FIRST CITIZEN What in the night? 325
SIMON How late is the night?
FIRST CITIZEN As late as between sunset and sunrise.
SIMON Rogue, what time is it?
FIRST CITIZEN Look at your watch-dial, it's the time when the pendulum swings to and fro between the sheets. 330
SIMON We must up! Forward, citizens! We answer with our heads for it! Dead or living! He has strong limbs! I will go first, citizens. Clear the way for freedom.—Take care of my wife! I will bequeath a crown of acorns* to her!
FIRST CITIZEN A crown of acorns! Enough acorns must fall in her lap every day without that. 335
SIMON Onward, citizens, you will have deserved well of the fatherland!
SECOND CITIZEN I wish the fatherland would deserve well of us. For all the holes we've made in other people's bodies not a single one has yet closed up in our trousers.
FIRST CITIZEN Do you want your fly-buttons closed up? Ha, ha, ha! 340
THE OTHERS Ha, ha, ha!
SIMON Forward, forward. (*They crowd into* DANTON'S *house*)

Scene 7

The National Convention. A group of Deputies, including LEGENDRE,
ROBESPIERRE, *and* SAINT-JUST
LEGENDRE Will the execution of deputies never cease? Who is safe if Danton falls? 345
A DEPUTY What's to be done?
ANOTHER He must be heard before the bar of the Convention. The success of this method is certain. What could they oppose to his voice?
ANOTHER Impossible. A decree prevents us. 350
LEGENDRE It must either be withdrawn or an exception allowed. I will propose the motion; I count on your support.
THE PRESIDENT The session is opened.

333 A crown of oak leaves and acorns was awarded to a Roman who had saved the life of another citizen.

LEGENDRE (*Ascends the tribune*) Four members of the National Convention were arrested during the past night. I know that Danton is one of them, the names of the remainder I do not know. Nevertheless, whoever they are, I demand that they be heard before the bar.

Citizens, I make this declaration: I hold Danton to be as innocent as myself, and I don't believe that any accusation can be made against me. I will attack no member of the Committee of Security or of the Committee of Public Safety, but well-founded reasons leave me afraid lest private hatred and private passions may deprive Liberty of men who have done her the greatest services. The man who through his energy saved France in the year 1792* deserves to be heard; he should be allowed to clear himself, if he is charged with high treason. (*Great excitement*)

SOME VOICES We support Legendre's motion.

A DEPUTY We are here in the name of the people; without the will of those who voted for us, no one can deprive us of our places.

ANOTHER Your words stink of corpses; you have taken them out of the mouths of the Girondists. Do you want privilege? The knife of the law sweeps over all heads.

ANOTHER We cannot allow our committees to send our lawgivers from the sanctuary of the law to the guillotine.

ANOTHER Crime has no sanctuary, only crowned criminals find one on the throne.

ANOTHER Only thieves appeal to their right of sanctuary.

ANOTHER Only murderers fail to recognize it.

ROBESPIERRE Such disorder, unknown for so long in this assembly, shows that great matters are under discussion. To-day will decide whether a few men will benefit by it to win a victory over their country.—How can you so far deny your fundamental principles as to grant a few individuals to-day that which yesterday you refused Chabot, Delaunai, and Fabre? What is the meaning of this discrimination in favour of a few men? Why should I concern myself with the complimentary speeches which people pay to themselves and their friends? Only too many experiences have shown us how much they are worth. We do not ask whether a man has brought to completion this or that task of patriotism; we ask after his whole political career.—Legendre appears to be ignorant of the names of the arrested men; the whole Convention knows them. His friend Lacroix is one of them. Why does Legendre seem ignorant of this? Because he knows that only shamelessness could defend Lacroix. Danton alone he named, because he thinks that a privilege has attached itself to this name. No, we want no privileges, we want no idols. (*Applause*)

What is there in Danton that places him before Lafayette, before Dumouriez, before Brissot, Fabre, Chabot, Hébert? What does one say of these that one cannot also say of him? And did you spare them? Through what service has he earned precedence over his fellow citizens? Perhaps because certain betrayed individuals, and others who had not let themselves be

---

364 In 1792 Danton raised armies in France to resist the threatened invasion by foreign powers.

betrayed, had ranged themselves behind him, so that in his train they might run into the arms of power and fortune? The more he has betrayed those 400 patriots who put trust in him, the more energetic must he find the strength of the friends of liberty.

They wish to inspire you with fear at the misuse of a power which you yourselves have exercised. They whine over the despotism of the Committees, as though the trust which the people have placed in you, and 405 which you have handed over to these committees, were not a sure guarantee of your patriotism. They pretend that everybody is trembling. But I tell you that whoever at this moment trembles is guilty, because innocence never trembles before public vigilance. (*General applause*)

They've tried to frighten me too; they gave me to understand that the 410 danger, if it neared Danton, could also reach as far as me. They wrote to me that Danton's friends held me besieged, believing that the memory of an old association, a blind faith in a simulated virtue could induce me to restrain my ardour and my passion for liberty.—So I declare that nothing will stop me, not even should Danton's danger become my own. We all 415 need a certain courage and a certain grandeur of soul. Only criminals and vulgar spirits fear to see those who resemble them fall at their side, because if a troop of accomplices no longer stuck to them, they would see themselves exposed in the light of truth. But if there are spirits such as these in this assembly, so also are there those who are heroic. The number of scoundrels 420 is not great; we have only to lop off a few heads and the country is saved.

(*Applause*)

I demand that Legendre's motion be rejected. (*The delegates rise together as a sign of general approbation*)

SAINT-JUST There seem to be in this assembly a few sensitive ears which 425 cannot hear the word "blood" with equanimity. A few general observations on the relations between nature and history should convince them that we are not crueller than Nature or than Time. Nature follows quietly and irresistibly her laws; Man is destroyed, wherever he comes in conflict with them. An alteration in the ingredients of the air, a flaring up of the tellurian* 430 fires, a vacillation in the balance of masses of water, and an epidemic, a volcanic eruption, a flood bury thousands. What is the result? A meaningless, on the whole, scarcely noticeable alteration of physical nature, which would have passed by scarcely leaving a trace, if corpses did not lie in its path.

I ask you: shall moral nature be more considerate than physics in making her revolutions? Shall not an idea, just as well as a law of physics, annihilate that which opposes it? Above all, shall an experience which alters the whole configuration of moral nature, which means humanity, not dare to wade through blood? The spirit of the world uses our arms in the spiritual 440 sphere just as in the physical it uses volcanoes and floods. What difference does it make whether one dies now through an epidemic or through the Revolution?

430 Emanating from the earth.

The strides of humanity are slow; one can only count them by centuries; behind each one rise the graves of generations. To arrive at the simplest 445 invention and fundamental truth has cost the lives of millions who died on the way. Is it not then simply that in a time where the pace of history is faster, more men lose their breath?

We conclude quickly and simply: since all men were created in the same circumstances, all are equal, apart from those differences which Nature 450 herself has made. Therefore every one has merits but none has privileges, either as individuals or as a smaller or larger class of individuals.—Every link in this argument translated into reality has killed its men. The 14th of July, the 10th of August, the 31st of May* are its punctuation marks. It required four years to be carried out in the physical world, and under 455 ordinary conditions it would have required centuries and been punctuated by generations. Is it so miraculous that the stream of the Revolution at every stop, at every new bend, discharges its corpses?

We still have a few inferences to add to our proposition; shall a few hundred corpses prevent us from making them? Moses led his people 460 through the Red Sea and into the desert, till the old corrupted generation had been annihilated, before he founded the new state. Legislators! We have neither Red Sea nor desert, but we have war and the guillotine.

The Revolution is like the daughter of Pelias;* she dismembers humanity to make it young. Humanity comes out of the cauldron of blood, like 465 earth out of the waters of the deluge, to raise itself with primordial limbs, as though it were first created. (*Long-sustained applause, some deputies rise in enthusiasm*) We call upon all the secret enemies of tyranny, who in Europe and the whole globe carry under their cloaks the dagger of Brutus, to share with us this exalted moment. (*The spectators and the deputies join in singing* 470 *the "Marseillaise."*)

Act Three

Scene 1

The Luxembourg. A hall with prisoners. CHAUMETTE, PAYNE, MERCIER, HÉRAULT-DE-SÉCHELLES *and other prisoners*

CHAUMETTE (*Takes* PAYNE'S *arm*) Listen, Payne, that might be it.. Before it came over me so clearly, to-day I have a headache; help me a little with your arguments, it seems to me quite uncannily difficult. 5

PAYNE Come, come, philosopher Anaxagoras,* I will catechize thee.—There is no God, for either God made the world, or he did not. If he did not create

---

454 July 14, 1789, the Fall of the Bastille; August 10, 1792, the revolt of the Paris Commune and the arrest of the royal family; May 31, 1793, the insurrection which brought the fall of the Girondins.

464 The daughters of Pelias, wishing to rejuvenate Pelias as Medea had rejuvenated Jason's father, Aeson, were persuaded by Medea to kill Pelias and to place his hacked body in a magic cauldron. At this point, however, Medea fled, leaving Pelias butchered. St. Just has apparently confused Medea's success with Aeson with the failure of Pelias' daughters.

6 Chaumette had taken the name of the Greek philosopher Anaxagoras (*c.*500–428 B.C.).

it, then the world contained its origins in itself, and there is no God, since God is only God through the fact that he contains the origins of all being. Now God cannot have created the world; for creation must either be 10 eternal like God, or it must have a beginning. If it had a beginning, God must have created it at a certain point in time. Thus God, having rested for an eternity, must once suddenly have become active, and must therefore have undergone an alteration in himself, which made him apply the conception of time, both of which conflict with the nature of God's being. 15 Thus it is impossible for God to have created the world. Now since we know very clearly that we exist or at least that our own ego exists and that, in accordance with what I have just told you, it also must have origins in itself or in something not itself which is not God, then it follows that there is no God. *Quod erat demonstrandum.** 20

CHAUMETTE Yes, indeed, that gives me light again. I thank you, I thank you.

MERCIER Wait, Payne! Supposing though that creation were eternal?

PAYNE Then it ceases to be creation any more, it becomes one with God or an attribute of him, as Spinoza* said, then God is present in everything, in thee, my worthiest philosopher Anaxagoras, and in me. That wouldn't be 25 so bad, but you must admit that it's not saying much for the heavenly majesty if the Lord God Almighty gets a headache in each one of us, or leprosy, or is buried alive, or at least experiences a very unpleasant impression of these things.

MERCIER But surely there must be a first cause? 30

PAYNE Who denies it? But who insists that this first cause must be that which we think of as God—that is to say, as perfection? Do you hold that the world is perfect?

MERCIER No.

PAYNE Then how do you arrive at an imperfect effect from a perfect cause? 35 —Voltaire* dared displease Gods as little as kings, and for that reason he did. He who has nothing except his reasoning, yet who does not know how or does not dare to use it consistently, is a blunderer.

MERCIER Against that, I ask can a perfect cause have a perfect effect, which means—can something perfect create something perfect? Is it not impos- 40 sible, because the created thing can never contain its origin within itself, which indeed, as you say, appertains to perfection?

CHAUMETTE Be quiet! Be quiet!

PAYNE Calm yourself, philosopher! You are quite right; but if God once starts creating, then if he can only create imperfect things he would have done 45 better to leave well alone. Isn't it very human of us that we can only think of God as creating? Since we must always stir and shake ourselves, only in order that we may ever be saying to ourselves that we exist! But must we ascribe to God as well this sickening need?—Must we, if our spirit is sunk

---

20 "Which was to be demonstrated."

24 Baruch Spinoza (1632-1677), a Dutch philosopher who taught that there is but one substance, God, which has two aspects, thought and extension.

36 The French satirist, philosopher, historian, and dramatist (1694-1778).

in a being harmoniously at rest with itself in eternal blessedness, at once 50
assume that it stretches out a finger over the table and kneads homunculi*
of bread—through immeasurable need for love, as we secretly whisper in
each other's ears? Must we do all this merely to make ourselves the sons
of God? I prefer a lesser father, at least I will not be able to say afterwards
that he let me be educated beneath his rank in the manger or amongst the 55
slaves.

Do away with imperfection: then alone can you demonstrate God—
Spinoza tried it. One can deny evil but not pain, only the understanding can
accept God, the feeling rebels against him. Mark well, Anaxagoras, why
do I suffer? That is the rock of atheism? The least twinge of pain, stir it 60
only an atom, rends your creation from top to bottom.

MERCIER And morality?

PAYNE First you prove God from morality and then morality from God. A nice
vicious circle that licks its own hindquarters. What do you want with your
morality? I don't know whether there is an intrinsic good or evil and have 65
no need to alter my way of life on that account. I act according to my nature;
what suits it is good for me and I do it, and what is bad for it is bad for me
and I don't do it and take sides against it when it lies in my way. You can
be virtuous, as they call it, and arm yourself against so-called vice, without
being obliged on that account to despise your opponents, which is a very 70
sad feeling to have!

CHAUMETTE True, very true!

HÉRAULT O, philosopher Anaxagoras, one can also say since God is everything,
he must also be his own opposite, that's to say perfect and imperfect, evil
and good, blessed and suffering; the result would admittedly then be nil, 75
it would cancel itself out, we should end with nothing.—Rejoice, you emerge
victorious, you can pray undisturbed to Madame Momoro* as nature's masterpiece; at least she's left you a crown of roses in the groin.

CHAUMETTE Gentlemen, I give you my heartiest thanks. (*Exit*)

PAYNE He still has no trust, he'll still give himself extreme unction,* set his 80
feet towards Mecca, and have himself circumcised, in order to lose no
opportunity.

(DANTON, LACROIX, CAMILLE, *and* PHILIPPEAU *are brought in*)

HÉRAULT (*Runs to* DANTON *and embraces him*) Good morning! No—I should
say—Good night! I can't ask how you slept? How will you sleep? 85

DANTON Well, well. One must go laughing to bed.

MERCIER (*To* PAYNE) These mastiffs with wings of doves! He's the evil genius
of the Revolution, he defied his mother but she was stronger than he.

PAYNE His life and his death are equal misfortunes.

LACROIX (*To* DANTON) I hadn't thought that you'd be here so soon. 90

---

51 Small models of human beings.

77 Mme. Mormoro, Chaumette's mistress, had played the goddess of reason in the ceremony by which Notre
Dame was converted to the Temple of Reason.

80 The last sacrament in Roman Catholic belief, hence a religious precaution, just as are "setting his feet
toward Mecca" in the Moslem faith, and circumcision in the Hebrew and Moslem faiths.

DANTON I knew, I was warned.

LACROIX And you said nothing?

DANTON To what? An apoplexy is the best death. Would you care to be ill first? And I thought they'd never dare. (*To* HÉRAULT) It's better to lie down in the earth than to walk on it with corns. I'd rather have her as a cushion 95 than as a footstool.

HÉRAULT At least we won't have warts on our fingers when we stroke the cheeks of the pretty lady putrefaction.

CAMILLE Only don't trouble yourself, you can hang your tongue out as far as your neck, but still you can't lick the death-sweat from your brow. 100 O Lucile! That is a great affliction. (*The prisoners crowd round the newcomers*)

DANTON (*To* PAYNE) What you did for the good of your country,* I have tried to do for mine. I was less fortunate; they send me to the scaffold; for my own part, I won't trip.

MERCIER (*To* DANTON) The blood of the twenty-two* drowns you. 105

A PRISONER (*To* HÉRAULT) The power of the people and the power of reason are one.

ANOTHER (*To* CAMILLE) Well, General Procurator of the Lanterns, your improvements in the lighting of the streets have not made France any lighter.

ANOTHER Leave him alone. His are the lips which spoke the word "pity." 110
(*He embraces* CAMILLE, *several other prisoners follow his example*)

PHILIPPEAU We are priests who have prayed with the dying. We have been infected and die of the same epidemic.

A FEW VOICES The blow that falls on you, kills us all.

CAMILLE Gentlemen, I grieve deeply that our efforts were so fruitless; I go 115 to the scaffold, because my eyes were wet at the fate of a few unfortunate ones.

Scene 2

     A room. FOUQUIER-TINVILLE *and* HERMAN

FOUQUIER All prepared?

HERMAN It will be difficult; if Danton weren't amongst them it would be 120 easy.

FOUQUIER He must open the ball.

HERMAN He will frighten the jury, he's the scarecrow of the revolution.

FOUQUIER The jury must will it.

HERMAN I thought of a way, but it would violate the letter of the law. 125

FOUQUIER Only say it!

HERMAN We don't draw by lot, but pick out our stalwarts.

FOUQUIER That must be done—that will provide a good bonfire. There are

---

[102] Thomas Payne, or Paine (1737–1809) was an American revolutionary writer and political thinker. He wrote the *Age of Reason* in prison.

[105] The twenty-two Girondins who were executed.

nineteen of them. They're cleverly mixed together. The four forgers, then a few bankers and foreigners. That's a piquant tribunal. The people 130 need such. Good then, let's have reliable people. Who, for example?

HERMAN   Leroi, he is deaf, so he hears nothing the accused say. With him there, Danton can scream himself hoarse.

FOUQUIER   Very good. Go on.

HERMAN   Vilatte and Lumière, the one sits in the pub all day, and the 135 other's always asleep. Both only open their mouths to say the word "Guilty!" Girard makes it a principle that no one can clear himself once he's been put before the Tribunal. Renaudin. . . .

FOUQUIER   He too? He once helped get some parsons off.

HERMAN   Don't worry, a few days ago he came to me and demanded that all 140 the condemned should be bled before their execution to make them a little pale; the defiant look of most of them annoys him.

FOUQUIER   Very good. Then I shall rely on you.

HERMAN   Leave it to me!

Scene 3

The Luxembourg. A Corridor. LACROIX, DANTON, MERCIER, *and other* 145
prisoners pacing to and fro

LACROIX (*To a prisoner*)   What, so many unfortunates, and in such a wretched situation?

PRISONER   Have the guillotine carts never told you that Paris is a slaughter-house?   150

MERCIER   Isn't it so, Lacroix? Equality swings its sickle over all heads, the lava of revolution flows; the guillotine makes Republicans. The gallery clap and the Romans rub their hands; but they don't hear in every one of these words the death rattle of a victim. Follow your slogans to the point at which they become incarnate. Stare around you, you have said it all, it is a mimic 155 translation of your words. These grief-stricken people, their hangmen and their guillotines are your speeches turned to life. You build your system, as Bajazet* his pyramids, from the heads of men.

DANTON   You're right! To-day one works out everything in human flesh. That is the curse of our time. My body also will be used now.   160

It's exactly a year since I established the Revolutionary Tribunal. I pray forgiveness of God and humanity for it; I wished to anticipate a new September massacre, I hoped to save the innocent, but this slow murder with its formalities is more cruel and just as inescapable. Gentlemen, I hoped to have you all out of this place.   165

MERCIER   Oh, we shall all get out of it!

DANTON   Now I am with you; Heaven knows how it will end!

---

158 A famous sultan of Turkey.

Scene 4

The Revolutionary Tribunal. HERMAN *and* DANTON

HERMAN (*To* DANTON) Your name, citizen?

DANTON The Revolution names my name. My dwelling will soon be in 170 nothing and my name in the Pantheon of history.

HERMAN Danton, the Convention accuses you of having conspired with Mirabeau, with Dumouriez, with Orleans, with the Girondists, with the foreigners, and with the factions of Louis XVII.*

DANTON My voice, which I have so often raised for the people's cause, will 175 easily refute this calumny. The wretches who accuse me should appear here, and I will cover them with shame. The Committee should present themselves here, I shall only answer in front of them. I need them as prosecutors and as witnesses. They ought to show themselves.

Apart from all this, what concern have I with you and your accusations? 180 I have told you already: the void will soon be my sanctuary. To me life is a load, they may tear it away from me, I long to shake it off.

HERMAN Danton, audacity is the mark of crime, calm the mark of innocence.

DANTON Private audacity is doubtless blameworthy, but that national audacity which I have so often shown, with which I have so often fought for 185 freedom, is the most meritorious of all the virtues. That is my audacity, that is what, for the good of the Republic, I use here against my miserable accusers. Can I control myself when I see myself calumniated in so shameful a manner? No one can expect cool pleading from a revolutionary like me. Men of my stamp are inestimable in revolutions, the genius of freedom 190 hovers on their brows. (*Signs of applause amongst the audience*)

I am accused of having conspired with Mirabeau, with Dumouriez, with Orleans, of having sat at the feet of sick despots; I am called upon to make my answer before inescapable, unbending justice! You, cowering Saint-Just, will be responsible to posterity for this blasphemy. 195

HERMAN I call upon you to answer calmly; think of Marat, he came before his judges with awe.

DANTON You have laid hands on my whole life; for that reason it rises and faces you. I will bury you under the weight of each one of my deeds.

I am not proud of this. Fate controlled our arms, but only powerful 200 natures are her instruments.—On the field of Mars* I declared war on the monarchy, I struck it on the 10th of August, on the 21st of January* I killed it and threw the head of a king as a gauntlet to kings. (*Repeated signs of applause; he becomes the accuser*) When I throw a glance at this shameful document, I feel my whole being quiver. Who then are those who had 205 to force Danton to show himself on that memorable 10th of August? Who are the privileged beings from whom he borrowed his energy?—My accusers should appear! I am quite in my senses when I make this demand! I will

---

174 That is, the party which supposedly hoped to place Louis XVII on the throne.

201 A mass demonstration had taken place on the Champs de Mars in Paris on July 17, 1791, at which the abdication of Louis XVI and a new form of government were demanded.

202 The date of Louis XVI's execution.

expose these worthless scoundrels and cast them back into the nothing out
of which they have crawled.   210
HERMAN (*Rings a bell*) Don't you hear the bell?
DANTON The voice of a man who defends his honour and his life must cry
louder than your bell.

    In September I fed the young brood of the Revolution with the dismem-
bered bodies of the aristocrats. My voice has forged weapons for the 215
People from the gold of the aristocrats and the rich. My voice was the hurricane which drowned the satellites of despotism under waves of bayonets.
                         (*Loud applause*)
HERMAN Danton, your voice is exhausted. You are too violently moved. You will
conclude your defence next time. You need rest.—The session is ended. 220
DANTON Now you still know Danton—a few hours more and he will slumber
in the arms of fame.

Scene 5

    The Luxembourg. A cell. DILLON,* LAFLOTTE, *and a* GAOLER
DILLON Fool, don't shine your nose in my face like that. Ha, ha, ha!
LAFLOTTE Keep your mouth shut, your sickle moon* has a stinking halo! 225
Ha, ha, ha, ha!
GAOLER Ha, ha, ha! Do you think, sir, that you could read by your light?
    (*He shows the writing on a paper which he holds in his hand*)
DILLON Give it to me!
GAOLER Sir, my sickle moon has ebbed.   230
LAFLOTTE Your trousers look as if it were the flood.
GAOLER No, they draw water. (*To* DILLON) She has waned at your sun, sir;
you must give me that which makes you fiery again, if you wish to see.
DILLON There, knave! Clear out! (*Gives him money. Exit* GAOLER)
    (*Reads*) Danton has terrified the tribunal, the jury hesitated, the 235
audience muttered. The crowd was extraordinary. The people pressed round
the Palace of Justice and stood right up to the benches. A handful of gold,
an arm to strike.—Hm! Hm! (*He walks to and fro and drinks from time to
time from a glass*) If only I had one foot on the pavement, I wouldn't allow
myself to be struck down like this. Yes, only one foot on the pavement. 240
LAFLOTTE And one in the tumbrils.
DILLON You think so? A couple of strides still lie between, long enough to
cover with the corpses of the Committee. The time has come at last when
right-thinking people should lift their heads.
LAFLOTTE (*To himself*) So that it's easier to cut them off. Go on, old man, 245
only a few glasses more and I'll be floating.
DILLON The rascals, the fools, in the end they'll guillotine themselves.
                  (*He paces to and fro*)
LAFLOTTE (*Aside*) One could love life again properly, like a child, if one gave

---

223 A Girondin general.
225 Crescent moon.

it to oneself. But that doesn't often happen, to commit incest with chance ²⁵⁰ and become one's own father. Father and child at the same time. A crazy Oedipus!*

DILLON You don't fodder the people with corpses. Let the wives of Danton and Camille throw banknotes among the people, that's better than heads.

LAFLOTTE (*Aside*) Unlike Oedipus, I won't tear my eyes out, I may need ²⁵⁵ them to weep for the good general.

DILLON Hands on Danton! Who's safe after that? Fear will unite them.

LAFLOTTE (*Aside*) Yes, he's lost. What does it matter then if I tread on a corpse in order to clamber out of the grave?

DILLON Only a foot on the pavement. I will find enough people, old soldiers, ²⁶⁰ Girondists, *ci-devants;* we'll break open the prisons, we must come to terms with the prisoners.

LAFLOTTE Certainly it smells a little of treachery. What does it matter? I should like to try that myself, until now I've been too one-sided. One gets remorse, that too is a change; it isn't so unpleasant to smell one's own stink. The ²⁶⁵ prospect of the guillotine has begun to bore me; to wait so long for the thing! I have been through it at least twenty times in my mind. There's nothing spicy about it any longer. It's become quite vulgar.

DILLON A letter must be got through to Danton's wife.

LAFLOTTE (*Aside*) And then—it isn't death I fear but the pain. It might hurt, ²⁷⁰ who can guarantee it doesn't? True they say it only lasts a moment; but pain has a finer measure for time; it splits up a fraction of a second. No, pain's the only sin, and suffering the only burden; I will stay virtuous.

DILLON Listen, Laflotte, where is that fellow gone to? I have money, it must succeed. We must strike while the iron is hot; my plan is ready.   ²⁷⁵

LAFLOTTE At once, at once! I know the turnkey, I'll speak to him; you can count on me, general. We'll get out of this hole (*To himself, going out*) to go into another: I into the broadest, the world—he into the narrowest, the grave.

Scene 6

The Committee of Public Safety. SAINT-JUST, BARÈRE, COLLOT D'HERBOIS, ²⁸⁰
and BILLAUD-VARENNES

BARÈRE What does Fouquier write?

SAINT-JUST The second hearing is over. The prisoners demand the appearance of several members of the Convention and the Committee of Public Safety; they appeal to the people against the silencing of witnesses. The excite- ²⁸⁵ ment seems to be indescribable. Danton parodied Jupiter and shook his locks.

COLLOT The easier for Samson to shear them.

BARÈRE We mustn't show ourselves, the fishwives and rag-collectors might find us less imposing.   ²⁹⁰

BILLAUD The people have an instinct for letting themselves be trodden on,

²⁵² Oedipus married his mother and had children by her.

even if it's only with glances: these insolent physiognomies please them. Such expressions are more awe-inspiring than a nobleman's coat of arms; the fine aristocracy of those who despise humanity sits on them. Every one whom it disgusts to be looked at up and down, should help to smash 295 them in.

BARÈRE He is like the horned Siegfried.* The blood of the Septembrists has made him invulnerable.—What does Robespierre say?

SAINT-JUST He behaves as though he had something to say. The jury must declare themselves sufficiently instructed and close the debate. 300

BARÈRE Impossible—that would never do.

SAINT-JUST They must be done away with—at any price—even if we have to throttle them with our hands. "Dare!"* Danton mustn't have taught us that word in vain. The Revolution won't stumble over their bodies; but if Danton stays alive—he will seize her by the skirt and he has something in his 305 face as though he might rape liberty. (*He is called away*)

(*The* GAOLER *enters*)

GAOLER Some prisoners in St. Pelagie* lie dying, they are asking for a doctor.

BILLAUD Unnecessary; so much the less trouble for the executioner.

GAOLER There are pregnant women amongst them— 310

BILLAUD So much the better. Their children will need no coffins.

BARÈRE The consumption of an aristocrat spares the Tribunal a session. Any medicine would be counter-revolutionary.

COLLOT (*Taking up a paper*) A petition! A woman's name!

BARÈRE Yes, from one of those who are compelled to choose between the 315 plank of a guillotine and the bed of a Jacobin. Those who, like Lucretia,* die at the loss of their honour, but somewhat later than the Roman . . . in childbirth or of old age. Perhaps it may not be so unpleasant to drive a Tarquin out of the virtuous Republic of a virgin.

COLLOT She is too old. Madame desires death, she knows how to express 320 herself, prison lies on her like the lid of a coffin. She's been there four weeks. The answer's easy. (*He writes and reads out*) "Citizeness, you have not yet wished long enough for death."

BARÈRE Well said! But Collot, it's not good that the guillotine begins to laugh; the people aren't afraid of it any more; one mustn't make oneself so 325 familiar.

(SAINT-JUST *returns*)

SAINT-JUST I have just received a denunciation. There is a conspiracy in the prison; a young man called Laflotte has discovered all. He was in the same cell as Dillon. Dillon got drunk and blabbed. 330

BARÈRE He cuts his own neck off with his bottle; that's happened often enough before.

---

297 The hero of the Germanic sagas, "horned" because he wore a horned helmet; "invulnerable" because he had been covered in the blood of the dragon he slew.

303 One of Danton's most memorable statements was: "We must dare, and dare again, and dare forever."

308 A prison in Paris.

316 A legendary Roman matron who was raped by Tarquin.

SAINT-JUST Danton's and Camille's wives must scatter money amongst the people; Dillon will break out; the prisoners will be freed; the Convention will be blown up. 335

BARÈRE Fairy stories!

SAINT-JUST We'll send them to sleep with these fairy tales. I hold the proofs in my hands; add to them the impudence of the accused, the muttering of the people, the dismay of the jury; I'll make a report.

BARÈRE Yes, go, Saint-Just, and spin your periods, where every comma is 340 the stroke of a sword and every period a head struck off.

SAINT-JUST The Convention must decree that the Tribunal carry through the session without interruption and that it exclude from the proceedings any witness who shows contempt for the judges or who creates a scene causing disturbance. 345

BARÈRE You have the revolutionary instinct; that sounds quite moderate and yet it will achieve its purpose. They cannot be silent, Danton is bound to cry out.

SAINT-JUST I count on your support. In the Convention there are people as ill as Danton, who fear the same cure. They've gained courage, they'll scream 350 about the irregular procedure . . .

BARÈRE (*Interrupting him*) I'll say to them: in Rome the consul who discovered the Catiline conspiracy and punished the criminals with instant death, was accused of irregular procedure. Who were his accusers?

COLLOT (*With pathos*) Go, Saint-Just, the lava of revolution flows! Liberty 355 will suffocate in her embrace those weaklings who wished to fertilize her mighty womb; the majesty of the people will appear in thunder and lightning, as Jupiter to Semele,* and change them into ashes. Go, Saint-Just, we will help you; the thunderbolt must strike on the heads of cowards.

(SAINT-JUST *exit*) 360

BARÈRE Did you hear the word "Cure"? They'll end by making the guillotine a specific* against syphilis. They don't fight the moderates, they fight vice.

BILLAUD Until now our ways have gone together.

BARÈRE Robespierre will make the Revolution a hall for preaching moral sermons and use the guillotine as a pulpit. 365

BILLAUD Or as a hassock.

COLLOT On which finally he'll not stand but lie.

BARÈRE That will happen easily enough. The world would be topsy turvy if the so-called wrong-doers were hanged by the so-called righteous folk.

COLLOT (*To* BARÈRE) When do you return to Clichy? 370

BARÈRE When the doctor stops visiting me.

COLLOT Doesn't a star stand over the place, under whose beams the marrow of your spine will be quite dried up?

BILLAUD Soon the pretty fingers of that charming Demaly* will tear it out of its sheath, and make it hang down over his back as a pigtail. 375

---

358 The mother of Dionysus-Bacchus by Jupiter.

362 A remedy.

374 Barère's mistress; usually spelled "Demailly."

BARÈRE (*Shrugs his shoulders*) Pooh! Virtue should know nothing of those things.

BILLAUD He's an impotent free-mason. (BILLAUD *and* COLLOT *exeunt*)

BARÈRE The monster! "You have not yet wished long enough for death!" These words should have withered the tongue that spoke them. 380
And I? When the Septembrists broke into the prisons, a prisoner seized his knife, joined with the assassins, and plunged it into the breast of a priest; he was saved! Who could object to that? Shall I now go join with the murderers or sit on the Committee of Public Safety? Shall I use the guillotine or a pocket knife? It's the same situation only under rather more complex 385 circumstances; the fundamentals are the same.—And dare he murder one, two, or three or even more of us? Where does it end? There come the barleycorns, do two make a heap, or three, or four, or how many? Come, my conscience, come, my chicken, cluck, cluck, cluck, here's your fodder.
Yet—if I also were a prisoner? If I were suspected, it would be the same 390 thing, my death would be certain. Come, my conscience, you and I still carry on all right! (*Exit*)

Scene 7

*The Conciergerie.** LACROIX, DANTON, PHILIPPEAU, *and* CAMILLE

LACROIX You have shrieked well, Danton; had you taken such pains earlier with your life, things would be different now. You realize now, don't you, 395 when death comes so shamelessly close to one, and has such stinking breath, and becomes more and more importunate?

CAMILLE If only she'd ravish one, and tear her prize from the hot limbs with fighting and struggle! But with such formality, like a marriage with an old woman, with the contracts set out, with the witnesses called, with the 400 amens said, and then with the counterpane lifted up when, with her cold limbs, she creaks slowly into bed.

DANTON Would it were a fight so that arms and teeth clutched at each other! But I feel as though I'd fallen into a mill-shaft and that my limbs were slowly and systematically being wrenched off by the cold physical power. 405 To be killed so mechanically!

CAMILLE And then to lie there, alone, cold, stiff, in the damp vapour of putrefaction. Perhaps death slowly torments the life out of one's fibres, with the knowledge, perhaps, that one's falling to pieces.

PHILIPPEAU Quiet, my friend. We are like the meadow saffron which first 410 bears seed after the winter. We only distinguish ourselves from flowers which are transplanted because in the attempt we stink a little. Is that so bad?

DANTON An edifying prospect! From one manure heap to another. Isn't that the theistic theory of classes? From first to second, second to third and so on? I've had enough of the school bench, I've got piles on my seat like an ape 415 from sitting on it.

PHILIPPEAU Then what would you like?

DANTON Rest.

PHILIPPEAU Rest is in God.

393 A prison in Paris.

DANTON In nothingness. What can you sink back in which is more restful 420 than nothingness, and if the highest peace is God, isn't nothingness God? But I'm an atheist; that accursed phrase! Something cannot become nothing! And I am something, that is the trouble! Creation has made itself so broad, nothing is empty. Everything full of multitude. Nothingness has killed itself, creation is its wound, we are the drops of its blood, the world is the 425 grave in which it decomposes. That sounds mad but there's some truth in it.

CAMILLE The world's the eternal Jew, nothingness is death, but that's impossible. Oh, not to be able to die, as the song goes!

DANTON We are all buried alive and set aside like kings in threefold or 430 fourfold coffins, under the sky, in our houses, in our coats and shirts. We scratch for fifty years on our coffin lids. If one could believe in annihilation! Yes, that would be a help.—There is no hope in death. It is only a simpler form of laziness, whilst life is one that is more complex, more organized. That's the whole difference! But it's exactly this form of indolence to 435 which I've become accustomed; the devil knows how I'll get used to another.

O, Julie, if I could go alone! If she would leave me in solitude! And if I could fall to pieces utterly, dissolve entirely—then I would be a handful of tormented dust—every one of my atoms could only find peace in her. 440 I cannot die, no, I cannot die. We aren't struck down yet. We must shriek, they must tear every drop of life-blood out of my limbs.

LACROIX We must stand by our demands. Our accusers and the Committee must appear before the Tribunal.

Scene 8

A room. FOUQUIER, AMAR, *and* VOULAND   445

FOUQUIER I no longer know what answer to make: they are demanding a commission.

AMAR We've got the scoundrels—here you have what you want.

(*Hands* FOUQUIER *a paper*)

VOULAND That will satisfy them.   450

FOUQUIER Certainly. We needed it.

AMAR Quickly then, so that we rid ourselves of this affair and of them. . . .

Scene 9

The Revolutionary Tribunal. DANTON

DANTON The Republic is in danger and is not instructed of it. We call upon the people; my voice is still strong enough to speak the funeral oration 455 of the Committee. I repeat—we demand a commission; we have important matters to reveal. I will re-establish myself in the citadel of reason, I will break through with the cannons of truth and pulverize my enemies.

(*Signs of applause*)

(*Enter* FOUQUIER, AMAR, *and* VOULAND)   460

FOUQUIER Silence in the name of the Republic and in the name of the law!

The Convention decrees: in view of the fact that signs of mutiny have been shown in the prisons; in view of the fact that the wives of Danton and Camille distribute money amongst the people and that General Dillon has plotted to escape and put himself at the head of an insurrection to free 465 the accused; lastly, in view of the fact that they themselves have endeavoured to provoke disturbances and to insult the Tribunal: the Tribunal will be empowered to carry out its inquiry without interruption and to exclude any of the accused who shall ignore the respect due to the law.

DANTON I ask all here whether we have derided the Tribunal, the People 470 or the Convention?

VOICES No! No!

CAMILLE Miserable wretches, they wish to murder my Lucile!

DANTON One day the truth will be known. I see a great misfortune over-whelming France. It is dictatorship; it has torn off its veils, it carries its 475 head high, it strides over our bodies. (*Pointing at* AMAR *and* VOULAND) See there the cowardly murderers, see the ravens of the Committee of Public Safety! I accuse Robespierre, Saint-Just and their hangmen of high treason. They want to suffocate the Republic in blood. The ruts of their guillotine carts are the roads by which the foreign armies will thrust into the heart 480 of the Fatherland.

How long will the footprints of liberty be graves? You need bread and you are thrown heads! You thirst, and they make you lap up the blood from the steps of the guillotine! (*Great emotion amongst the audience, cries of applause*)

MANY VOICES Long live Danton! Down with the Committee! 485
(*The prisoners are led away by force*)

Scene 10

A square in front of the Palace of Justice. A crowd

VOICES Down with the Committee! Long live Danton!

FIRST CITIZEN Yes, that's right. Heads instead of bread, blood instead of wine.

WOMEN The guillotine is a bad mill and Samson a bad baker. We want 490 bread, bread!

SECOND CITIZEN Your bread—Danton's devoured it. His head will give bread to all of you. He was right.

FIRST CITIZEN Danton was with us on the 10th of August. Danton was with us in September. Where were the people who make accusations against 495 him?

SECOND CITIZEN And Lafayette was with you in Versailles, and was a traitor just the same.

FIRST CITIZEN Who says that Danton is a traitor?

SECOND CITIZEN Robespierre. 500

FIRST CITIZEN Then Robespierre is a traitor!

SECOND CITIZEN Who says that?

FIRST CITIZEN Danton.

SECOND CITIZEN Danton has beautiful clothes, Danton has a beautiful house, Danton has a beautiful wife, he bathes himself in Burgundy, eats phea- 505 sants off silver plates and sleeps with your wives and daughters when he's drunk. Danton was poor like you. From where has he got it all? The Royal Veto has bought him with it, so that he may save his crown for him with it! The Duke of Orléans has made him a present of it, so that he may steal a crown for him. The foreigner has given it to him, so that he may betray 510 you all. What has Robespierre? The virtuous Robespierre! All of you know him.

ALL Long live Robespierre! Down with Danton! Down with the traitor.

Act Four

Scene 1

A Room. JULIE, *and a boy*

JULIE It's all over. They trembled before him. They kill him out of fear. Go! I have seen him for the last time; tell him I could not see him as he is now. (*Gives him a lock of hair*) There, give him this and tell him he will not go alone—he will understand. And come back quickly, I will read his look in 5 your eyes. (*The boy exits*)

Scene 2

A street. Enter DUMAS *and a citizen*

CITIZEN How can they condemn so many unfortunates to death after such a trial?

DUMAS Indeed it's extraordinary; but revolutionaries have a sense other men 10 lack, and their instinct never betrays them.

CITIZEN It's the instinct of the tiger.—You have a wife?

DUMAS Soon I shall have had one.

CITIZEN So it's true?

DUMAS The Revolutionary Tribunal will pronounce our divorce; the guil- 15 lotine will divide us from bed and board.

CITIZEN You are a monster!

DUMAS Idiot! You admire Brutus?

CITIZEN With all my soul.

DUMAS Must one be a Roman consul and be able to hide one's head in a 20 toga, to sacrifice one's dearest to the Fatherland? I shall wipe my eyes with the sleeve of my red coat; that's the only difference.

CITIZEN That is horrible!

DUMAS Go, you don't understand me. (*Exeunt*)

Scene 3

(*The Conciergerie.* LACROIX, HÉRAULT SÉCHELLES *on one bed,* DANTON, 25 CAMILLE *an another*)

LACROIX One's hair grows long, and one's fingernails, really one's ashamed of oneself.

HÉRAULT Take care what you're doing, you sneeze sand all over my face!

LACROIX   And don't tread on my feet, my dear fellow, I've got corns. 30
HÉRAULT   You've got lice too.
LACROIX   Ah! If only I were free of the worms.
HÉRAULT   Anyhow, sleep well! We must see how we get on with each other, there's not much room.—Don't scratch me with your nails in your sleep! —So!—Don't pull at the shroud like that, it's cold down there! 35
DANTON   Yes, Camille, to-morrow we're worn out shoes, thrown into the lap of the beggar woman Earth.
CAMILLE   The cowhide which Plato says the angels make slippers out of, when they grope their way about the earth. But there's more to come hereafter. —My Lucile! 40
DANTON   Be calm, my boy!
CAMILLE   How can I? What do you think, Danton? Can I? They can't lay their hands on her, it's impossible! The light of beauty that pours from her lovely body can't be put out. Look, the Earth would not dare to bury her; it would arch itself above her, the damp of the grave would sparkle like dew on 45 her eyelashes, crystals would shoot up like flowers about her limbs and bright springs murmur to her in sleep.
DANTON   Sleep, my boy, sleep.
CAMILLE   Listen, Danton, between ourselves, it's so miserable to have to die. And it does no good. I'll still steal from life a last look from her pretty 50 eyes, I will have my eyes open.
DANTON   They will stay open anyhow. Samson does not close one's eyes. Sleep is more merciful. Sleep, my boy, sleep!
CAMILLE   Lucile, your kisses play tricks upon my lips, every kiss becomes a dream, my eyelids drop and close fast upon it. 55
DANTON   Will the clock not be quiet? With every tick it pushes the walls closer round me, till they're as close as a coffin—I read such a story as a child, my hair stood on end. Yes, as a child! It wasn't worth their trouble to fatten me up and keep me warm. Only work for the grave-diggers!

I feel as if I stank already. My dear body, I will hold my nose and pretend 60 you're a woman sweating and stinking after a dance and pay you compliments. We've often passed the time together in other ways.

To-morrow you're a broken violin; the melody is played out. To-morrow you're an empty bottle; the wine is finished but hasn't made me drunk and I go soberly to bed—lucky people who can still get tight. To-morrow 65 you're a worn-out pair of trousers; you'll be thrown into the wardrobe and the moths will eat you, you may smell as much as you like.

Ugh, it's no good! Yes, it is miserable to have to die. Death mimics birth, and dying we're as helpless and naked as new-born children. Of course, we're given a shroud for swaddling-clothes, but how will that help? In 70 the grave we can whimper just as well as in the cradle.

Camille! He's asleep; (*Bends over him*) a dream plays between his eyelashes. I will not brush the golden dew of sleep from his eyes.

(*Rises and goes to the window*) I shall not go alone; I thank you, Julie! And yet I should have liked to die differently, without any effort, as a star 75 falls, as a note expires, kissing itself dead with its own lips, as a ray of light buries itself in the clear stream.— Like glimmering tears the stars are sprinkled through the night; there must be some great sorrow in the eyes from which they fall.

CAMILLE Oh! (*He has sat up and reaches towards the ceiling*) 80

DANTON What is it, Camille?

CAMILLE Oh, oh!

DANTON (*Shakes him*) Do you want to scratch the roof down.

CAMILLE Oh you, you, hold me, speak to me!

DANTON You're trembling in every limb, there's sweat on your forehead. 85

CAMILLE It is you, it is me—so? This is my hand! Yes, now I remember. Oh Danton, it was terrible!

DANTON What was?

CAMILLE I lay between dream and waking. Then the roof disappeared, and the moon sank into the room, close and thick, my arm took hold of it. The 90 roof of heaven with its lights had sunk lower, I knocked on it, I touched the stars, I reeled like a drunken man under the roof of ice. It was terrible, Danton.

DANTON The lamp throws a round shadow on the ceiling, that's what you saw.

CAMILLE As for me, it doesn't need much to make me lose my scrap of 95 reason. Madness grasped me by the hair. (*He rises*) I won't sleep any more, I don't want to go mad. (*He reaches for a book*)

DANTON What are you taking?

CAMILLE The *Night Thoughts.**

DANTON Do you want to die beforehand? I'll take *La Pucelle.** I'll steal away 100 from life not as from a praying-desk but as from the bed of a sister of mercy. Life is a whore; she fornicates with the whole world.

Scene 4

Before the Conciergerie. A gaoler, two carters with tumbrils, and women

GAOLER Who said you were to come here?

FIRST CARTER I'm not "To-Come-Here," what a curious name. 105

GAOLER Fool, who gave you the commission?

FIRST CARTER I don't get any commission, nothing except ten sous a head.

SECOND CARTER The villain takes the bread out of my mouth.

FIRST CARTER What do you call your bread? (*Pointing to the window of the prisoners*) That's food for worms. 110

SECOND CARTER My children are worms too, and they also want their share. Oh, things are going badly with our business and yet we're the best carters.

FIRST CARTER Why's that?

SECOND CARTER Who is the best carter?

FIRST CARTER He who carries furthest and fastest. 115

---

99 *Night Thoughts on Life, Death, and Immortality,* a poem by Edward Young.

100 An epic poem by Jean Chapelain on the life and death of Joan of Arc; also an obscene mock-heroic piece by Voltaire.

SECOND CARTER Well, donkey, who can carry further than to carry you out of the world, and who can carry faster than one who does it in quarter of an hour! It's exactly a quarter of an hour from here to the Place de la Révolution.

GAOLER Quickly, you villains! Nearer to the door; make way, my girl! 120

FIRST CARTER Don't move! A man doesn't go round a girl, he always goes through her.

SECOND CARTER I'll bet he does; you can drive your cart and horses through her, you'll find the ruts easy; but you'll have to go into quarantine when you come out. (*They drive forward*) 125

SECOND CARTER (*To the women*) What are you staring at?

A WOMAN We're waiting for old customers.

SECOND CARTER Do you mean my cart is going to be turned into a brothel? It's a respectable cart, it carried the King and all the fine gentlemen of Paris to the scaffold. 130

(LUCILE *enters. She sits on a stone under the prisoners' window*)

LUCILE Camille! Camille! (CAMILLE *appears at the window*)

Listen, Camille, you make me laugh with that long coat of stone and that iron mask before your face; can't you bend down? Where are your arms?—I'll entice you, sweet bird. 135

(*Sings*) Two stars stand in the sky
        Shining brighter than the moon,
        One shines at my darling's window
        The other at her door.

Come, come, my friend! Softly up the steps, they're all asleep. The moon 140 has helped me to wait. But you can't get through the door, your clothes are impossible. The joke's gone too far, give it up. You don't move, why don't you speak to me? You frighten me.

Listen, the people say that you must die, and they make such serious faces over it. Die! I can't help laughing at their faces. "Die!" What kind of a 145 word is that? Tell me, Camille. "Die!" I will think it over. There it is, there! I'll run after it, come, sweet friend, help me catch it, come, come!

(*She runs away*)

CAMILLE (*Calls*) Lucile, Lucile!

Scene 5

The Conciergerie. DANTON, *at a window which looks into the next room.* 150
CAMILLE, PHILIPPEAU, LACROIX, *and* HÉRAULT

DANTON You're quiet now, Fabre.

A VOICE (*From within*) As death.

DANTON Do you know what we are doing now?

A VOICE Well? 155

DANTON What you've done all your life; making verses—*des vers.**

---

156 He puns on a second meaning of *"vers,"* worms.

CAMILLE (*To himself*) Madness sat behind her eyes. More people have gone mad already. It's the way of the world. What can we do? We wash our hands of them.—It is better so.

DANTON I leave everything in terrible confusion. Not one of them knows 160 how to govern. Things might still be managed if I left Robespierre my whores and Couthon my legs.

LACROIX We'd have turned liberty into a whore!

DANTON And what else is it? Liberty and whores are the most cosmopolitan things under the sun. Liberty will now prostitute herself decently in the 165 marriage bed of the lawyer from Arras. But I think she will be a Clytemnestra* to him; I don't give him more than six months' respite, I drag him with me.

CAMILLE (*To himself*) Heaven help her to some comfortable *idée fixe!** The universal *idée fixe* which is called good sense is intolerably boring. The 170 happiest man would be he who could persuade himself that he was God the Father, the Son, and the Holy Ghost.

LACROIX The fools will cry "Long live the Republic!" as we pass by.

DANTON What does it matter? The deluge of the Revolution may carry our corpses where it likes; with our fossilized bones men can always break the 175 heads of all kings.

HÉRAULT Yes, so long as there's a Samson to use our jaw-bones.

DANTON They bear the brand of Cain.

LACROIX Nothing shows more clearly that Robespierre is a Nero* than that he was never so friendly to Camille as two days before his arrest. Isn't it 180 so, Camille?

CAMILLE What does it matter, so far as I'm concerned?—(*To himself*) What an attractive thing she has made of madness. Why must I go away now? We'd have laughed over it together, have nursed it and kissed it.

DANTON If History once opens her vaults, Despotism may still suffocate 185 from the vapours of our corpses.

HÉRAULT We stank quite sufficiently in our lifetime.—These are phrases for posterity, aren't they, Danton? They have nothing to do with us.

CAMILLE He makes a face, as if it ought to turn to stone and be dug up by posterity as an antique. 190

That isn't worth the trouble either, to pull faces and put on red and speak with a good accent; once in a while we should take off the masks, then we should see everywhere, as in a room of mirrors, the one, primeval, toothless, everlasting sheep's head,* no more and no less. The differences are not so big, we are all villains and angels, fools and geniuses, and indeed all of 195 them in one; the four find plenty of room in one body, they are not so large as people pretend. Sleep, digest, breed children—every one does that; other things are only variations in different keys on the same theme. And

---

167 Clytaemnestra, the wife of Agamemnon, killed him after his victorious return from Troy.
169 "Fixed idea."
179 A mad Roman tyrant (37–68 A.D.) notorious for his atrocities.
194 Image of utter stupidity.

yet men have to walk on tiptoes and make faces, still they have to be embarrassed in front of each other. We have all eaten ourselves sick at the 200 same table and have now got the gripes; why do you hold your napkins before your faces? Scream and cry as the fancy takes you! But don't make such virtuous and such witty and such heroic and such brilliant grimaces. After all, we know each other; spare yourselves the trouble.

HÉRAULT Yes, Camille, let us sit beside each other and scream; nothing 205 stupider than pressing your lips together if something is hurting you.—Greeks and Gods screamed, Romans and Stoics* made heroic grimaces.

DANTON The second were as good Epicureans as the first. They gave themselves a very comforting self-respect. It's not so bad to drape your toga and look around to see if you throw a long shadow. What should we aim at? 210 To hide our shame with laurel leaves, rose wreaths or vine leaves or to show the ugly thing openly and let it be licked by the dogs?

PHILIPPEAU My friends, one need not stand very high above the earth to see nothing more of all the confused flux and glimmer and have one's eye filled by a few great godlike outlines. There is an ear for which the clamour 215 and discordance which deafen us are a stream of harmonies.

DANTON But we are the poor musicians and our bodies the instruments. Do the ugly sounds that are ground out of them only exist so that rising higher and higher and finally softly echoing they expire in a voluptuous sigh in the ear of heaven?   220

HÉRAULT Are we sucking-pigs which are whipped to death for princely tables, so that their flesh is tastier?

DANTON Are we children, roasted in the glowing Moloch* arms of this world and tickled with rays of light so that the Gods may enjoy their laugh?

CAMILLE Is the air with its golden eyes a dish full of golden carp that stands 225 on the table of the blissful Gods, and the blissful Gods laugh eternally, and the fish die eternally, and the Gods rejoice eternally at the play of colour in the death struggle.

DANTON The world is chaos. The Nothing is its too fertile Deity.

(*Enter the* GAOLER)   230

GAOLER Gentlemen, you may go, the carriages wait at the door.

PHILIPPEAU Good night, my friends! Let us quietly draw over our heads the great coverlet, under which all hearts burn out and all eyes close.

(*They embrace each other*)

HÉRAULT (*Takes* CAMILLE'S *arm*) Rejoice, Camille, we shall have a good 235 night. The clouds hang in the calm evening sky like a burnt-out Olympus* with the fading sinking forms of the Gods. (*They leave*)

---

207 The followers of a philosophy which advocated austerity, reason, and freedom from desire and passion.
223 A pagan god with the head of a calf; third in rank in the satanic hierarchy.
236 A mountain in Greece, thought to be the home of the gods.

Scene 6

A room. JULIE.

JULIE The people ran into the street, now all is quiet. I should not like to keep him waiting a moment. (*She takes out a phial*) Come, dearest priest, whose 240 Amen sends us to bed. (*Goes to the window*) It is so lovely to say good-bye; now I have only to close the door behind me (*Drinks*)
One would like to stand like this for ever.—The sun has gone down. The earth's features were so sharp in her light, but now her face is as calm and grave as a dying woman's.—How beautifully the evening light plays 245 about her forehead and her cheeks.—Paler and paler she becomes, like a corpse she drives downwards on the flood of the air. Will no arm seize her by the golden hair and take her from the stream and bury her?
I go softly. I do not kiss her, so that no breath, no sigh may wake her from her slumber.—Sleep, sleep! (*Dies*) 250

Scene 7

Place de la Révolution. The tumbrils are driven on and halt at the guillotine.
Men and women sing and dance the Carmagnole. The prisoners sing the
Marseillaise.

WOMAN (*With children*) Make room, make room! The children are crying, they're hungry. I must make them watch, so they'll be quiet. Make room! 255
A WOMAN Hey, Danton, now you can go to bed with the worms.
ANOTHER Hérault, I'll get myself a wig made from your lovely hair.
HÉRAULT I haven't enough bush to cover so denuded a Mound of Venus.
CAMILLE Damned witches! You shall still cry: may the mountains fall upon us.
A WOMAN The mountain has fallen on you, or rather you've fallen beneath it. 260
DANTON (*To* CAMILLE) Quiet, my boy! You've shouted yourself hoarse.
CAMILLE (*Gives the driver money*) There, old Charon,* your cart is a fine platter!
—Gentlemen, I shall serve myself first. This is a classical banquet; we lie in our places and scatter a little blood as a libation. Adieu, Danton! (*He ascends the scaffold, the Prisoners follow him one by one,* DANTON *last*) 265
LACROIX (*To the people*) You kill us on the day when you've lost your reason; you'll kill them on the day you recover it.
SOME VOICES That's been said before; how tiresome!
LACROIX The tyrants will break their necks over our graves.
HÉRAULT (*To* DANTON) He thinks his corpse a breeding-ground of Freedom. 270
PHILIPPEAU (*On the scaffold*) I forgive you; I hope that your hour of death may be no bitterer than mine.
HÉRAULT I knew it! He has to reach into his bosom once more to show the people down there that he has clean linen.
FABRE Good luck, Danton! I die twice over. 275
DANTON Adieu, my friend! The guillotine is the best doctor.
HÉRAULT (*Tries to embrace* DANTON) Ah, Danton, I can't even make a joke. The time has come. (*An* EXECUTIONER *separates them*)

262 In classical story the ferryman of the Styx, the river of the underworld.

DANTON (*To the* EXECUTIONER) Do you wish to be more cruel than death? Can you prevent our heads from kissing at the bottom of the basket? 280

Scene 8

A Street. LUCILE.

LUCILE And yet there's something serious in it. I must think about it. I'm beginning to understand a little.

To die—to die!—Yet everything may live, yes, everything, the little fly there, the birds. Why not he? The river of life would cease to flow if but 285 one drop were spilled. The earth would have a wound from such a blow.

Everything moves, the clocks tick, the bells peal, the people run, the water flows, and everything else goes on except there, there—! No, it shall not happen, no, I will sit upon the ground and scream, so that everything will stand still in fear, everything come to a stop, nothing move any 290 more. (*She sits down, covers her eyes, and gives one cry. Then after a pause she gets up*)

It doesn't help, everything remains as before; the houses, the street, the wind blows, the clouds pass.—We have to bear it.

(*Some women come down the street*) 295

FIRST WOMAN A handsome man, Hérault!

SECOND WOMAN When he stood at the triumphal arch at the Feast of the Constitution, I thought to myself, he'd look well on the guillotine, that's what I said. It was a presentiment, as you might say.

THIRD WOMAN Yes, one must see people under all conditions; it's a good 300 thing dying's become so public. (*They pass by*)

LUCILE My Camille! Where shall I look for you now?

Scene 9

Place de la Révolution. Two executioners at work on the guillotine

FIRST EXECUTIONER (*Stands on the guillotine and sings*)

    And when home go I 305
    The moon shines so shy . . .

SECOND EXECUTIONER Hey, hallo! Will you finish soon?

FIRST EXECUTIONER In a minute! (*Sings*)

    Shines in my old father's window—
    Boy, where have you been for so long? 310

Hey, give us my coat. (*They go singing away*)

    And when home go I
    The moon shines so shy. . . .

LUCILE (*Enters and sits on the steps of the guillotine*) I lay myself in your lap, quiet angel of death. 315

(*Sings*) There is a reaper, his name is Death,
    Has power from Almighty God. . . .

Dear cradle, who lulled my Camille to sleep, who stifled him beneath your roses. You bells of death, whose sweet tongue sang him to the grave. (*Sings*)

Hundreds of thousands without number 320
Fall beneath the sickle only.

(Enter a patrol)

A CITIZEN   Hey, who goes there?

LUCILE   Long live the King!

CITIZEN   In the name of the Republic! 325

(She is surrounded by the watch and taken away)

ABOVE: François Joseph Talma (1763–18
in the title role as *Charles VI.*
His use of costume and
style of acting foreshadowed
the romantic and realistic
dramatic styles of the
later 19th-century French theater.
Harvard Theatre Collection.
LEFT: Talma in one of the first
uses of historically accurate
costuming, in Voltaire's *Brutus.*
Courtesy A. M. Nagler

Percy Bysshe Shelley

Percy Bysshe Shelley (1792–1822), *though far better known as one of England's foremost poets, wrote several plays including* THE CENCI, *the best play to be produced by the Romantic movement in England. With his contemporaries, most of whom tried at least one play in the course of their careers, Shelley was acutely aware of the low estate of British drama in his time and he was convinced that a dramatic renaissance lay in taking the Elizabethan dramatists (especially Shakespeare) and the German romantics (especially Schiller) as models. Unfortunately, most of the drama produced by this effort was, despite brilliant passages, too untheatrical to qualify for production. Only* THE CENCI *has occasionally been produced, and, though it will probably never achieve the popularity Shelley would have wished for it, it remains a powerful, skillfully turned example of the type of historical tragedy popular with Romantic writers of all countries.*

Chronology

1792 Born at Field Place, Sussex, the son of a country squire of aristocratic family.

1804 Entered Eton.

1810 Published *Zastrozzi,* a romance, and wrote *Original Poetry by Victor and Cazire* in collaboration with his sister. He entered Oxford, where he became friendly with Jefferson Hogg and enthusiastic about chemistry, philosophy, and political radicalism, as well as poetry. He published a collection called *Posthumous Fragments of Margaret Nicholson.*

1811 Collaborated with Hogg to publish the pamphlet *The Necessity of Atheism.* Expelled from Oxford, he travelled to London, where he met Harriet Westbrook, with whom he eloped to Edinburgh.

1811–13 Travelled to York, Sussex, Cumberland, Dublin, and Wales. He met William Godwin.

1813 His daughter, Ianthe, was born. He wrote *Queen Mab* and moved to Windsor Forest.

1814 He met Mary Wollstonecraft Godwin and travelled with her and Jane Clairmont to France and Switzerland.

1815 Inherited his father's property.

1816 Harriet gave birth to a son, Charles. Shelley wrote *Alastor, or the Spirit of Solitude.* Mary gave birth to a son, William. Shelley travelled to Switzerland, where he met Byron.

1817 Harriet committed suicide. Shelley wrote *The Revolt of Islam.* On Mr. Westbrook's suit, Lord Chancellor Eldon judged Shelley unfit to have custody of his first two children.

1818 Travelled to Italy with Mary and wrote *Rosalind and Helen* and *Julian and Maddado.*

1819 Wrote *The Cenci* and *Prometheus Unbound.*

1820 Wrote *The Witch of Atlas.*

1821 Wrote *Epipsychidion, Adonais,* an elegy on Keats, and *Hellas,* a drama. He translated selections from Homer, Euripides, Calderon, and Goethe.

1822 Drowned in a sailing accident in July.

Selected Bibliography

Adams, Charles L., "The Structure of *The Cenci,*" *Drama Survey,* IV (1965), 139–48.

Bates, E. S., *A Study of Shelley's Drama "The Cenci,"* New York, 1908.

Cameron, K. N., and Horst Frenz, "The Stage History of Shelley's *The Cenci,*" *PMLA,* LX (1945), 1080–1105.

Evans, B., *Gothic Drama From Walpole to Shelley,* Berkeley, Calif., 1947.

States, Bert O., "Addendum: The Stage History of Shelley's *The Cenci,*" *PMLA,* LXXII (1957), 633–44.

Whitman, Robert F., "Beatrice's 'Pernicious Mistake' in *The Cenci,*" *PMLA,* LXXIV (1959), 249–53.

THE CENCI

by Percy Bysshe Shelley

Characters

COUNT FRANCESCO CENCI

GIACOMO *his Sons*
BERNARDO

CARDINAL CAMILLO

ORSINO, *a Prelate*

SAVELLA, *the Pope's Legate*

OLIMPIO *Assassins*
MARZIO

ANDREA, *Servant to Cenci*

Nobles, Judges, Guards, Servants

LUCRETIA, *Wife of Cenci, and Step-mother of his Children*

BEATRICE, *his Daughter*

The Scene lies principally in Rome during the Pontificate of Clement VIII, but changes during the Fourth Act to Petrella, a castle among the Apulian Apennines

Act One

Scene 1

An apartment in the Cenci Palace

(*Enter* COUNT CENCI, *and* CARDINAL CAMILLO)

CAMILLO That matter of the murder is hushed up
If you consent to yield his Holiness
Your fief* that lies beyond the Pincian gate.*
It needed all my interest in the conclave
To bend him to this point: he said that you   5
Bought perilous impunity with your gold;
That crimes like yours if once or twice compounded
Enriched the Church, and respited from hell
An erring soul which might repent and live;
But that the glory and the interest   10
Of the high throne he fills, little consist
With making it a daily mart of guilt
As manifold and hideous as the deeds
Which you scarce hide from men's revolted eyes.

---

3 (*a*) A piece of property which a feudal lord would allow his vassal to use in return for service. (*b*) One of the gates in the old walls of Rome.

CENCI   The third of my possessions—let it go!   15
        Ay, I once heard the nephew of the Pope
        Had sent his architect to view the ground,
        Meaning to build a villa on my vines
        The next time I compounded with his uncle:
        I little thought he should outwit me so!   20
        Henceforth no witness—not the lamp—shall see
        That which the vassal threatened to divulge,
        Whose throat is choked with dust for his reward.
        The deed he saw could not have rated higher
        That his most worthless life:—it angers me!   25
        "Respited me from Hell!"—So may the Devil
        Respite their souls from Heaven. No doubt Pope Clement,
        And his most charitable nephews, pray
        That the Apostle Peter and the saints
        Will grant for their sake that I long enjoy   30
        Strength, wealth, and pride, and lust, and length of days
        Wherein to act the deeds which are the stewards
        Of their revenue.—But much yet remains
        To which they show no title.
CAMILLO   Oh, Count Cenci!   35
        So much that thou mightst honourably live
        And reconcile thyself with thine own heart
        And with thy God, and with the offended world.
        How hideously look deeds of lust and blood
        Thro' those snow white and venerable hairs!   40
        Your children should be sitting round you now,
        But that you fear to read upon their looks
        The shame and misery you have written there.
        Where is your wife? Where is your gentle daughter?
        Methinks her sweet looks, which make all things else   45
        Beauteous and glad, might kill the fiend within you.
        Why is she barred from all society
        But her own strange and uncomplaining wrongs?
        Talk with me, Count,—you know I mean you well.
        I stood beside your dark and fiery youth   50
        Watching its bold and bad career, as men
        Watch meteors, but it vanished not: I marked
        Your desperate and remorseless manhood; now
        Do I behold you, in dishonoured age,
        Charged with a thousand unrepented crimes.   55
        Yet I have ever hoped you would amend,
        And in that hope have saved your life three times.
CENCI   For which Aldobrandino owes you now
        My fief beyond the Pincian. Cardinal,
        One thing, I pray you, recollect henceforth,   60

And so we shall converse with less restraint.
A man you knew spoke of my wife and daughter:
He was accustomed to frequent my house;
So the next day *his* wife and daughter came
And asked if I had seen him; and I smiled: 65
I think they never saw him any more.
CAMILLO   Thou execrable man, beware!—
CENCI   Of thee?
     Nay, this is idle: we should know each other.
As to my character for what men call crime,   70
Seeing I please my senses as I list,*
And vindicate that right with force or guile,
It is a public matter, and I care not
If I discuss it with you. I may speak
Alike to you and my own conscious heart;   75
For you give out that you have half reformed me,
Therefore strong vanity will keep you silent
If fear should not; both will, I do not doubt.
All men delight in sensual luxury,
All men enjoy revenge; and most exult   80
Over the tortures they can never feel;
Flattering their secret peace with others' pain.
But I delight in nothing else. I love
The sight of agony, and the sense of joy,
When this shall be another's and that mine.   85
And I have no remorse and little fear,
Which are, I think, the checks of other men.
This mood has grown upon me, until now
Any design my captious fancy makes
The picture of its wish, and it forms none   90
But such as men like you would start to know,
Is as my natural food and rest debarred
Until it be accomplished.
CAMILLO   Art thou not
Most miserable?   95
CENCI   Why miserable?—
     No. I am what your theologians call
Hardened; which they must be in impudence,
So to revile a man's peculiar taste.
True, I was happier than I am, while yet   100
Manhood remained to act the thing I thought;
While lust was sweeter than revenge; and now
Invention palls: ay, we must all grow old:
And but that there yet remains a deed to act

---

71 Wish.

Whose horror might make sharp an appetite 105
Duller than mine—I'd do,—I know not what.
When I was young I thought of nothing else
But pleasure; and I fed on honey sweets:
Men, by St. Thomas, cannot live like bees,
And I grew tired: yet, till I killed a foe, 110
And heard his groans, and heard his children's groans,
Knew I not what delight was else on earth,
Which now delights me little. I the rather
Look on such pangs as terror ill conceals:
The dry, fixed eyeball; the pale, quivering lip, 115
Which tell me that the spirit weeps within
Tears bitterer than the bloody sweat of Christ.
I rarely kill the body, which preserves,
Like a strong prison, the soul within my power,
Wherein I feed it with the breath of fear 120
For hourly pain.
CAMILLO   Hell's most abandoned fiend
Did never, in the drunkenness of guilt,
Speak to his heart as now you speak to me;
I thank my God that I believe you not. 125
                    (*Enter* ANDREA)
ANDREA My Lord, a gentleman from Salamanca*
Would speak with you.
CENCI Bid him attend me in the grand saloon.* (*Exit* ANDREA)
CAMILLO Farewell; and I will pray 130
Almighty God that thy false, impious words,
Tempt not his spirit to abandon thee. (*Exit* CAMILLO)
CENCI The third of my possessions! I must use
Close husbandry,* or gold, the old man's sword,
Falls from my withered hand. But yesterday 135
There came an order from the Pope to make
Fourfold provision for my cursed sons;
Whom I had sent from Rome to Salamanca,
Hoping some accident might cut them off;
And meaning if I could to starve them there. 140
I pray thee, God, send some quick death upon them!
Bernardo and my wife could not be worse
If dead and damned: then, as to Beatrice—(*Looking around him suspiciously*)
I think they cannot hear me at that door;
What if they should? And yet I need not speak, 145
Though the heart triumphs with itself in words.
O, thou most silent air, that shalt not hear

---

127 A province in western Spain.
129 A large reception hall.
134 Thrift.

What now I think! Thou, pavement, which I tread
Towards her chamber,—let your echoes talk
Of my imperious step, scorning surprise,
But not of my intent! Andrea!

(*Enter* ANDREA)

ANDREA   My lord!
CENCI   Bid Beatrice attend me in her chamber
This evening:—no, at midnight, and alone. (*Exeunt*)

Scene 2

A garden of the Cenci Palace
(*Enter* BEATRICE *and* ORSINO, *as in conversation*)

BEATRICE   Pervert not truth,
Orsino. You remember where we held
That conversation;—nay, we see the spot
Even from this cypress;—two long years are past
Since, on an April midnight, underneath
The moonlight ruins of mount Palatine,*
I did confess to you my secret mind.

ORSINO   You said you loved me then.
BEATRICE   You are a priest,
Speak to me not of love.

ORSINO   I may obtain
The dispensation of the Pope to marry.
Because I am a priest do you believe
Your image, as the hunter some struck deer,
Follows me not whether I wake or sleep?

BEATRICE   As I have said, speak to me not of love;
Had you a dispensation, I have not;
Nor will I leave this home of misery
Whilst my poor Bernard, and that gentle lady
To whom I owe life and these virtuous thoughts,
Must suffer what I still have strength to share.
Alas, Orsino! All the love that once
I felt for you, is turned to bitter pain.
Ours was a youthful contract, which you first
Broke, by assuming vows no Pope will loose.
And thus I love you still, but holily,
Even as a sister or a spirit might;
And so I swear a cold fidelity.
And it is well perhaps we shall not marry.
You have a sly, equivocating vein
That suits me not. Ah, wretched that I am!
Where shall I turn? Even now you look on me

150

155

160

165

170

175

180

185

---

163 That is, the ancient ruins on the Palatine in moonlight.

As you were not my friend, and as if you 190
Discovered that I thought so, with false smiles
Making my true suspicion seem your wrong.
Ah! No, forgive me; sorrow makes me seem
Sterner than else my nature might have been;
I have a weight of melancholy thoughts, 195
And they forbode,—but what can they forbode
Worse than I now endure?
ORSINO All will be well.
Is the petition yet prepared? You know
My zeal for all you wish, sweet Beatrice; 200
Doubt not but I will use my utmost skill,
So that the Pope attend to your complaint.
BEATRICE Your zeal for all I wish; Ah me, you are cold!
Your utmost skill——speak but one word——(*Aside*) Alas!
Weak and deserted creature that I am, 205
Here I stand bickering with my only friend!
(*To* ORSINO) This night my father gives a sumptuous feast,
Orsino; he has heard some happy news
From Salamanca, from my brothers there,
And with this outward show of love he mocks 210
His inward hate. 'Tis bold hypocrisy,
For he would gladlier celebrate their deaths,
Which I have heard him pray for on his knees:
Great God! That such a father should be mine!
But there is mighty preparation made, 215
And all our kin, the Cenci, will be there,
And all the chief nobility of Rome.
And he has bidden me and my pale mother
Attire ourselves in festival array.
Poor lady! She expects some happy change 220
In his dark spirit from this act; I none.
At supper I will give you the petition:
Till when—farewell.
ORSINO Farewell. (*Exit* BEATRICE)
               I know the Pope 225
Will ne'er absolve me from my priestly vow
But by absolving me from the revenue
Of many a wealthy see;* and, Beatrice,
I think to win thee at an easier rate.
Nor shall he read her eloquent petition: 230
He might bestow her on some poor relation
Of his sixth cousin, as he did her sister,
And I should be debarred from all access.

228 That is, by taking as bribe the revenue of certain church properties.

Then as to what she suffers from her father,
In all this there is much exaggeration: 235
Old men are testy and will have their way;
A man may stab his enemy, or his vassal,
And live a free life as to wine or women,
And with a peevish temper may return
To a dull home, and rate* his wife and children; 240
Daughters and wives call this foul tyranny.
I shall be well content, if on my conscience
There rest no heavier sin than what they suffer
From the devices of my love.—A net
From which she shall escape not. Yet I fear 245
Her subtle mind, her awe-inspiring gaze,
Whose beams anatomize me, nerve by nerve,
And lay me bare, and make me blush to see
My hidden thoughts.—Ah, no! A friendless girl
Who clings to me, as to her only hope:— 250
I were a fool, not less than if a panther
Were panic-stricken by the antelope's eye,
If she escape me. (*Exit*)

Scene 3

A magnificent hall in the Cenci Palace. A banquet
(*Enter* CENCI, LUCRETIA, BEATRICE, ORSINO, CAMILLO, NOBLES) 255
CENCI Welcome, my friends and kinsmen; welcome ye
Princes and Cardinals, pillars of the church,
Whose presence honours our festivity.
I have too long lived like an anchorite,*
And, in my absence from your merry meetings, 260
An evil word is gone abroad of me:
But I do hope that you, my noble friends,
When you have shared the entertainment here,
And heard the pious cause for which 'tis given,
And we have pledged a health or two together, 265
Will think me flesh and blood as well as you;
Sinful indeed, for Adam made all so,
But tender-hearted, meek and pitiful.
1ST GUEST In truth, my Lord, you seem too light of heart,
Too sprightly and companionable a man, 270
To act the deeds that rumour pins on you.
(*To his companion*) I never saw such blithe and open cheer
In any eye!
2ND GUEST Some most desired event,

240 Berate.
259 Religious hermit.

In which we all demand a common joy, 275
Has brought us hither; let us hear it, Count.
CENCI It is indeed a most desired event.
 If, when a parent, from a parent's heart,
 Lifts from this earth to the great father of all
 A prayer, both when he lays him down to sleep 280
 And when he rises up from dreaming it;
 One supplication, one desire, one hope,
 That he would grant a wish for his two sons,
 Even all that he demands in their regard—
 And suddenly, beyond his dearest hope, 285
 It is accomplished, he should then rejoice,
 And call his friends and kinsmen to a feast,
 And task their love to grace his merriment,
 Then honour me thus far—for I am he.
BEATRICE (*To* LUCRETIA) Great God! How horrible! Some dreadful ill 290
 Must have befallen my brothers.
LUCRETIA Fear not, child,
 He speaks too frankly.
BEATRICE Ah! My blood runs cold.
 I fear that wicked laughter round his eye, 295
 Which wrinkles up the skin even to the hair.
CENCI Here are the letters brought from Salamanca;
 Beatrice, read them to your mother. God,
 I thank thee! In one night didst thou perform,
 By ways inscrutable, the thing I sought. 300
 My disobedient and rebellious sons
 Are dead!—Why dead!—What means this change of cheer?
 You hear me not, I tell you they are dead;
 And they will need no food or raiment more:
 The tapers that did light them the dark way 305
 Are their last cost. The Pope, I think, will not
 Expect I should maintain them in their coffins.
 Rejoice with me, my heart is wondrous glad.
BEATRICE (LUCRETIA *sinks, half fainting;* BEATRICE *supports her*)
 It is not true!—Dear lady, pray look up. 310
 Had it been true, there is a God in Heaven,
 He would not live to boast of such a boon.
 Unnatural man, thou knowest that it is false.
CENCI Ay, as the word of God; whom here I call
 To witness that I speak the sober truth; 315
 And whose most favouring Providence was shown
 Even in the manner of their deaths. For Rocco
 Was kneeling at the mass, with sixteen others,
 When the church fell and crushed him to a mummy;
 The rest escaped unhurt. Cristofano 320

Was stabbed in error by a jealous man,
Whilst she he loved was sleeping with his rival;
All in the self-same hour of the same night;
Which shows that Heaven has special care of me.
I beg those friends who love me, that they mark   325
The day a feast upon their calendars.
It was the twenty-seventh of December:
Ay, read the letters if you doubt my oath. (*The assembly appears confused;
                                          several of the guests rise*)

1ST GUEST   Oh, horrible! I will depart.   330

2ND GUEST   And I.

3RD GUEST   No, stay!
I do believe it is some jest; though faith,
'Tis mocking us somewhat too solemnly.
I think his son has married the Infanta,*   335
Or found a mine of gold in Eldorado;*
'Tis but to season some such news; stay, stay!
I see 'tis only raillery by his smile.

CENCI (*Filling a bowl of wine, and lifting it up*)
Oh, thou bright wine, whose purple splendour leaps   340
And bubbles gaily in this golden bowl
Under the lamp-light, as my spirits do,
To hear the death of my accursed sons!
Could I believe thou wert their mingled blood,
Then would I taste thee like a sacrament,   345
And pledge with thee the mighty Devil in Hell;
Who, if a father's curses, as men say,
Climb with swift wings after their children's souls,
And drag them from the very throne of Heaven,
Now triumphs in my triumph!—But thou art   350
Superfluous; I have drunken deep of joy,
And I will taste no other wine to-night.
Here, Andrea! Bear the bowl around.

A GUEST (*Rising*)   Thou wretch!
Will none among this noble company   355
Check the abandoned villain?

CAMILLO   For God's sake
Let me dismiss the guests! You are insane,
Some ill will come of this.

2ND GUEST   Seize, silence him!   360

1ST GUEST   I will!

3RD GUEST   And I!

CENCI (*Addressing those who rise with a threatening gesture*)
Who moves? Who speaks?

335 Princess of Spain or Portugal.
336 Legendary city of gold in South America.

(*Turning to the company*) 'Tis nothing,   365
Enjoy yourselves.—Beware! For my revenge
Is as the sealed commission of a king,
That kills, and none dare name the murderer.
            (*The banquet is broken up; several of the guests are departing*)
BEATRICE I do entreat you, go not, noble guests;   370
What, although tyranny and impious hate
Stand sheltered by a father's hoary hair?
What, if 'tis he who clothed us in these limbs
Who tortures them, and triumphs? What, if we,
The desolate and the dead, were his own flesh,   375
His children and his wife, whom he is bound
To love and shelter? Shall we therefore find
No refuge in this merciless wide world?
Oh, think what deep wrongs must have blotted out
First love, then reverence in a child's prone mind,   380
Till it thus vanquish shame and fear! O, think!
I have borne much, and kissed the sacred hand
Which crushed us to the earth, and thought its stroke
Was perhaps some paternal chastisement!
Have excused much, doubted; and when no doubt   385
Remained, have sought by patience, love and tears,
To soften him; and when this could not be,
I have knelt down through the long sleepless nights,
And lifted up to God, the father of all,
Passionate prayers: and when these were not heard   390
I have still borne;—until I meet you here,
Princes and kinsmen, at this hideous feast
Given at my brothers' deaths. Two yet remain,
His wife remains and I, whom if ye save not,
Ye may soon share such merriment again   395
As fathers make over their children's graves.
Oh! Prince Colonna, thou art our near kinsman;
Cardinal, thou art the Pope's chamberlain;
Camillo, thou art chief justiciary;
Take us away!   400
CENCI (*He has been conversing with* CAMILLO *during the first part of* BEATRICE'S
      speech; he hears the conclusion, and now advances) I hope my good
      friends here
Will think of their own daughters—or perhaps
Of their own throats—before they lend an ear   405
To this wild girl.
BEATRICE (*Not noticing the words of* CENCI) Dare no one look on me?
None answer? Can one tyrant overbear
The sense of many best and wisest men?
Or is it that I sue not in some form   410
Of scrupulous law, that ye deny my suit?

Oh, God! That I were buried with my brothers!
And that the flowers of this departed spring
Were fading on my grave! And that my father
Were celebrating now one feast for all!   415
CAMILLO   A bitter wish for one so young and gentle;
Can we do nothing?
COLONNA   Nothing that I see.
Count Cenci were a dangerous enemy:
Yet I would second any one.   420
A CARDINAL   And I.
CENCI   Retire to your chamber, insolent girl!
BEATRICE   Retire thou, impious man! Ay, hide thyself
Where never eye can look upon thee more!
Wouldst thou have honour and obedience,   425
Who art a torturer? Father, never dream,
Though thou mayst overbear this company,
But ill must come of ill.—Frown not on me!
Haste, hide thyself, lest with avenging looks
My brothers' ghosts should hunt thee from thy seat!   430
Cover thy face from every living eye,
And start if thou hear a human step:
Seek out some dark and silent corner, there
Bow thy white head before offended God,
And we will kneel around, and fervently   435
Pray that he pity both ourselves and thee.
CENCI   My friends, I do lament this insane girl
Has spoiled the mirth of our festivity.
Good night, farewell; I will not make you longer
Spectators of our dull domestic quarrels.   440
Another time.—(*Exeunt all but* CENCI *and* BEATRICE)
            My brain is swimming round;
Give me a bowl of wine!
(*To* BEATRICE)   Thou painted viper!
Beast that thou art! Fair and yet terrible!   445
I know a charm shall make thee meek and tame,
Now get thee from my sight! (*Exit* BEATRICE)
            Here, Andrea,
Fill up this goblet with Greek wine. I said
I would not drink this evening; but I must;   450
For, strange to say, I feel my spirits fail
With thinking what I have decreed to do. (*Drinking the wine*)
Be thou the resolution of quick youth
Within my veins, and manhood's purpose stern,
And age's firm, cold, subtle villainy;   455
As if thou wert indeed my children's blood
Which I did thirst to drink. The charm works well;
It must be done; it shall be done, I swear! (*Exit*)

Act Two

Scene 1

An apartment in the Cenci Palace
(*Enter* LUCRETIA *and* BERNARDO)

LUCRETIA Weep not, my gentle boy; he struck but me,
Who have borne deeper wrongs. In truth, if he
Had killed me, he had done a kinder deed.   5
O, God Almighty, do thou look upon us,
We have no other friend but only thee!
Yet weep not; though I love you as my own,
I am not your true mother.

BERNARDO Oh more, more,   10
Than ever mother was to any child,
That have you been to me! Had he not been
My father, do you think that I should weep?

LUCRETIA Alas! Poor boy, what else couldst thou have done?
(*Enter* BEATRICE)   15

BEATRICE (*In a hurried voice*) Did he pass this way? Have you seen him,
                                              brother?
Ah! No, that is his step upon the stairs;
'Tis nearer now; his hand is on the door;
Mother, if I to thee have ever been
A duteous child, now save me! Thou, great God,   20
Whose image upon earth a father is,
Dost thou indeed abandon me? He comes;
The door is opening now; I see his face;
He frowns on others, but he smiles on me,   25
Even as he did after the feast last night.
(*Enter a Servant*)
Almighty God, how merciful thou art!
'Tis but Orsino's servant.—Well, what news?

SERVANT My master bids me say, the Holy Father   30
Has sent back your petition thus unopened. (*Giving a paper*)
And he demands at what hour 'twere secure
To visit you again?

LUCRETIA At the Ave Mary. (*Exit Servant*)
So, daughter, our last hope has failed; Ah me,   35
How pale you look; you tremble, and you stand
Wrapped in some fixed and fearful meditation,
As if one thought were over strong for you:
Your eyes have a chill glare; O, dearest child!
Are you gone mad? If not, pray speak to me.   40

BEATRICE You see I am not mad; I speak to you.

LUCRETIA You talked of something that your father did
After that dreadful feast? Could it be worse

Than when he smiled, and cried, My sons are dead!
And every one looked in his neighbour's face   45
To see if others were as white as he?
At the first word he spoke I felt the blood
Rush to my heart, and fell into a trance;
And when it past I sat all weak and wild;
Whilst you alone stood up, and with strong words   50
Checked his unnatural pride; and I could see
The devil was rebuked that lives in him.
Until this hour thus you have ever stood
Between us and your father's moody wrath
Like a protecting presence: your firm mind   55
Has been our only refuge and defence:
What can have thus subdued it? What can now
Have given you that cold melancholy look,
Succeeding to your unaccustomed fear?

BEATRICE   What is it that you say? I was just thinking   60
'Twere better not to struggle any more.
Men, like my father, have been dark and bloody,
Yet never—O! Before worse comes of it
'Twere wise to die: it ends in that at last.

LUCRETIA   Oh, talk not so, dear child! Tell me at once   65
What did your father do or say to you?
He stayed not after that accursed feast
One moment in your chamber.—Speak to me.

BERNARDO   Oh, sister, sister, prithee, speak to us!

BEATRICE (*Speaking very slowly with a forced calmness*)   70
It was one word, mother, one little word;
One look, one smile.
    (*Wildly*)   Oh! He has trampled me
Under his feet, and made the blood stream down
My pallid cheeks. And he has given us all   75
Ditch water, and the fever-stricken flesh
Of buffaloes, and bade us eat or starve,
And we have eaten. He has made me look
On my beloved Bernardo, when the rust
Of heavy chains has gangrened his sweet limbs,   80
And I have never yet despaired—but now!
What would I say?
    (*Recovering herself*)   Ah! No, 'tis nothing new.
The sufferings we all share have made me wild:
He only struck and cursed me as he passed;   85
He said, he looked, he did;—nothing at all
Beyond his wont,* yet it disordered me.
Alas! I am forgetful of my duty,

———
87 Custom.

I should preserve my senses for your sake.

LUCRETIA   Nay, Beatrice; have courage, my sweet girl.   90
If any one despairs it should be I,
Who loved him once, and now must live with him
Till God in pity call for him or me.
For you may, like your sister, find some husband,
And smile, years hence, with children round your knees;   95
Whilst I, then dead, and all this hideous coil,*
Shall be remembered only as a dream.

BEATRICE   Talk not to me, dear lady, of a husband.
Did you not nurse me when my mother died?
Did you not shield me and that dearest boy?   100
And had we any other friend but you
In infancy, with gentle words and looks,
To win our father not to murder us?
And shall I now desert you? May the ghost
Of my dead mother plead against my soul   105
If I abandon her who filled the place
She left, with more, even, than a mother's love!

BERNARDO   And I am of my sister's mind. Indeed
I would not leave you in this wretchedness,
Even though the Pope should make me free to live   110
In some blithe place, like others of my age,
With sports, and delicate food, and the fresh air.
Oh, never think that I will leave you, mother!

LUCRETIA   My dear, dear children!

                    (Enter CENCI, suddenly)   115

CENCI   What, Beatrice here!
Come hither! (She shrinks back, and covers her face)
              Nay, hide not your face, 'tis fair;
Look up! Why, yesternight you dared to look
With disobedient insolence upon me,
Bending a stern and an inquiring brow   120
On what I meant; whilst I then sought to hide
That which I came to tell you—but in vain.

BEATRICE   (Wildly, staggering towards the door)
Oh, that the earth would gape! Hide me, oh God!   125

CENCI   Then it was I whose inarticulate words
Fell from my lips, and who with tottering steps
Fled from your presence, as you now from mine.
Stay, I command you: from this day and hour
Never again, I think, with fearless eye,   130
And brow superior, and unaltered cheek,
And that lip made for tenderness or scorn,

96 Disturbance.

Shalt thou strike dumb the meanest of mankind;
Me least of all. Now get thee to thy chamber!
Thou too, loathed image of thy cursed mother,   135
                    (*To* BERNARDO)
Thy milky, meek face makes me sick with hate! (*Exeunt* BEATRICE *and*
                    BERNARDO)
(*Aside*)   So much has past between us as must make
Me bold, her fearful. 'Tis an awful thing   140
To touch such mischief as I now conceive:
So men sit shivering on the dewy bank,
And try the chill stream with their feet; once in—
How the delighted spirit pants for joy!
LUCRETIA (*Advancing timidly towards him*)   145
Oh, husband! Pray forgive poor Beatrice,
She meant not any ill.
CENCI   Nor you perhaps?
Nor that young imp, whom you have taught by rote
Parricide with his alphabet? Nor Giacomo?   150
Nor those two most unnatural sons, who stirred
Enmity up against me with the Pope?
Whom in one night merciful God cut off:
Innocent lambs! They thought not any ill.
You were not here conspiring? You said nothing   155
Of how I might be dungeoned as a madman;
Or be condemned to death for some offence,
And you would be the witnesses?—This failing,
How just it were to hire assassins, or
Put sudden* poison in my evening drink?   160
Or smother me when overcome by wine?
Seeing we had no other judge but God,
And he had sentenced me, and there were none
But you to be the executioners
Of his decree enregistered in heaven?   165
Oh, no! You said not this?
LUCRETIA   So help me God,
I never thought the things you charge me with!
CENCI   If you dare speak that wicked lie again
I'll kill you. What! It was not by your counsel   170
That Beatrice disturbed the feast last night?
You did not hope to stir some enemies
Against me, and escape, and laugh to scorn
What every nerve of you now trembles at?
You judged that men were bolder than they are: 175
Few dare to stand between their grave and me.

160 Swift.

LUCRETIA Look not so dreadfully! By my salvation,
  I knew not aught that Beatrice designed;
  Nor do I think she designed any thing
  Until she heard you talk of her dead brothers.   180
CENCI Blaspheming liar! You are damned for this!
  But I will take you where you may persuade
  The stones you tread on to deliver you:
  For men shall there be none but those who dare
  All things; not question that which I command.   185
  On Wednesday next I shall set out: you know
  That savage rock, the Castle of Petrella:
  'Tis safely walled, and moated round about:
  Its dungeons under-ground, and its thick towers,
  Never told tales; though they have heard and seen   190
  What might make dumb things speak. Why do you linger?
  Make speediest preparation for the journey! (*Exit* LUCRETIA)
  The all-beholding sun yet shines; I hear
  A busy stir of men about the streets;
  I see the bright sky through the window panes: 195
  It is a garish, broad and peering day;
  Loud, light, suspicious, full of eyes and ears;
  And every little corner, nook, and hole,
  Is penetrated with the insolent light.
  Come, darkness! Yet, what is the day to me?   200
  And wherefore should I wish for night, who do
  A deed which shall confound both night and day?
  'Tis she shall grope through a bewildering mist
  Of horror: if there be a sun in heaven
  She shall not dare to look upon its beams,   205
  Nor feel its warmth. Let her then wish for night;
  The act I think shall soon extinguish all
  For me: I bear a darker deadlier gloom
  Than the earth's shade, or interlunar* air,
  Or constellations quenched in murkiest cloud,   210
  In which I walk secure and unbeheld
  Towards my purpose.—Would that it were done! (*Exit*)

Scene 2

A *chamber in the Vatican*
(*Enter* CAMILLO *and* GIACOMO, *in conversation*)
CAMILLO There is an obsolete and doubtful law   215
  By which you might obtain a bare provision
  Of food and clothing—
GIACOMO Nothing more? Alas!

---

[209] Pertaining to the period between the old and new moon.

Bare must be the provision which strict law
Awards, and aged, sullen avarice pays.   220
Why did my father not apprentice me
To some mechanic trade? I should have then
Been trained in no high-born necessities
Which I could meet not by my daily toil.
The eldest son of a rich nobleman   225
Is heir to all his incapacities;
He has wide wants, and narrow powers. If you,
Cardinal Camillo, were reduced at once
From thrice-driven* beds of down, and delicate food,
An hundred servants, and six palaces,   230
To that which nature doth indeed require?—
CAMILLO Nay, there is reason in your plea; 'twere hard.
GIACOMO 'Tis hard for a firm man to bear: but I
Have a dear wife, a lady of high birth,
Whose dowry in ill hour I lent my father,   235
Without a bond or witness to the deed:
And children, who inherit her fine senses,
The fairest creatures in this breathing world;
And she and they reproach me not. Cardinal,
Do you think the Pope would interpose,   240
And stretch authority beyond the law?
CAMILLO Though your peculiar case is hard, I know
The Pope will not divert the course of law.
After that impious feast the other night
I spoke with him, and urged him then to check   245
Your father's cruel hand; he frowned and said,
"Children are disobedient, and they sting
Their father's hearts to madness and despair,
Requiting years of care with contumely.
I pity the Count Cenci from my heart;   250
His outraged love perhaps awakened hate,
And thus he is exasperated to ill.
In the great war between the old and young,
I, who have white hairs and a tottering body,
Will keep at least blameless neutrality."   255
                        (*Enter* ORSINO)
You, my good Lord Orsino, heard those words.
ORSINO What words?
GIACOMO Alas, repeat them not again!
There then is no redress for me; at least
None but that which I may achieve myself,   260
Since I am driven to the brink. But, say,

---

229 Down was thrown or cast to separate the heavier from the lighter. A "thrice-driven bed" would be very
luxurious.

My innocent sister and my only brother
Are dying underneath my father's eye.
The memorable tortures of this land,   265
Galeaz Visconti, Borgia, Ezzelin,*
Never inflicted on their meanest slave
What these endure; shall they have no protection?
CAMILLO   Why, if they would petition to the Pope
I see not how he could refuse it—yet   270
He holds it of most dangerous example
In aught to weaken the paternal power,
Being, as 'twere, the shadow of his own.
I pray you now excuse me. I have business
That will not bear delay. (*Exit* CAMILLO)   275
GIACOMO   But you, Orsino,
Have the petition: wherefore not present it?
ORSINO   I have presented it, and backed it with
My earnest prayers, and urgent interest;
It was returned unanswered. I doubt not   280
But that the strange and execrable deeds
Alleged in it (in truth they might well baffle
Any belief) have turned the Pope's displeasure
Upon the accusers from the criminal:
So I should guess from what Camillo said.   285
GIACOMO   My friend, that palace-walking devil, Gold,
Has whispered silence to his Holiness:
And we are left, as scorpions ringed with fire,*
What should we do but strike ourselves to death?
For he who is our murderous persecutor   290
Is shielded by a father's holy name,
Or I would— (*Stops abruptly*)
ORSINO   What? Fear not to speak your thought.
Words are but holy as the deeds they cover:
A priest who has forsworn the God he serves;   295
A judge who makes truth weep at his decree;
A friend who should weave counsel, as I now,
But as the mantle of some selfish guile;
A father who is all a tyrant seems,
Were the profaner for his sacred name.   300
GIACOMO   Ask me not what I think; the unwilling brain
Feigns often what it would not; and we trust
Imagination with such fantasies
As the tongue dares not fashion into words;
Which have no words, their horror makes them dim   305

266 Gian Galeazzo Visconti (1378-1402), Cesare Borgia (1476-1507), Ezzelino da Romano (1194-1259),
all notorious for their crimes.
288 It was thought that scorpions stung themselves to death if exposed to fire.

To the mind's eye. My heart denies itself
To think what you demand.
ORSINO   But a friend's bosom
Is as the inmost cave of our own mind,
Where we sit shut from the wide gaze of day,   310
And from the all-communicating air.
You look what I suspected:
GIACOMO   Spare me now!
I am as one lost in a midnight wood,
Who dares not ask some harmless passenger   315
The path across the wilderness, lest he,
As my thoughts are, should be—a murderer.
I know you are my friend, and all I dare
Speak to my soul, that will I trust with thee.
But now my heart is heavy, and would take   320
Lone counsel from a night of sleepless care.
Pardon me, that I say farewell—farewell!
I would that to my own suspected self
I could address a word so full of peace.
ORSINO   Farewell!—Be your thoughts better or more bold. (*Exit* GIACOMO) 325
I had disposed the Cardinal Camillo
To feed his hope with cold encouragement:
It fortunately serves my close designs
That 'tis a trick of this same family
To analyse their own and other minds.   330
Such self-anatomy shall teach the will
Dangerous secrets: for it tempts our powers,
Knowing what must be thought, and may be done,
Into the depth of darkest purposes:
So Cenci fell into the pit; even I,   335
Since Beatrice unveiled me to myself,
And made me shrink from what I cannot shun,
Show a poor figure to my own esteem,
To which I grow half reconciled. I'll do
As little mischief as I can; that thought   340
Shall fee* the accuser conscience.
(*After a pause*)   Now what harm
If Cenci should be murdered?—Yet, if murdered,
Wherefore by me? And what if I could take
The profit, yet omit the sin and peril   345
In such an action? Of all earthly things
I fear a man whose blows outspeed his words;
And such is Cenci: and while Cenci lives
His daughter's dowry were a secret grave,

341 Bribe.

If a priest wins her.—Oh, fair Beatrice!
Would that I loved thee not, or loving thee
Could but despise danger and gold, and all
That frowns between my wish and its effect,
Or smiles beyond it! There is no escape:
Her bright form kneels beside me at the altar,
And follows me to the resort of men,
And fills my slumber with tumultuous dreams,
So, when I wake, my blood seems liquid fire;
And if I strike my damp and dizzy head,
My hot palm scorches it: her very name,
But spoken by a stranger, makes my heart
Sicken and pant; and thus unprofitably
I clasp the phantom of unfelt delights,
Till weak imagination half possesses
The self-created shadow. Yet much longer
Will I not nurse this life of feverous hours:
From the unravelled hopes of Giacomo
I must work out my own dear purposes.
I see, as from a tower, the end of all:
Her father dead; her brother bound to me
By a dark secret, surer than the grave;
Her mother scared and unexpostulating
From the dread manner of her wish achieved:
And she!—Once more take courage, my faint heart;
What dares a friendless maiden matched with thee?
I have such foresight as assures success:
Some unbeheld divinity doth ever,
When dread events are near, stir up men's minds
To black suggestions; and he prospers best,
Not who becomes the instrument of ill,
But who can flatter the dark spirit, that makes
Its empire and its prey of other hearts,
Till it become his slave—as I will do. (*Exit*)

Act Three

Scene 1

An apartment in the Cenci Palace
(LUCRETIA, *to her enter* BEATRICE)
BEATRICE (*She enters staggering, and speaks wildly*)
Reach me that handkerchief!—My brain is hurt;
My eyes are full of blood; just wipe them for me—
I see but indistinctly:—
LUCRETIA   My sweet child,

You have no wound; 'tis only a cold dew
That starts from your dear brow—Alas! Alas!
What has befallen?   10
BEATRICE   How comes this hair undone?
Its wandering strings must be what blind me so,
And yet I tied it fast.—O, horrible!
The pavement sinks under my feet! The walls
Spin round! I see a woman weeping there,   15
And standing calm and motionless, whilst I
Slide giddily as the world reels.—My God!
The beautiful blue heaven is flecked with blood!
The sunshine on the floor is black! The air
Is changed to vapours such as the dead breathe   20
In charnel pits! Pah! I am choked! There creeps
A clinging, black, contaminating mist
About me—'tis substantial, heavy, thick,
I cannot pluck it from me, for it glues
My fingers and my limbs to one another,   25
And eats into my sinews, and dissolves
My flesh to a pollution, poisoning
The subtle, pure, and inmost spirit of life!
My God! I never knew what the mad felt
Before; for I am mad beyond all doubt!   30
(*More wildly*)   No, I am dead! These putrefying limbs
Shut round and sepulchre the panting soul,
Which would burst forth into the wandering air! (*A pause*)
What hideous thought was that I had even now?
'Tis gone; and yet its burthen remains here   35
O'er these dull eyes—upon this weary heart!
O, world! O, life! O, day! O, misery!
LUCRETIA   What ails thee, my poor child? She answers not:
Her spirit apprehends the sense of pain,
But not its cause; suffering has dried away   40
The source from which it sprung.
BEATRICE (*Franticly*)   Like parricide—
Misery has killed its father: yet its father
Never like mine.—O, God! What thing am I?
LUCRETIA   My dearest child, what has your father done?   45
BEATRICE (*Doubtfully*)   Who art thou, questioner? I have no father.
(*Aside*)   She is the mad-house nurse who tends on me,
It is a piteous office.
(*To* LUCRETIA, *in a slow, subdued voice*)   Do you know
I thought I was that wretched Beatrice   50
Men speak of, whom her father sometimes hales*

---

51 Pulls.

From hall to hall by the entangled hair;
At others, pens up naked in damp cells
Where scaly reptiles crawl, and starves her there,
Till she will eat strange flesh. This woeful story　　　　55
So did I overact in my sick dreams,
That I imagined—no, it cannot be!
Horrible things have been in this wild world,
Prodigious mixtures, and confusions strange
Of good and ill; and worse have been conceived　　　　60
Than ever there was found a heart to do.
But never fancy imaged such a deed
As— (*Pauses, suddenly recollecting herself*)
Who art thou? Swear to me, ere I die
With fearful expectation, that indeed　　　　65
Thou art not what thou seemest—mother!

LUCRETIA　Oh!
My sweet child, know you—

BEATRICE　Yet speak it not:
For then if this be truth, that other too　　　　70
Must be a truth, a firm enduring truth,
Linked with each lasting circumstance of life,
Never to change, never to pass away.
Why so it is. This is the Cenci Palace;
Thou art Lucretia; I am Beatrice.　　　　75
I have talked some wild words, but will no more.
Mother, come near me: from this point of time,
I am— (*Her voice dies away faintly*)

LUCRETIA　Alas! What has befallen thee, child?
What has thy father done?　　　　80

BEATRICE　What have I done?
Am I not innocent? Is it my crime
That one with white hair, and imperious brow,
Who tortured me from my forgotten years,
As parents only dare, should call himself　　　　85
My father, yet should be!—Oh, what am I?
What name, what place, what memory shall be mine?
What retrospects, outliving even despair?

LUCRETIA　He is a violent tyrant, surely, child:
We know that death alone can make us free;　　　　90
His death or ours. But what can he have done
Of deadlier outrage or worse injury?
Thou art unlike thyself; thine eyes shoot forth
A wandering and strange spirit. Speak to me,
Unlock those pallid hands whose fingers twine　　　　95
With one another.

BEATRICE　'Tis the restless life

Tortured within them. If I try to speak
I shall go mad. Ay, something must be done;
What, yet I know not—something which shall make   100
The thing that I have suffered but a shadow
In the dread lightning which avenges it;
Brief, rapid, irreversible, destroying
The consequence of what it cannot cure.
Some such thing is to be endured or done: 105
When I know what, I shall be still and calm,
And never any thing will move me more.
But now!—Oh blood, which art my father's blood,
Circling through these contaminated veins,
If thou, poured forth on the polluted earth,   110
Could wash away the crime, and punishment
By which I suffer—no, that cannot be!
Many might doubt there were a God above
Who sees and permits evil, and so die:
That faith no agony shall obscure in me.   115

LUCRETIA   It must indeed have been some bitter wrong;
Yet what, I dare not guess. Oh, my lost child,
Hide not in proud impenetrable grief
Thy sufferings from my fear.

BEATRICE   I hide them not.   120
What are the words which you would have me speak?
I, who can feign no image in my mind
Of that which has transformed me: I, whose thought
Is like a ghost shrouded and folded up.
In its own formless horror: of all words,   125
That minister to mortal intercourse,
Which wouldst thou hear? For there is none to tell
My misery; if another ever knew
Aught like to it, she died as I will die,
And left it, as I must, without a name.   130
Death! Death! Our law and our religion call thee
A punishment and a reward.—Oh, which
Have I deserved?

LUCRETIA   The peace of innocence;
Till in your season you be called to heaven.   135
Whate'er you may have suffered, you have done
No evil. Death must be the punishment
Of crime, or the reward of trampling down
The thorns which God has strewed upon the path
Which leads to immortality.   140

BEATRICE   Ay, death—
The punishment of crime. I pray thee, God,
Let me not be bewildered while I judge.

If I must live day after day, and keep
These limbs, the unworthy temple of thy spirit,   145
As a foul den from which what thou abhorrest
May mock thee, unavenged—it shall not be!
Self-murder? No, that might be no escape,
For thy decree yawns like a Hell between
Our will and it. O! In this mortal world   150
There is no vindication and no law
Which can adjudge and execute the doom
Of that through which I suffer.

(*Enter* ORSINO)

(*She approaches him solemnly*) Welcome, friend!   155
I have to tell you that, since last we met,
I have endured a wrong so great and strange,
That neither life nor death can give me rest.
Ask me not what it is, for there are deeds
Which have no form, sufferings which have no tongue.   160

ORSINO And what is he who has thus injured you?

BEATRICE The man they call my father: a dread name.

ORSINO It cannot be—

BEATRICE What it can be, or not,
Forbear to think. It is, and it has been;   165
Advise me how it shall not be again.
I thought to die, but a religious awe
Restrains me, and the dread lest death itself
Might be no refuge from the consciousness
Of what is yet unexpiated. Oh, speak!   170

ORSINO Accuse him of the deed, and let the law
Avenge thee.

BEATRICE Oh, ice-hearted counsellor!
If I could find a word that might make known
The crime of my destroyer; and that done,   175
My tongue should, like a knife, tear out the secret
Which cankers my heart's core; ay, lay all bare,
So that my unpolluted fame should be
With vilest gossips a stale mouthed story;
A mock, a bye-word, an astonishment:—   180
If this were done, which never shall be done,
Think of the offender's gold, his dreaded hate,
And the strange horror of the accuser's tale,
Baffling belief, and overpowering speech;
Scarce whispered, unimaginable, wrapped   185
In hideous hints.—Oh, most assured redress!

ORSINO You will endure it then?

BEATRICE Endure! Orsino,
It seems your counsel is small profit.

(*Turns from him, and speaks half to herself*) Ay,   190

All must be suddenly resolved and done.
What is this undistinguishable mist
O thoughts, which rise, like shadow after shadow,
Darkening each other?

ORSINO   Should the offender live?   195
Triumph in his misdeed? And make, by use,
His crime, whate'er it is, dreadful no doubt,
Thine element; until thou mayest become
Utterly lost; subdued even to the hue
Of that which thou permittest?   200

BEATRICE (*To herself*) Mighty death!
Thou double-visaged shadow! Only judge!
Rightfullest arbiter! (*She retires absorbed in thought*)

LUCRETIA   If the lightning
Of God has e'er descended to avenge—   205

ORSINO   Blaspheme not! His high Providence commits
Its glory on this earth, and their own wrongs
Into the hands of men; if they neglect
To punish crime—

LUCRETIA   But if one, like this wretch,   210
Should mock, with gold, opinion, law, and power?
If there be no appeal to that which makes
The guiltiest tremble? If, because our wrongs,
For that they are unnatural, strange, and monstrous,
Exceed all measure of belief? Oh, God!   215
If, for the very reasons which should make
Redress most swift and sure, our injurer triumphs?
And we, the victims, bear worse punishment
Than that appointed for their torturer?

ORSINO   Think not   220
But that there is redress where there is wrong,
So we be bold enough to seize it.

LUCRETIA   How?
If there were any way to make all sure,
I know not—but I think it might be good   225
To—

ORSINO   Why, his late outrage to Beatrice;
For it is such, as I but faintly guess,
As makes remorse dishonour, and leaves her
Only one duty, how she may avenge: 230
You, but one refuge from ills ill endured;
Me, but one counsel—

LUCRETIA   For we cannot hope
That aid, or retribution, or resource,
Will arise thence, where every other one   235
Might find them with less need.

(BEATRICE *advances*)

ORSINO Then—

BEATRICE Peace, Orsino!
 And, honoured Lady, while I speak, I pray,   240
 That you put off, as garments overworn,
 Forbearance and respect, remorse and fear,
 And all the fit restraints of daily life,
 Which have been borne from childhood, but which now
 Would be a mockery to my holier plea.   245
 As I have said, I have endured a wrong,
 Which, though it be expressionless, is such
 As asks atonement, both for what is past,
 And lest I be reserved, day after day,
 To load with crimes an overburthened soul,   250
 And be—what ye can dream not. I have prayed
 To God, and I have talked with my own heart,
 And have unravelled my entangled will,
 And have at length determined what is right.
 Art thou my friend, Orsino? False or true?   255
 Pledge thy salvation ere I speak.

ORSINO I swear
 To dedicate my cunning, and my strength,
 My silence, and whatever else is mine,
 To thy commands.   260

LUCRETIA You think we should devise
 His death?

BEATRICE And execute what is devised,
 And suddenly. We must be brief and bold.

ORSINO And yet most cautious.   265

LUCRETIA For the jealous laws
 Would punish us with death and infamy
 For that which it became themselves to do.

BEATRICE Be cautious as ye may, but prompt. Orsino,
 What are the means?   270

ORSINO I know two dull, fierce outlaws,
 Who think man's spirit as a worm's, and they
 Would trample out, for any slight caprice,
 The meanest or the noblest life. This mood
 Is marketable here in Rome. They sell   275
 What we now want.

LUCRETIA To-morrow, before dawn,
 Cenci will take us to that lonely rock,
 Petrella, in the Apulian Apennines.
 If he arrive there—   280

BEATRICE He must not arrive.

ORSINO Will it be dark before you reach the tower?

LUCRETIA The sun will scarce be set.

BEATRICE   But I remember
    Two miles on this side of the fort, the road   285
    Crosses a deep ravine; 'tis rough and narrow,
    And winds with short turns down the precipice;
    And in its depth there is a mighty rock,
    Which has, from unimaginable years,
    Sustained itself with terror and with toil   290
    Over a gulf,* and with the agony
    With which it clings seems slowly coming down;
    Even as a wretched soul hour after hour,
    Clings to the mass of life; yet clinging, leans;
    And leaning, makes more dark the dread abyss   295
    In which it fears to fall: beneath this crag,
    Huge as despair, as if in weariness,
    The melancholy mountain yawns; below,
    You hear but see not an impetuous torrent
    Raging among the caverns, and a bridge   300
    Crosses the chasm; and high above there grow,
    With intersecting trunks, from crag to crag,
    Cedars, and yews, and pines; whose tangled hair
    Is matted in one solid roof of shade
    By the dark ivy's twine. At noon-day here   305
    'Tis twilight, and at sunset blackest night.
ORSINO   Before you reach that bridge make some excuse
    For spurring on your mules, or loitering
    Until—
BEATRICE   What sound is that?   310
LUCRETIA   Hark! No, it cannot be a servant's step;
    It must be Cenci, unexpectedly
    Returned—Make some excuse for being here.
BEATRICE (*To* ORSINO, *as she goes out*)
    That step we hear approach must never pass   315
    The bridge of which we spoke. (*Exeunt* LUCRETIA *and* BEATRICE)
ORSINO   What shall I do?
    Cenci must find me here, and I must bear
    The imperious inquisition of his looks
    As to what brought me hither: let me mask   320
    Mine own in some inane and vacant smile.
            (*Enter* GIACOMO, *in a hurried manner*)
    How! Have you ventured hither? Know you then
    That Cenci is from home?
GIACOMO   I sought him here;   325
    And now must wait till he returns.
ORSINO   Great God!
    Weigh you the danger of this rashness?

291 A wide, deep chasm.

GIACOMO Ay!

    Does my destroyer know his danger? We 330
    Are now no more, as once, parent and child,
    But man to man; the oppressor to the oppressed;
    The slanderer to the slandered; foe to foe.
    He has cast Nature off, which was his shield,
    And Nature casts him off, who is her shame; 335
    And I spurn both. Is it a father's throat
    Which I will shake, and say, I ask not gold;
    I ask not happy years; nor memories
    Of tranquil childhood; nor home-sheltered love;
    Though all these hast thou torn from me, and more; 340
    But only my fair fame; only one hoard
    Of peace, which I thought hidden from thy hate,
    Under the penury heaped on me by thee;
    Or I will—God can understand and pardon,
    Why should I speak with man? 345
ORSINO Be calm, dear friend.
GIACOMO Well, I will calmly tell you what he did.
    This old Francesco Cenci, as you know,
    Borrowed the dowry of my wife from me,
    And then denied the loan; and left me so 350
    In poverty, the which I sought to mend
    By holding a poor office in the state.
    It had been promised to me, and already
    I bought new clothing for my ragged babes,
    And my wife smiled; and my heart knew repose; 355
    When Cenci's intercession, as I found,
    Conferred this office on a wretch, whom thus
    He paid for vilest service. I returned
    With this ill news, and we sate sad together
    Solacing our despondency with tears 360
    Of such affection and unbroken faith
    As temper life's worst bitterness; when he,
    As he is wont, came to upbraid and curse,
    Mocking our poverty, and telling us
    Such was God's scourge for disobedient sons. 365
    And then, that I might strike him dumb with shame,
    I spoke of my wife's dowry; but he coined
    A brief yet specious tale, how I had wasted
    The sum in secret riot; and he saw
    My wife was touched, and he went smiling forth. 370
    And when I knew the impression he had made,
    And felt my wife insult with silent scorn
    My ardent truth, and look averse and cold,
    I went forth too: but soon returned again;

Yet not so soon but that my wife had taught 375
My children her harsh thoughts, and they all cried,
"Give us clothes, father! Give us better food!
What you in one night squander were enough
For months!" I looked, and saw that home was hell;
And to that hell will I return no more 380
Until mine enemy has rendered up
Atonement, or, as he gave life to me
I will, reversing nature's law—
ORSINO Trust me,
The compensation which thou seekest here 385
Will be denied.
GIACOMO Then—are you not my friend?
Did you not hint at the alternative,
Upon the brink of which you see I stand,
The other day when we conversed together? 390
My wrongs were then less. That word "parricide,"
Although I am resolved, haunts me like fear.
ORSINO It must be fear itself, for the bare word
Is hollow mockery. Mark, how wisest God
Draws to one point the threads of a just doom, 395
So sanctifying it: what you devise
Is, as it were, accomplished.
GIACOMO Is he dead?
ORSINO His grave is ready. Know that since we met
Cenci has done an outrage to his daughter. 400
GIACOMO What outrage?
ORSINO That she speaks not, but you may
Conceive such half conjectures as I do,
From her fixed paleness, and the lofty grief
Of her stern brow, bent on the idle air, 405
And her severe unmodulated voice,
Drowning both tenderness and dread; and last
From this; that whilst her step-mother and I,
Bewildered in our horror, talked together
With obscure hints; both self-misunderstood, 410
And darkly guessing, stumbling, in our talk,
Over the truth, and yet to its revenge,
She interrupted us, and with a look
Which told before she spoke it, he must die:—
GIACOMO It is enough. My doubts are well appeased; 415
There is a higher reason for the act
Than mine; there is a holier judge than me,
A more unblamed avenger. Beatrice,
Who in the gentleness of thy sweet youth
Hast never trodden on a worm, or bruised 420

A living flower, but thou hast pitied it
With needless tears! Fair sister, thou in whom
Men wondered how such loveliness and wisdom
Did not destroy each other! Is there made
Ravage of thee? O, heart, I ask no more   425
Justification! Shall I wait, Orsino,
Till he return, and stab him at the door?
ORSINO Not so; some accident might interpose
To rescue him from what is now most sure;
And you are unprovided where to fly,   430
How to excuse or to conceal. Nay, listen:
All is contrived; success is so assured
That—

                    (*Enter* BEATRICE)
BEATRICE 'Tis my brother's voice! You know me not?   435
GIACOMO My sister, my lost sister!
BEATRICE Lost indeed!
I see Orsino has talked with you, and
That you conjecture things too horrible
To speak, yet far less than the truth. Now, stay not,   440
He might return: yet kiss me; I shall know
That then thou hast consented to his death.
Farewell, farewell! Let piety to God,
Brotherly love, justice, and clemency,
And all things that make tender hardest hearts,   445
Make thine hard, brother. Answer not: farewell. (*Exeunt severally*)

Scene 2

       A mean apartment in Giacomo's House. GIACOMO *alone*
GIACOMO 'Tis midnight, and Orsino comes not yet. (*Thunder, and the sound
                    of a storm*)
What! Can the everlasting elements   450
Feel with a worm like man? If so, the shaft
Of mercy-winged lightning would not fall
On stones and trees. My wife and children sleep:
They are now living in unmeaning dreams:
But I must wake, still doubting if that deed   455
Be just, which was most necessary. O,
Thou unreplenished lamp! Whose narrow fire
Is shaken by the wind, and on whose edge
Devouring darkness hovers! Thou small flame,
Which, as a dying pulse rises and falls,   460
Still flickerest up and down, how very soon,
Did I not feed thee, wouldst thou fail, and be
As thou hadst never been! So wastes and sinks

Even now, perhaps, the life that kindled mine:
But that no power can fill with vital oil, 465
That broken lamp of flesh. Ha! 'Tis the blood
Which fed these veins, that ebbs till all is cold:
It is the form that moulded mine, that sinks
Into the white and yellow spasms of death:
It is the soul by which mine was arrayed 470
In God's immortal likeness, which now stands
Naked before Heaven's judgment seat! (*A bell strikes*)
                                        One! Two!
The hours crawl on; and, when my hairs are white,
My son will then perhaps be waiting thus, 475
Tortured between just hate and vain remorse;
Chiding the tardy messenger of news
Like those which I expect. I almost wish
He be not dead, although my wrongs are great;
Yet—'tis Orsino's step— 480
                (*Enter* ORSINO)
            Speak!
ORSINO   I am come
    To say he has escaped.
GIACOMO   Escaped! 485
ORSINO   And safe
    Within Petrella. He passed by the spot
    Appointed for the deed an hour too soon.
GIACOMO   Are we the fools of such contingencies?
    And do we waste in blind misgivings thus 490
    The hours when we should act? Then wind and thunder,
    Which seemed to howl his knell, is the loud laughter
    With which Heaven mocks our weakness! I henceforth
    Will ne'er repent of aught, designed or done,
    But my repentance. 495
ORSINO   See, the lamp is out.
GIACOMO   If no remorse is ours when the dim air
    Has drank this innocent flame, why should we quail
    When Cenci's life, that light by which ill spirits
    See the worse deeds they prompt, shall sink for ever? 500
    No, I am hardened.
ORSINO   Why, what need of this?
    Who feared the pale intrusion of remorse
    In a just deed? Although our first plan failed,
    Doubt not but he will soon be laid to rest. 505
    But light the lamp; let us not talk i' the dark.
GIACOMO (*Lighting the lamp*)   And yet, once quenched, I cannot thus relume*

---

507 Re-light.

My father's life: do you not think his ghost
Might plead that argument with God?

ORSINO   Once gone, 510
You cannot now recall your sister's peace;
Your own extinguished years of youth and hope;
Nor your wife's bitter words; nor all the taunts
Which, from the prosperous, weak misfortune takes;
Nor your dead mother; nor— 515

GIACOMO   O, speak no more!
I am resolved, although this very hand
Must quench the life that animated it.

ORSINO   There is no need of that. Listen: you know,
Olimpio, the castellan* of Petrella 520
In old Colonna's time; him whom your father
Degraded from his post? And Marzio,
That desperate wretch, whom he deprived last year
Of a reward of blood, well earned and due?

GIACOMO   I knew Olimpio; and they say he hated 525
Old Cenci so, that in his silent rage
His lips grew white only to see him pass.
Of Marzio I know nothing.

ORSINO   Marzio's hate
Matches Olimpio's. I have sent these men, 530
But in your name, and as at your request,
To talk with Beatrice and Lucretia.

GIACOMO   Only to talk?

ORSINO   The moments which even now
Pass onward to tomorrow's midnight hour 535
May memorise* their flight with death: ere then
They must have talked, and may perhaps have done,
And made an end—

GIACOMO   Listen! What sound is that?

ORSINO   The house-dog moans, and the beams crack: nought else. 540

GIACOMO   It is my wife complaining in her sleep:
I doubt not she is saying bitter things
Of me; and all my children round her dreaming
That I deny them sustenance.

ORSINO   Whilst he 545
Who truly took it from them, and who fills
Their hungry rest with bitterness, now sleeps
Lapped in bad pleasures, and triumphantly
Mocks thee in visions of successful hate
Too like the truth of day. 550

GIACOMO   If e'er he wakes
Again, I will not trust to hireling hands—

520 Officer in charge.
536 That is, make memorable.

ORSINO Why, that were well. I must be gone; good night:
When next we meet may all be done!
GIACOMO And all
Forgotten: Oh, that I had never been! (*Exeunt*)   555

Act Four

Scene 1

An apartment in the Castle of Petrella
(*Enter* CENCI)

CENCI She comes not; yet I left her even now
Vanquished and faint. She knows the penalty
Of her delay: yet what if threats are vain?   5
Am I not now within Petrella's moat?
Or fear I still the eyes and ears of Rome?
Might I not drag her by the golden hair?
Stamp on her? Keep her sleepless till her brain
Be overworn? Tame her with chains and famine?   10
Less would suffice. Yet so to leave undone
What I most seek! No, 'tis her stubborn will,
Which, by its own consent, shall stoop as low
As that which drags it down.
                                   (*Enter* LUCRETIA)   15
                          Thou loathed wretch!
Hide thee from my abhorrence; fly, begone!
Yet stay! Bid Beatrice come hither.
LUCRETIA Oh,
Husband! I pray, for thine own wretched sake,   20
Heed what thou dost. A man who walks like thee
Through crimes, and through the danger of his crimes,
Each hour may stumble o'er a sudden grave.
And thou art old; thy hairs are hoary gray;
As thou wouldst save thyself from death and hell,   25
Pity thy daughter; give her to some friend
In marriage: so that she may tempt thee not
To hatred, or worse thoughts, if worse there be.
CENCI What! Like her sister who has found a home
To mock my hate from with prosperity?   30
Strange ruin shall destroy both her and thee
And all that yet remain. My death may be
Rapid, her destiny outspeeds it. Go,
Bid her come hither, and before my mood
Be changed, lest I should drag her by the hair.   35
LUCRETIA She sent me to thee, husband. At thy presence
She fell, as thou dost know, into a trance;
And in that trance she heard a voice which said,

"Cenci must die! Let him confess himself!
Even now the accusing angel waits to hear   40
If God, to punish his enormous crimes,
Harden his dying heart!"
CENCI Why—such things are:
No doubt divine revelings may be made.
'Tis plain I have been favoured from above,   45
For when I cursed my sons they died.—Ay—so.
As to the right or wrong that's talk—repentance—
Repentance is an easy moment's work,
And more depends on God than me. Well—well—
I must give up the greater point, which was   50
To poison and corrupt her soul. (*A pause;* LUCRETIA *approaches anxiously,*
and then shrinks back as he speaks)
One, two;
Ay—Rocco and Cristofano my curse
Strangled: and Giacomo, I think, will find   55
Life a worse Hell than that beyond the grave:
Beatrice shall, if there be skill in hate,
Die in despair, blaspheming: to Bernardo,
He is so innocent, I will bequeath
The memory of these deeds, and make his youth   60
The sepulchre of hope, where evil thoughts
Shall grow like weeds on a neglected tomb.
When all is done, out in the wide Campagna*
I will pile up my silver and my gold;
My costly robes, paintings, and tapestries;   65
My parchments and all records of my wealth;
And make a bonfire in my joy, and leave
Of my possessions nothing but my name;
Which shall be an inheritance to strip
Its wearer bare as infamy. That done,   70
My soul, which is a scourge, will I resign
Into the hands of him who wielded it;
Be it for its own punishment or theirs,
He will not ask it of me till the lash
Be broken in its last and deepest wound;   75
Until its hate be all inflicted. Yet,
Lest death outspeed my purpose, let me make
Short work and sure—(*Going*)
LUCRETIA (*Stops him*) Oh, stay! It was a feint:
She had no vision, and she heard no voice.   80
I said it but to awe thee.
CENCI That is well.

63 The plain surrounding Rome.

Vile palterer with the sacred truth of God,
Be thy soul choked with that blaspheming lie!
For Beatrice, worse terrors are in store,   85
To bend her to my will.
LUCRETIA Oh! To what will?
What cruel sufferings, more than she has known,
Canst thou inflict?
CENCI Andrea! Go call my daughter,   90
And if she comes not tell her that I come.
What sufferings? I will drag her, step by step,
Through infamies unheard of among men:
She shall stand shelterless in the broad noon
Of public scorn, for acts blazoned abroad,   95
One among which shall be—What? Canst thou guess?
She shall become (for what she most abhors
Shall have a fascination to entrap
Her loathing will) to her own conscious self
All she appears to others; and when dead,   100
As she shall die unshrived* and unforgiven,
A rebel to her father and her God,
Her corpse shall be abandoned to the hounds;
Her name shall be the terror of the earth;
Her spirit shall approach the throne of God   105
Plague-spotted with my curses. I will make
Body and soul a monstrous lump of ruin.
                    (*Enter* ANDREA)
ANDREA The lady Beatrice—
CENCI Speak, pale slave! What   110
Said she?
ANDREA My Lord, 'twas what she looked she said:
"Go tell my father that I see the gulf
Of Hell between us two, which he may pass,
I will not." (*Exit* ANDREA)   115
CENCI Go thou quick, Lucretia,
Tell her to come; yet let her understand
Her coming is consent; and say, moreover,
That if she come not I will curse her. (*Exit* LUCRETIA)
                    Ha!   120
With what but with a father's curse doth God
Panic-strike armed victory, and make pale
Cities in their prosperity? The world's Father
Must grant a parent's prayer against his child,
Be he who asks even what men call me.   125
Will not the deaths of her rebellious brothers

___

101 Without confession or absolution.

Awe her before I speak? For I on them
Did imprecate quick ruin, and it came.

(*Enter* LUCRETIA)

Well; what? Speak, wretch!   130

LUCRETIA   She said, "I cannot come;
Go tell my father that I see a torrent
Of his own blood raging between us."

CENCI (*Kneeling*)   God!
Hear me! If this most specious mass of flesh,   135
Which thou hast made my daughter; this my blood,
This particle of my divided being;
Or rather, this my bane and my disease,
Whose sight infects and poisons me; this devil
Which sprung from me as from a hell, was meant   140
To aught good use; if her bright loveliness
Was kindled to illumine this dark world;
If nursed by thy selectest dew of love
Such virtues blossom in her as should make
The peace of life, I pray thee, for my sake,   145
As thou the common God and Father art
Of her, and me, and all; reverse that doom!
Earth, in the name of God, let her food be
Poison, until she be encrusted round
With leprous stains! Heaven, rain upon her head   150
The blistering drops of the Maremma's* dew,
Till she be speckled like a toad; parch up
Those love-enkindled lips, warp those fine limbs
To loathed lameness! All beholding sun,
Strike in thine envy those life-darting eyes   155
With thine own blinding beams!

LUCRETIA   Peace! Peace!
For thine own sake unsay those dreadful words.
When high God grants, he punishes such prayers.

CENCI (*Leaping up, and throwing his right hand towards Heaven*)   He does his   160
will, I mine! This in addition,
That if she have a child—

LUCRETIA   Horrible thought!

CENCI   That if she ever have a child; and thou,
Quick Nature, I adjure thee by thy God,   165
That thou be fruitful in her, and increase
And multiply, fulfilling his command,
And my deep imprecation! May it be
A hideous likeness of herself; that, as
From a distorting mirror, she may see   170

---

¹⁵¹ Marshes north of Rome.

Her image mixed with what she most abhors,
Similing upon her from her nursing breast.
And that the child may from its infancy
Grow, day by day, more wicked and deformed,
Turning her mother's love to misery: 175
And that both she and it may live, until
It shall repay her care and pain with hate,
Or what may else be more unnatural.
So he may hunt her through the clamorous scoffs
Of the loud world to a dishonoured grave.   180
Shall I revoke this curse? Go, bid her come,
Before my words are chronicled in heaven. (*Exit* LUCRETIA)
I do not feel as if I were a man,
But like a fiend appointed to chastise
The offences of some unremembered world.   185
My blood is running up and down my veins;
A fearful pleasure makes it prick and tingle:
I feel a giddy sickness of strange awe;
My heart is beating with an expectation
Of horrid joy.   190
                    (*Enter* LUCRETIA)
            What? Speak!
LUCRETIA   She bids thee curse;
    And if thy curses, as they cannot do,
    Could kill her soul—   195
CENCI   She would not come. 'Tis well,
    I can do both: first take what I demand,
    And then extort concession. To thy chamber!
    Fly ere I spurn thee: and beware this night
    That thou cross not my footsteps. It were safer   200
    To come between the tiger and his prey. (*Exit* LUCRETIA)
    It must be late; mine eyes grow weary dim
    With unaccustomed heaviness of sleep.
    Conscience! Oh, thou most insolent of lies!
    They say that sleep, that healing dew of heaven,   205
    Steeps not in balm the foldings of the brain
    Which thinks thee an impostor. I will go,
    First to belie thee with an hour of rest,
    Which will be deep and calm, I feel: and then—
    O, multitudinous Hell, the fiends will shake   210
    Thine arches with the laughter of their joy!
    There shall be lamentation heard in Heaven
    As o'er an angel fallen; and upon Earth
    All good shall droop and sicken, and ill things
    Shall, with a spirit of unnatural life,   215
    Stir and be quickened; even as I am now. (*Exit*)

Scene 2

Before the Castle of Petrella

(Enter BEATRICE and LUCRETIA above on the ramparts)

BEATRICE They come not yet.

LUCRETIA 'Tis scarce midnight. 220

BEATRICE How slow
Behind the course of thought, even sick with speed,
Lags leaden-footed time!

LUCRETIA The minutes pass—
If he should wake before the deed is done? 225

BEATRICE O, mother! He must never wake again.
What thou hast said persuades me that our act
Will but dislodge a spirit of deep hell
Out of a human form.

LUCRETIA 'Tis true he spoke 230
Of death and judgment with strange confidence
For one so wicked; as a man believing
In God, yet recking not of good or ill.
And yet to die without confession!

BEATRICE Oh! 235
Believe that Heaven is merciful and just,
And will not add our dread necessity
To the amount of his offences.

(Enter OLIMPIO and MARZIO below)

LUCRETIA See, 240
They come.

BEATRICE All mortal things must hasten thus
To their dark end. Let us go down. (Exeunt LUCRETIA and BEATRICE
from above)

OLIMPIO How feel you to this work? 245

MARZIO As one who thinks
A thousand crowns excellent market price
For an old murderer's life. Your cheeks are pale.

OLIMPIO It is the white reflection of your own,
Which you call pale. 250

MARZIO Is that their natural hue?

OLIMPIO Or 'tis my hate, and the deferred desire
To wreak it, which extinguishes their blood.

MARZIO You are inclined then to this business?

OLIMPIO Ay, 255
If one should bribe me with a thousand crowns
To kill a serpent which had stung my child,
I could not be more willing.

(Enter BEATRICE and LUCRETIA below)

Noble ladies! 260

BEATRICE Are ye resolved?
OLIMPIO Is he asleep?
MARZIO Is all
Quiet?
LUCRETIA I mixed an opiate with his drink: 265
He sleeps so soundly—
BEATRICE That his death will be
But as a change of sin-chastising dreams,
A dark continuance of the Hell within him,
Which God extinguish! But ye are resolved? 270
Ye know it is a high and holy deed?
OLIMPIO We are resolved.
MARZIO As to how this act
Be warranted, it rests with you.
BEATRICE Well, follow! 275
OLIMPIO Hush! Hark! What noise is that?
MARZIO Ha! Some one comes!
BEATRICE Ye conscience-stricken cravens,* rock to rest
Your baby hearts. It is the iron gate,
Which ye left open, swinging to the wind, 280
That enters whistling as in scorn. Come, follow!
And be your steps like mine, light, quick, and bold. (*Exeunt*)

Scene 3

An apartment in the Castle
(*Enter* BEATRICE *and* LUCRETIA)

LUCRETIA They are about it now. 285
BEATRICE Nay, it is done.
LUCRETIA I have not heard him groan.
BEATRICE He will not groan.
LUCRETIA What sound is that?
BEATRICE List! 'Tis the tread of feet 290
About his bed.
LUCRETIA My God!
If he be now a cold stiff corpse.
BEATRICE O, fear not
What may be done, but what is left undone: 295
The act seals all.
(*Enter* OLIMPIO *and* MARZIO)
Is it accomplished?
MARZIO What?
OLIMPIO Did you not call? 300
BEATRICE When?
OLIMPIO Now.

278 Cowards.

BEATRICE   I ask if all is over?

OLIMPIO   We dare not kill an old and sleeping man;   305
    His thin grey hair, his stern and reverent brow,
    His veined hands crossed on his heaving breast,
    And the calm innocent sleep in which he lay,
    Quelled me. Indeed, indeed, I cannot do it.

MARZIO   But I was bolder; for I chid Olimpio,
    And bade him bear his wrongs to his own grave   310
    And leave me the reward. And now my knife
    Touched the loose wrinkled throat, when the old man
    Stirred in his sleep, and said, "God! Hear, O, hear
    A father's curse! What art thou not our father?"
    And then he laughed. I knew it was the ghost   315
    Of my dead father speaking through his lips,
    And could not kill him.

BEATRICE   Miserable slaves!
    Where, if ye dare not kill a sleeping man,
    Found ye the boldness to return to me
    With such a deed undone? Base palterers!*   320
    Cowards and traitors! Why, the very conscience
    Which ye would sell for gold and for revenge
    Is an equivocation: it sleeps over
    A thousand daily acts disgracing men;   325
    And when a deed where mercy insults heaven—
    Why do I talk? (*Snatching a dagger from one of them and raising it*)
            Hadst thou a tongue to say,
    She murdered her own father, I must do it!
    But never dream ye shall outlive him long!   330

OLIMPIO   Stop, for God's sake!

MARZIO   I will go back and kill him.

OLIMPIO   Give me the weapon, we must do thy will.

BEATRICE   Take it! Depart! Return! (*Exeunt* OLIMPIO *and* MARZIO)
                How pale thou art!   335
    We do but that which 'twere a deadly crime
    To leave undone.

LUCRETIA   Would it were done!

BEATRICE   Even whilst
    That doubt is passing through your mind, the world   340
    Is conscious of a change. Darkness and hell
    Have swallowed up the vapour they sent forth
    To blacken the sweet light of life. My breath
    Comes, methinks, lighter, and the jellied blood
    Runs freely through my veins. Hark!   345
            (*Enter* OLIMPIO *and* MARZIO)
               He is—

---

[321] One who delays or shuffles about.

OLIMPIO Dead!

MARZIO We strangled him that there might be no blood;
And then we threw his heavy corpse i' the garden   350
Under the balcony; 'twill seem it fell.

BEATRICE (*Giving them a bag of coin*) Here, take this gold, and hasten to
your homes.
And, Marzio, because thou wast only awed
By that which made me tremble, wear thou this!
(*Clothes him in a rich mantle*)   355
It was the mantle which my grandfather
Wore in his high prosperity, and men
Envied his state: so may they envy thine.
Thou wert a weapon in the hand of God   360
To a just use. Live long and thrive! And, mark,
If thou hast crimes, repent: this deed is none. (*A horn is sounded*)

LUCRETIA Hark! 'Tis the castle horn; my God! It sounds
Like the last trump.

BEATRICE Some tedious guest is coming.   365

LUCRETIA The drawbridge is let down; there is a tramp
Of horses in the court; fly, hide yourselves! (*Exeunt* OLIMPIO *and* MARZIO)

BEATRICE Let us retire to counterfeit deep rest;
I scarcely need to counterfeit it now:
The spirit which doth reign within these limbs   370
Seems strangely undisturbed. I could even sleep
Fearless and calm: all ill is surely past. (*Exeunt*)

Scene 4

Another apartment in the Castle
(*Enter on one side the Legate* SAVELLA, *introduced by a Servant, and on the
other* LUCRETIA *and* BERNARDO)   375

SAVELLA Lady, my duty to his Holiness
Be my excuse that thus unseasonably
I break upon your rest. I must speak with
Count Cenci; doth he sleep?

LUCRETIA (*In a hurried and confused manner*) I think he sleeps;   380
Yet, wake him not, I pray, spare me awhile,
He is a wicked and a wrathful man;
Should he be roused out of his sleep to-night,
Which is, I know, a hell of angry dreams,
It were not well; indeed it were not well.   385
Wait till day break—
(*Aside*)   O, I am deadly sick!

SAVELLA I grieve thus to distress you, but the Count
Must answer charges of the gravest import,
And suddenly; such my commission is.   390

LUCRETIA ᐟ(*With increased agitation*)   I dare not rouse him:
    I know none who dare:
    'Twere perilous;—you might as safely waken
    A serpent; or a corpse in which some fiend
    Were laid to sleep.   395
SAVELLA   Lady, my moments here
    Are counted. I must rouse him from his sleep,
    Since none else dare.
LUCRETIA (*Aside*)   O, terror! O, despair!
    (*To* BERNARDO)   Bernardo, conduct you the Lord Legate to   400
    Your father's chamber. (*Exeunt* SAVELLA *and* BERNARDO)
                     (*Enter* BEATRICE)
BEATRICE   'Tis a messenger
    Come to arrest the culprit who now stands
    Before the throne of unappealable God.   405
    Both Earth and Heaven, consenting arbiters,
    Acquit our deed.
LUCRETIA   Oh, agony of fear!
    Would that he yet might live! Even now I heard
    The Legate's followers whisper, as they passed,   410
    They had a warrant for his instant death.
    All was prepared by unforbidden means,
    Which we must pay so dearly, having done.
    Even now they search the tower, and find the body;
    Now they suspect the truth; now they consult   415
    Before they come to tax us with the fact:
    O, horrible, 'tis all discovered!
BEATRICE   Mother,
    What is done wisely, is done well. Be bold
    As thou art just. 'Tis like a truant child   420
    To fear that others know what thou hast done,
    Even from thine own strong consciousness, and thus
    Write on unsteady eyes and altered cheeks
    All thou wouldst hide. Be faithful to thyself,
    And fear no other witness but thy fear.   425
    For if, as cannot be, some circumstance
    Should rise in accusation, we can blind
    Suspicion with such cheap astonishment,
    Or overbear it with such guiltless pride,
    As murderers cannot feign. The deed is done,   430
    And what may follow now regards not me.
    I am as universal as the light;
    Free as the earth-surrounding air; as firm
    As the world's centre. Consequence, to me,
    Is as the wind which strikes the solid rock   435
    But shakes it not. (*A cry within and tumult*)

VOICES Murder! Murder! Murder!

(*Enter* BERNARDO *and* SAVELLA)

SAVELLA (*To his followers*) Go search the castle round; sound the alarm;
  Look to the gates that none escape! 440

BEATRICE What now?

BERNARDO I know not what to say: my father's dead!

BEATRICE How? Dead? He only sleeps: you mistake, brother.
  His sleep is very calm, very like death;
  'Tis wonderful how well a tyrant sleeps. 445
  He is not *dead?*

BERNARDO Dead! Murdered!

LUCRETIA (*With extreme agitation*) Oh, no, no,
  He is not murdered, though he may be dead;
  I have alone the keys of those apartments. 450

SAVELLA Ha! Is it so?

BEATRICE My Lord, I pray excuse us;
  We will retire; my mother is not well:
  She seems quite overcome with this strange horror. (*Exeunt* LUCRETIA
                                        and BEATRICE) 455

SAVELLA Can you suspect who may have murdered him?

BERNARDO I know not what to think.

SAVELLA Can you name any
  Who had an interest in his death?

BERNARDO Alas! 460
  I can name none who had not, and those most
  Who most lament that such a deed is done;
  My mother, and my sister, and myself.

SAVELLA 'Tis strange! There were clear marks of violence.
  I found the old man's body in the moonlight 465
  Hanging beneath the window of his chamber,
  Among the branches of a pine: he could not
  Have fallen there, for all his limbs lay heaped
  And effortless; 'tis true there was no blood.
  Favour me, Sir, (it much imports your house 470
  That all should be made clear) to tell the ladies
  That I request their presence. (*Exit* BERNARDO)

(*Enter Guards, bringing in* MARZIO)

GUARD We have one.

OFFICER My lord, we found this ruffian and another 475
  Lurking among the rocks; there is no doubt
  But that they are the murderers of Count Cenci:
  Each had a bag of coin; this fellow wore
  A gold-inwoven robe, which, shining bright
  Under the dark rocks to the glimmering moon, 480
  Betrayed them to our notice: the other fell
  Desperately fighting.

SAVELLA What does he confess?

OFFICER He keeps firm silence; but these lines found on him
Than speak. 485

SAVELLA Their language is at least sincere.
(*Reads*) "To the Lady Beatrice.
That the atonement of what my nature sickens to conjecture may soon arrive,
I send thee, at thy brother's desire, those who will speak and do more than I
dare write— 490

Thy devoted servant,
Orsino."

(*Enter* Lucretia, beatrice, *and* bernardo)
Knowest thou this writing, Lady?

BEATRICE No. 495

SAVELLA Nor thou?

LUCRETIA (*Her conduct throughout the scene is marked by extreme agitation*)
Where was it found? What is it? It should be
Orsino's hand! It speaks of that strange horror
Which never yet found utterance, but which made 500
Between that hapless child and her dead father
A gulf of obscure hatred.

SAVELLA Is it so?
Is it true, Lady, that thy father did
Such outrages as to awaken in thee 505
Unfilial hate?

BEATRICE Not hate, 'twas more than hate:
This is most true, yet wherefore question me?

SAVELLA There is a deed demanding question done;
Thou hast a secret which will answer not. 510

BEATRICE What sayest? My Lord, your words are bold and rash.

SAVELLA I do arrest all present in the name
Of the Pope's Holiness. You must to Rome.

LUCRETIA O, not to Rome! Indeed we are not guilty.

BEATRICE Guilty! Who dares talk of guilt? My Lord, 515
I am more innocent of parricide
Than is a child born fatherless. Dear mother,
Your gentleness and patience are no shield
For this keen-judging world, this two-edged lie,
Which seems, but is not. What! Will human laws, 520
Rather will ye who are their ministers,
Bar all access to retribution first,
And then, when heaven doth interpose to do
What ye neglect, arming familiar things
To the redress of an unwonted crime, 525
Make ye the victims who demanded it
Culprits? 'Tis ye are culprits! That poor wretch
Who stands so pale, and trembling, and amazed,

If it be true he murdered Cenci, was
A sword in the right hand of justest God.   530
Wherefore should I have wielded it? Unless
The crimes which mortal tongue dare never name
God therefore scruples to avenge.
SAVELLA   You own
That you desired his death?   535
BEATRICE   It would have been
A crime no less than his, if, for one moment,
That fierce desire had faded in my heart.
'Tis true I did believe, and hope, and pray,
Ay, I even knew—for God is wise and just,   540
That some strange sudden death hung over him.
'Tis true that this did happen, and most true
There was no other rest for me on earth,
No other hope in Heaven: now what of this?
SAVELLA   Strange thoughts beget strange deeds; and here are both: 545
I judge thee not.
BEATRICE   And yet, if you arrest me,
You are the judge and executioner
Of that which is the life of life: the breath
Of accusation kills an innocent name,   550
And leaves for lame acquittal the poor life
Which is a mask without it. 'Tis most false
That I am guilty of foul parricide;
Although I must rejoice, for justest cause,
That other hands have sent my father's soul   555
To ask the mercy he denied to me.
Now leave us free: stain not a noble house
With vague surmises of rejected crime;
Add to our sufferings and your own neglect
No heavier sum; let them have been enough;   560
Leave us the wreck we have.
SAVELLA   I dare not, Lady.
I pray that you prepare yourselves for Rome:
There the Pope's further pleasure will be known.
LUCRETIA   O, not to Rome! O, take us not to Rome!   565
BEATRICE   Why not to Rome, dear mother? There as here
Our innocence is as an armed heel
To trample accusation. God is there
As here, and with his shadow ever clothes
The innocent, the injured, and the weak;   570
And such are we. Cheer up, dear Lady, lean
On me; collect your wandering thoughts. My Lord,
As soon as you have taken some refreshment,
And had all such examinations made

Upon the spot, as may be necessary   575
    To the full understanding of this matter,
    We shall be ready. Mother, will you come?
LUCRETIA Ha! They will bind us to the rack, and wrest
    Self-accusation from our agony!
    Will Giacomo be there? Orsino? Marzio?   580
    All present; all confronted; all demanding
    Each from the others countenance the thing
    Which is in every heart! O, misery! (*She faints, and is borne out*)
SAVELLA She faints: an ill appearance this.
BEATRICE My Lord,   585
    She knows not yet the uses of the world.
    She fears that power is as a beast which grasps
    And loosens not: a snake, whose look transmutes
    All things to guilt which is its nutriment;
    She cannot know how well the supine slaves   590
    Of blind authority read the truth of things
    When written on a brow of guilelessness:
    She sees not yet triumphant Innocence
    Stand at the judgment-seat of mortal man,
    A judge and an accuser of the wrong   595
    Which drags it there. Prepare yourself, my Lord;
    Our suite will join yours in the court below. (*Exeunt*)

Act Five

Scene 1

An apartment in Orsino's palace
(*Enter* ORSINO *and* GIACOMO)

GIACOMO Do evil deeds thus quickly come to end?
    O, that the vain remorse which must chastise
    Crimes done, had but as loud a voice to warn   5
    As its keen sting is mortal to avenge!
    O, that the hour when present had cast off
    The mantle of its mystery, and shown
    The ghastly form with which it now returns
    When its scared game is roused, cheering the hounds   10
    Of conscience to their prey! Alas! Alas!
    It was a wicked thought, a piteous deed,
    To kill an old and hoary-headed father.
ORSINO It has turned out unluckily, in truth.
GIACOMO To violate the sacred doors of sleep;   15
    To cheat kind nature of the placid death
    Which she prepares for over-wearied age;
    To drag from Heaven an unrepentant soul

Which might have quenched in reconciling prayers
A life of burning crimes—   20

ORSINO   You cannot say
I urged you to the deed.

GIACOMO   O, had I never
Found in thy smooth and ready countenance
The mirror of my darkest thoughts; hadst thou   25
Never with hints and questions made me look
Upon the monster of my thought, until
It grew familiar to desire—

ORSINO   'Tis thus
Men cast the blame of their unprosperous acts   30
Upon the abettors of their own resolve;
Or any thing but their weak, guilty selves.
And yet, confess the truth, it is the peril
In which you stand that gives you this pale sickness
Of penitence; confess 'tis fear disguised   35
From its own shame that takes the mantle now
Of thin remorse. What if we yet were safe?

GIACOMO   How can that be? Already Beatrice,
Lucretia, and the murderer, are in prison.
I doubt not officers are, whilst we speak,   40
Sent to arrest us.

ORSINO   I have all prepared
For instant flight. We can escape even now,
So we take fleet occasion by the hair.

GIACOMO   Rather expire in tortures, as I may.   45
What! Will you cast by self-accusing flight
Assured conviction upon Beatrice?
She, who alone in this unnatural work,
Stands like God's angel ministered upon
By fiends; avenging such a nameless wrong   50
As turns black parricide to piety;
Whilst we for basest ends—I fear, Orsino,
While I consider all your words and looks,
Comparing them with your proposal now,
That you must be a villain. For what end   55
Could you engage in such a perilous crime,
Training me on with hints, and signs, and smiles,
Even to this gulf? Thou art no liar? No,
Thou art a lie! Traitor and murderer!
Coward and slave! But, no, defend thyself; (*Drawing*)   60
Let the sword speak what the indignant tongue
Disdains to brand thee with.

ORSINO   Put up your weapon.
Is it the desperation of your fear

Makes you thus rash and sudden with a friend, 65
Now ruined for your sake? If honest anger
Have moved you, know, that what I just proposed
Was but to try you. As for me, I think
Thankless affection led me to this point,
From which, if my firm temper could repent, 70
I cannot now recede. Even whilst we speak
The ministers of justice wait below:
They grant me these brief moments. Now if you
Have any word of melancholy comfort
To speak to your pale wife, 'twere best to pass 75
Out at the postern,* and avoid them so.

GIACOMO   O, generous friend! How canst thou pardon me?
Would that my life could purchase thine!

ORSINO   That wish
Now comes a day too late. Haste; fare thee well! 80
Hear'st thou not steps along the corridor? (*Exit* GIACOMO)
I'm sorry for it; but the guards are waiting
At his own gate, and such was my contrivance
That I might rid me both of him and them.
I thought to act a solemn comedy 85
Upon the painted scene of this new world,
And to attain my own peculiar ends
By some such plot of mingled good and ill
As others weave; but there arose a Power
Which grasped and snapped the threads of my device, 90
And turned it to a net of ruin—Ha! (*A shout is heard*)
Is that my name I hear proclaimed abroad?
But I will pass, wrapped in a vile disguise;
Rags on my back, and a false innocence
Upon my face, through the misdeeming* crowd 95
Which judges by what seems. 'Tis easy then
For a new name and for a country new,
And a new life, fashioned on old desires,
To change the honours of abandoned Rome.
And these must be the masks of that within, 100
Which must remain unaltered. Oh, I fear
That what is past will never let me rest!
Why, when none else is conscious but myself
Of my misdeeds, should my own heart's contempt
Trouble me? Have I not the power to fly 105
My own reproaches? Shall I be the slave
Of—what? A word? Which those of this false world
Employ against each other, not themselves;

76 Private gate.
95 Possessed of wrong opinions.

As men wear daggers not for self-offence.
But if I am mistaken, where shall I   110
Find the disguise to hide me from myself,
As now I skulk from every other eye? (*Exit*)

Scene 2

A Hall of Justice. CAMILLO, *Judges, and other officials are discovered seated*
(MARZIO *is led in*)
1ST JUDGE   Accused, do you persist in your denial?   115
I ask you, are you innocent, or guilty?
I demand who were the participators
In your offence? Speak truth and the whole truth.
MARZIO   My God! I did not kill him; I know nothing;
Olimpio sold the robe to me from which   120
You would infer my guilt.
2ND JUDGE   Away with him!
1ST JUDGE   Dare you, with lips yet white from the rack's kiss,
Speak false? Is it so soft a questioner,
That you would bandy lover's talk with it   125
Till it wind out your life and soul? Away!
MARZIO   Spare me! O, spare! I will confess.
1ST JUDGE   Then speak.
MARZIO   I strangled him in his sleep.
1ST JUDGE   Who urged you to it?   130
MARZIO   His own son Giacomo, and the young prelate
Orsino sent me to Petrella; there
The ladies Beatrice and Lucretia
Tempted me with a thousand crowns, and I
And my companion forthwith murdered him.   135
Now let me die.
1ST JUDGE   This sounds as bad as truth. Guards, there,
Lead forth the prisoners.
                (*Enter* LUCRETIA, BEATRICE, *and* GIACOMO, *guarded*)
                              Look upon this man;   140
When did you see him last?
BEATRICE   We never saw him.
MARZIO   You know me too well, Lady Beatrice.
BEATRICE   I know thee! How? Where? When?
MARZIO   You know 'twas I   145
Whom you did urge with menaces and bribes
To kill your father. When the thing was done
You clothed me in a robe of woven gold
And bade me thrive: how I have thriven, you see.
You, my Lord Giacomo, Lady Lucretia,   150
You know that what I speak is true.

(BEATRICE *advances towards him; he covers his face, and shrinks back*)
O, dart
The terrible resentment of those eyes
On the dead earth! Turn them away from me! 155
They wound: 'twas torture forced the truth. My Lords,
Having said this, let me be led to death.

BEATRICE Poor wretch, I pity thee: yet stay awhile.

CAMILLO Guards, lead him not away.

BEATRICE Cardinal Camillo, 160
You have a good repute for gentleness
And wisdom: can it be that you sit here
To countenance a wicked farce like this?
When some obscure and trembling slave is dragged
From sufferings which might shake the sternest heart, 165
And bade to answer, not as he believes,
But as those may suspect or do desire,
Whose questions thence suggest their own reply;
And that in peril of such hideous torments
As merciful God spares even the damned. Speak now 170
The thing you surely know, which is, that you
If your fine frame were stretched upon that wheel,
And you were told: "Confess that you did poison
Your little nephew; that fair blue-eyed child
Who was the lodestar* of your life:"—and though 175
All see, since his most swift and piteous death,
That day and night, and heaven and earth, and time,
And all the things hoped for or done therein
Are changed to you, through your exceeding grief,
Yet you would say, "I confess any thing": 180
And beg from your tormentors, like that slave,
The refuge of dishonourable death.
I pray thee, Cardinal, that thou assert
My innocence.

CAMILLO (*Much moved*) What shall we think, my Lords? 185
Shame on these tears! I thought the heart was frozen
Which is their fountain. I would pledge my soul
That she is guiltless.

JUDGE Yet she must be tortured.

CAMILLO I would as soon have tortured mine own nephew: 190
(If he now lived he would be just her age;
His hair, too, was her colour, and his eyes
Like her's in shape, but blue and not so deep)
As that most perfect image of God's love
That ever came sorrowing upon the earth. 195
She is as pure as speechless infancy!

---

[175] Guiding star.

JUDGE   Well, be her purity on your head, my Lord,
If you forbid the rack. His Holiness
Enjoined us to pursue this monstrous crime
By the severest forms of law; nay, even   200
To stretch a point against the criminals.
The prisoners stand accused of parricide
Upon such evidence as justifies
Torture.
BEATRICE   What evidence? This man's?   205
JUDGE   Even so.
BEATRICE (*To* MARZIO)   Come near. And who art thou thus chosen forth
Out of the multitude of living men
To kill the innocent?
MARZIO   I am Marzio,   210
Thy father's vassal.
BEATRICE   Fix thine eyes on mine;
Answer to what I ask. (*Turning to the Judges*)
I prithee mark
His countenance: unlike bold calumny   215
Which sometimes dares not speak the thing it looks,
He dares not look the things he speaks, but bends
His gaze on the blind earth.
(*To* MARZIO)   What! Wilt thou say
That I did murder my own father?   220
MARZIO   Oh!
Spare me! My brain swims round—I cannot speak—
It was that horrid torture forced the truth.
Take me away! Let her not look on me!
I am a guilty, miserable wretch;   225
I have said all I know; now, let me die!
BEATRICE   My Lords, if by my nature I had been
So stern, as to have planned the crime alleged,
Which your suspicions dictate to this slave,
And the rack makes him utter, do you think   230
I should have left this two-edged instrument
Of my misdeed; this man, this bloody knife
With my own name engraven on the heft*
Lying unsheathed amid a world of foes,
For my own death? That with such horrible need   235
For deepest silence, I should have neglected
So trivial a precaution, as the making
His tomb the keeper of a secret written
On a thief's memory? What is his poor life?
What are a thousand lives? A parricide   240
Had trampled them like dust; and see, he lives!

233 Handle.

(*Turning to* MARZIO)   And thou—

MARZIO   Oh, spare me! Speak to me no more!
That stern yet piteous look, those solemn tones,
Wound worse than torture.   245
(*To the Judges*)   I have told it all;
For pity's sake lead me away to death.

CAMILLO   Guards, lead him nearer the Lady Beatrice,
He shrinks from her regard like autumn's leaf
From the keen breath of the serenest north.   250

BEATRICE   Oh, thou who tremblest on the giddy verge
Of life and death, pause ere thou answerest me;
So mayst thou answer God with less dismay:
What evil have we done thee? I, alas!
Have lived but on this earth a few sad years   255
And so my lot was ordered, that a father
First turned the moments of awakening life
To drops, each poisoning youth's sweet hope; and then
Stabbed with one blow my everlasting soul;
And my untainted fame; and even that peace   260
Which sleeps within the core of the heart's heart.
But the wound was not mortal; so my hate
Became the only worship I could lift
To our great father, who in pity and love,
Armed thee, as thou dost say, to cut him off;   265
And thus his wrong becomes my accusation;
And art thou the accuser? If thou hopest
Mercy in heaven, show justice upon earth:
Worse than a bloody hand is a hard heart.
If thou hast done murders, made thy life's path   270
Over the trampled laws of God and man,
Rush not before thy Judge, and say: "My Maker,
I have done this and more; for there was one
Who was most pure and innocent on earth;
And because she endured what never any   275
Guilty or innocent, endured before;
Because her wrongs could not be told, not thought;
Because thy hand at length did rescue her;
I with my words killed her and all her kin."
Think, I adjure you, what it is to slay   280
The reverence living in the minds of men
Towards our ancient house, and stainless fame!
Think what it is to strangle infant pity,
Cradled in the belief of guileless looks,
Till it become a crime to suffer. Think   285
What 'tis to blot with infamy and blood
All that which shows like innocence, and is,
Hear me, great God! I swear, most innocent,

So that the world lose all discrimination
Between the sly, fierce, wild regard of guilt,   290
And that which now compels thee to reply
To what I ask: Am I, or am I not
A parricide?

MARZIO Thou art not!

JUDGE What is this?   295

MARZIO I here declare those whom I did accuse
Are innocent. 'Tis I alone am guilty.

JUDGE Drag him away to torments; let them be
Subtle and long drawn out, to tear the folds
Of the heart's inmost cell. Unbind him not   300
Till he confess.

MARZIO Torture me as ye will:
A keener pang has wrung a higher truth
From my last breath. She is most innocent!
Bloodhounds, not men, glut yourselves well with me;   305
I will not give you that fine piece of nature
To rend and ruin. (*Exit* MARZIO, *guarded*)

CAMILLO What say ye now, my Lords?

JUDGE Let tortures strain the truth till it be white
As snow thrice sifted by the frozen wind.   310

CAMILLO Yet stained with blood.

JUDGE (*To* BEATRICE) Know you this paper, Lady?

BEATRICE Entrap me not with questions. Who stands here
As my accuser? Ha! Wilt thou be he,
Who art my judge? Accuser, witness, judge,   315
What, all in one? Here is Orsino's name;
Where is Orsino? Let his eye meet mine.
What means this scrawl? Alas! Ye know not what,
And therefore on the chance that it may be
Some evil, will ye kill us?   320

(*Enter an Officer*)

OFFICER Marzio's dead.

JUDGE What did he say?

OFFICER Nothing. As soon as we
Had bound him on the wheel, he smiled on us,   325
As one who baffles a deep adversary;
And holding his breath, died.

JUDGE There remains nothing
But to apply the question to those prisoners,
Who yet remain stubborn.   330

CAMILLO I overrule
Further proceedings, and in the behalf
Of these most innocent and noble persons
Will use my interest with the Holy Father.

JUDGE Let the Pope's pleasure then be done. Meanwhile   335

Conduct these culprits each to separate cells;
And be the engines* ready: for this night,
If the Pope's resolution be as grave,
Pious, and just as once, I'll wring the truth
Out of those nerves and sinews, groan by groan. (*Exeunt*) 340

Scene 3

The cell of a prison. BEATRICE *is discovered asleep on a couch*
(*Enter* BERNARDO)

BERNARDO How gently slumber rests upon her face,
Like the last thoughts of some day sweetly spent
Closing in night and dreams, and so prolonged. 345
After such torments as she bore last night,
How light and soft her breathing comes. Ay, me!
Methinks that I shall never sleep again.
But I must shake the heavenly dew of rest
From this sweet folded flower, thus—wake! Awake! 350
What, sister, canst thou sleep?

BEATRICE (*Awaking*) I was just dreaming
That we were all in Paradise. Thou knowest
This cell seems like a kind of Paradise
After our father's presence. 355

BERNARDO Dear, dear sister,
Would that thy dream were not a dream! O, God!
How shall I tell?

BEATRICE What wouldst thou tell, sweet brother?

BERNARDO Look not so calm and happy, or even whilst 360
I stand considering what I have to say
My heart will break.

BEATRICE See now, thou mak'st me weep:
How very friendless thou wouldst be, dear child,
If I were dead. Say what thou hast to say. 365

BERNARDO They have confessed; they could endure no more
The tortures—

BEATRICE Ha! What was there to confess?
They must have told some weak and wicked lie
To flatter their tormentors. Have they said 370
That they were guilty? O, white innocence,
That thou shouldst wear the mask of guilt to hide
Thine awful and serenest countenance
From those who know thee not!
(*Enter* JUDGE, *with* LUCRETIA *and* GIACOMO, *guarded*) 375
                    Ignoble hearts!
For some brief spasms of pain, which are at least

---

[337] Instruments of torture.

As mortal as the limbs through which they pass,
Are centuries of high splendour laid in dust?
And that eternal honour which should live   380
Sun-like, above the reek of mortal fame,
Changed to a mockery and a bye-word? What!
Will you give up these bodies to be dragged
At horses' heels, so that our hair should sweep
The footsteps of the vain and senseless crowd,   385
Who, that they may make our calamity
Their worship and their spectacle, will leave
The churches and the theatres as void
As their own hearts? Shall the light multitude
Fling, at their choice, curses or faded pity,   390
Sad funeral flowers to deck a living corpse,
Upon us as we pass to pass away,
And leave—what memory of our having been?
Infamy, blood, terror, despair? O thou,
Who wert a mother to the parentless,   395
Kill not thy child! Let not her wrongs kill thee!
Brother, lie down with me upon the rack,
And let us each be silent as a corpse;
It soon will be as soft as any grave.
'Tis but the falsehood it can wring from fear   400
Makes the rack cruel.
GIACOMO   They will tear the truth
Even from thee at last, those cruel pains:
For pity's sake say thou art guilty now.
LUCRETIA   O, speak the truth! Let us all quickly die;   405
And after death, God is our judge, not they;
He will have mercy on us.
BERNARDO   If indeed
It can be true, say so, dear sister mine;
And then the Pope will surely pardon you,   410
And all be well.
JUDGE   Confess, or I will warp
Your limbs with such keen tortures—
BEATRICE   Tortures! Turn
The rack henceforth into a spinning wheel!   415
Torture your dog, that he may tell when last
He lapped the blood his master shed—not me!
My pangs are of the mind, and of the heart,
And of the soul; ay, of the inmost soul,
Which weeps within tears as of burning gall   420
To see, in this ill world where none are true,
My kindred false to their deserted selves.
And with considering all the wretched life

Which I have lived, and its now wretched end,
And the small justice shown by Heaven and Earth   425
To me or mine; and what a tyrant thou art,
And what slaves these; and what a world we make,
The oppressor and the oppressed—such pangs compel
My answer. What is it thou wouldst with me?

JUDGE   Art thou not guilty of thy father's death?   430

BEATRICE   Or wilt thou rather tax* high judging God
That he permitted such an act as that
Which I have suffered, and which he beheld;
Made it unutterable, and took from it
All refuge, all revenge, all consequence,   435
But that which thou hast called my father's death?
Which is or is not what men call a crime,
Which either I have done, or have not done;
Say what ye will. I shall deny no more.
If ye desire it thus, thus let it be.   440
And so an end of all. Now do your will;
No other pains shall force another word.

JUDGE   She is convicted, but has not confessed.
Be it enough. Until their final sentence
Let none have converse with them. You, young Lord,   445
Linger not here!

BEATRICE   O, tear him not away!

JUDGE   Guards, do your duty.

BERNARDO   (*Embracing* BEATRICE)   Oh! Would ye divide
Body from soul?   450

OFFICER   That is the headsman's business.
          (*Exeunt all but* LUCRETIA, BEATRICE, *and* GIACOMO)

GIACOMO   Have I confessed? Is it all over now?
No hope! No refuge! O weak, wicked tongue,
Which hast destroyed me, would that thou hadst been   455
Cut out and thrown to dogs first? To have killed
My father first, and then betrayed my sister;
Ay, thee! The one thing innocent and pure
In this black guilty world, to that which I
So well deserve! My wife! My little ones!   460
Destitute, helpless, and I—Father! God!
Canst thou forgive even the unforgiving,
When their full hearts break thus, thus! (*Covers his face, and weeps*)

LUCRETIA   O, my child!
To what a dreadful end are we all come!   465
Why did I yield? Why did I not sustain
Those torments? Oh, that I were all dissolved

---

431 Charge or censure.

Into these fast and unavailing tears,
Which flow and feel not!

BEATRICE   What 'twas weak to do,   470
'Tis weaker to lament, once being done;
Take cheer! The God who knew my wrong, and made
Our speedy act the angel of his wrath,
Seems, and but seems to have abandoned us.
Let us not think that we shall die for this.   475
Brother, sit near me; give me your firm hand,
You had a manly heart. Bear up! Bear up!
O, dearest Lady, put your gentle head
Upon my lap, and try to sleep awhile:
Your eyes look pale, hollow, and overworn,   480
With heaviness of watching and slow grief.
Come, I will sing you some low, sleepy tune,
Not cheerful, nor yet sad; some dull old thing,
Some outworn and unused monotony,
Such as our country gossips sing and spin,   485
Till they almost forget they live: lie down!
So, that will do. Have I forgot the words?
Faith! They are sadder than I thought they were.

                    (*Song*)
    False friend, wilt thou smile or weep   490
    When my life is laid asleep?
    Little cares for a smile or a tear,
    They clay-cold corpse upon the bier!
        Farewell! Heigho!
        What is this whispers low?   495
    There is a snake in thy smile, my dear;
    And bitter poison within thy tear.

    Sweet sleep, were death like to thee,
    Or if thou couldst mortal be,
    I would close these eyes of pain;   500
    When to wake? Never again.
        O, World! Farewell!
        Listen to the passing bell!
    It says, thou and I must part,
    With a light and a heavy heart. (*The scene closes*)   505

Scene 4

                    A hall of the prison
                (*Enter* CAMILLO *and* BERNARDO)

CAMILLO   The Pope is stern; not to be moved or bent.
He looked as calm and keen as is the engine

Which tortures and which kills, exempt itself 510
From aught that it inflicts; a marble form,
A rite, a law, a custom: not a man.

He frowned, as if to frown had been the trick
Of his machinery, on the advocates
Presenting the defences, which he tore 515
And threw behind, muttering with hoarse, harsh voice:
"Which among ye defended their old father,
Killed in his sleep?" Then to another: "Thou
Dost this in virtue of thy place; 'tis well."
He turned to me then, looking deprecation, 520
And said these three words, coldly: "They must die."

BERNARDO And yet you left him not?

CAMILLO I urged him still;
Pleading, as I could guess, the devilish wrong
Which prompted your unnatural parent's death. 525
And he replied: "Paolo Santa Croce
Murdered his mother yester evening,
And he is fled. Parricide grows so rife,
That soon, for some just cause no doubt, the young
Will strangle us all, dozing in our chairs. 530
Authority, and power, and hoary hair,
Are grown crimes capital. You are my nephew,
You come to ask their pardon; stay a moment;
Here is their sentence; never see me more
Till, to the letter, it be all fulfilled." 535

BERNARDO O, God, not so! I did believe indeed
That all you said was but sad preparation
For happy news. O, there are words and looks
To bend the sternest purpose! Once I knew them,
Now I forget them at my dearest need. 540
What think you if I seek him out, and bathe
His feet and robe with hot and bitter tears?
Importune him with prayers, vexing his brain
With my perpetual cries, until in rage
He strike me with his pastoral cross,* and trample 545
Upon my prostrate head, so that my blood
May stain the senseless dust on which he treads,
And remorse waken mercy? I will do it!
O, wait till I return! (*Rushes out*)

CAMILLO Alas! Poor boy! 550
A wreck-devoted* seaman thus might pray
To the deaf sea.

(Enter LUCRETIA, BEATRICE, and GIACOMO, guarded)

545 Pertaining to the shepherd of souls.
551 Doomed.

BEATRICE I hardly dare to fear
    That thou bring'st other news than a just pardon.   555
CAMILLO May God in heaven be less inexorable
    To the Pope's prayers, than he has been to mine.
    Here is the sentence and the warrant.
BEATRICE (*Wildly*) Oh,
    My God! Can it be possible I have   560
    To die so suddenly? So young to go
    Under the obscure, cold, rotting, wormy ground!
    To be nailed down into a narrow place;
    To see no more sweet sunshine; hear no more
    Blithe voice of living thing; muse not again   565
    Upon familiar thoughts, sad, yet thus lost—
    How fearful! To be nothing! Or to be—
    What? O, where am I? Let me not go mad!
    Sweet Heaven, forgive weak thoughts! If there should be
    No God, no Heaven, no Earth in the void world;   570
    The wide, grey, lampless, deep, unpeopled world!
    If all things then should be—my father's spirit,
    His eye, his voice, his touch, surrounding me;
    The atmosphere and breath of my dead life!
    If sometimes, as a shape more like himself,   575
    Even the form which tortured me on earth,
    Masked in grey hairs and wrinkles, he should come
    And wind me in his hellish arms, and fix
    His eyes on mine, and drag me down, down, down!
    For was he not alone omnipotent   580
    On Earth, and ever present? Even tho' dead,
    Does not his spirit live in all that breathe,
    And work for me and mine still the same ruin,
    Scorn, pain, despair? Who ever yet returned
    To teach the laws of death's untrodden realm?   585
    Unjust perhaps as those which drive us now,
    O, whither, whither?
LUCRETIA Trust in God's sweet love,
    The tender promises of Christ: ere night,
    Think we shall be in Paradise.   590
BEATRICE 'Tis passed!
    Whatever comes, my heart shall sink no more.
    And yet, I know not why, your words strike chill:
    How tedious, false, and cold seem all things. I
    Have met with much injustice in this world;   595
    No difference has been made by God or man,
    Or any power moulding my wretched lot,
    'Twixt good or evil, as regarded me.
    I am cut off from the only world I know,

From light, and life, and love, in youth's sweet prime. 600
You do well telling me to trust in God,
I hope I do trust in him. In whom else
Can any trust? And yet my heart is cold.
(*During the latter speeches* GIACOMO *has retired conversing with* CAMILLO,
who now goes out. GIACOMO *advances*) 605

GIACOMO   Know you not, mother—sister, know you not?
Bernardo even now is gone to implore
The Pope to grant our pardon.

LUCRETIA   Child, perhaps
It will be granted. We may all then live 610
To make these woes a tale for distant years:
O, what a thought! It gushes to my heart
Like the warm blood.

BEATRICE   Yet both will soon be cold.
O, trample out that thought! Worse than despair, 615
Worse than the bitterness of death, is hope:
It is the only ill which can find place
Upon the giddy, sharp and narrow hour
Tottering beneath us. Plead with the swift frost
That it should spare the eldest flower of spring: 620
Plead with awakening earthquake, o'er whose couch
Even now a city stands, strong, fair and free;
Now stench and blackness yawn, like death. O, plead
With famine, or wind-walking pestilence,
Blind lightning, or the deaf sea, not with man! 625
Cruel, cold, formal man! Righteous in words,
In deeds a Cain. No, mother, we must die:
Since such is the reward of innocent lives;
Such the alleviation of worst wrongs.
And whilst our murderers live, and hard, cold men, 630
Smiling and slow, walk thro' a world of tears
To death as to life's sleep; 'twere just the grave
Were some strange joy for us. Come, obscure Death,
And wind me in thine all-embracing arms!
Like a fond mother hide me in thy bosom, 635
And rock me to the sleep from which none wake.
Live ye, who live, subject to one another
As we were once, who now—
                    (BERNARDO *rushes in*)

BERNARDO   Oh, horrible! 640
That tears, that looks, that hope poured forth in prayer,
Even till the heart is vacant and despairs,
Should all be vain! The ministers of death
Are waiting round the doors. I thought I saw
Blood on the face of one—what if 'twere fancy? 645
Soon the heart's blood of all I love on earth

Will sprinkle him, and he will wipe it off
As if 'twere only rain. O, life! O, world!
Cover me! Let me be no more! To see
That perfect mirror of pure innocence   650
Wherein I gazed, and grew happy and good,
Shivered to dust! To see thee, Beatrice,
Who made all lovely thou didst look upon—
Thee, light of life—dead, dark! While I say, sister,
To hear I have no sister; and thou, Mother,   655
Whose love was a bond to all our loves—
Dead! The sweet bond broken!
                    (*Enter* CAMILLO *and Guards*)
                              They come! Let me
Kiss those warm lips before their crimson leaves   660
Are blighted—white—cold. Say farewell, before
Death chokes that gentle voice! O, let me hear
You speak!
BEATRICE   Farewell, my tender brother. Think
Of our sad fate with gentleness, as now: 665
And let mild pitying thoughts lighten for thee
Thy sorrow's load. Err not in harsh despair,
But tears and patience. One thing more, my child,
For thine own sake be constant to the love
Thou bearest us; and to the faith that I,   670
Though wrapped in a strange cloud of crime and shame,
Lived ever holy and unstained. And though
Ill tongues shall wound me, and our common name
Be as a mark stamped on thine innocent brow
For men to point at as they pass, do thou   675
Forbear, and never think a thought unkind
Of those, who perhaps love thee in their graves.
So mayest thou die as I do; fear and pain
Being subdued. Farewell! Farewell! Farewell!
BERNARDO   I cannot say, farewell!   680
CAMILLO   O, Lady Beatrice!
BEATRICE   Give yourself no unnecessary pain,
My dear Lord Cardinal. Here, Mother, tie
My girdle for me, and bind up this hair
In any simple knot; ay, that does well.   685
And yours I see is coming down. How often
Have we done this for one another! Now
We shall not do it any more. My Lord,
We are quite ready. Well, 'tis very well.

The Stone Theater at St. Petersburg. Early 19th-century print.
Photo Radio Times Hulton Picture Library

Nicolai Gogol

Nicolai Gogol (*1809–1852*), *Russia's first great realist writer,
wrote several plays, as well as numerous stories and the novel*
DEAD SOULS, *but his reputation as a dramatist rests almost entirely
on his first and most successful play,* THE INSPECTOR GENERAL.
*In its time this ebullient satire on provincial life heralded both
a new attitude and a new mode of writing and served for decades
as a model of what could be done by writers willing to break with
the rhapsodic Romanticism of the time. Its sturdiness of structure,
its frankness of outlook, and its comic vitality have served,
moreover, to make it one of the most popular plays in the Russian
repertory ever since.*

Chronology

1809   Born in Sarochinsk in the Ukraine.

1828   Left school and travelled to St. Petersburg.

c.1829   Discouraged by his failures to find work, he decided to go to America, but turned around in Sweden.

1830   Secured a position with the Department of Royal Estates.

1831   Wrote a volume of Ukrainian tales, *Evenings on a Farm Near Dekanka,* met Pushkin, and began writing a history of the Ukraine.

1834   Appointed as Reader of Medieval History at the University of St. Petersburg.

1835   Published two volumes of short stories and articles and finished *The Inspector General.*

1836   Published *The Nose* and *The Carriage;* wrote *Marriage,* a play,
and *Alfred the Great,* a historical play. He left St. Petersburg for Lübeck to remain abroad for twelve years. He returned to Russia only in 1838 and 1841.

1834–42   Wrote the first part of *Dead Souls.*

1841   Wrote *The Overcoat.*

1842–52   Wrote the second part of *Dead Souls.*

1847   Published a collection of letters, most of them in defense of serfdom and the policies of Nicholas I.

1848   Made a pilgrimage to Jerusalem.

c.1850   Fell under the influence of the religious fanatic Matthew Konstantinovski, who persuaded him to burn the second part of *Dead Souls.*

1852   He burned the second part of *Dead Souls* and died in March.

Selected Bibliography

Dupuy, Ernest, *The Great Masters of Russian Literature in the Nineteenth Century,* trans. Nathan Haskell Dole, London, 1886.

Lavrin, Janko, *Gogol,* London, 1926.

————, *Nicolai Gogol, 1809–1852; A Centenary Survey,* London, 1951.

Magarshack, David, *Gogol,* New York, 1957.

Nabokov, Vladimir, *Gogol,* Norfolk, Conn., 1944.

Perry, Henry Ten Eyck, *Masters of Dramatic Comedy,* Cambridge, Mass., 1939.

Wilson, Edmund, "Gogol: The Demon in the Overgrown Garden," *The Nation,* CLXXV (1952), 520–24.

THE
INSPECTOR GENERAL

by Nicolai Gogol

Translated by B. G. Guerney

Characters

ANTON ANTONOVICH SKVOZNIKDMUHANOVSKI, *the Mayor*

He has already grown grey in serving the public, and in his own way is very, very far from being a foolish man. Even though he is a taker of bribes, he nevertheless carries himself with very great dignity; he is rather serious—even a moralist, to some extent; he speaks neither too loudly nor too softly, neither too much nor too little. His every word is fraught with significance. His features are coarse and harsh, like those of every man who has started in an exacting service at the bottom of the ladder. His transitions from fear to joy, from abasement to arrogance, are quite rapid—those of a man with but roughly developed spiritual tendencies. He is generally togged out in his uniform frock coat, the buttons and buttonholes being prominent features, and in jackboots, highly polished and spurred. His hair is grizzled and closely cropped.

LUKA LUKICH HLOPOV, *Superintendent of Schools*

AMOS FEDOROVICH LYAPKINTYAPKIN, *the Judge*

A man who has read five or six books and is hence somewhat inclined to freethinking. A great hand for making conjectures, and for that reason lends profundity to his every word. The actor portraying him must always preserve a significant mien. He speaks in a bass, with a rather excessive drawl, hoarsely and strangled, like one of those grandfather clocks that go through a great deal of hissing as a preliminary to striking.

ARTEMII PHILIPOVICH ZEMIY ANIKA, *Director of Charities*

A very stout, unwieldy, and clumsy man but, for all that, as foxy as they come and a knave. No end obliging and as active as can be.

IVAN KUZMICH SHPEKIN, *the Postmaster*

So simple-hearted that he is naïve.

PETER IVANOVICH BOBCHINSKI *and* PETER IVANOVICH DOBCHINSKI

Both landowners—but of those who prefer to live in town instead of on their estates. Both are rather squat, rather short, both inquisitive and extraordinarily like each other. Both have neat little bay-windows. Both speak in a patter, helping that patter along with gestures and their hands—excessively so. DOBCHINSKI is a trifle taller and more serious than BOBCHINSKI, but BOBCHINSKI is more free and easy and lively than DOBCHINSKI.

IVAN ALEXANDROVICH HLESTACOV, *a government clerk from the capital*
A young man (twenty-three), very slender, very thin—somewhat on the silly side and, as the saying goes, there's nobody home. One of those fellows who, in the Civil Service, are called the lamest of lame-brains. He speaks and acts without any consideration of anything. He is utterly incapable of giving undivided attention to any one idea. His speech is jerky, and his words pop out in an utterly unexpected way. The more ingenuousness and simplicity the actor evinces in this role the more successful he will be. HLESTACOV'S dress is the last word in style.

OSSIP, *Hlestacov's Servant*
Like all servants who are getting on in years. He is serious of speech; his eyes are somewhat cast down; he is a moralist and fond of sermonizing to himself moral lectures intended for his master. His voice is almost always even; when he speaks with his master it takes on a stern, abrupt, and even a somewhat rude tone. He is far more intelligent than his master and therefore catches on to things more quickly, but he doesn't like to talk too much and, as a knave, prefers to keep his mouth shut. He is dressed in a long jacket, either grey or blue, and much worn.

CHRISTIAN IVANOVICH HÜBNER, *District Doctor*

FEDOR ANDREIEVICH LULUCOV, IVAN LAZAREVICH RASTACOVSKI, STEPAN IVANOVICH KOROBKIN, *Retired Officials*
Prominent citizens in the town.

STEPAN ILYICH UHOVERTOV, *Inspector of Police*

SVISTUNOV, PUGOVITZIN, DERZHIMORDA, *Policemen*
Typical bullies—while DERZHIMORDA is the prototype of all uniformed, small-town bullies.
ABDULIN, *a Shopkeeper*
MISHKA, *the Mayor's Servant*
WAITER *at the inn*
A GENDARME

ANNA ANDREIEVNA, *the Mayor's Wife*
A provincial coquette, not entirely elderly yet, her education about evenly divided between romantic novels and album verse, and cares about the pantry and the maidservants. Very inquisitive, and evinces vanity and conceit whenever there is a chance. Occasionally gets the upper hand of her husband, merely because he cannot find a ready answer. But this dominance is utilized only for trifles and consists of lectures and sneers. She has four complete changes of costume during the play.

MARIA ANTONOVNA, *the Mayor's Daughter*
WIFE OF THE SUPERINTENDENT OF SCHOOLS
KOROBKIN'S WIFE
THEVRONIA PETROVNA POSHLEPKINA, *the Locksmith's Wife*
CORPORAL'S WIDOW
Guests (both sexes); Shopkeepers; Townspeople; Petitioners

The parts not commented upon above do not require any special explanations. Their originals are almost always before our eyes.

The cast should pay particular attention to the last tableau. The concluding speech (the GENDARME'S*) must stun everybody, suddenly and simultaneously, like an electric shock. The entire group must shift its poses in an instant. The exclamation of astonishment must escape all the feminine characters simultaneously, as if from but a single pair of lungs. Failure to carry out this business exactly may ruin the whole effect.*

No use blaming the mirror if it's your own mug that's crooked.

FOLK SAYING.

Act One

Scene 1

A room in the Mayor's house. Early morning.
At rise: MISHKA *is dusting hurriedly; straightens out chairs and table, looks over room, exits.*
ANNA *enters, casts housewifely look over room, unnecessarily shifts a vase and adjusts a curtain, and, after another look, exits.*
MARIA *runs on girlishly, looks around her, peeps through windows, and, hearing someone approaching, scampers off in girlish fright.*
The MAYOR *stomps on; looks over the room absent-mindedly; he seems worried and takes a few steps through the room.*
Enter two POLICEMEN; *they flank the door. They are followed by the* DIRECTOR
OF CHARITIES, *the* SUPERINTENDENT OF SCHOOLS, *the* JUDGE, *and the*
DISTRICT DOCTOR.
They gather around the table amid a general atmosphere of expectancy)

MAYOR I've called you together, gentlemen, to let you in on a most unpleasant bit of news. There's an Inspector General on his way here. And not only that, but he has secret instructions too.
DIRECTOR OF CHARITIES What! An Inspector General?
JUDGE An Inspector General?
MAYOR An Inspector General, straight from the capital, and travelling incognito.
JUDGE There's a fix for you.
DIRECTOR OF CHARITIES Well, there hasn't been much trouble lately, so now we'll have plenty and to spare.

SUPERINTENDENT OF SCHOOLS Good Lord! And with secret instructions, 10 mind you!

MAYOR It's just as though I felt this coming. I kept dreaming all last night of a couple of rats—and most unusual they were somehow. Really, I'd never seen anything like them—all black, and of a most unnatural size! They came, sniffed around, and then ran off. Here, I'll read you a letter I've 15 received from Chmihov (*Turning to* DIRECTOR OF CHARITIES)—you know him. Here's what he writes: "Dear friend and benefactor"—(*Mumbles in a low voice to himself, his eyes running quickly through the letter*)—"to inform you . . ." Ah, here it is: "hasten to inform you, among other things, of the arrival of a governmental official with instructions to inspect the whole 20 province and particularly (*Raises his right index finger with great significance*) our district. I have learned this from most reliable sources, even though he pretends to be a private individual. Since I know that you are no more innocent of certain little transgressions than other people, inasmuch as you are a clever fellow and dislike to let slip anything that may come to hand." 25 (*Pause*) Oh well, we're all friends here! (*Resumes reading*) "I advise you to take certain precautions, for he may arrive at any moment—if he has not arrived already and is not stopping somewhere incognito. Yesterday I———" Well, from there on he deals with family matters: "Sister Anne has come to visit us with her husband; her brother has grown very fat but still plays 30 the fiddle"—and so on. There, that's the situation!

JUDGE Yes, the situation is an extraordinary one—simply extraordinary! There's something back of all this.

SUPERINTENDENT OF SCHOOLS (*To* MAYOR) But what's all this for? What brought this on? Why should the Inspector General be coming here? 35

MAYOR Why indeed! It must be fate evidently! (*Sighs*) Up to now, glory be, they were getting after the other towns; now they've caught up with us.

JUDGE (*To* MAYOR) I think there's a deeper motive here, and one of a political nature rather. This visit means that this country is . . . yes . . . this country is about to declare war and the Department of State, now—you see?— 40 has sent an official to find out if there is any disloyalty anywhere.

MAYOR You sure have taken in a lot of territory! And yet you're supposed to be intelligent! Disloyalty—in a county seat! Where do you think our town is, on a foreign border? Why, if you were to gallop at top speed for three years in any direction you wouldn't come to any other country! 45

JUDGE No, I must tell you you haven't grasped . . . you don't . . . the Government . . . the Government has some thoroughly considered ends in view; it doesn't matter that we're so far in the sticks—the Government still has something in the back of its mind———

MAYOR Whether it has or not, at least I've warned you, gentlemen. Look 50 sharp; I've taken certain steps as far as those things under my jurisdiction are concerned; I advise you to do likewise in your departments. (*Turning to* DIRECTOR OF CHARITIES) You especially! Beyond a doubt the official, as he is passing through, will want to see before anything else the charitable institutions under your supervision—therefore do everything possible to 55 make things look decent; you might put clean gowns on the patients in the hospital—and the patients themselves ought not to look as if they'd just been through a blacksmith's shop—the way they usually do when no visitors are expected.

DIRECTOR OF CHARITIES Oh well, that's a small matter. The clean gowns 60 can be managed if you like.

MAYOR Right! Also the patient's case-history ought to be written out on a card at the head of the bed, in Latin—or even in Greek. (*Turning to* DISTRICT DOCTOR) That's your department, since you're the District Doctor. Write down who the patient is, what day and month—and year—the patient 65 was admitted. It's a pity your patients smoke such strong tobacco that you sneeze your head off the minute you set foot in the hospital. Also it mightn't be a bad idea if there weren't so many of them—their number will immediately be put down to poor management or the inefficiency of the Doctor.

DIRECTOR OF CHARITIES Oh, as far as treatment goes, we (*Patting* DISTRICT 70 DOCTOR'S *arm*) don't go in for any fancy medicines—the more chances you give nature the better. Our patients are all simple folk: if any one of 'em is going to pop off, pop off he will anyway; and if he's going to get well, he'll get well just so. And besides, it would be rather difficult for our friend here (*Patting* DISTRICT DOCTOR'S *back*) to make himself understood—he 75 doesn't know a damned word in our language.

DISTRICT DOCTOR (*Mouths out something that sounds like a cross between*): "*Ja*" and "*Oui.*"

MAYOR (*To* JUDGE) And I'd advise you also to turn your attention to our administrative buildings. Take your ante-room, now, where the litigants 80 usually come—your court attendants have gotten into keeping their geese there, together with the goslings, and they're for ever getting underfoot. It's a praiseworthy thing, of course, for any man to go in for poultry-raising and things like that, and really, why shouldn't a man go in for raising poultry, even if he is a court attendant? Only, don't you know, it sort 85 of doesn't look right to do so in such a place. I meant to remark on this to you even before, but somehow it kept slipping my mind all the time.

JUDGE Why, I'll issue immediate orders to have every fowl removed to my kitchen this very day. You might drop in for dinner if you like.

MAYOR Besides that, it really looks bad to have all sorts of ragged wash 90 hanging out to dry in the courtroom itself. And right over the closet where you keep all the papers you've got your hunting crop hung up. I know you're fond of hunting, but just the same, for the time being, it might be better to remove it and then, when the Inspector General will have gone on his way, you can hang it up again if you like. Then there's your clerk. 95 (*Sighs*) Of course he's a walking, or rather staggering, encyclopaedia of the law, but he always smells as if he had just crawled out of a distillery—and that's not so good either. I meant to tell you about this too, ages ago, but my mind was taken off by something—I can't recall just what. There are certain palliatives if, as he claims, that is his natural odour; you might 100 suggest that he go in for garlic, or scallions, or some similar vegetable diet. The District Doctor might help out in this case with some preparation.

DISTRICT DOCTOR (*Mouths out same cross between*) *"Ja"* and *"Oui."*

JUDGE No, this is something beyond all help by now. He claims his nurse injured him when he was a child and that he's been giving off a slight reek of whisky ever since. 105

MAYOR Well, I merely remarked on it. As for internal arrangements and what the letter calls "slight transgressions," there's really nothing much I can say. Why, it's an odd thing even to talk about. There isn't a man living that hasn't some . . . irregularities on his conscience. Surely all that must 110 have been so arranged by the Lord God Himself, and it's all in vain that the freethinkers talk against it.

JUDGE Well, what do you consider transgressions? There are transgressions— and transgressions. I tell the whole world I take bribes—but what do those bribes consist of? Why, greyhound pups! That's an entirely different 115 matter!

MAYOR Well, whether you take them in the form of pups or of something else, they're all bribes.

JUDGE Oh, never! On the other hand, if somebody gets a fur-lined coat worth half a thousand, and his wife gets a shawl—— 120

MAYOR Well, suppose you do take your bribes in greyhound pups—what of it? But to make up for that you don't believe in God, you never set foot in a church, whereas I at least am firm in my faith and go to church every Sunday. But you—oh, I'm on to you! If you just start talking about the creation of the world it's enough to make one's hair stand on end. 125

JUDGE Why, I arrived at all that by my own self—through my own intelligence.

MAYOR All I have to say is that there are some cases where too much intelli- gence is worse than none at all. However, I merely mentioned the county courthouse in passing, whereas, if the truth were told, hardly anyone will ever look in there. It's such an enviable spot—the Lord God Himself watches 130 over it. On the other hand, you (*Turning to the* SUPERINTENDENT OF SCHOOLS), as the Superintendent of Schools, ought to be particularly careful as far as the teachers are concerned. They are, of course, men of learning and received their education in different colleges, and so on, but just the same they have some mighty queer ways about them—things that go hand in 135 hand with their learned calling, naturally. One of them—the fellow with the fat face, for instance, I can't recall his name—well, he simply can't get along without making a face every time he gets up on the platform. Like this (*Mugging*). And then he starts in fiddling with his necktie and ironing out his beard. Of course if he pulls a face like that at a pupil it isn't so bad; per- 140 haps that's even just as it should be—I'm no judge of that. But you just judge for yourself: if he should ever pull anything like that on a visitor, things might go very badly. The Inspector General, or somebody else, might con- sider that the face was meant for his benefit. And the devil alone knows what the upshot might be. 145

SUPERINTENDENT OF SCHOOLS But really, what am I to do with him? I've spoken to him several times already. Why, just the other day, when one of our foremost citizens happened to drop in on his class, this teacher pulled a face that was a masterpiece even for him. His heart was in the right place when he did it, but just the same it meant a bawling-out for me: Why were radical ideas being implanted in the minds of our young people, and so on?

MAYOR I am compelled to make a similar remark to you about the professor of history. He has a slew of learning in that head of his—anybody can see that; and he has accumulated no end of information—only why does he have to explain things with such earnestness that he forgets himself? I happened to hear one of his lectures; well, while he was speaking about the Assyrians and the Babylonians things weren't so very bad; but when he came to Alexander of Macedonia—well, I simply couldn't begin telling you what came over him! I thought there was a fire, by God! He dashes off the platform and, with all his might and main, smashes a chair against the floor! Well now, Alexander the Great is a hero and all that—but why smash chairs? The public funds are bound to suffer thereby——

SUPERINTENDENT Yes, he's a hot-headed fellow! I've already reprimanded him several times for this trait of his. "Well," he says, "do whatever you like, but I'm willing to lay down my life for scholarship!"

MAYOR Yes. Such, evidently, is the inexplicable decree of the fates: the man of learning is bound to be either a drunkard or to pull faces that are enough to curdle milk.

SUPERINTENDENT May God save me from ever having to teach! You're afraid of everything then; everyone interferes, everyone wants to show that he too has scholarship.

MAYOR Things wouldn't be so bad if it weren't for that damned incognito! Suppose he were to drop in? "Ah, so you're all here, my dear sirs? And who," he'll say, "who is the Judge?"—"Lyapkin-Tyapkin."—"Well, fetch this Lyapkin-Tyapkin here! And who is the Director of Charities?"—"Zemlyanika."—"Well, fetch this Zemlyanika here!"—There, that's what's bad!

POSTMASTER (*Entering*) Will you please explain to me, gentlemen, just what's what? Who's the official on his way here?

MAYOR Why, haven't you heard?

POSTMASTER I did hear something from Bobchinski. He dropped into see me at the Post Office.

MAYOR Well, what do you think of all this?

POSTMASTER What do I think? Why, I think it means we're going to be at war with the Turks.

JUDGE Just what I said! I was thinking the very same thing.

MAYOR Both of you are shooting at the moon!

POSTMASTER No, really—we're going to have a war with the Turks. It's those damned Frenchmen, always messing things up.

MAYOR What's all this talk of a war with the Turks? It's all very simple; it'll be us that will catch it and not the Turks. That's something we already know—I have a letter.

POSTMASTER Ah, in that case the war with the Turks is all off.

MAYOR (*To* POSTMASTER) Well, now, where do you stand?

POSTMASTER Well, what about me? Where do *you* stand?

MAYOR Where do I stand now? It isn't that I'm afraid exactly, but still, to a very slight extent . . . I'm uneasy about the business men and the gentry. They're saying that they're fed up with me; but, by God, even if I did accept a little something from this one or that one, it really was without any prejudice. I'm even wondering (*Taking the* POSTMASTER *by the arm and leading* 200 *him off to one side*)—I'm even wondering if there weren't some complaints against me. For really, now, why should an Inspector General be heading this way? I say, couldn't you—for all our sakes—take every letter that goes through the Post Office—both the incoming and the outgoing, and sort of . . . unseal each one a little, don't you know, and kind of glance it through, to 205 see if it doesn't contain some complaint or other, or simply an exchange of information? If it doesn't, it can be sealed up again—or it may be delivered just as it is, "opened by mistake," don't you know——

POSTMASTER Oh, I know, I know. You don't have to teach me. I do it not so much out of precaution but more out of curiosity; I'm no end fond of find- 210 ing out if there's anything new going on in the world. And it's mighty interesting reading, let me tell you. Now and then there's a letter that's simply delightful to read—what vivid descriptions, what tender passages! And what lofty morality—better than in any metropolitan daily!

MAYOR Well, now, tell me—haven't you read anything about a certain 215 official coming from the capital?

POSTMASTER No, there wasn't a word about any official from the capital—but there's a great deal about two other officials from two other cities. What a pity it is though that you don't get to look over the mail; there are some dandy items. One, for instance, where a certain lieutenant describes a ball to a 220 friend of his, in a most playful mood. Very, very good. He described that ball with great feeling—very great feeling. I've purposely kept that letter by me. Would you like to have me read it to you?

MAYOR Well, this is hardly the time for it. So do me that favour—if you should come across a complaint, or someone informing, just hold the letter back, 225 without the least hesitation.

POSTMASTER With the greatest of pleasure.

JUDGE Watch out; you'll get into trouble some day over that.

POSTMASTER Oh, Lord!

MAYOR (*Glaring at the* JUDGE) It's nothing, it's nothing! It would be another 230 matter if you were to use such letters publicly—but this is all in the family.

JUDGE Yes, this is beginning to look like a grand mess! I must own up I was coming to you (*Turning to* MAYOR) to present you with a fine pup. Own sister to the hound, you know. You must have heard about the lawsuit that two of our landowners have started recently—and now I'm in the seventh 235 heaven: I hunt rabbits with dogs on both their lands.

MAYOR My dear fellow, I have no heart now for your rabbits; I've got that damned incognito stuck in my head. I expect the door to fly open any minute —and bingo!

BOBCHINSKI (*Piling in with* DOBCHINSKI; *both are out of breath*) Something 240 extraordinary has happened!

DOBCHINSKI The news is so utterly unexpected!

ALL What is it? What is it?

DOBCHINSKI Whoever would have thought it? We come to the hotel——

BOBCHINSKI (*Breaking in on him*) Peter Ivanovich here and I come to the 245 hotel——

DOBCHINSKI (*Breaking in in his turn*) Oh now, Peter Ivanovich, if you'll only let me I'll tell everything——

BOBCHINSKI Oh no, if you'll only let me, now! Let me, do! You'd hardly be able to tell it, if it comes to that—— 250

DOBCHINSKI And you'll get all muddled up and won't remember everything.

BOBCHINSKI Yes, I'll remember—I will, so help me! Don't interrupt now—let me tell the story. Don't interrupt! Do me a favour, gentlemen—tell Peter Ivanovich not to interrupt——

MAYOR Come, speak, for the love of God! What's up? My heart is down in 255 my boots. Sit down, gentlemen! Help yourselves to chairs. Here's one for you, Bobchinski, and one for you, Dobchinski. (*All seat themselves around the two* PETER IVANOVICHES) Well now, out with it!

BOBCHINSKI Allow me, allow me—I'll tell everything in order. No sooner did I leave you, after you received the letter that confused you so much, than I 260 immediately dropped in on—now please don't interrupt, Peter Dobchinski! I already know everything—*everything*—EVERYTHING! Well then, if you please, I dropped in on Korobkin. But not finding this Korobkin at home, I turned in at Rastacovski's, and not finding Rastacovski in either, I dropped in on Shpekin, the Postmaster, you see, so's to tell him of the news you 265 received, and as I was coming from there, I met Peter Dobchinski——

DOBCHINSKI Near that place where they sell hot cakes——

BOBCHINSKI Right—near the place where they sell hot cakes. Very well. Having met Dobchinski, I said to him: "Have you heard the news our Mayor has received by mail, from a most reliable source?" But he'd already heard this 270 (*Turning to* MAYOR) from your housekeeper, whom you had sent to Poche-chuev's house to fetch something—I don't know just what it was——

DOBCHINSKI A small brandy keg——

BOBCHINSKI (*Pushing* DOBCHINSKI'S *hand away*) A small brandy keg. And so Dobchinski and I started off for Pochechuev's house—come, Dobchinski, 275 don't you interrupt me now! Please don't interrupt! So we started off for Pochechuev's house, but on the way Dobchinski says to me, he says: "You've no idea what a rumpus my stomach is raising! I haven't eaten a thing since morning, and my stomach is simply crying for food"—that's Dobchinski's stomach, mind you. "And," he says, "they've just delivered some fresh 280 salmon at the hotel, so we might just as well have a bite." No sooner had we stepped into the hotel than a young man——

DOBCHINSKI Not at all of a bad appearance, in civilian clothes——

BOBCHINSKI Yes, yes—not at all of a bad appearance, and in civilian clothes. Well, he strolls through the room, don't you know, with such a thought- 285 ful expression—such a serious face. And the way he carried himself! And (*Fluttering his fingers near his forehead*) he seems to have a lot up here—oh, a lot! It was just as though I had a hunch, and I said to Dobchinski here, I said: "There's more here than meets the eye! Yes, sir! By that time Dobchinski had already made a sign to the owner—you know him: his name is Vlass; 290

his wife was confined three weeks ago—a boy, it was, and what a lively one, to be sure—he's going to run an hotel, just like his daddy. So, having called this Vlass over, Dobchinski here ups and asks him, on the quiet: "Who," he asks, "may that young man be?" To which Vlass answers: "This young man," he says—I wish you wouldn't interrupt now, Dobchinski; please don't 295 interrupt! You could never tell the story, so help me—never. You lithp! You have but one tooth in your head, I know, and that one whistles. "This young man," Vlass says, "is a government official"—that's just what he said! "He's come from the capital now, and his name," Vlass says, "is Hlestacov, and he's on his way north, and," he says, "he's behaving mighty queer; he's staying 300 here for the second week now, hardly ever sets foot outside the place, calls for everything on credit, and won't lay out as much as a copper in cash." The minute he said that to me, it was just as though a light broke in on me from up above. "Ah!" I says to Dobchinski——

DOBCHINSKI No. Bobchinski, it was me that said "Ah!" 305

BOBCHINSKI All right, you said "Ah!" first, and then I said "Ah!" too. "Ah!" said Dobchinski and I. "And what reason would he have for staying here if his way lies north?" Yes, sir! Well, now, he and none other is that very official——

MAYOR What official? 310

BOBCHINSKI The official you were notified about, if you please—the Inspector General.

MAYOR (*Thoroughly frightened*) Whatever are you saying—the Lord be with you! It can't be he!

DOBCHINSKI It is he! He'll neither pay nor go away. Even his transportation 315 pass specifies that he's travelling north.

BOBCHINSKI It is he, it is he—honest to God it is he! What an observant fellow —he took in everything. He noticed that Dobchinski and I were eating salmon—the main reason we had chosen salmon was on account of Dobchinski's stomach—well, he looked right into our plates too. Why, I was 320 simply scared stiff!

MAYOR Lord have mercy on us sinners! What room has he got at the hotel?

DOBCHINSKI Number Five—under a flight of stairs.

BOBCHINSKI The same room where those army officers had a fight last year, the day they arrived. 325

MAYOR And has he been here long?

DOBCHINSKI Why, it must be two weeks by now.

MAYOR Two weeks! (*Aside*) May the Lord and all His saints deliver us! The corporal's widow was flogged within these two weeks! No provisions were issued to the convicts! The people are carrying on in the streets—and the 330 streets themselves are downright filthy! It's a disgrace and a shame!

(*Clutches his head*)

DIRECTOR OF CHARITIES (*To* MAYOR) Well, what do you say? Shall we start for the hotel and pay him a formal call?

JUDGE No, no! Let the clergy and the business men of the town call on him 335 first. Even according to procedure——

MAYOR No, no! Let me attend to everything in my own way. Life has had its difficult moments before this—but they passed, and there were even times when I was thanked. Who knows, perhaps God will deliver us this time as well. (*To* BOBCHINSKI) He's a young man, you say? 340

BOBCHINSKI Yes, a young man; twenty-three, or a little over twenty-four.

MAYOR So much the better; you can get things out of a youngster much quicker. It's hell when you come up against an old devil, but with a young fellow everything is right on the surface. You get everything set in your own bailiwicks, gentlemen, while I'll go by myself—or even with Dobchinski here, 345 if you like—privately, sort of strolling by, don't you know, and just dropping in to find out if our transient visitors are having any unpleasant experiences in our town. Hey there, Svistunov!

SVISTUNOV (*Rushing forward from his post near the door*) What do you wish, sir?

MAYOR Go this minute and fetch the Inspector of Police—or no, I'll need 350 you. Tell somebody else to go and bring the Inspector of Police to me here, as soon as possible, and then you come back here. (SVISTUNOV *bustles out, almost at a run*)

DIRECTOR OF CHARITIES (*To* JUDGE) Come, come! There really may be some trouble. 355

JUDGE Why, what have you to be afraid of? All you have to do is slap clean gowns on your patients and you've covered up everything.

DIRECTOR OF CHARITIES Gowns my eye! The patients are supposed to be on a strict diet, but there's such a reek of cabbage in all the corridors that you have to hold your nose. 360

JUDGE As for me, I feel quite calm. Really, now, who'd ever think of dropping in at a county courthouse? And if anyone should ever get it into his head to look over any of the papers, he'd curse the day he was ever born. It's fifteen years now that I've been on the bench, yet if I ever as much as glance at a report I just sigh and give it up as a bad job. Solomon himself wouldn't be 365 able to decide what's true in it and what isn't (*Exeunt* JUDGE, DIRECTOR OF CHARITIES, SUPERINTENDENT OF SCHOOLS, *and* POSTMASTER; *in the doorway they collide with the returning* SVISTUNOV)

MAYOR Well, is the carriage ready?

SVISTUNOV Right at the door. 370

MAYOR Go outside and—or, no, hold on! Go and fetch me . . . why, where are all the other police? Didn't I give orders for Prohorov to be here too? Where is he?

SVISTUNOV He's at the station house; the only thing is he's out of the running.

MAYOR What do you mean by that? 375

SVISTUNOV Why, just this—he was brought in this morning dead drunk. We've thrown two buckets of water over him so far, but he hasn't come to yet.

MAYOR (*Clutching his hair*) Oh, my God, my God! Go on out, fast as you can— or wait; run up to my room first—do you hear—and bring me my sword and my new hat. (*To* DOBCHINSKI) Well, let's go. 380

BOBCHINSKI Me too, me too! Let me go along too!

MAYOR No, no, Bobchinski—you can't, you can't! It'd be awkward, and, be- sides, there'd be no room for you in the carriage.

BOBCHINSKI That's nothing, that's nothing, I'll manage somehow; I could even trot behind your carriage, if you'll let me hold on. All I want is just one 385 tiny peep through the crack of the door, don't you know, to see how the young man acts——

MAYOR (*To* SVISTUNOV, *as he takes sword from him*) Run right away, take some of the police, and let each one of them take . . . Just see how nicked and banged up that sword is! That damned little shopkeeper Abdulin sees right well 390 that the boss of the town has an old sword but never thinks of sending him a new one! Oh, what a wise crowd! As it is, I'm thinking they're already drawing up complaints on the sly. (*Turning to* SVISTUNOV *again*) Let each one of your men take a street in hand—what in hell am I saying? Not a street but a broom—let each man take a broom in hand and sweep the whole street 395 that leads to the hotel, and sweep it clean—the street, I mean—do you hear me? And you watch out—you, you, I mean! I'm on to you; you pretend to be friendly but steal silver spoons and shove them in your bootleg. Watch out! I've got my ear to the ground. What did you pull on that shopkeeper Chernayev—eh? He gave you two yards of broadcloth for a uniform—so what 400 did you do but swipe the whole bolt? Watch out! You're taking bribes 'way above what your rank entitles you to! On your way now! (*Exit* SVISTUNOV)

(*Enter* INSPECTOR OF POLICE, *whom the* MAYOR *addresses*)

Ah, there you are! Tell me, for God's sake—did you get lost in the shuffle? What does it look like for the Inspector of Police to be away at such a time? 405

INSPECTOR OF POLICE I was here all the time—right at your gate.

MAYOR Very well, listen: The official from the capital has arrived. What steps have you taken?

INSPECTOR OF POLICE Why, I've followed your instructions exactly. I sent Pugovitzin and a few policemen under him to clean up the sidewalks. 410

MAYOR And where's Derzhimorda?

INSPECTOR OF POLICE Derzhimorda has gone off with the fire engine.

MAYOR And Prohorov is drunk?

INSPECTOR OF POLICE Drunk as a lord.

MAYOR How did you ever allow such a thing to happen? 415

INSPECTOR OF POLICE Why, the Lord only knows how it all came about. There was a brawl just outside the town yesterday; Prohorov went out there to preserve law and order, but was shipped back fried somehow.

MAYOR Tell you what you do: Pugovitzin, now, is a pretty tall fellow, even for a cop; so, for the looks of things, you station him at the bridge. And then 420 break up the old fence around where the shoemaker lives, as fast as you can, and make it look as if we were planning to build something there. The more demolition there's going on, the greater the inference that the head of the town is active. Oh, my God—why, I forgot that there are about forty cartloads of all sorts of garbage dumped behind that fence. What an atrocious 425 town this is! No sooner is a monument put up on any spot—or even a fence, for that matter—than they'll pile up all sorts of rubbish there! The devil alone knows where it all comes from! (*Sighs*) And another thing: should this newly arrived official get to asking anybody working for the city if they're

satisfied, let 'em say: "Yes, Your Honour"—but if any one of 'em should 430
turn out to be dissatisfied—well, I'll really give him something to be dissatisfied about later on. Ah me, but I have sinned; I have sinned much! (*Picks
up cardboard hatbox instead of his hat*) May God grant that all this blow over
as soon as possible, and after that I'll put up such a candle as no one has ever
yet put up; I'll make each son of a bitch of a shopkeeper in this town come 435
across with a hundred pounds of wax for that candle. Oh, my God, my God!
Come, let's go, Dobchinski! (*Puts on hatbox instead of hat*)

INSPECTOR OF POLICE Sir, that's a hatbox and not a hat.

MAYOR (*Hurling hatbox to one side*) So it is, so it is—and to hell with it! Yes,
and if he should ask why the chapel for the hospital hasn't been built yet— 440
for which a certain sum was appropriated five years ago—don't forget to say
that construction was begun on it but that it burned down. I even submitted
a report to that effect. Otherwise, like as not, somebody may get absent-
minded and blab his fool head off and say that it was never as much as
started. And you might tell Derzhimorda not to be so free with his fists; 445
that fellow gives shiners to everybody, just on general principles—both to the
just and the unjust. Let's go, let's go, Dobchinski! (*Goes out but immediately
returns*) Yes, and don't let the soldiers out into the street without their full
equipment; they're such a crummy lot they'll put their uniforms on, true
enough—but there won't be a thing underneath. (*Exeunt all*)   450

(ANNA, *wife of the* MAYOR, *and* MARIA, *his daughter, dash on*)

ANNA Where are they now? Where are they? Oh, Lord! (*Opening door*) Where's
my husband? Anton! Tony! (*Speaks fast*) And it's all your fault! It's all on
account of you! You had to start fussing around. "Just this pin! Just this
collar!" (*Runs up to window, leans out, and calls*) Tony, where are you going? 455
Where? What? Did he come? You mean it's the Inspector General? Has he a
moustache? What kind of a moustache?

MAYOR (*Off*) Later on, later on, my love!

ANNA Later on? What an idea—he'll tell me later! I won't have it later! Just
one word is all I want—what is he, a colonel? Eh? (*Contemptuously, with-* 460
drawing from window) He went off. Oh, I'll make him pay for this! And it's
all this girl's fault: "Mamma dear, Mamma dear, wait, I'll just pin up my
collar! I'll be ready right away!" There, that's what you get for your "Right
away!" And we didn't get to find out anything. And it's all her confounded
coquetry: she heard that the Postmaster was here and right off started 465
primping before the mirror—now from this side, now from the other. She
imagines he's after her! In reality he only makes a face at you the minute
your back is turned.

MARIA Well, Mother dear, what can we do about it now? We'll find out everything in a couple of hours anyway.   470

ANNA In a couple of hours? Thanks, no end! I'm ever so much obliged to you
for that answer! How is it you never thought of saying that in a month we
can find out still better? (*Leans out of window*) Avdotya! Eh? Well, Avdotya,
have you heard somebody has just come to town? You haven't? How stupid
you are! He shoos you away? Let him! You just go ahead and get it out 475

of him! You couldn't? That's the trouble with you—all you have on your mind is men and all that sort of nonsense. Eh? They went off too fast? Why, you should have run after the carriage. Go on, go on with you—this very minute! Do you hear me? Run and find out where they went. And be sure to find out everything, to the last detail. Find out who the stranger is and 480 what he looks like—you hear me? Look through the keyhole and find out everything—and also what colour his eyes are, whether they're dark or not, and come back in a minute or so—do you hear? Hurry, hurry, hurry hurry!

(She keeps shouting until the curtain comes down upon her and MARIA, *both of them standing at the window)* 485

Scene 2

(An attic room at the hotel—little more than a cubby-hole. A bed, a table, and a chair comprise practically all the furnishings.
A valise, an empty bottle, boots, a clothes-brush, and other such articles are strewn about the room)

OSSIP *(Discovered lounging on his master's bed with his boots on)* Oh hell, but I 490 want to eat! My stomach is raising as much of a racket as a whole regimental band! There, we'll never manage to reach home—and that's that. Well, what can you do about it? It's going on two months now that the great man left the capital. He squandered all his money on the way, the little darling; now he's stuck here with his tail betwixt his legs and is lying low. Why, there 495 was plenty—plenty and to spare—for travelling expenses; but no, he has to show off in every town we come to, you see. *(Mimics* HLESTACOV) "I say, Ossip, go and look at the rooms, and pick out the best; and you might order the very best they have for dinner—I can't dine poorly, I must dine well." It wouldn't matter so much if he really amounted to something—but then 500 he's nothing but a common pen-pusher, at the very bottom of the Civil Service! He'll scrape up an acquaintance with every passing stranger and then sit down to cards with him—and now just see what his cards have brought him to! Eh, I'm fed up with such a life! On the level, it's much better in the country; there may not be so much going on but, on the other hand, 505 there's less to worry you: you get yourself a wench, and loll in bed all day and eat dumplings. Of course, if the truth were told, there's no disputing that life in the capital is best of all. You must have money, naturally, but living there is grand and refined—theayters, and trained dogs dancing for your amusement, and everything else your heart may desire. And then there's 150 housemaids and such, flirting with you now and then—what girls! *(Smirks and shakes his head)* Hell, everybody treats you fine; you never hear an impolite word. If you get tired of walking, you just jump in a cab and sit there like a lord—and if you don't feel like paying the driver you don't have to really—there's hardly a house that hasn't got an exit on some other street; 515 all you've got to do is to give him the slip, quick, and then the devil himself won't ever find you. There's one bad thing though: one day you eat swell but the next you all but pass away from hunger—like now, f'r instance. And it's him that's to blame for everything. What can one do with a fellow like that? His old man sends him money for living expenses—and that's all he needs: 520 he's off on a spree the minute he gets it. He won't go a step on foot; not a day passes but he sends me out to get theayter tickets for him; but inside of a week, the first thing you know he's sending me out to sell a brand-new suit as a cast off. Sometimes he'll let everything go, down to his last shirt, until he's got nothing left but his worn-out uniform. Honest to God! The finest 525 cloth, mind you; he'll spend as much as a hundred and fifty for the coat alone —and then sell it for twenty; as for the pants, there's no need even mentioning them—they're practically given away. And what's the reason for all this? It's all because he won't get down to business; instead of going to his office he traipses around or plays cards. Oh, if your old man was ever to find out! 530 He wouldn't give a damn that you're working for the Government but just let your pants down and let you have it so hot you'd be eating your meals off a mantel for a week. If you've got a job, attend to it. Why, just now the proprietor said he wouldn't send up any more meals till you've settled for what you've had up to now; well, and what'll happen if we don't? (*Sighs*) Oh, 535 Lord, what wouldn't I do for a bowl of soup! I feel I could eat up the whole world now. I think there's somebody coming; it must be he, for sure.

(*Hastily gets off the bed*)

HLESTACOV (*Entering*) Here, take these (*Hands cap and cane to* OSSIP) Ah, loafing on my bed again? 540

OSSIP What would I want to be loafing on your bed for? Do you think I never saw a bed before, or what?

HLESTACOV You're lying; you were so loafing on it—see how you mussed it all up.

OSSIP Why, what would I be wanting with it? Do you think I don't know 545 what a bed is? I have me own legs and I can stand—what do I need your bed for?

HLESTACOV (*Pacing the room*) Take a look—maybe there's a pinch of tobacco left in the wrapper.

OSSIP Well now, how should there be any left there? You smoked the last 550 shred four days ago.

HLESTACOV (*Still pacing the room, twists his mouth in all sorts of ways, then in a loud and assured voice*) Listen, Ossip! I say, now——

OSSIP What do you want?

HLESTACOV (*In a voice just as loud but no longer as assured*) You go there—— 555

OSSIP Where?

HLESTACOV (*In a voice not at all assured nor loud—in fact very near begging*) Why, go down to the dining-room . . . tell them . . . to send up something for my dinner——

OSSIP Well, no, I don't feel like going there at all. 560

HLESTACOV How dare you, you idiot!

OSSIP Why, just so; it won't make no difference even if I was to go—nothing will come of it. The proprietor said not to serve you no more dinner.

HLESTACOV How dare you refuse? What sort of nonsense is this?

OSSIP And that's not all neither, "I," he says, "will even go to the Mayor; it's 565 the third week now that I haven't seen the colour of your master's money. Why, you and your master," he says, "are both dead beats, and your master is up to all sorts of tricks. We now," he says, "have seen plenty of such con-men and scoundrels."

HLESTACOV Well, I can see you're only too happy to be telling me all this, 570 you brute.

OSSIP "If things go on like this," he says, "every man jack will be coming to this place, make himself at home, run up a bill, and in the end you won't be able to kick him out even. I got no intentions of fooling around," he says. "I'm going straight off to lodge a complaint, so's to get him out of here— 575 and into jail."

HLESTACOV There, there, you fool, that'll do! Go on, go on—tell him what I said. What a coarse brute!

OSSIP Why, I'd better call the proprietor himself to come up to you.

HLESTACOV Who wants the proprietor now? You go and tell him yourself. 580

OSSIP Oh now, really——

HLESTACOV Go ahead then, and the devil take you! Go on—call the proprietor! (*Exit* OSSIP) Oh, but I'm famished! Dreadfully famished. I took a little walk, just so, thinking maybe my hunger would pass—but no, it won't, the devil take it! Well, if I hadn't gone off on a bat on the way here, there would 585 have been money enough to take me home. That damned infantry captain all but knocked the props from under me—he can deal the most amazing hands to himself at stuss!* He sat in at the game for no more than a quarter of an hour or so—and did he trim me! But completely. And yet, for all that, how I'd have liked to have another go at him! Only circumstances were against 590 it. Circumstances are everything. What a vile hick town this is! They won't give you a thing on credit at the food stores. Why, that's downright mean. (*Whistles: at first an aria from "Robert le Diable," then the "Red Sarafan,"* and finally trails off into something that's neither here nor there*) Well, I guess nobody wants to come up. 595

WAITER (*Entering*) The proprietor told me to ask what you wanted.

HLESTACOV Ah there, my good fellow! And how are you?

WAITER Well enough, glory be.

HLESTACOV And how's everything around the place? Everything going nicely, eh? 600

WAITER Yes, glory be—quite nicely.

HLESTACOV Place all filled up?

WAITER Oh yes, quite—glory be.

HLESTACOV I say, my good man, my lunch hasn't been sent up yet; so won't you hurry things up a bit, please; you see, I've something to attend to right 605 after lunch.

WAITER Well now, the proprietor said he weren't going to send up nothing more on the cuff. Why, he was all set to go and lodge a complaint with the Mayor today.

---

588 A card game.

593 *Robert le Diable* (1831) is an opera by Giacomo Meyerbeer; the "Red Sarafan" a waltz by Luigi Arditi. A sarafan is a long mantle, often worn by Russian peasant women.

HLESTACOV Why, what's the idea of complaining? Judge for yourself, my 610
dear fellow—what's to be done now? Why, I *must* eat. If things go on like this
I'm liable to waste away to nothing. I'm as hungry as hungry can be—and
that's no joke either.

WAITER Right, sir. But the boss said: "I ain't giving him no more dinners till
he's paid for those he's already et." Them's his very words. 615

HLESTACOV Come now, reason with him—persuade him.

WAITER Why, what kind of arguments could I give him?

HLESTACOV You just explain to him, in all seriousness, that I must eat. Money
isn't everything! He thinks just because it may do no harm for a coarse lout
like himself to go hungry for a day, others can go hungry as well. Who 620
ever heard of such a thing!

WAITER I'll talk with him if you like. (*Exit*)

HLESTACOV (*Solo*) It'll be rotten if he refuses outright to give me anything to eat.
Never have I wanted to eat so much as now. Should I put some of my clothes
in circulation perhaps? Sell my trousers maybe? No; it's better to starve 625
but come home with the latest outfit from the capital. What a pity that I
couldn't get a carriage on credit from some first-class livery stable, for it would
have been a fine thing, deuce take it, to arrive in the old home town in a fine
carriage, to drive up at a devilish speed to the grand entrance of some neigh-
bouring squire, with all the carriage lanterns lit and Ossip perched behind, 630
tagged out as a flunkey. I can imagine what a stir that would create! "Who's
that? What's up?" And just then a footman enters. (*Drawing himself up and
impersonating a footman*) "Ivan Alexandrovich Hlestacov, from Petersburg;
are you at home?" Why, the yokels don't even know what "at home" means!
If some country bumpkin of a squire does come to see them, he barges 635
right into the drawing-room, bear that he is. A fellow can walk up to one of
the neighbour's pretty little daughters: "How delighted I am, madam———"
(*Rubs his hands, bowing and scraping*) Ugh! (*Makes a wry face*) I'm actually
nauseated, that's how badly I want to eat.

(*Enter* OSSIP) 640

Well, how did you make out?

OSSIP They're bringing up lunch.

HLESTACOV (*Clapping his hands and bouncing on a chair*) Goody, goody, goody!

WAITER (*Entering with a loaded tray*) This is the last time, now, that the boss is
giving you anything. 645

HLESTACOV Oh, your boss! I don't give a whoop for your boss! What have you
there?

WAITER Soup and a roast.

HLESTACOV What, only two courses?

WAITER That's all, sir. 650

HLESTACOV How preposterous! I refuse to accept that! You just tell your boss this
will never do! What does he think he's doing? This isn't enough———

WAITER No, the boss says even this is much too much.

HLESTACOV And why is there no gravy?

WAITER There just isn't any. 655

HLESTACOV And why isn't there? I saw with my own eyes as I was passing through the kitchen that there were a great many things being prepared. And in the dining-room this morning I saw two chubby little men putting away salmon and lots of other things.

WAITER Well, there is gravy—and at the same time there ain't. 660

HLESTACOV What do you mean by that?

WAITER Why, there just ain't.

HLESTACOV But what about the salmon and the steaks and the chops?

WAITER That's for them as are the real thing——

HLESTACOV Oh, you fool! 665

WAITER Yes, sir.

HLESTACOV You're something of a swine. How is it they eat those things and I don't? Why can't I have the same, the devil take it? Aren't they just guests, the same as I'am?

WAITER Why, everybody knows they ain't in the same class. 670

HLESTACOV What class are they in then?

WAITER They're real guests. Everybody knows they pay hard cash.

HLESTACOV I don't want to argue with you, you fool. (*Ladles out some soup and eats*) You call this soup? You must have put plain dish-water into the tureen; it hasn't the least taste—but plenty of smell! I don't want this soup—bring 675 me a different kind!

WAITER I'll take it away then. The boss said if you didn't like it, it was all right with him.

HLESTACOV (*Protecting the food with his arms*) There, there, there! Leave it alone, you fool. You must have gotten used to treating others like that—I'm 680 different, fellow! You can't do this to me—and I advise you not to try. (*Eats*) Oh, Lord, what soup! (*But he continues to eat*) I don't think anybody in all this world has ever yet tasted a soup like that; there are some feathers floating around in it instead of good, honest fat. (*Fishes out a bit of chicken and cuts it up*) Oh, oh, oh—what chicken! Let me have the roast. There's a little soup 685 left over—you may have it, Ossip. (*Tackling the roast*) What kind of roast is this? This is no roast.

WAITER Well, what would you call it?

HLESTACOV The devil alone knows what it is, only it's not a roast. It's just a boot sole, well done. (*Eating*) What cheats, what scoundrels! Look at the 690 food they give you! One mouthful is enough to make your jaw ache for a week. (*Picking his teeth with his fingers*) What low-down creatures! Just like splinters—can't pull them out even, no matter how you try; stuff like that will ruin your teeth. What cheats! (*Wipes mouth with napkin*) Anything else?

WAITER No. 695

HLESTACOV Scoundrels! Cheats! Why, if there were only a little gravy, at least, or a bit of pastry—the good-for-nothings! All they know is to take the stranger in. (WAITER *and* OSSIP *clear off the dishes and carry them out*) Honestly, it's just as if I hadn't eaten at all; I've simply whetted my appetite. If I had any change at all I'd send out for a loaf. 700

OSSIP (*Entering*) The Mayor has just arrived for some reason, and is making inquiries about you.

HLESTACOV (*Frightened*) There it is! What a damned beast that proprietor is—

he's already managed to start proceedings! What if he should really lug me off to jail? Well, what of it? As long as I'm treated as a gentleman I may 705 as well go. . . . No, no, I don't want to go! The town is chock-full of officers and natives promenading around—and, as if for spite, I've been putting on airs and winking at a certain merchant's daughter. She winked right back at me, if it comes to that. No, I don't want to go. Why, who does the proprietor think he is? When you come to think of it, how dare he do such a thing? 710 Really, what does he take me for now? A plain business man or a manual labourer? (*Screwing up courage and drawing himself up*) I'll walk right up to him and tell him to his face: "How dare you! How——" (*A knock on the door, door knob turns*—HLESTACOV *turns pale and shrinks into himself*) (MAYOR *enters, followed by* DOBCHINSKI, *and stops.* HLESTACOV *and the* 715 MAYOR, *both equally frightened, stare at each other for a few moments, their eyes popping*)

MAYOR (*Recovering a little and standing at attention*)   Hope you are well, sir!

HLESTACOV (*Bowing*)   My respects, sir!

MAYOR   Pardon my intrusion——

HLESTACOV   Not at all. 720

MAYOR   It is my duty, as Chief Magistrate of this town, to see that no advantage is taken of transients and people of standing——

HLESTACOV (*Stammering a little at first but, towards the end of the speech, quite loudly*) Well, what can one do. . . . It's hardly my fault. . . . I really intend to pay— 725 I expect money from home—(BOBCHINSKI *peers in at the door*) He is far more at fault than I am; he serves me beef as tough as shoe leather; as for his soups, the devil knows what he puts in 'em; I just had to throw some out of the window. He starves me for days at a time. And his tea is most peculiar; you could never tell it's tea by its smell—it stinks of fish. Why should I then 730 . . . I never heard of such a thing!

MAYOR (*Taken aback*)   Do forgive me—I'm not to blame really. The beef I inspect at the markets is always good. It's brought in by reliable dealers, sober and well-behaved people. I really don't know where he gets his. But if anything isn't just so, why, then . . . May I suggest that you come with 735 me to other quarters——

HLESTACOV   No, I don't want to. I know just what you mean by other quarters —the jail. Why, what right have you got to say that to me? How dare you? Why, I'll . . . I work for the Government at the capital! (*Putting on a bold front*) Why, I—I—I—— 740

MAYOR (*Aside*)   Oh, good Lord, how angry he is! He has found out everything— those damned shopkeepers have spilled everything.

HLESTACOV (*Blustering*)   Why, if you were to come down with all your men I wouldn't go! I'll take the matter directly to the Prime Minister! (*Thumping the table*) Who do you think you are, you . . . you—— 745

MAYOR (*Drawing himself up at attention, with his whole body trembling*)   Have pity on me—don't ruin me! I have a wife and little ones . . . You don't have to ruin a man!

HLESTACOV   I simply won't have it! What's all that got to do with me? Just because you have a wife and little ones I have to sit in prison? That's just 750 dandy! (BOBCHINSKI *peeks in through door and, thoroughly frightened, hides himself*) No, thanks ever so much, but I won't have it!

MAYOR (*Trembling*) It's all due to my inexperience—by God, it's all my inexperience. And shortage of funds. . . . You may judge for yourself: my official salary wouldn't keep me in tea and what goes with it. And if there 755 have been any bribes, why, they were the merest trifles—something for the table, or enough cloth for a suit. As for that corporal's widow who runs a shop, and whom I'm supposed to have flogged—why, that's just slander, by God! It was invented by those who would wrong me; they're the sort who are ready to attempt my life—— 760

HLESTACOV Well, what of it? I have nothing to do with them. (*Thoughtfully*) However, I don't know why you talk of those who would wrong you and of some corporal's widow or other. A corporal's wife is something else entirely; but as for me, you dare not flog me—you've a long way to go before you can do that. What else? Look whom we have here! I'll pay—I'll pay 765 my hotel bill, but I haven't anything just now. That's precisely why I'm stuck here—because I haven't got a copper on me.

MAYOR (*Aside*) Oh, what a fox! Just see what he's aiming at! What a smoke screen he puts up! Let anybody that wants to try to make him out. A fellow doesn't know what side to tackle him from. Oh well, come what may, let's 770 have a try at him! Can't lose much by making a blind stab. (*Aloud*) If you are really short of cash, or anything else, why I'm at your service, at a moment's notice. It's my duty to help out transients.

HLESTACOV Yes, yes, lend me some money. I'll pay off the proprietor. All I'd like to have is a couple of hundred—or even less. 775

MAYOR (*Offering him a sheaf of bank notes*) Exactly two hundred; you don't even have to bother counting them.

HLESTACOV (*Accepting the money*) Thanks ever so much. I'll send this back to you the minute I get to my country estate. I don't put off things like that. You're a noble fellow, I can see that. Things are entirely different now. 780

MAYOR (*Aside*) Well, glory be to God, he took the money. Looks as if things will go smoothly from here on. Just the same, I shoved four hundred on him instead of two.

HLESTACOV Hey there, Ossip! (*Enter* OSSIP) Call that waiter in here! (*Exit* OSSIP. HLESTACOV *turns to the* MAYOR *and* DOBCHINSKI) But why are you stand- 785 ing? Be good enough to sit down. (*Urging the reluctant* DOBCHINSKI) Do sit down, I beg of you!

MAYOR It doesn't matter; we'll just stand.

HLESTACOV Be good enough to sit down. I can now see perfectly the goodness of your natures and your hospitality; for I must confess that I was already 790 thinking that you had come to—— (*To* DOBCHINSKI) Do sit down! (MAYOR *and* DOBCHINSKI *take seats.* BOBCHINSKI *peeks in at the door and listens*)

MAYOR (*Aside*) I should have acted more boldly. He wants to be considered incognito. Very well, we too will put up a bluff; we'll act as if we weren't at all aware just who and what he is. (*Aloud*) As we—Peter Ivanovich 795

Dobchinski here—he's a landowner hereabouts—and I—as we were walking by in the line of duty, we purposely dropped in here, to find out whether the guests were being treated right, because I'm not like some other mayors, who'll have nothing to do with anything; but, outside of any call of duty, out of Christian regard for my fellow men, I want a good reception to be 800 extended to every mortal, and in this instance, as if in reward, chance has afforded me such a pleasant acquaintance!

HLESTACOV Same here—I'm very happy also. Had it not been for you, I confess I'd have been stuck here for a long time; I had no earthly idea how I was to square the bill.   805

MAYOR (*Aside*) Tell us another! He didn't know how he was to pay the bill! (*Aloud*) May I make so bold as to ask you—where, and to what places, you wish to travel?

HLESTACOV I'm on my way to the Saratov* province—to my own country estate.   810

MAYOR (*Aside, his face assuming an ironic expression*) To the Saratov province indeed! Why, he doesn't even blush! Oh, you've got to be up your toes with this fellow! (*Aloud*) That's a very good idea, travelling. As for reaching there, they're saying that on the one hand there's a lot of bother in getting horses but, on the other hand, there's nothing like a trip for diverting 815 the mind. For I guess it's mostly for your own pleasure that you're going there?

HLESTACOV No, my father demands that I come; the old gentleman is angry because up to now I haven't worked myself up to anything worth while at the capital. He's under the impression that the minute you get there 820 they start out handing decorations to you. Yes, I'd like to send him there and see how much headway he'd make in some department.

MAYOR (*Aside*) Just listen, if you please, to the line he hands out—he even dragged in his old man! (*Aloud*) And are you planning to stay there long?

HLESTACOV Really, I don't know. For my father is a stubborn old pepper-pot 825 and as stupid as a log. I'll let him have it straight from the shoulder: "Do as you like," I'll tell him, "but I can't live out of the capital. For after all, for what earthly reason should I ruin my life among a lot of hayseeds? The demands of the present day aren't what they used to be; my soul longs for civilized ways."   830

MAYOR (*Aside*) What a masterly liar! He lies and he lies, but there's never a loose end to give him away. And yet he isn't much to look at, and a kind of short little fellow—looks as if you could squash him on your thumbnail. But you just wait—I'll catch you slipping up yet. I'll sure make you tell us more! (*Aloud*) That was a very just remark you were pleased to 835 make. What can one accomplish out in the sticks? Why, take this very town; you don't sleep of nights, trying to do your best for your country, without sparing anything, but as for any reward, nobody knows when it'll come. (*Looks over the room*) This room seems sort of damp, doesn't it?

HLESTACOV It's a rat hole, and I've never seen the like of the bed-bugs here 840 —they bite like dogs.

809 In southeastern Russia.

MAYOR Well now! Such a distinguished guest—and he has to suffer! And from whom, mind you? From worthless bed-bugs, who should never have come into this world! Like as not, this room is dark as well?

HLESTACOV Oh yes, pitch dark. The proprietor has gotten into the habit 845 of not giving me any candles. At times one feels like doing something, or reading; you may get a notion of writing something, but you can't; it's dark in here—so dark!

MAYOR Dare I request that you . . . But no, I'm not worthy of it——

HLESTACOV Why, what is it? 850

MAYOR No, no! I'm not worthy of it—I'm not worthy of it!

HLESTACOV Come, what's it all about?

MAYOR If I may make so bold—I've a fine room for you in my house, light, and so comfortable. . . . But no; I myself feel that it would be too great an honour. . . . Don't be angry at me! Really, by God, I suggested it to 855 you out of sheer simple-heartedness——

HLESTACOV On the contrary, I'll accept with pleasure if you like. It would be far more pleasant for me in a private home than in this pot-house.*

MAYOR Oh, that would make me ever so happy! And it'll make my wife ever so happy too! For that's just my nature: I've been taught to practise 860 hospitality ever since my childhood—especially if the guest is a civilized person. Don't get the idea that I'm saying this just out of flattery. No, that's one vice I'm free from; I say this with all my soul.

HLESTACOV Thank you ever so much. I'm the same way myself: I've no great love for two-faced people. I find your frankness and cordiality very much to 865 my liking, and I'll confess I never ask for anything more than loyalty and respect—and respect and loyalty.

(*Enter* WAITER *and* OSSIP. BOBCHINSKI *peeks in at door*)

WAITER Did you call, sir?

HLESTACOV Yes, let's have the bill. 870

WAITER I already handed you a second bill just a while back.

HLESTACOV I no longer remember what your silly bills were. Come now, what did they amount to?

WAITER You ordered a full dinner the first day, while on the second you had just a snack of smoked salmon, and after that you began putting every- 875 thing on the cuff——

HLESTACOV You fool—are you going to start itemizing everything? How much do I owe altogether?

MAYOR (*To* HLESTACOV) Don't upset yourself—he can wait. (*To* WAITER) Go on, git! The money will be sent you. 880

HLESTACOV An excellent idea that! (*Puts away his money. Exit* WAITER. BOBCHINSKI *peeks in through door*)

MAYOR Would you care to inspect some of the institutions in the town, such as the Department of Public Charities and so on?

HLESTACOV Why, what would I find there? 885

MAYOR Oh, look them over just so; you'll see how the administration carries on . . . the general system . . . it might be of interest to a visitor——

858 An ale-house of low repute.

HLESTACOV With the greatest pleasure; I'm at your service. (BOBCHINSKI *puts his head in through door*)

MAYOR Also, you may wish, later on, to go from there to the District School, to see our methods of teaching the various subjects.

HLESTACOV By all means, by all means.

MAYOR After that, if you like, you can visit the prison and the town hoosegows —I mean jails—to see how we treat our prisoners.

HLESTACOV But why pick on jails? It would be better if we inspected just the charitable institutions.

MAYOR Whatever you wish. Do you intend to go in your carriage, or will you share my buggy with me?

HLESTACOV Why, I'd better go with you in your buggy.

MAYOR (*To* DOBCHINSKI) Well, there won't be any room for you now.

DOBCHINSKI It doesn't matter; I'll manage.

MAYOR (*To* DOBCHINSKI, *in a low voice*) Listen, you run along—but, what I mean, run as fast as your legs will carry you—and deliver two notes for me; one to Zemlyanika, at the Department of Public Charities, and the other to my wife. (*To* HLESTACOV) I'll make so bold as to ask your permission to dash off just a line to my wife in your presence, so that she may prepare herself to receive our distinguished guest——

HLESTACOV Oh, but whatever for? However, here's the ink; the only thing is, I don't know about paper . . . unless you use this bill——

MAYOR It won't take me but a minute. (*Writes, at the same time talking to himself*) There, we'll see how things will go after a good lunch and a nice, pot-bellied bottle. Yes, we have a provincial Madeira—not much to look at, but it's strong enough to knock an elephant off its feet. If only I could find out just who he is and to what extent I must be on my guard against him! (*Having finished, the* MAYOR *hands the notes to* DOBCHINSKI, *who approaches the door, but at that moment it flies open and* BOBCHINSKI, *who had been eavesdropping on the other side, tumbles in. General exclamations.* BOBCHINSKI *picks himself up*)

HLESTACOV I say, you haven't hurt yourself by any chance?

BOBCHINSKI Not at all, not at all—nothing out of the way—just a bump on the bridge of my nose. I'll run over to the Doctor's; he's got a certain kind of plaster, and the bump will go away in no time.
(*Exit* DOBCHINSKI, *clucking*)

MAYOR (*Makes a gesture of disapproval to* BOBCHINSKI, *then turns to* HLESTACOV) It's really nothing. This way, please, I beg you! And I'll tell your man to bring your things over. (*To* OSSIP) You bring everything over to my place —the Mayor's now; anybody will show you the way. (*To* HLESTACOV) Right this way! (*Lets* HLESTACOV *precede him, but, before following him, manages to turn around and say reproachfully to* BOBCHINSKI) What a man you are! You couldn't find any other place to flop? And you had to stretch out at full length—it looked like hell! (*Exits, followed by* BOBCHINSKI. *Curtain*)

Act Two

(Setting same as Act One, Scene 1. At rise: ANNA *and* MARIA *are standing near the window, in the same poses as at Curtain of Act One, Scene 1)*

ANNA There, we've been waiting a whole hour, and it's all your fault, with your stupid primping. You were all dressed, but no, you had to fuss around. I shouldn't have listened to the girl at all! How provoking! Not a soul in 5 sight; you might think it was on purpose. You'd think the whole town died out.

MARIA But really, Mamma dear, we'll find out everything in just a minute or two. Why, Avdotya is bound to be back soon. *(Looks attentively through window and emits a little scream)* Ah, Mamma dear, Mamma dear, some- 10 body's coming! There, at the end of the street!

ANNA Where do you see anybody coming? You're for ever imagining one thing or another. Well yes, there is somebody coming. But just who can it be? Rather short . . . in a frock-coat . . . whoever could it be? Eh? I must say it's provoking! Who in the world could it be? 15

MARIA It's Dobchinski, Mamma dear

ANNA How could it be Dobchinski? You're always making things up out of thin air. It's not Dobchinski at all. *(Waves her handkerchief)* I say, walk a little faster! A little faster!

MARIA Really, Mamma dear, it is Dobchinski. 20

ANNA There you go—just to be arguing! I'm telling you it isn't Dobchinski.

MARIA Well now? Well now, Mamma dear? You can see for yourself it's Dobchinski.

ANNA Well, yes, it's Dobchinski. I can see that now—so what are you arguing about? *(Shouting through window)* Walk faster! Faster! You walk so slowly! 25 Well now, where are they? Eh? Oh, you can tell me from there—it doesn't matter. What? Is he very stern? Eh? And what about my husband? My husband, I said! *(Stepping away from window a little, with vexation)* What a stupid creature—he won't tell me a thing until he's inside! *(Enter* DOB-CHINSKI, *all out of breath)* There, now, tell me please—doesn't your con- 30 science bother you? I depended upon you as the only decent man, but everybody dashed out and you had to go right after them! And up to this minute I can't get a sensible word out of anybody. Aren't you ashamed of yourself? Why, I was godmother to your little boy and girl, and that's how you acted towards me! 35

DOBCHINSKI As God is my witness, dear lady, I ran so hard to pay my respects to you that I can't catch my breath. Greetings, Maria Antonovna.

MARIA How d'you do?

ANNA Well, what's what? Come, tell me all about it.

DOBCHINSKI Your husband sent you this little note—— 40

ANNA *(Taking note)* Well, who is he? A general?

DOBCHINSKI No, he isn't, but he's every bit as good as any general. So well educated, and his every action is so impressive.

ANNA Ah, then it must be the very same man they wrote my husband about.

DOBCHINSKI He's the real thing. I was the first one to find this out—together 45
with Bobchinski.

ANNA Do tell me everything at last! What happened, and how did it happen?

DOBCHINSKI Well, glory be to God, everything went off auspiciously. At first
he received your husband a trifle sternly, true enough; he was huffy and said
that nothing about the hotel suited him, for one thing, but he wouldn't 50
come here either, and that he didn't feel like sitting in jail for his sake; but
later on, when he found out how innocent your husband was and when
he had talked a little more intimately with him, he at once changed his
ideas, and, glory be, everything went well. They've gone off now to inspect
the charitable institutions. But I really must tell you that your husband 55
was thinking whether a secret complaint hadn't been lodged against him;
I myself had a bit of a scare too.

ANNA Why, what have you to be afraid of? You aren't in any government
service.

DOBCHINSKI Oh, just on general principles. You know how it is—when a 60
high dignitary speaks you naturally feel scared.

ANNA Oh well! However, all this is nonsense—tell me what he looks like?
Is he old or young now?

DOBCHINSKI He's young—a young man of twenty-three or close to it, yet he
talks just as if he were an old man. "I'll come to your house," he says, "if 65
you like," and (*Gesturing vaguely*) this and that—it was all done so grandly.
"I," he says, "am fond both of reading and writing; but I find it's a nuisance
because this room is a trifle dark."

ANNA But what's he like, you provoking man—dark-haired or light?

DOBCHINSKI No, he's more on the auburn side, and his eyes dart here and 70
there ever so quickly, like little animals of some sort—it actually makes you
feel uneasy.

ANNA Let's see what Tony writes me. (*Reads*) "I write you in haste, dearest,
to inform you that my situation was a most lamentable one; but, placing my
trust in the mercy of God, for two pickles, extra, and a half-portion of 75
caviare, one-twenty-five——" (*Stops reading*) I can't understand a thing:
what have pickles and caviare to do with all this?

DOBCHINSKI Why, your husband wrote on scrap paper, he was in such a hurry;
there must have been some bill written on it.

ANNA Ah yes—that's it. (*Resumes reading*) ". . . but, placing my trust in the 80
mercy of God . . . it seems as if everything will come out right. Get a room
ready as quickly as you can for a distinguished guest—the one with the yellow
wallpaper; as for dinner, don't bother preparing anything extra, because we
are going to have a bite at the Department of Public Charities, with its
Director. But as for wines, order as much as possible; tell that shopkeeper 85
Abdulin to send his best, for otherwise I will turn his whole wine cellar
upside-down myself. Kissing your hand, my dearest, I remain yours, Anton
Skvoznik-Dmuhanovski——" Oh, my God, this must surely be attended
to as soon as possible. Hey, who's there? Mishka!

DOBCHINSKI (*Making a dash for the door and shouting*) Mishka! Mishka! 90
Mishka! (*Enter* MISHKA)

ANNA Look here, dash over to Abdulin's shop . . . hold on, I'll give you a note. (*Sitting down at a desk and speaking as she writes*) You give this note to Sidor, the coachman; let him run over to Abdulin's shop and bring the wine back from there. And you yourself get that room (*Pointing*) ready for the guest 95 and do it right! Put a bed in there, and a wash-basin, and everything else. (*Exit* MISHKA)

DOBCHINSKI Well, I'll run along now to see how they're doing with their inspection——

ANNA Go ahead, go ahead—I'm not detaining you. (*Exit* DOBCHINSKI) 100 Well, daughter, we'll have to get busy dressing. He's from the capital; God forbid he should make fun of us over something or other. Your blue dress with the little pleats would be the most becoming——

MARIA (*With disgust*) No, Mamma dear; I don't like that blue dress at all. Not only does Lyapkin-Tyapkin's wife dress in blue, but so does Zemlyanika's 105 daughter too. No, I'd better put on something bright.

ANNA Something bright indeed! Really, you're saying that only to be contrary. The blue will look ever so much better on you, because I want to wear straw-yellow. I'm very fond of straw-yellow.

MARIA Ah, Mamma dear, straw-yellow is so unbecoming to you! 110

ANNA Straw-yellow is unbecoming to me?

MARIA Yes. I'll stake anything you like it won't become you. One must have absolutely dark eyes to wear straw-yellow.

ANNA That's just dandy! And aren't my eyes dark? As dark as dark can be! What nonsense the girl spouts! How can they be anything but dark when 115 I always take the queen of clubs for myself whenever I tell fortunes by cards?*

MARIA Ah, Mamma dear, you're more like the queen of hearts!

ANNA Bosh—absolute bosh! I never was a queen of hearts. (*Exit hurriedly with* MARIA, *but is still heard, off*) What things pop into your head! Queen of 120 hearts indeed! God knows what nonsense you talk! (*As they exit, the door of the room* ANNA *had indicated opens and* MISHKA *sweeps out rubbish*) (OSSIP *comes in through main door, lugging a valise on his head*)

OSSIP Where do I put this?

MISHKA This way, Uncle—right this way. 125

OSSIP Hold on; give us a chance to rest. What a dog's life! Every load seems heavy on an empty belly.

MISHKA Tell me, Uncle—will the general be here soon?

OSSIP What general?

MISHKA Why, your master. 130

OSSIP My master? But what sort of a general is he?

MISHKA Why ain't he a general?

OSSIP (*Hedging*) He is—only the other way around.

MISHKA Well, is he more important than a real general or less?

OSSIP More! 135

MISHKA So that's it! No wonder they're raising such a fuss in our house!

---

[117] The queen of hearts is fair and is associated with love; the queen of clubs is dark and associated with hard work and practical effectiveness.

OSSIP Look here, young fellow—I can see you're a bright lad; suppose you fix up a bite of something for me.

MISHKA Why, Uncle, there's nothing ready yet that would be to your liking. You wouldn't want to eat anything plain; but when your master sits down at table you'll get some of the same food.

OSSIP Well now, what have you got in the way of plain fare?

MISHKA Cabbage soup, buckwheat groats, and meat pies.

OSSIP Bring on your soup, your groats, and meat pies! It don't matter—we'll eat anything. Come on, let's lug this in. Is there another way out from there?

MISHKA There is. (*Exit both, carrying the large suitcase into the adjoining room*) (*Both halves of main door are flung open by two* POLICEMEN, *who flank the entrance. Enter* HLESTACOV, *followed by* MAYOR, *then the* DIRECTOR OF CHARITIES, *the* SUPERINTENDENT OF SCHOOLS, *and* DOBCHINSKI *and* BOB-CHINSKI, *the latter with a plaster on the bridge of his nose.* MAYOR *makes a Jove-like gesture at a scrap of paper on the floor; the* POLICEMEN *rush helter-skelter to pick it up, colliding with each other*)

HLESTACOV Fine institutions you've got here. What I like is that you let your visitors see everything; in other towns they wouldn't show me a thing.

MAYOR In other towns, if I may make so bold as to inform you, the town administrators and officials are more concerned with their own welfare, as it were; but here, if one may say so, we have no other thought save to earn the recognition of our superiors by good order and vigilance.

HLESTACOV That was a very fine lunch; I ate entirely too much. Why, do you have lunches like that every day?

MAYOR It was especially arranged for so pleasant a guest.

HLESTACOV I love a good meal. For that's what one lives for—to pluck the blossoms of pleasure. What do they call that fish we had?

DIRECTOR OF CHARITIES (*Trotting up to* HLESTACOV) Salted scrod, sir.

HLESTACOV Very tasty. Where was it we lunched? At the hospital, wasn't it?

DIRECTOR Right, sir! Just one of our eleemosynary* institutions.

HLESTACOV I remember, I remember. There were a lot of cots standing empty there. And have all the patients recovered? There didn't seem to be many of them around.

DIRECTOR There's half a score or so of them left; all the others have recovered. That's the way it goes—it's the way things are arranged. Ever since I've assumed the post—perhaps this may seem actually incredible to you—all the patients recover like . . . like flies. No sooner does a patient set foot in the infirmary than he gets well—and not so much through the aid of any medicines as through sheer honesty and efficient organization.

MAYOR And, if I may make so bold as to inform you, the responsibility of being Mayor is ever so harrowing! There are so many problems—take sanitation alone, and repairs, and rectifications. . . . In short, the most intelligent of men might find himself in difficulties; yet, God be thanked, everything

---

[167] Charitable.

runs smoothly. Another Mayor, of course, might strive for his own benefit; but, believe me, that even when one lies down to sleep one keeps thinking —Lord God, how can I arrange things so that my superiors may perceive my zeal? I ask for nothing more. Whether they reward me or not, at least I shan't be perturbed at heart. When good order is maintained throughout 185 the town, when all the streets are swept, the prisoners well kept, and there are only a few drunkards—what more could I desire? I swear I want no honours. Of course that sort of thing is enticing, but before virtue all else is but dross and vanity.

DIRECTOR (*Aside*) Listen to that scallywag laying it on! It's a gift from 190 Heaven!

HLESTACOV Very, very true. I confess I myself am occasionally fond of intellectual pursuits—at times in prose, and at others tossing off some slight verse.

BOBCHINSKI (*To* DOBCHINSKI) Quite right, Peter Ivanovich, quite right! 195 His remarks are so . . . so . . . you know! One can see that he has studied the humanities.

HLESTACOV Tell me, please, don't you go in for diversions of any sort? Haven't you gatherings where one may, for instance, indulge in a little game of cards? 200

MAYOR (*Aside*) Oho, brother, I know what you're driving at! (*Aloud*) God save us from anything of the sort! There isn't even a hint at such gatherings here. I never as much as held a card in my hands; I couldn't play cards if my life actually depended on it. I never could bear to look at them with indifference; why, if I should but happen somehow to catch sight of a 205 king of diamonds, let's say, I'm overcome with such disgust that I simply have to spit. One time it so happened that I built a house of cards, just to amuse the children, don't you know—and all that night the accursed things kept plaguing me in my dreams. God be with them that play—how can anyone kill precious time over cards? 210

SUPERINTENDENT OF SCHOOLS (*Aside*) And yet that scoundrel took me over for a hundred on points only three days ago!

MAYOR I'd rather utilize the time for the good of the State.

HLESTACOV Oh, really now, you're making a fuss over nothing at all. It all depends on how you look at a thing. If, for instance, you were to start 215 hedging when you've lost three-quarters of your stakes, then naturally . . . No, it's no use talking, it's intriguing to play a game of cards now and then.

(*Enter* ANNA *and* MARIA)

MAYOR May I make so bold as to present my family: my wife and my daughter.

HLESTACOV (*Bowing and scraping*) Delighted, madam, in having the pleasure, 220 as it were, of meeting you——

ANNA It's still a greater pleasure for us to meet such a personage.

HLESTACOV (*Posturing*) Pardon me, but mine is so much greater!

ANNA How can that be! You're pleased to say so only for the sake of a compliment. Be seated, I beg of you. 225

HLESTACOV Merely to stand near you constitutes happiness; however, since you absolutely insist, I'll sit down. How happy I am to be sitting near you at last!

ANNA Pardon me, but I dare not accept the compliment as being really intended for me. .... I think you must have found travelling very unpleasant after life in the capital? 230

HLESTACOV Extremely unpleasant. Having become used to living in society, *comprenez vous,** and then to find yourself suddenly on the road—the filthy inns, the surrounding gloom of boorishness. I must confess, if it weren't for such good fortune which (*Glancing at* ANNA *and showing off before her*) has 235 rewarded me for everything . . .

ANNA Really, it must be so unpleasant for you!

HLESTACOV However, madam, at this moment I am in a most pleasant mood!

ANNA But that's out of the question—you do me too much honour. I do not merit it. 240

HLESTACOV But why in the world not? You do merit it!

ANNA I live in the backwoods——

HLESTACOV Yes, but the backwoods, by the by, also has its points—knolls, brooks, and rills. Well, naturally, no one would compare it with the capital. Ah, the capital! What life really! You may think perhaps that I'm merely 245 a pen-pusher; but no, the Head of the Department is on a friendly footing with me. He'll slap me on the back, like this: "Come and have dinner with me, dear fellow!" I drop in at the office for only a couple of minutes a day, merely to tell 'em to do this thing that way and that thing this way. And immediately a special clerk—and what an old rat he is!—starts scraping 250 away with his pen. (*Imitates a scratchy pen*) They even wanted to give me a much higher rank, but, I thought to myself, what's the use? And the doorman runs after me with a brush: "Permit me, sir—I want to shine your shoes!" (*To* MAYOR) But why are you standing! Please do sit down, gentlemen! 255

(*The following three speeches are spoken simultaneously*)

MAYOR Your rank is such that we can well keep on standing——

DIRECTOR We'll stand——

SUPERINTENDENT Please don't mind us——

HLESTACOV Never mind ranks—I'm asking you to sit down. (MAYOR *and* 260 *the others sit down*) I'm not fond of ceremonies; on the contrary, I actually try to slip by without attracting attention—so I do. But you simply can't hide yourself—you can't, you can't! All I have to do is to go out somewhere, and they all start saying at once: "There," they say, "goes Hlestacov!" And on one occasion they actually took me for a commander-in-chief. The 265 soldiers rushed right out of the guardroom and presented arms. It was only later on that an officer, whom I know very well, explained to me: "Why, brother, we actually took you for the commander-in-chief!"

ANNA Do tell!

HLESTACOV I know ever so many pretty little actresses. For, after all, I've 270 written all sorts of amusing little pieces for the stage. I mingle with all the

233 "You understand."

writers. Pushkin* and I are like that. (*Puts middle finger over index finger*)
Many's the time I've said to him: "Well, how are things going, Pushkin,
old thing?"—And he'd come right back at me with, "Why, old thing, things
are just so-so somehow!" Most original fellow!   275
ANNA So you write too? It must be so pleasant to feel oneself a writer. You
probably publish in the magazines as well?
HLESTACOV Oh yes—in the magazines as well. However, I've done ever so
many things: *The Marriage of Figaro, Robert Le Diable, Norma.** . . . By now
I don't remember even the titles. And it all came about by sheer chance; 280
I didn't want to write, but the theatrical managers kept pestering me, "Please,
dear fellow, write something for us!" So I thought to myself: "All right,
dear fellows, so I will—just to get rid of you!" And right then and there—
I don't think it took me more than a single evening, I dashed off everything
—and did I astonish all of them! (*Slight pause*) I have an exceptional 285
facility of imagination. I am really the backbone of the *Morning Telegraph;**
my sea novel, *The Frigate Hope,** is still a best seller, and everything that
came out under the name of Baron Brambeus*——
ANNA (*Breaking in on him*) Do tell! So you were that famous columnist?
HLESTACOV Why, of course. Why, there isn't a poet whose poems I don't 290
doctor. The biggest publisher in the country pays me a retainer of forty
thousand a year for that alone.
ANNA Then *Yuri Miloslavski** must also be your work——
HLESTACOV Yes, it is.
ANNA There, I guessed it right off!   295
MARIA Ah, Mamma dear, it says right on the titlepage it was written by some
Zagoskin.
ANNA There you go! I simply knew you'd start an argument even over that——
HLESTACOV (*Hardly batting an eye*) Oh yes, that's right; that's really by Zagoskin;
but there's another novel by the same name—well, that one is mine.   300
ANNA Well, it surely must be yours I read. How well written it is!
HLESTACOV To confess the truth, I live by my pen. My house is the best in
the whole capital. Everybody knows it! They call it Hlestacov House—just
like that. (*Addressing everybody*) If you're ever in the capital, gentlemen, do
me a favour and drop in on me; I urge you, most heartily. And then, 305
I also give grand affairs.
ANNA I can imagine how tasteful and magnificent they must be.
HLESTACOV Well, really they're past all description. In the centre of the table
is a water-melon—and that water-melon costs a mere seven hundred. Soup

---

272 Alexander Pushkin (1799–1837), Russian poet and dramatist.
279 *The Marriage of Figaro* (1784) is a comedy by Beaumarchais; *Norma* (1831) is an opera by Vincenzo
Bellini.
286 A newspaper in St. Petersburg.
287 A story by A. A. Bestuzhev-Marlinsky (1797–1837), then a very popular Romantic novelist and short
story writer.
288 The pen name of Josef-Julian Senkowski (1800–1859), a Pole by birth, who was important as a journal-
ist in St. Petersburg.
293 A historical novel (1829) in the manner of Sir Walter Scott by Mikail Zagoskin (1789–1854).

in special cans, just arrived by steamer direct from Paris—open a can, 310 and the steam is like—like nothing on earth. Not a day passes without my having to attend dances. There, in the capital, we have formed our own circle for whist.* The Minister of Foreign Affairs, the French Ambassador, and the British, and the German, and me. And you get so fagged out playing it's really a shame. When you run up to the fourth floor all you have 315 strength to say to the cook is, "Here, old girl, take my coat"—hold on though: why, I'm mixing everything up; I've actually forgotten I live on the first floor. My staircase alone is—well, simply priceless! And it's ever so curious to peep in at my reception hall, at an hour when I haven't even opened my eyes. The counts and dukes are milling about and buzz like 320 so many bumble-bees; all you can hear is their *bzz, bzz, bzz!* Occasionally you'll find the Premier there—just hanging around. . . . (*The* MAYOR *and the others are so awed that they rise from their chairs*) Even my letters are addressed "Your Excellency." Once I had charge of a whole department actually. Most odd, that was. The Director had gone off—but where to 325 nobody seemed to know. Well, naturally, all sorts of discussions sprang up: How was his place to be filled, who was going to fill it, what was to be done. Many of the generals were willing enough and tackled the job, but, when they got right down to it—we-e-ell, no, the matter was entirely too complicated. It was easy enough, at first glance, but when you got a 330 closer look at it, it turned out to be the devil and all. Later on they see that there's no help for it—so they turn to me. And that very moment all the streets are simply swarming with dashing messengers, and messengers, and more messengers—no end of messengers, and all of 'em dashing about like mad. You can just imagine, there were thirty-five thousand mes- 335 sengers alone! Wasn't that some situation, I ask you? "Ivan Alexandrovich, come and take charge of that department!" I was somewhat taken aback, I confess; I had come out in my dressing-gown and was just about to turn 'em down, but then I thought to myself: Suppose word of my refusal reaches the Emperor? And then there's my service record to be considered too . . . 340 "Very well, gentlemen," I said, "if you like I'll accept the post; I accept it," I tell 'em; "The only thing is, watch out! I don't stand for any guff from anybody. You've got to be up on your toes when you work for me. You know me!" And really, whenever I used to pass through the department it was simply like an earthquake; there wasn't a soul there that didn't 345 quake and quiver like an aspen leaf. (*The* MAYOR *and the others quake in apprehension;* HLESTACOV *works himself up to a real fever pitch*) Oh, I don't like to fool around! I hauled all of them over the coals. (*Pause*) Why, even the Imperial Council* is afraid of me. And really, why not? That's the sort of man I am! I don't let anybody stand in my way. I always tell everybody 350 "I, I myself know my own self." I'm all over—all over! I drop in at the palace every day. They'd make me field-marshal on the morrow—at a mo- ment's notice from me—— (*Slips, and all but flops on the floor, but is deferen- tially caught and supported by the* OFFICIALS)

313 A card game.
349 The Emperor's cabinet.

MAYOR (*Approaching him and trying to speak, his whole body quaking*) B-b-ut 355
. . . Yo . . . yo . . . yo . . .
HLESTACOV (*Sharply*) What is it?
MAYOR B-b-ut . . . Yo . . . yo . . . yo . . .
HLESTACOV (*As before*) I can't make out a word. It doesn't make sense.
MAYOR Yo . . . yo . . . Your Lexecency—Your Excellency may wish to rest. 360
Here's your room, and everything you need——
HLESTACOV Rest? Nonsense! However, if you like, I'm ready to take a rest.
Your lunch was eckshellent gemmen! I'm gratified—I'm gratified. (*Declaiming*) Scrod, scrod, SCROD! (*Exit, solicitously followed by the* MAYOR, *into the
side room*) 365
BOBCHINSKI (*To* DOBCHINSKI) There's a man for you, Peter Ivanovich. There's
a man that's a man! Never in my life have I been in the presence of so
important a personage—I all but passed out, I was that scared. What do you
think, Peter Ivanovich: who is he? What's his rank, I mean?
DOBCHINSKI I think he's nothing short of a general, Peter Ivanovich. 370
BOBCHINSKI Well, in my opinion no general is fit to lace the shoes of this
fellow! But if he is a general, then he must be a generalissimo at the very
least. You heard him: he's got the whole Imperial Council backed up against
the wall. Let's go and tell everything to the judge and to Korobkin. Goodbye,
Anna Andreievna! 375
DOBCHINSKI Goodbye, dearest lady! (*Exeunt* DOBCHINSKI *and* BOBCHINSKI)
DIRECTOR OF CHARITIES (*To* SUPERINTENDENT OF SCHOOLS) It's simply frightening! But just why, a body can't tell. Why, we aren't even wearing our
uniforms! Well now, suppose he gets up after a good night's sleep and
then dashes off a confidential report to the capital? (*Walks thoughtfully* 380
to door with SUPERINTENDENT OF SCHOOLS, *then turns to* ANNA) Goodbye,
Ma'am!
SUPERINTENDENT OF SCHOOLS Goodbye! (*Exeunt both*)
ANNA Ah, what an agreeable fellow!
MARIA Ah! The darling! 385
ANNA But mind you, what fine deportment! One can perceive a man from the
capital right off. His ways, and all that sort of thing. . . . Ah, but that's fine!
I'm awfully fond of young men like that. I've simply lost my head over
him. However, I proved very much to his liking; I noticed he was eyeing
me all the time—— 390
MARIA Ah, Mamma dear—it was me he was looking at!
ANNA Oh, get away from me with your impertinence! That remark is entirely
out of place in this instance.
MARIA No, Mamma dear, he really was.
ANNA There you go! God forbid that you should ever keep from arguing! It 395
just couldn't be, and that's that. When did he look at you? And what reason
did he have to look at you?
MARIA Really, Mamma dear, he kept looking at me all the time. Why, he
glanced at me the moment he began talking about literature, and when he
was telling us about how he played whist with the ambassadors he looked 400
at me also.

ANNA Well, maybe he did, one little time, and even then he did it just so, just to be nice. "Eh," he must have said to himself, "let's take a look at her—might as well."

MAYOR (*Tiptoeing in from* HLESTACOV'S *room*) Shhhh—sh! 405

ANNA What is it?

MAYOR Really, I'm none too happy now I got him drunk. Well, now, supposing even half of what he said is true? (*Falls into thought*) But still, how could it be anything but the truth? Once you've got plenty of drink under your belt you come right out with everything. Whatever you've got in your 410 heart is right at the tip of your tongue. Of course, he did touch things up a bit. But then, nobody ever says anything without some added touches. He plays whist with prime ministers and is a regular visitor at Court. So really, now, the more I think of it—the devil knows what's going on in my head, for I'm sure I don't know; it's just as if I were standing up on 415 some belfry, or as if they were about to hang me.

ANNA But me, now—I wasn't in the least put out; I simply saw him as a well-brought-up man of the world, a man of the highest quality, but as for his rank and position, why, I simply don't take them into consideration even.

MAYOR Oh, you women! That one word is enough to settle all argument. 420 All you think of is fuss and feathers. And you'll always pop up with some silly thing or other. You will get off with nothing but a flogging—but your husband's goose will be gone and done for. You, my darling, treated him just as familiarly as if he were some Dobchinski or other.

ANNA That's something I'd advise you not to worry your head about. There's 425 a little something we know about him. (*Looks at her daughter*)

MAYOR (*Solo*) Oh, what's the use of talking with you! What a thing to happen, really! I still can't get over my fright. (*Opening door and calling*) Mishka, call Svistunov and Derzhimorda; their beat is just a little beyond the gates. (*Short pause after closing door*) Odd how mixed up everything has become 430 in the world; if only people would be impressive to look at, but no, every man is puny and small and as thin as a match—how can a body tell who he is? You take a military man, now—at least his uniform tells you what he is; but even he, when he puts on civilian dress, will look like a fly with its wings snipped off. However, he sure did hold back at that hotel. 435 He sprang such allegories and equivocations on me that it looked as if I'd never get anything sensible out of him. But there, he did give in in the end. And he actually let spill more than he should have. You can see right off he's still a youngster. (*Enter* OSSIP, *polishing a boot. All make a dash for him, beckoning with their fingers*) 440

ANNA Come here, old fellow!

MAYOR Shhh! Well? Is he sleeping?

OSSIP No, not yet; he's still stretching himself every once in a while.

ANNA Look here . . . what's your name?

OSSIP Ossip, ma'am. 445

MAYOR (*To his wife and daughter*) There, that'll do you, that'll do you! (*To* OSSIP) Now then, my friend, have they fed you well?

OSSIP They did that, thanking you most humbly—they fed me right well.

ANNA Well, now, tell me: there must be ever so many counts and dukes calling on your master? 450

OSSIP (*Aside*) What's the use of saying anything! If they fed me well now, it means they're going to feed me still better later on. (*Aloud*) Yes, there's counts calling on him, amongst others.

MARIA Ossip darling, your master is such a good-looking little fellow!

ANNA But tell me please, Ossip—is your master—— 455

MAYOR Now stop that, please! You merely hinder me with such idle talk. Come, what can you tell me, friend?

ANNA And what might your master's rank be?

OSSIP His rank? Why, the usual thing——

MAYOR Oh, my God, how you keep on with your silly pumping! You won't 460 give me a chance to ask anything that matters. (*To* OSSIP) Well, my friend, what sort of man is your master? Strict? Is he fond of bawling people out, or isn't he? Eh?

OSSIP Yes, he's fond of having everything in order. What he's after is having everything regular-like. 465

MAYOR Why, I like your face, so I do! You must be a kind-hearted fellow, friend. Well, now——

ANNA See here, how does your master look in his uniform?

MAYOR Come, that'll do you two chatterboxes. This is a most urgent matter. It concerns life and death! (*To* OSSIP) As I was saying, I do like you, 470 ever so much. When you're travelling it can't do the least harm to have an extra glass of tea or something; it's cold now. So here's a couple of cart-wheels* for tea.

OSSIP (*Accepting the coins*) Thank you, ever so humbly. May God grant you all good health for helping a poor man. 475

MAYOR Fine, fine; that makes me happy too. Well, now, friend——

ANNA I say, Ossip, what sort of eyes does your master prefer, now?

MARIA Ossip darling! What a cute little nose your master has!

MAYOR Hold on, now, give me a chance! (*To* OSSIP) And now, friend—to what things does your master pay the most attention? What appeals to 480 him most when he's travelling, that is?

OSSIP It all depends on whatever turns up. He likes best of all to be well received —he likes good entertainment.

MAYOR Good entertainment?

OSSIP Yes, good entertainment. There, now, I may be nothing but a serf, 485 yet even so he looks out that I'm treated right too. By God, whenever we used to stop anywhere, he'd always ask me, "Well, Ossip, were you treated right?"—"Not so well, Your Excellency," I might tell him. "Eh," he'd say, "our host has a mean nature, Ossip. You remind me," he'd say, "when we get back to the capital." But I'd think to myself: "Eh, (*Makes a resigned* 490 *gesture*) God be with that fellow; I'm a simple man."

MAYOR Fine, fine, and what you're saying is good common sense. I gave you something for tea just now—so here's something else for cookies to go with it.

473 Large coins.

OSSIP   Why are you so good to me, Your Honour? (*Pocketing the coin*) In 495 that case I'll drink to Your Honour's health.

ANNA   You come to me, Ossip; you'll get something additional.

MARIA   Ossip darling, kiss your master for me! (HLESTACOV *is heard coughing slightly in the adjoining room*)

MAYOR   Shhh! (*Gets up on tiptoes; rest of scene in* sotto voce*) God save you 500 from making a noise! That'll do you two; go to your rooms.

ANNA   Come along, Maria! I'll tell you exactly what I noticed about our guest; it's something I can tell you only when we're alone.

(*Exeunt* ANNA *and* MARIA)

MAYOR   Oh, they'll have plenty to talk about! I think if you were to listen 505 you'd have to stick your fingers in your ears. (*Turning to* OSSIP) Well, friend—— (DERZHIMORDA *and* SVISTUNOV *clump in*) Shhh! What clumsy bears, clumping with their boots! Barging in with as much noise as if somebody was dumping a load off a cart! Where in the hell were you?

DERZHIMORDA   I wuz carryin' out orders—— 510

MAYOR   Shhhh! (*Clapping hand over* DERZHIMORDA'S *mouth*) Listen to him cawing like a crow! (*Mimicking*) "I wuz carryin' out orders!" Sounds like a foghorn. (*To* OSSIP) Well, friend, you run along and get whatever your master needs. You can call for anything and everything in the house. (*Exit* OSSIP) As for you two, you stand on the front steps and don't stir from the spot! And 515 don't let a single stranger into the house—especially the storekeepers! If you let even one of 'em in, I'll skin you alive. The minute you see anyone at all coming with a complaint—or even without a complaint, but maybe the fellow looks like the kind of a fellow that would want to lodge a complaint against me—you must let him have it right in the neck! Like this! 520 Let him have it good and hot! (*Kicks, to demonstrate*) You hear me? Shh! Shhhhhh! (*Tiptoes out, after* DERZHIMORDA *and* SVISTUNOV. *Curtain*)

Act Three

Scene 1

(*Scene same. Next morning. Enter, cautiously and almost on tiptoes,* JUDGE, DIRECTOR OF CHARITIES, POSTMASTER, SUPERINTENDENT OF SCHOOLS, *and* DOBCHINSKI *and* BOBCHINSKI. *All act as if on dress parade, and the officials are in their uniforms. The whole scene, until* HLESTACOV'S *entrance, is in* sotto voce) 5

JUDGE (*Arranging everybody in a semicircle*) For God's sake, gentlemen, get in a circle without wasting time, and try to be as orderly as possible! God be with him—he not only attends at Court but also bawls out the Imperial Council! Straighten up! A soldier-like bearing, gentlemen—you mustn't fall down on that soldier-like bearing! You, Peter Ivanovich—trot over to 10 this side; and you, Peter Ivanovich, stand right here. (DOBCHINSKI *and* BOBCHINSKI *trot over to the places indicated*)

500 "In a subdued voice."

DIRECTOR OF CHARITIES Have it your way, Judge, but we really ought to take some . . . action.

JUDGE And what, precisely?

DIRECTOR OF CHARITIES Well, you know what.

JUDGE Palm oil?

DIRECTOR OF CHARITIES Well, yes—why not palm oil?——

JUDGE A dangerous thing, devil take it; he may raise a hullabaloo, working for the State as he does. Unless, perhaps, we were to do it in the guise of a contribution from the gentry, for some sort of a monument?

POSTMASTER Or else: "Here, now, some money has come through the mails —and no one knows to whom it belongs!"

DIRECTOR OF CHARITIES Watch out he doesn't post you somewhere to hell and back again. Look here, that's not the way things are done in a well-regulated State. Why is there a whole squadron of us here? We ought to present ourselves one by one and, when each is eye to eye with him, then . . . do whatever has to be done, and there are no ears to overhear. That's how things are done in a well-regulated social order. There, now, Judge— you'll be the first to start the ball rolling.

JUDGE Why, it would be better if you did; it was in your department that our important visitor broke bread.

DIRECTOR OF CHARITIES Well, it might be better, after all, if the Superintendent of Schools took the initiative—as one who enlightens the youth and all that.

SUPERINTENDENT OF SCHOOLS I can't, gentlemen, I simply can't. To tell you the truth, my upbringing has been such that if anyone, even one step above me in rank, starts talking to me my heart simply sinks into my boots and it's as if the cat has stolen my tongue. No, gentlemen, you must excuse me —you really must.

DIRECTOR OF CHARITIES Well, Judge, it looks like there's nobody to do it outside of yourself. You never utter a word but it sounds as if Cicero* himself were speaking with your tongue.

JUDGE Come now! Come now—Cicero indeed! What will you think of next? Just because once in a while one becomes deeply interested in discussing a pack of house-dogs or a racing bloodhound——

ALL (*Badgering him*) No, dogs aren't all you can talk about—you could have straightened out the trouble at the building of the Tower of Babel!* No, Judge, don't leave us in a lurch! Be like a father to us! Really, Judge——

JUDGE Do let me alone, gentlemen! (*At this moment* HLESTACOV *is heard clearing his throat and walking about in his room. All try to head off one another in a panic rush to the door—which, naturally, leads to certain casualties.*
    But, for all that, the protests are also in sotto voce)

BOBCHINSKI'S VOICE Ouch! Dobchinski, Dobchinski, you're standing on my foot!

---

⁴² Roman statesman and orator (106–43 B.C.), famous for his intricate rhetorical style.
⁴⁸ The tower in biblical history which was never completed because Jehovah cursed the builders with many languages and communication became impossible.

VOICE OF DIRECTOR OF CHARITIES Gentlemen, let me out of here before I pass away! You've crushed me completely—— (*A few more "Ouch!" 's; finally all push through, leaving stage empty for a few seconds*)

HLESTACOV (*Solo, entering with sleep-laden eyes*) I must have had some snooze, it looks like. Wherever do they get such soft mattresses and feather beds? 60 I was actually roasting. It looks as if they'd given me something stronger than water; my head is still throbbing. A man can pass his time most pleasantly here, I can see that. I love open-handed hospitality and it pleases me all the more, I must admit, when I'm being entertained from the bottom of the heart and not out of any selfish interest. Then, too, the Mayor's 65 daughter isn't at all hard to look at, and her mother, for that matter, is an old fiddle on which one could still play a tune. . . . Yes, I don't know why, but really this sort of life is to my liking.

JUDGE (*Entering and stopping, in an aside*) Lord God, see me through this safely! My knees are simply caving in. (*Aloud, straightening up and clutching the* 70 *sword at his side*) I have the honour of presenting myself: Lyapkin-Tyapkin, Collegiate Assessor and Judge of the District Court in this town!

HLESTACOV Be seated, please. So you're the Judge here?

JUDGE I was chosen for a three-year term by the gentry, ever so long ago, and I've continued on the bench right up to now. 75

HLESTACOV I say, though, is there much in being a judge?

JUDGE During my three-year terms I was proposed for the Order of St. Vladimir,* Fourth Class, with the commendation of my superiors. (*Aside*) I've got the money right in my fist—and my fist feels as if it were on fire.

HLESTACOV Why, I like the Order of St. Vladimir. The Order of St. Anna, 80 Third Class, isn't so much by comparison.

JUDGE (*Aside, thrusting out his fist little by little*) Lord God, I don't know what I'm sitting on. Just as though I were on pins and needles.

HLESTACOV What's that you've got in your hand?

JUDGE (*Losing his head and dropping the bank-notes on the floor*) Not a thing, 85 sir——

HLESTACOV What do you mean, not a thing? Isn't that money I see on the floor?

JUDGE (*Shivering from head to foot*) By no means, sir. (*Aside*) Oh, God, I'm as good as up on charges right now! I can hear the Black Maria* rattling up 90 to fetch me away.

HLESTACOV (*Picking up the bank-notes*) Yes, it's money sure enough.

JUDGE (*Aside*) Well, it's all over; I'm lost—lost!

HLESTACOV Tell you what: suppose you let me have this as a loan——

JUDGE (*Hastily*) Of course, sir, of course—with the greatest of pleasure! 95 (*Aside*) A little more boldly now! Get me out of this, Most Holy Mother of God!

HLESTACOV I've sort of run low on funds on my travels, don't you know, what with one thing and another. However, I'll send this right back to you from my country estate—— 100

---

⁷⁷ Decoration for distinguished service.

⁹⁰ The black van used to transport prisoners.

JUDGE Good gracious, don't give it a thought! Why, this is such an honour. . . .
Of course, with all my feeble powers . . . my striving and zeal for my superiors
. . . I shall try to merit—— (*Gets up from chair and stands at attention, his hands at his sides*) I dare not impose my presence on you any further. Have you any
instructions for me perhaps?   105
HLESTACOV What instructions?
JUDGE I mean, aren't you issuing any instructions for the District Court here?
HLESTACOV Whatever for? For I have absolutely no concern with it at present;
no, there are no instructions. Thanks, ever so much.
JUDGE (*Aside, bowing and scraping as he makes his getaway*) Well, the town is 110
all ours now!
HLESTACOV Fine fellow, the Judge.
POSTMASTER (*Drawing himself up as he enters and clutching the sword at his side*)
I have the honour of presenting myself: Court Councillor Shpekin, the Post-
master.   115
HLESTACOV Ah, do come in. I'm very fond of pleasant company. Sit down!
You've always lived in this town—isn't that right?
POSTMASTER Just so, sir.
HLESTACOV Why, I like this little town. Of course, it hasn't got so much of a
population—well, what of that? After all, it isn't a capital. Isn't that so— 120
it isn't a capital, after all?
POSTMASTER Absolutely so, sir.
HLESTACOV For it's only at the capital that you'll find the *bon ton**—and no
provincial geese. What's your opinion—isn't that so?
POSTMASTER Just so, sir. (*Aside*) I must say, though, that he isn't at all 125
uppity; he asks about everything.
HLESTACOV But just the same, you must admit that even in a small town it's
possible to live one's life happily.
POSTMASTER Just so, sir.
HLESTACOV What, to my way of thinking, does a man need? All one needs 130
is to be respected, to be loved sincerely—isn't that so?
POSTMASTER That is absolutely correct.
HLESTACOV To tell you the truth, I'm glad you are of the same opinion as my-
self. Of course, they'll call me an odd stick, but then that's the sort of nature
I have. (*Soliloquizes, even while he is looking right into the* POSTMASTER'S *eyes*) 135
Guess I might as well make a touch from this Postmaster! (*Aloud*) What an
odd thing to happen to me; I ran absolutely short of funds during my travels.
Could you possibly let me have three hundred as a loan?
POSTMASTER Why not? I would deem it the greatest happiness. There you are,
sir. At your service, with all my heart.   140
HLESTACOV Very grateful to you. For, I must confess, I have a mortal dislike of
denying myself anything while I'm travelling—and, besides, why in the world
should I? Isn't that so?
POSTMASTER Just so, sir. (*Stand up, draws himself erect, and holds on to his sword*)
I dare not impose my presence on you any longer. . . . Perhaps you have 145
some criticism as to the management of the Post Office, sir?

123 "High tone."

HLESTACOV   No, not at all. (*Exit* POSTMASTER, *bowing and scraping*) Postmaster, it seems to me that you too are a very fine fellow. At least you're obliging; I like people like that.

VOICE (*Off, quite audibly*)   What are you so scared about?   150

SUPERINTENDENT OF SCHOOLS (*He doesn't exactly enter, but is practically shoved through the door, right after the above speech; draws himself up, not without trembling, and clutches the sword at his side*)   I have the honour of presenting myself: Titular Councillor Hlopov, Superintendent of Schools——

HLESTACOV   Ah, do come in! Sit down, sit down! Care for a cigar?   155

(*Offering cigar*)

SUPERINTENDENT OF SCHOOLS (*Soliloquizing as he hesitates*)   There's comeuppance! That's something I'd never foreseen. To take or not to take?

HLESTACOV   Take it, take it! It's a rather decent smoke. Of course not the same thing as at the capital. There, my friend, I'm used to corona-corona- 160 coronas, at twenty-five the hundred; you simply have to blow a kiss after smoking one. Here's a light—get it going. (*Offers light.* SUPERINTENDENT OF SCHOOLS *tries to light cigar, at the same time trembling all over*) You're lighting it from the wrong end.

SUPERINTENDENT OF SCHOOLS (*Soliloquizing, as he drops the cigar from sheer* 165 *fright and gives up, with a hopeless gesture*)   The devil take it all! My damned timidity has been the ruin of me!

HLESTACOV   You, I can see, are no great lover of cigars. Yet I confess they're a weakness of mine. And also as far as the feminine sex is concerned—I simply can't remain indifferent. What about you? Which do you prefer—blondes 170 or brunettes? (*The* SUPERINTENDENT OF SCHOOLS *is at a total loss as to what to say*) Now, do be frank with me—is it blondes or brunettes?

SUPERINTENDENT OF SCHOOLS   I dare not venture on an opinion.

HLESTACOV   No, no—don't try to wriggle out of it. I want to find out your taste, without fail.   175

SUPERINTENDENT OF SCHOOLS   I make so bold as to report . . . (*Aside*) Why, I myself don't know what I'm saying!

HLESTACOV   Ah, ah! So you won't tell me. Probably some little brunette has already smitten your heart. Confess—hasn't she? (*The* SUPERINTENDENT OF SCHOOLS *can't utter a word*) Ah, ah! You've turned red—you see, you see! 180 But why don't you say something?

SUPERINTENDENT OF SCHOOLS   I'm overcome with timidity, Your Hon . . . Excell . . . High. . . . (*Aside*) My confounded tongue has sold me out! It has sold me out!

HLESTACOV   Overcome by timidity, are you? Well, there really is something 185 about my eyes that inspires timidity. At least I know that there isn't a woman living who can resist them—isn't that so?

SUPERINTENDENT OF SCHOOLS   Just so, sir.

HLESTACOV   However, a deucedly odd thing has happened to me: I've run entirely out of funds on the road. Could you possibly let me have a loan of 190 three hundred?

SUPERINTENDENT OF SCHOOLS (*Soliloquizing as he gropes in his pocket*)   What a fix I'll be in if I haven't the money on me! I have it, I have it! (*Takes out bank-notes and offers them with fear and trembling*)

HLESTACOV   Thanks, ever so much.   195

SUPERINTENDENT OF SCHOOLS (*Drawing himself up and clutching his sword*)   I dare not impose my presence on you any longer——

HLESTACOV   Goodbye!

SUPERINTENDENT OF SCHOOLS (*Aside, as he scuttles out, practically at a run*) There, glory be to God! Chances are he won't as much as look in at my   200 classes.

DIRECTOR OF CHARITIES (*Drawing himself up as he enters and clutching his sword*) I have the honour of presenting myself: Court Councillor Zemlyanika, Director of Charities!

HLESTACOV   How d'you do; I beg you to be seated.   205

DIRECTOR OF CHARITIES   I had the honour of accompanying you on your tour of inspection and of receiving you personally in the eleemosynary institutions entrusted to my care.

HLESTACOV   Ah yes, I remember. You tendered me a most excellent luncheon.

DIRECTOR OF CHARITIES   Only too happy to exert myself in the service of our   210 native land!

HLESTACOV   It's a weakness of mine, I confess, but I do love good food. Tell me, please—it seems to me that you were somewhat shorter yesterday—isn't that so?

DIRECTOR OF CHARITIES   That's very possible. (*After a brief silence*) I may say   215 that I spare no effort and fulfil my duties zealously. (*Inching forward together with his chair and speaking in a low voice*) It's the Postmaster here who does absolutely nothing; all his affairs are much neglected; the outgoing mail is always held up . . . you can find out the specific details yourself, if you wish. The Judge too—he's the one who was here a little while before me—all he   220 knows is to go riding after rabbits; he keeps dogs in the courthouse, and his whole conduct—if I may be frank with you—of course it's for the good of the State that I must do this, even though he's related to me and is a friend of mine—his conduct is most prejudicial. There's a certain landowner hereabouts; they call him Dobchinski—you've seen him around, I dare say.   225 Well, no sooner does this Dobchinski step out of his house than the Judge is already there, sitting with Dobchinski's wife. I'm ready to take my oath on that. And make a point of looking the little Dobchinskis over; there isn't a one that looks like Dobchinski, but every one of them, even the little girl, is the spit and image of the Judge——   230

HLESTACOV   You don't say! Why, I'd never even think that.

DIRECTOR OF CHARITIES   And then there's the Superintendent of the Schools here. I don't know how the Administration could ever entrust him with such a post. He's worse than any Red,* and he instills the youth with such pernicious doctrines as it would be difficult even to describe. If you care to give   235 me instructions to that effect, I could report on all this ever so much better in black and white——

234 Radical or revolutionary.

HLESTACOV   Very well—let it be done in black and white. It'll please me very much. I'm sort of fond, don't you know, of reading something amusing whenever I'm bored. What's your name? I keep forgetting it.   240

DIRECTOR OF CHARITIES   Zemlyanika.

HLESTACOV   Ah yes—Zemlyanika. Well, now, tell me, please: have you any little ones?

DIRECTOR OF CHARITIES   Why, naturally, sir: five—two of them are grown up by now.   245

HLESTACOV   You don't say! Already grown up? And what do you . . . how are they——

DIRECTOR OF CHARITIES   You are pleased to ask, I take it, what they are called?

HLESTACOV   That's it; how are they called?

DIRECTOR OF CHARITIES   Nicolai, Ivan, Elizaveta, Maria, and Perepetuya.   250

HLESTACOV   Fine, fine!

DIRECTOR OF CHARITIES   I dare not impose my presence upon you any further . . . to infringe upon the time dedicated to your consecrated duties——
         (*Bowing and scraping as a preliminary to leaving*)

HLESTACOV (*Seeing him to the door*)   No, not at all. All that you've told me is   255 most amusing. Please pay me another call some time. I love that sort of thing, very much. (DIRECTOR OF CHARITIES *steps through door;* HLESTACOV *closes it but immediately goes back and, opening it, calls after him*) Hey, there! What do they call you? I keep forgetting your full name.

DIRECTOR OF CHARITIES (*In doorway*)   Artemii Philipovich Zemlyanika.   260

HLESTACOV   If you'll be so kind, Artemii Philipovich: I'm in an odd fix—I've run all out of funds during my travels. Have you four hundred on you by any chance that you could lend me——

DIRECTOR OF CHARITIES (*Proffering bank-notes*)   I have.

HLESTACOV   It comes in quite handy, I must say. Thanks, ever so much.   265
         (*Exit* DIRECTOR OF CHARITIES. *Enter* BOBCHINSKI *and* DOBCHINSKI)

BOBCHINSKI   I have the honour of presenting myself: Peter Ivanovich Bobchinski. I'm a landowner, living in this town.

DOBCHINSKI   Peter Ivanovich Dobchinski, a landowner.

HLESTACOV   Ah, I've already seen you around. (*To* BOBCHINSKI) I believe you   270 fell that time—and how is your nose now?

BOBCHINSKI   Glory be—Please don't worry on that score; there's a scab on it now—a perfect scab.

HLESTACOV   A fortunate thing, that scab. Happy to hear about it. (*With unexpected abruptness*) Got any money on you?   275

BOBCHINSKI   Money? What money?

HLESTACOV   A thousand—to lend me.

BOBCHINSKI   I swear to God I have no such sum on me. But perhaps you have, Peter Ivanovich?

DOBCHINSKI   Not on me, I haven't. All my funds, I must inform you, are   280 placed with the Board of Guardians.

HLESTACOV   Well, if you haven't all of a thousand, have you a hundred or so perhaps?

BOBCHINSKI (*Rummaging through his pockets*)   Have you a hundred on you, Peter
Ivanovich? All I have is forty, in bank-notes.   285

DOBCHINSKI (*Looking in his wallet*)   All I have is twenty-five.

BOBCHINSKI   Oh, look a little better, Peter Ivanovich! I know you have a hole
in your right-hand pocket—surely something must have slipped down the
lining of the coat.

DOBCHINSKI   No, really, there's nothing even in the lining.   290

HLESTACOV   Well, it doesn't really matter. I thought I'd ask. Very well—sixty-
five will do. It doesn't matter. (*Accepts money*)

DOBCHINSKI   I make so bold as to make a request of you, concerning a certain
very delicate matter.

HLESTACOV   Just what is it?   295

DOBCHINSKI   It's of a very delicate nature; my eldest son, may it please you, was
born to me before my marriage.

HLESTACOV   Really?

DOBCHINSKI   In a manner of speaking, that is; but he was born to me just as if in
wedlock, and I consummated everything properly afterwards, through the   300
legal bonds of matrimony, sir. So, may it please you, I would like him to be
an entirely legitimate son of mine, as it were, sir, and to have him bear the
same name as myself: Dobchinski, sir.

HLESTACOV   Very well, let him be called thus! It can be done.

DOBCHINSKI   I wouldn't trouble you, but I feel sorry for him, on account of   305
his capabilities. He's a lad of great promise; he can recite all sorts of verse and,
if a jack-knife is handy, he can whittle out a tiny carriage right on the spot, as
deftly as any sleight-of-hand artist. There, Peter Ivanovich knows that too.

BOBCHINSKI   Yes, he's quite a capable lad.

HLESTACOV   Fine, fine—I'll exert myself in this matter; I'll put in a word or   310
two. All this will be managed—I hope. Yes, yes! (*To* BOBCHINSKI) Perhaps
there's something you wish to say to me?

BOBCHINSKI   Of course—I have a most important request——

HLESTACOV   Well, what is it? What about?

BOBCHINSKI   I beg of you most humbly, when you go to the capital tell all   315
those different high dignitaries, all those senators and admirals, now—tell
them that, now, "Your Serenity—or Your Excellency—there's a Peter Ivanovich Bobchinski living in such-and-such a town." Tell 'em just that: "There's
a Peter Ivanovich Bobchinski living in such-and-such a town."

HLESTACOV   Very good.   320

BOBCHINSKI   And should you have occasion to speak to the Sovereign, then tell
it to the Sovereign as well; that, now, "Your Imperial Majesty, there's a Peter
Ivanovich Bobchinski living in such-and-such a town——"

HLESTACOV   Very good!

DOBCHINSKI   Excuse us for having put you out so with our presence.   325

BOBCHINSKI   Excuse us for having put you out so with our presence.

HLESTACOV   Not at all, not at all. It has been a great pleasure for me. (*Gets rid
of them. Solo*) There's certainly a slew of officials here. I seems to me, however, that they must take me for a State dignitary. I must have thrown plenty

of dust in their eyes yesterday. What a pack of fools! I guess I'll write 330
about all this to the capital, to Tryapichkin. He dashes off articles and things
now and then; let him give them a thorough going-over. Hey there, Ossip!
(OSSIP *pops his head through doorway*) Fetch me paper and ink.

OSSIP Right away! (*Disappears*)

HLESTACOV And as for Tryapichkin, really, if he ever sinks his teeth into 335
anybody, he's a caution! He wouldn't spare his own father to put a joke over.
And he's fond of the coin too. However, these officials are a kindly lot; that's
a good trait of theirs, making me all those loans. Let's see, now, how much
money I have exactly. There's three hundred—that's from the Judge. There's
another three hundred—that's from the Postmaster. Six hundred, seven 340
hundred, eight hundred—what a filthy bill! Eight hundred, nine hundred . . .
Oho, it's over a thousand! Well, now, my captain of infantry! Well, you just
cross my path now! We'll see who will trim whom at stuss!

(*Enter* OSSIP, *with paper and ink*)

Well, you fool, you see how they receive and entertain me? (*Begins writing*) 345

OSSIP Yes, glory be to God! The only thing is . . . You know what?

HLESTACOV Well, what is it?

OSSIP Make your getaway. Honest to God, it's time.

HLESTACOV (*Writing*) What bosh! Why should I?

OSSIP Oh, just so. God be with all of them! You've had a fine time here for a 350
couple of days; well, let that do you. What's the use of getting tangled up
with them for long? Give 'em up! Cut it too fine—and somebody else will
come along. By God, that's so, Ivan Alexandrovich! And you can hire such
dandy horses here—how they'd dash off with you!

HLESTACOV (*Writing*) No. I want to stay on here for a while. We'll go to- 355
morrow perhaps.

OSSIP Don't talk of tomorrow! Really, Ivan Alexandrovich, let's get away from
here. It's sure a great honour for you, but just the same, you know, it would
be better to make tracks as quickly as we can. They must have taken you for
somebody else, sure enough—and your father will be ever so angry at you 360
for delaying so long. So really, we ought to dash away in a blaze of glory!
And they'd give us fine horses here——

HLESTACOV (*Writing*) Very well then. Only first of all send off this letter, and
you might as well get an order for the post horses at the same time. But watch
out that you get good horses. Tell the drivers that I'll give a cart-wheel to 365
each one of 'em—so's they'll dash along as if I were an Imperial Courier! And
so's they'll sing their songs for me! (*Continuing to write*) I can just imagine it:
Tryapichkin will die laughing——

OSSIP I'll send it off with one of the men here, sir, whilst I'd better be packing,
so's not to waste time.   370

HLESTACOV (*Writing*) Good idea. But bring me a candle.

OSSIP (*Going out and speaking off*) Hey there, brother! You'll bring a letter over
to the Post Office, and tell the Postmaster to frank it, and tell 'em to bring

---

374 A vehicle drawn by three horses.

up their best troika* for my master—a courier's troika—and they'd best be quick about it; as for the mileage, tell 'em my master rides free; tell 'em the mileage is at government expense. And snap it up, all around, for otherwise, now, my master will be angry. Hold on, the letter isn't ready yet.

HLESTACOV (*Still writing*) I'm curious—where's he living now? On Post Office Street or Gorohovaya? For he too likes to change his rooms often—it's cheaper than paying rent. I'll take a chance and address this to Post Office Street. (*Folds letter, forming it into an envelope, and addresses it*)
(OSSIP *brings in candle.* HLESTACOV *seals letter*)

DERZHIMORDA'S VOICE (*Off*) Hey there, you with the beard! The orders is not to let nobody in, I'm telling you!

HLESTACOV (*Handing letter to* OSSIP) There, get that off.

SHOPKEEPERS (*Off*) Let us through, like a good man! You can't keep us out! We're here on business——

DERZHIMORDA'S VOICE Move on, move on now! Break it up! He ain't seeing nobody; he's sleeping now. (*Hubbub increases*)

HLESTACOV What's going on there, Ossip? See what that noise is.

OSSIP (*Looking through window*) Some shopkeepers or other; they want to come in but the policeman won't let them through. They're waving papers—probably want to see you.

HLESTACOV (*Walking up to window*) Well, what is it you wish, my dear friends?

SHOPKEEPERS (*Off*) We appeal to Your Worship! Sir, order them to accept our petition!

HLESTACOV Let 'em in—let 'em in! Let 'em come in. Ossip, tell 'em they can come in. (*Exit* OSSIP. HLESTACOV *receives the petitions through the window, unrolls one of them and reads it aloud*) "To His Nobly Born Serenity, Master of Finance, from Abdulin the Merchant——" what the devil is all this; there isn't any such rank or title, as a matter of fact! (*The* SHOPKEEPERS *troop in*) Well, what is it you wish, my dear friends?

SHOPKEEPERS (*Bowing very low*) We prostrate ourselves before Your Worship! We appeal to your mercy!

HLESTACOV But just what is it you want?

SHOPKEEPERS Save us from ruin, sir!—We suffer grievous and most unjust oppression!

HLESTACOV From whom?

ABDULIN Why, it's all because of the Mayor of this here town. Sir, there has never been such another Mayor as this one. He puts such wrongs upon us as are past all describing. He's been the death of us, entirely, what with his billeting and all—we might as well put our heads in the noose. He don't act rightly, he don't. He grabs you by the beard and calls you a furriner and a vagabond. Honest to God! If it were a matter of our not having paid him proper respects, now, in anything; but no, we always does the right thing; we never kick about comin' across with whatever's owin' to him, cloth for his wife's dresses, say, or his daughter's. But no; all that is too little for him, you see. So help us God—so help us! He'll barge into the store and take whatever comes to his hand; if he lays his eyes on a bolt of cloth, he'll say: "Eh, my

dear fellow, that's a fine piece of cloth—bring it over to my house!" Well, ⁴²⁰
naturally, you bring it over—and yet there may be all of fifty yards in that
bolt.

HLESTACOV Really now? Ah, what a swindler he is!

ABDULIN Honest to God, there's nobody can recall such another Mayor! You
simply gotta hide everything in the shop as soon as you catch sight of ⁴²⁵
him——

ANOTHER SHOPKEEPER We're not saying anything, even, about delicacies of
any sort—but he'll grab at all sorts of trash: prunes that may have been
mouldering in a barrel for seven years, that no clerk of mine would touch,
even—but no, he'll sink his whole paw in that there barrel—— ⁴³⁰

THIRD SHOPKEEPER When his birthday rolls around, on St. Anthony's Day, it
sure don't look like we'd overlooked him in any way; there's nary a thing
lacking. But no, you gotta come across with more offerings later—he's got a
birthday for every saint on the calendar! So what can a body do? You give
him birthday presents on all the other days as well. ⁴³⁵

HLESTACOV Why, he's no better than a highwayman!

ABDULIN Aye, aye, by God! But you just dare to let a peep out of you, and he'll
march a whole regiment up to your house and billet them on you. And, if
there's the least objections, he gives orders to put a lock on the shop door.
"I," he says, "ain't goin' to subject you to no corporal punishment, nor to ⁴⁴⁰
put you to no torture. Them things," he says, "is forbidden by law, but, my
dear friend, I'll have you livin' off of herring—and that without a drop of
water!"

HLESTACOV Oh, what a swindler! Why, he ought to be sent straight to Siberia
for that! ⁴⁴⁵

ABDULIN Why, it don't really matter where Your Worship may pack him off
to—so long, that is, as he's as far from us as possible. Don't disdain our marks
of hospitality, our Father. We offer you these here heads of sugar, and this
hamper of wine.

HLESTACOV No, you really must not think that of me; I never take any bribes ⁴⁵⁰
whatsoever. On the other hand, if you were to suggest lending me three
hundred, for example, it might be an entirely different matter; a loan is something I can accept.

SHOPKEEPERS If you will favour us, our Father! (*Dig up bills and coins*) Better
take five hundred, only help us out! ⁴⁵⁵

HLESTACOV I won't have a word to say against a loan. If you like, I'll accept it.

ABDULIN (*Offering* HLESTACOV *the money on a silver platter*) There, if it please
you—take the silver platter at the same time.

HLESTACOV Very well; I can take the little silver platter as well.

SHOPKEEPERS (*Bowing*) Do take the sugar, too, at the same time. ⁴⁶⁰

HLESTACOV Oh no; I never take any bribes of any sort——

OSSIP Why don't you take them things, Your Honour? Take 'em! They'll come
in handy on the road. Let's have them sugar loaves here, and that hamper!
Let's have everything. It'll all come in useful. What you got there—a bit of
rope? Let's have that bit of rope too! Even a bit of rope can come in handy; ⁴⁶⁵
if a cart breaks down, or something like that, it can be spliced together.

ABDULIN So do us that favour, Your Serenity. For if you don't help us out with our petition, now, then we really don't know what's to become of us; we might as well put our heads in a noose.

HLESTACOV Absolutely, absolutely! I'll do my best. (*Exit* SHOPKEEPERS) 470

WOMAN'S VOICE (*Off*) No, you dassen't keep me out! I'll complain against you to the great man himself! Don't you push me so hard—it hurts!

HLESTACOV Who's that? (*Walks up to window*) And what's the matter with you, mother?

VOICES OF TWO WOMEN I ask for your mercy, Father! Master, order them to 475 let us in—hear us out!

HLESTACOV (*Through window*) Let 'em come in.

KEYSMITH'S WIFE (*Bowing very low before* HLESTACOV *as she rushes on*) I ask your mercy!

CORPORAL'S WIDOW (*Same business*) I ask your mercy! 480

HLESTACOV Why, who might you women be?

CORPORAL'S WIDOW I'm the widow of Ivanov—a corporal, he was.

KEYSMITH'S WIFE I'm a keysmith's wife, living in this town—Thebronia Petrova Poshlepkina; my father was——

HLESTACOV Hold on; speak one at a time. (*To* KEYSMITH'S WIFE) What is it 485 you want?

KEYSMITH'S WIFE I crave your mercy! I am complaining against the Mayor! May God send him every sort of evil, so that neither his children, nor he himself, swindler that he is, nor his uncles, nor his aunts, may have good or gain in anything! 490

HLESTACOV Come, what is it?

KEYSMITH'S WIFE Why, he ordered my husband to be clipped short for a soldier, and yet it weren't our turn yet, swindler that he is! And besides, it's agin the law: my husband's a married man.

HLESTACOV How could he ever do such a thing? 495

KEYSMITH'S WIFE He done it! The swindler, he done it! May God strike him down in this world and the next! And if he's got an aunt, may every nasty thing befall her, and if his father be living, may he croak, the dog, or choke for ever and ever, swindler that he is. It was the tailor's son that should have been took, and he's a miserable little drunkard to boot, only his parents 500 come across with an expensive present, so the Mayor he went after the son of Panteleievna, the merchant's wife; well, Panteleievna in her turn sent the Mayor's wife three bolts of linen; so then he tackles me: "What do you want with a husband?" he says. "He's of no use to you any more." But I'm the one that knows whether he's of any use or not; that's my affair, you scallywag, 505 you. "He's a thief," he says, "he mayn't have stolen nothing yet, but that don't make no difference," he says, "he's goin' to steal; and even without that he'll be took for a recruit next year." Why, what will it be like for me without a husband, you scallywag, you? I'm a weak human critter, you low-down thief, you! May all your kin and kindred never see God's own daylight, 510 and if you've got a mother-in-law, may even your mother-in-law——

HLESTACOV (*Getting the old woman out of the room*) Very good, very good! (*Turning to the* CORPORAL'S WIDOW) Well, and what about you?

KEYSMITH'S WIFE (*Leaving*) So don't forget, our Father! Be merciful to us! (*Exit*) ⁵¹⁵

CORPORAL'S WIDOW I've come to complain against the Mayor, Father——

HLESTACOV Yes, but what is it? For what reason? Tell me in a few words.

CORPORAL'S WIDOW He flogged me, Father.

HLESTACOV How did that happen?

CORPORAL'S WIDOW Through a mistake, my Father. Us women folk, now, ⁵²⁰ got in a free-for-all on the marketplace, but the police didn't get there in time and they caught me instead. And they let me have it so good and hot that I couldn't sit down for two days.

HLESTACOV But what can one do about it now?

CORPORAL'S WIDOW Well, naturally, there's nothing to be done now. But ⁵²⁵ you might order him to pay a fine for that there mistake. There ain't no use of me turning down any bit of good luck, and the money would come in right handy now.

HLESTACOV Very good, very good. Run along, run along. I'll look into it. (*Shoos her out. Hands, waving petitions, are thrust in through window*) Who else is ⁵³⁰ out there? (*Walks up to window*) I don't want 'em, I don't want 'em! Don't need 'em, don't need 'em! (*Leaving window*) I'm fed up with 'em, the devil take it! Don't let anybody in, Ossip!

OSSIP (*Shouting out of the window*) Get going! Get going! Come around to-morrow. (*Door is pushed open and some sort of woebegone figure in a shoddy* ⁵³⁵ *overcoat emerges—unshaven, with a swollen lip and his cheek tied up. Several others appear behind him*) Get out, get out! What's the idea of barging in here? (*Shoves against intruder's belly and squeezes through door together with him, at the same time slamming door to*)

MARIA (*Entering girlishly*) Ah! ⁵⁴⁰

HLESTACOV What has frightened you so, ma'am?

MARIA No, I wasn't frightened——

HLESTACOV (*Posturing*) I must say, ma'am, I'm very much pleased at being taken for the sort of man who . . . Where did you intend to go, if I may ask?

MARIA Really, I wasn't going anywhere in particular. ⁵⁴⁵

HLESTACOV But just why weren't you going anywhere in particular?

MARIA I thought perhaps Mamma dear was here——

HLESTACOV No, I'd really like to know why you weren't going anywhere in particular——

MARIA I've intruded on you. You must have been engaged in important ⁵⁵⁰ matters.

HLESTACOV (*Posturing more than ever*) Why, what are important matters compared with your eyes? . . . You couldn't possibly intrude on me; on the contrary, your presence is such a pleasure!

MARIA You talk just the way they do in the capital—— ⁵⁵⁵

HLESTACOV Only to such a bewitching person as yourself. May I offer you a chair—it would make me so happy. But no, you ought to have a throne and not a mere chair——

MARIA Really, I don't know . . . I really did have to go. (*Sits down*)

HLESTACOV What a beautiful kerchief!

MARIA Oh, now you're making fun of me! Anything to have a laugh at us provincials!

HLESTACOV Oh, how I wish I were your kerchief, that I might clasp your little lily-white neck!

MARIA I absolutely can't understand what you're admiring so; it's just an 565 ordinary kerchief. . . . What queer weather we're having today——

HLESTACOV But what does any weather matter, ma'am, compared with your lips?

MARIA You persist in saying such odd things. . . . I'd like to ask you to write some sort of a little poem for my album instead. You probably know a lot of poems. 570

HLESTACOV For you, ma'am—anything you desire. Merely demand whatever sort of poem you wish.

MARIA Something sort of . . . Something good—new.

HLESTACOV Oh, what do poems matter! I know no end of them.

MARIA Yes, but tell me—just what will you write? 575

HLESTACOV Oh, what's the use of repeating the lines—I can write them down without that!

MARIA I'm ever so fond of poems——

HLESTACOV Yes, I've a great stock of them, of all sorts. Well, if you like, I'll give you this one of mine: "All the world's a stage, and all the men and 580 women merely players." Well, now, I've written others too. Can't remember 'em all now; however, it doesn't really matter. Instead of that I'd rather symbolize my love which, because of your glance—— (*Edges his chair nearer*)

MARIA Love! I don't understand love. I've never even known what love is—— (*Moves her chair away*) 585

HLESTACOV But why do you move your chair away? It'll be better if we sit closer to each other.

MARIA (*Moving her chair away*) But why closer? It's just as well if there's some distance between us.

HLESTACOV (*Edging his chair nearer*) But why the distance—it's just as well if 590 we're closer.

MARIA (*Moving away*) But what's all this for?

HLESTACOV (*Edging nearer*) Why, it merely seems to you that the chairs are close together, but what you ought to do is imagine that they're at a distance from each other. How happy it would make me, ma'am, if I could clasp you in 595 my embraces——

MARIA (*Glancing out of the window*) What was that? Something seems to have flown past. Is it a magpie? Or some other bird?

HLESTACOV (*Kissing her shoulder and glancing through window*) That's a magpie.

MARIA (*Getting up indignantly*) No, this is too much! What impudence! 600

HLESTACOV (*Detaining her*) Forgive me, ma'am! I did it out of love, purely out of love.

MARIA You must consider me some sort of a country girl—— (*Makes an effort to leave*)

HLESTACOV (*Still detaining her*) Yes, out of love—really, it was out of love. 605

Don't be angry at me, Maria Antonovna—I was only joking! I'm ready to get down on my knees to beg your forgiveness. (*Falls on his knees*) Forgive me—do forgive me! There, you see, I'm on my knees before you!

ANNA (*Entering and catching sight of* HLESTACOV *kneeling*) Ah, what a situation!

HLESTACOV (*Scrambling to his feet*) Eh, the devil take it! 610

ANNA (*Turning on her daughter*) What is the meaning of this, miss? What sort of behaviour is this?

MARIA Why, Mamma dear, I——

ANNA Get out of here! Do you hear me—out, out, and don't dare show me your face again! (*Exit* MARIA, *in girlish tears.* ANNA *turns to* HLESTACOV) Excuse 615 me, please, but I must confess I am so astonished——

HLESTACOV (*Aside*) She too is most appealing—very far from bad. (*Throws himself on his knees before* ANNA) Madam, you can see that I am consumed by love!

ANNA What, you're on your knees? Ah, get up, get up; the floor is so dusty here! 620

HLESTACOV I must learn on my knees—absolutely on my knees!—what my fate is to be: life or death!

ANNA Really, you must excuse me, but I still can't grasp fully the significance of your words. If I'm not mistaken you're making a request for my daughter's hand—— 625

HLESTACOV No, it's you I'm in love with! My life hangs on a thread. If you do not crown my undying love, then I am unworthy of earthly existence. With my heart being consumed by flames I supplicate your hand——

ANNA But, if you will permit me to remark, I am, in a sort of a way . . . married!

HLESTACOV Oh, that! Love knows no such distinctions, and one of our 630 greatest poets has said: " 'Tis but the laws that condemn." We shall withdraw to some shady stream. Your hand—I crave your hand!

MARIA (*Dashing in unexpectedly*) Mamma dear, Papa dear said for you to—— (*Cries out as she sees* HLESTACOV *kneeling*) Ah, what a situation!

ANNA Well, what's got into you? You run in all of a sudden like a cat with 635 conniption fits. There, what do you find so astonishing? What ideas have you gotten into your head? Really, you're like some three-year-old child. It doesn't look in the least as if the girl were eighteen—it doesn't, it doesn't at all! I don't know when you'll become more prudent, when you're going to conduct yourself like a decently brought up young lady, when you will 640 know what the properties are, or what decorous demeanour is.

MARIA (*Through her tears*) Really, Mamma dear, I had no idea——

ANNA There's a draught or something blowing through your head all the time; you are taking Judge Lyapkin-Tyapkin's daughters as your example. Why should you look at them? You shouldn't look at them. You have other 645 examples before you; you have your own mother before your own eyes. There, that's the sort of example you ought to follow.

HLESTACOV (*Seizing* MARIA'S *hand but addressing the mother*) Do not oppose our well-being—bless a constant love!

ANNA (*In astonishment*) So it's she whom you—— 650

HLESTACOV Decide: is it life or death?

ANNA (*To* MARIA) There, you see, you fool? There, you see, it's because of you, because of such an insignificant little baggage, that our guest was pleased to get down on his knees. But no, you have to burst in all of a sudden like a madwoman. There, really, it would serve you right if I were deliberately 655 to refuse him; you aren't worthy of such good fortune. (HLESTACOV *gets up, brushes his knees*)

MARIA I won't act like that in the future, Mamma dear; I won't, honest!

MAYOR (*Dashing in, much upset, to* HLESTACOV) Your Excellency! Do not ruin me! Do not ruin me! 660

HLESTACOV What is the matter with you?

MAYOR Those shopkeepers were complaining to Your Excellency. I assure you on my honour that not even half of what they're saying is true. They themselves deceive the public and give false weights and measures. The corporal's widow told you a pack of lies if she claimed I flogged her. She lies! I swear 665 to God she lies. She flogged her own self.

HLESTACOV The corporal's widow be damned. I have other things on my mind.

MAYOR Don't you believe her—don't you believe her! They're all such liars— not even a child that high would believe them. Why, the whole town knows them for liars by now. And as for swindling, I make so bold as to inform 670 you that they're swindlers whose like the world hasn't yet produced.

ANNA Do you know what honour Ivan Alexandrovich is bestowing upon us? He is asking for the hand of our daughter.

MAYOR What? What? You're out of your head, Mother! Please restrain your wrath, Your Excellency! She's a little touched—and her mother was the 675 same way.

HLESTACOV Yes, I really am asking for your daughter's hand. I am in love with her.

MAYOR I find it impossible to believe, Your Excellency.

ANNA Not even when you're told so? 680

HLESTACOV I'm telling you this in all seriousness. I may go out of my head because of love!

MAYOR I dare not believe; I am unworthy of such an honour.

HLESTACOV Yes. If you won't consent to give me Maria Antonovna's hand, I'm ready to do the devil knows what. 685

MAYOR I cannot believe it; you are pleased to jest, Your Excellency.

ANNA Ah, what a blockhead you really are! When he's trying to get the idea into your head!

MAYOR I cannot believe it.

HLESTACOV Give her to me—give her to me! I am a desperate man; I am 690 ready for anything; if I shoot myself you'll be hauled up for trial before the court.

MAYOR Ah, my God! I'm innocent, body and soul—I swear it, I swear it. Please don't be angry! I'll do whatever your mercy may command me to do! To tell you the truth, my head right now is . . . I don't rightly know myself what's 695 going on in there. I've become such an utter fool now as never before——

ANNA Well, give them your blessing! (HLESTACOV *approaches the* MAYOR, *leading* MARIA *by the hand*)

MAYOR Ay; may God bless you both—but I'm innocent, I tell you! (HLESTACOV *kisses* MARIA, *while the* MAYOR *stares at them*) What the devil! It's really true! 700 (*Rubs his eyes*) They're kissing. Ah, my sainted aunt, they're kissing! He's her bridegroom, sure enough! (*Shouts and hops about in joy*) Ah, Tony! Ah, Tony! Ah, you Mayor! So that's the way things are going now!

OSSIP (*Entering*) The horses are waiting.

HLESTACOV Ah . . . very well. I'll be ready right away. 705

MAYOR What? Are you leaving us?

HLESTACOV Yes, I'm leaving.

MAYOR But just when, may I ask? You yourself were pleased to hint, it seems, at a wedding.

HLESTACOV Why, it'll be for just a minute, so to say. For a single day, to see 710 an uncle of mine—a rich old codger—and I'll start back no later than tomorrow.

MAYOR I dare not detain you in any way and hope for your propitious return.

HLESTACOV Of course, of course, I'll be back in a wink. Goodbye, my love . . . no, I simply can't express all I feel. Goodbye, dearest! 715
(Kisses MARIA'S *hand)*

MAYOR Isn't there anything you need for your trip perhaps? You were pleased to say, I think, that you were short of cash.

HLESTACOV Oh no, no need of that at all. (*After a moment's reflection*) On the other hand, why not, if you feel so inclined— 720

MAYOR How much would you like?

HLESTACOV Well, you gave me two hundred that time—that is, not two hundred but four—I wouldn't want to take advantage of your error; so, if you like, give me the same amount now, so's to make it an even eight hundred.

MAYOR In a moment! (*Takes bills out of his wallet*) And, as if on purpose, it's 725 all in crisp, new bills.

HLESTACOV Ah yes, just so. (*Takes bills and examines them*) A very good thing, that. For they do say it brings new luck to be given new bills.

MAYOR Precisely, sir.

HLESTACOV Goodbye, Anton Antonovich! I'm very much indebted to you for 730 your hospitality. I confess with all my heart that I've never been so well received anywhere. Goodbye, Anna Andreievna! Goodbye, Maria Antonovna, my love! (*Exit, followed by* OSSIP *and all the others*)
(Off)

HLESTACOV'S VOICE Goodbye, Maria Antonovna, my soul's angel! 735

MAYOR'S VOICE But how can you ride in that wretched post carriage?

HLESTACOV'S VOICE Why, I've gotten used to that. Springs make my head ache.

DRIVER'S VOICE Whoa, there!

MAYOR'S VOICE Cover the seat with something at least—even a mat. Would you care to? I'll order a mat to be brought. 740

HLESTACOV'S VOICE No, what in the world for? It's a trifling matter. On the other hand—yes, let 'em bring a mat, if you like.

MAYOR'S VOICE Hey there, Avdotya! Go to the storeroom and take out a rug. The best one, the Persian one with the blue background! And be quick about it. 745

DRIVER'S VOICE Whoa, there!

MAYOR'S VOICE When may we expect you then?

HLESTACOV'S VOICE Tomorrow, or the day after.

OSSIP'S VOICE Is that the rug? Let's have it here. Put it down—that's it! Now let's have some hay on this side.   750

DRIVER'S VOICE Whoa, there!

OSSIP'S VOICE Here, put some hay on this side. Right here! Some more! That's fine. Now it'll be grand! (*Slaps rug*) Now you can take your seat, Your Honour!

HLESTACOV'S VOICE Goodbye, Anton Antonovich!   755

MAYOR'S VOICE Goodbye, Your Excellency!

FEMININE VOICES Goodbye, Ivan Alexandrovich!

HLESTACOV'S VOICE Goodbye, Mamma dear!

> (*Sound of a short kiss. Pause. Sound of a prolonged kiss*)

DRIVER'S VOICE Giddap, me darlin'! (*Sound of jingle bells, receding. Slow* 760 *curtain, coming down completely only as the last sound of the jingle bells dies away*)

Scene 2

Scene: Same evening. At Rise: MAYOR, ANNA, *and* MARIA

MAYOR Well, now, Anna Andreievna? Eh? Did you ever think of such a thing as this? What a rich prize, devil take it! There, own up—you never even dreamt of it. From an ordinary Mayor's lady and then—holy hell— to be- 765 come related to such a devil of a fellow!

ANNA Not at all. I knew it all along. It's such a rarity for you because you're so common; you've never met any decent people.

MAYOR Mother, I myself am a decent person. But really, now, when one stops to think of it, Anna Andreievna—what fine-feathered birds you and I have 770 now become! Eh, Anna Andreievna? We can fly high now, the devil take it! You just wait—now's the time when I'll make it hot for all those who were so ready to lodge complaints and denunciations against me! (*Opening door a trifle*) Hey, who's there? (*Enter* PUGOVITZIN) Ah, it's you, Pugovitzin! Brother, you just summon all the shopkeepers here. I'll fix those dogs! 775 So they're going to complain against me, are they? Why, the damned pack of Judases! You just wait, my darlings! Up to now I've been just going easy with you; you'll find out what real hell is now! Make a list of every man jack who as much as came here to complain against me. And, above all, make a note of all those writing fellows—all those writing gents, now, who made up 780 the petitions for the others. And proclaim it to everybody, so that all men may know: that, now, just look at what an honour God has bestowed upon your Mayor; he's going to marry his daughter off not to just any old commoner, but to such a grand man as the world has never yet seen, and who can do everything—everything, everything, everything! Proclaim it to every- 785 body, so that all men may know. Cry it out to all the people; ring all the bells till they crack, the devil take it! If there's going to be a celebration, let it be an all-out one! (PUGOVITZIN *withdraws*) So that's the way things are going, eh, Anna Andreievna? Well, what are our plans now—where are we going to live? Here or at the capital? 790

ANNA At the capital, naturally. How could we ever stay on here?

MAYOR Well, if it's the capital, the capital it is! But it would be well to stay on right here. Well, now, I guess we'll send mayoring to the devil, eh, Anna Andreievna?

ANNA Naturally! The idea of being a mere Mayor now! 795

MAYOR Sure; we can go after a big position in society now. Don't you think, Anna Andreievna? For he's like that (*Crosses index and middle fingers of right hand*)—with all the prime ministers and calls at Court; with a pull like that one can work things so's to get in right among the generals. What do you think, Anna Andreievna, can I get in among all those generals, or can't I? 800

ANNA I should say so! Of course you can!

MAYOR Ah, the devil take it, it's swell to be a general! They'll sling a pretty ribbon over my shoulder—and which do you think is better, Anna Andreievna: the red, for the Order of St. Anna, or the blue, for the White Eagle?

ANNA The blue, of course. 805

MAYOR See what the woman has set her heart on! Even a red ribbon would be good enough. Do you know why one wants to be a general? Because, if you have occasion to travel anywhere, you have aides and state couriers galloping ahead of you everywhere you go, demanding horses! And when you get to a post station there won't be anybody getting any horses; 810 every living soul has to bide its turn. All those titled persons, and captains and mayors. But you don't give a good damn even. You're dining at some governor's—and you simply snub a mayor if you see one standing around! (*Sniggers; sends out peal after peal of laughter; his laughter is simply killing him*) There, damn it, that's what's so attractive! 815

ANNA Anything that is coarse always appeals to you. You must remember that we'll have to change our course of life entirely, that our friends will no longer consist of a hound-loving Judge with whom you go chasing rabbits, or a charity-monger like Zemlyanika; on the contrary, your friends will be of the most ree-fined deportment: counts, and all sorts of society people. 820 The only thing is, I'm really worried about you. At times you'll come out with some such phrase as is never heard in good society.

MAYOR Damn it, what of it? Words will never hurt you.

ANNA That sort of thing was well enough when you were Mayor. But life in the capital is altogether different. 825

MAYOR Why, they say you can get two particular kinds of fish there so tasty they make your mouth water at the first bite—sea-eels and smelts—

ANNA All he thinks of is seafood! I absolutely will have things my way. Our house must be the first one at the capital, and my boudoir must be so exquisitely lighted and so scented with ambergris* that nobody will be able 830 to set foot in it without puckering up the eyes—like this! (*Blinks her eyes and sniffs daintily*) Ah, how splendid all this is! (*Enter* SHOPKEEPERS, *sheepishly*)

MAYOR Ah, greetings to you, my fine-feathered friends!

---

830 A substance taken from the sperm-whale and used as perfume.

SHOPKEEPERS (*Bowing deeply*) Greetings to you, Father!

MAYOR Well, my darlings, how are you getting along? How are your goods 835
moving? So, you tea-swilling, yardstick-swinging swine got a notion of
complaining against me, did you? You archknaves, you super-swindlers, you
master-cheats and sea-monsters! You're going to complain, eh? Well? Did
it get you much? Thought they'd just grab me and clap me into jail! Do
you know, may seven devils and a witch take you, that— 840

ANNA Ah, my God, what language you're using!

MAYOR (*Ruffled*) Eh, I have more than language to think of right now! (*Goes
back to badgering the* SHOPKEEPERS) Do you know that the very same official
to whom you were complaining is now going to marry my daughter? What?
Eh? What have you got to say now? Now I'll show you! Ooo-oo-oo-ooh! 845
(*Singles out* ABDULIN) You cheat the public. You'll get a contract from the
Treasury, swindle it to the tune of a hundred thousand by supplying rotten
cloth, and then sacrifice twenty yards to me—and you expect a medal for it?
Why, if they were to know that, they'd take you and . . . Look at the way
he shoves his belly out! He's a business man; you dassen't touch him; 850
"We won't take no back seat even for no gentry!" Why, a gentleman—
damn your ugly looking puss—a gentleman goes in for learning; even
though they may beat him at school it's for a good purpose, so's he'll know
whatever is useful. But what about you? You begin with knavish tricks; your
boss beats you if you aren't skilled at cheating. While you're still a brat 855
and don't know your paternoster yet, you're already giving short measure,
and, soon as your belly fills out and you've got your pockets stuffed, you
start in putting on airs! My, my, what a rare fellow! Just because you can
drink seventeen samovars* dry in a day you think it entitles you to put on
airs? Why, I spit in your face, you and your airs! 860

ABDULIN (*Leading the chorus of deeply bowing* SHOPKEEPERS) We're at fault,
Anton Antonovich!

MAYOR Complain, will you? (*Again singling out* ABDULIN) But who was it
helped you to put over that crooked deal when you were building the bridge,
and who entered twenty thousand for lumber when there wasn't even a 865
hundred's worth? It was me that helped you, you goat-beard! That's something you forgot. If I'd told on you it would have been my turn to pack
you off to Siberia. What have you to say to that? Eh?

ABDULIN We're at fault before God, Anton Antonovich. The sly Evil One
tripped us up. And we'll take our oaths not to complain from now on. 870
We'll make it up to in any way you like, only don't be angry!

MAYOR Don't be angry, eh? There, you're grovelling at my feet now. Why?
Because I've got the upper hand. But if things were going ever so little
your way, why, you dog, you'd grind me into the very mud—and sink me
in with a piledriver, on top of everything! 875

SHOPKEEPERS (*Bowing to the* MAYOR'S *very feet*) Don't ruin us, Anton Antonovich!

MAYOR "Don't ruin us!" Now it's "Don't ruin us!" But what were you saying

859 Russian tea-urn.

before? (*Ferociously menacing*) Why, I ought to take you and—— (*With an "I-give-you-up!" gesture*) Well, let God forgive you! Enough! I'm not 880 the sort to bear a grudge. Only, mind you, walk the chalk line from now on! I'm not marrying my daughter off to just any ordinary squire. So let your congratulations be in keeping—d'you understand? Don't think you can get away with some measly side of salted sturgeon or a head of sugar! There, go, and God go with ye! (SHOPKEEPERS *crawl out*) 885

(*Enter* JUDGE *and* DIRECTOR OF CHARITIES)

JUDGE (*In the very doorway*) Am I to believe the rumours, Anton Antonovich? Fortune has been very good to you!

DIRECTOR OF CHARITIES I have the honour of congratulating you on your exceptional good fortune! I was sincerely glad when I heard of it! (*Approaches* 890 ANNA *and kisses her hand*) Anna Andreievna! (*Repeats business with* MARIA) Maria Antonovna!

RASTACOVSKI (*Entering*) I congratulate Anton Antonovich! May God prolong the lives of yourself and the young couple and give you a numerous posterity —grandchildren and great-grandchildren! Anna Andreievna! (*Approaches* 895 ANNA *and kisses her hand*) Maria Antonovna! (*Repeats business*)

(*Enter* KOROBKIN *and his* WIFE, *and* LULUCOV)

KOROBKIN I have the honour of congratulating Anton Antonovich! (*Approaching* ANNA *and kissing her hand*) Anna Andreievna! (*Repeating business with* MARIA) Maria Antonovna! 900

KOROBKIN'S WIFE I congratulate you with all my heart on your new good fortune, Anna Andreievna!

LULUCOV I have the honour of congratulating you, Anna Andreievna! (*Kisses her hand; then, turning to spectators, clicks his tongue with a devil-of-a-fellow air*) Maria Antonovna, I have the honour of congratulating you! (*Kisses her* 905 *hand and repeats rest of business. Numerous* GUESTS, *of both sexes, in informal dress, who have been drifting in steadily, crowd around, the men first kissing* ANNA'S *hand, then* MARIA'S, *with exclamations of* "Anna Andreievna!" *and* "Maria Antonovna!" *and the women gushing and kissing* ANNA *and* MARIA. BOBCHINSKI *and* DOBCHINSKI *bustle in, making their way through the thronging guests*) 910

BOBCHINSKI I have the honour of congratulating you, Anton Antonovich!

DOBCHINSKI Anton Antonovich, I have the honour of congratulating you!

BOBCHINSKI Congratulations on your good fortune!

DOBCHINSKI Anna Andreievna!

BOBCHINSKI Anna Andreievna! (*Both approach at the same time for the hand-* 915 *kissing ritual and bump their foreheads together*)

DOBCHINSKI (*Kissing* MARIA'S *hand*) Maria Antonovna, I have the honour of congratulating you! You'll be ever so happy; you'll wear a dress of gold and eat all sorts of exquisite soups; you'll have a most amusing time—

BOBCHINSKI (*Breaking in*) Maria Antonovna! (*Kissing her hand*) I have the 920 honour of congratulating you! May God grant you all wealth, lots of gold pieces, and a little rascal of a son, so-o big (*Spreading his arms*) so that you may dandle him on the palm of your hand—yes, ma'am! And the little one will keep on bawling all the time. (*Imitates a baby crying. A few more guests go through kissing business with* ANNA *and* MARIA) 925

SUPERINTENDENT OF SCHOOLS (*Entering with his* WIFE) I have the honour—
HIS WIFE (*Running ahead of him*) I congratulate you, Anna Andreievna! (*She and* ANNA *kiss each other*) Really, now, I was overjoyed. "Anna Andreievna is marrying off her daughter," they tell me. "Ah, my God!" I think to myself, and I was that overjoyed I say to my husband: "Listen, Luka dear 930 —what good luck has come to Anna Andreievna! There," I think to myself, "glory be to God!" And I say to him, I say: "I'm so delighted I'm simply burning up with impatience to let Anna Andreievna know. . . . Ah, my God," I think to myself, "Anna Andreievna was just waiting for a good match for her daughter, and now fate has been so good to her, things fell out 935 just the way she wanted them," and really, I was so overjoyed that I couldn't utter a word. I cry and cry—there, I simply sobbed. So then Luka Lukich he says to me: "What are you sobbing about, Nastenka?"—"Luka, dear," I say to him, "I don't rightly know myself why"—and my tears keep flowing like a river— 940
MAYOR I beg you to be seated, ladies and gentlemen. (*Through door*) Hey, Mishka! Fetch a lot of chairs in here! (GUESTS *seat themselves.* MISHKA *brings in more chairs. Enter* INSPECTOR OF POLICE *and three* POLICEMEN)
INSPECTOR OF POLICE I have the honour of congratulating you, Your Honour, and of wishing you a long and prosperous life. 945
MAYOR Thank you, thank you. Please be seated, ladies and gentlemen. (*More* GUESTS *seat themselves*)
JUDGE Now tell us please, Anton Antonovich, just how all this began—the gradual progress of this matter.
MAYOR The progress was extraordinary: he was pleased to make a personal 950 proposal—
ANNA (*Taking the ball away from him*) Most respectfully, and in the most refined manner. Everything was extraordinarily well put. "I, Anna Andreievna," he says, "am doing this solely' out of respect for your personal qualities." And such a splendid, cultured person, of the noblest principles. "Anna 955 Andreievna," he says, "would you believe it, I don't value my life at a bent pin; I am doing this only because I respect your rare qualities."
MARIA Ah, Mamma dear, it was to me he said that!
ANNA Stop that; you don't know anything, and don't mix into what is none of your affair! "Anna Andreievna," he said, "I am astonished . . ." He was 960 profuse with such flattering things. . . . And when I wanted to tell him that we simply dared not hope for such an honour, he suddenly fell down on his knees, and that in the most genteel manner: "Anna Andreievna! Don't make me the most miserable of men! Consent to respond to my feelings, otherwise I'll put a violent end to my life!" 965
MARIA Really, Mamma dear, he was saying that concerning me.
ANNA Why, of course. It concerned you also; I don't deny that in the least.
MAYOR And he even scared us no end, actually—said he would shoot himself. "I'll shoot myself, so I will!" he says.
CHORUS OF GUESTS You don't say! 970
JUDGE What an odd thing to happen!
SUPERINTENDENT OF SCHOOLS Ay, verily, Fate must have guided things so.

DIRECTOR OF CHARITIES No, not Fate, my Father. Fate is a tough old turkey; it's Anton Antonovich's meritorious services that have brought him this. (*Aside*) Luck will always pop into the snout of a swine like that. ⁹⁷⁵

JUDGE I'd just as lief sell you that young hound we were dickering about, Anton Antonovich.

MAYOR No, I've bigger fish to fry now than that hound pup.

JUDGE Well, if you don't want it, we'll come to terms on some other dog.

KOROBKIN'S WIFE Ah, Anna Andreievna, how glad I am over your good ⁹⁸⁰ luck! You simply can't imagine!

KOROBKIN And where, if I may ask, is your distinguished guest at present? I heard that he has left for some reason.

MAYOR Yes, he has gone away for a day on a very important matter—

ANNA To see an uncle of his, and ask his blessing— ⁹⁸⁵

MAYOR And ask his blessing; but no later than tomorrow. (*Sneezes. The "God bless you's!" blend and swell into a mighty chorus*) Thank you all! But no later than on the morrow he's coming back. (*Sneezes. Again a swelling chorus of "God bless you's!" Certain voices are heard above the others*)

POLICE INSPECTOR'S I wish you health, Your Honour! ⁹⁹⁰

BOBCHINSKI'S A hundred years and a sackful of gold pieces!

DOBCHINSKI'S May God prolong your life to forty times forty years!

DIRECTOR OF CHARITIES Drop dead, you skunk!

KOROBKIN'S WIFE'S May the devil take you!

MAYOR I humbly thank you. And I wish you the same. ⁹⁹⁵

ANNA We intend to live in the capital now. For here, I confess, the atmosphere is so . . . far too countrified! Most uncongenial, I confess. And my husband, now—he'll get a general's rank there.

MAYOR Yes, ladies and gentlemen, I confess I very much want to be a general, the devil take it! ¹⁰⁰⁰

SUPERINTENDENT OF SCHOOLS And may God grant that you get to be one!

RASTACOVSKI What's impossible through human means is possible through the Divine.

JUDGE A great ship needs deep waters.

DIRECTOR OF CHARITIES All honour to them that have earned honour. ¹⁰⁰⁵

JUDGE (*Aside*) There, he'll show 'em a thing or two if he ever gets to be a general! There's somebody whom a general's rank fits the way a saddle fits a cow! No, brother, you haven't gotten there yet, not by a long shot. There are folks in this town far better than you, and they aren't generals to this day. ¹⁰¹⁰

DIRECTOR OF CHARITIES (*Aside*) Look at what's actually trying to worm himself in among the generals, devil take it! For all you know, he may really get to be one. For there are enough high airs about him—may the cunning Evil One take him. (*Turning to* MAYOR) When the time comes, Anton Antonovich, don't forget all about us. ¹⁰¹⁵

JUDGE And if anything should turn up—some opportunity in administrative matters—don't leave us without your favour.

KOROBKIN Next year I'm bringing my youngster to the capital so that he may serve the government; so do me a favour, extend your patronage to him, take the place of a father to the poor lonely lad. 1020

MAYOR I'm quite ready; for my part, I'm quite ready to exert myself.

ANNA Tony dear, you're always ready with your promises. In the first place, you won't have time to think of such things. And how can you, and for what reason should you, burden yourself with promises?

MAYOR But why not, dearest? One can do so, now and then. 1025

ANNA Of course one can, but then there's no use extending patronage to all the small fry.

KOROBKIN'S WIFE (Sotto voce, *to another* LADY GUEST) Did you hear how she rates us?

LADY GUEST Why, she was always like that; I know her—you give her an 1030 inch and she'll take a yard—

POSTMASTER (*Rushing in, all out of breath and waving an open letter*) An amazing thing, ladies and gentlemen! The official whom we took for the Inspector General wasn't the Inspector General—

ALL What? He wasn't the Inspector General? 1035

POSTMASTER Not the Inspector General at all; I found this out through a letter—

MAYOR What are you saying? What are you saying? From what letter?

POSTMASTER Why, from a letter which he himself wrote. A letter was brought to me at the Post Office. I look at the address, and I see that it's directed 1040 to Post Office Street. I was simply stunned. "Well," I thinks to myself, "he must have come across irregularities in my department and is informing the Administration." So I went and unsealed it.

MAYOR But how could you ever do it?

POSTMASTER I don't rightly know myself. Some unnatural force must have 1045 impelled me. I had already summoned a special courier in order to send it off posthaste—but such curiosity as I had never before experienced overcame me. I couldn't, I couldn't do it—I felt that I simply couldn't, yet at the same time it was drawing me, simply drawing me to open it. In one ear I hear nothing but: "Hey there, don't break that seal; your goose is cooked if 1050 you do!"—but in the other ear there seems to be some demon sitting: "Break the seal! Break the seal! Break the seal!" And no sooner had I pressed down on the wax than fire seemed to shoot right through my veins, and when I had actually unsealed the letter, by God, I was frozen stiff; my hands were trembling and everything turned black before my eyes. 1055

MAYOR But how dared you unseal the letter of such an influential personage?

POSTMASTER Why, that's just where the trick comes in: he's not influential and he's no personage!

MAYOR What is he then, according to you?

POSTMASTER Nor fish nor flesh nor good red herring; the devil knows 1060 what he is.

MAYOR (*Flaring up*) What do you mean by that? How dare you call him nor fish nor flesh nor good red herring and the devil knows what, on top of that? I'll place you under arrest—

POSTMASTER Who? You?

MAYOR Yes, me!

POSTMASTER You're not big enough.

MAYOR Are you aware that he is marrying my daughter, that I myself am going to be a high dignitary—that I'll bottle you up in Siberia, no less?

POSTMASTER Eh, Anton Antonovich! Why talk of Siberia—Siberia's a long way off. I'd better read the letter to you. Ladies and gentlemen! May I have your permission?

ALL Read it! Read it!

POSTMASTER (*Reading letter*) "I hasten to inform you, my dearest friend Tryapichkin, of what wonders have befallen me. On my travels I was cleaned out—but thoroughly!—by a certain captain of infantry, so that mine host of the local hostelry was all set to put me in the cooler, when out of a clear sky, owing to my physiognomy and dress being those of a citizen of the capital, the whole town took me for a governor-general, or something. And now I am living at the home of the Mayor, having the time of my life, and running after the Mayor's wife and daughter for all I am worth. The only thing is, I haven't made up my mind which one to start up with; I think I'll tackle the mother first, because it looks as if she were ready to grant one any favours right off the bat. Do you remember what tough times you and I used to have, trying to get our meals without paying for them, and how once, in a pastry shop, the proprietor grabbed me by the collar because I had eaten some tarts and wanted to charge them to the account of His Britannic Majesty? Things are altogether different now. They all lend me money, as much as I wish. And they're all frightfully quaint here. You'd die laughing. I know you write short things of all sorts; find a place for them in your work. First of all, there's the Mayor; he's as stupid as a grey gelding——"

MAYOR Impossible! There's nothing of the sort in the letter—

POSTMASTER (*Showing* MAYOR *the letter*) Read it yourself!

MAYOR "—as stupid as a grey gelding——" Impossible! You wrote that yourself.

POSTMASTER How could I possibly sit down to write a letter like that?

DIRECTOR OF CHARITIES Read on!

POSTMASTER (*Resumes reading*) "—there's the Mayor; he's as stupid as a grey gelding——"

MAYOR Oh, to hell with all that! Must you keep on repeating it—just as though it weren't there without all that repetition!

POSTMASTER (*Resumes reading*) Hmm . . . hmm . . . hmm . . . hmm! "—as a grey gelding. The Postmaster too is a good-hearted fellow——" (*Cuts short his reading*) Well, at this point he expresses himself disrespectfully about me as well—

MAYOR No, you read it!

POSTMASTER But what for?

MAYOR No, devil take it, if you're going to read, then read—read everything!

DIRECTOR OF CHARITIES Allow me, I'll read it (*Takes letter, puts on spectacles,* *and reads aloud*) "The Postmaster is, down to the least detail, just like Mihei, the watchman in our department; and, just like Mihei he must be fond of gin-and-bitters, the scoundrel——"

POSTMASTER (*To spectators*) Well, he's just an atrocious brat who ought to be whipped—that's all! 1115

DIRECTOR OF CHARITIES (*Going on with his reading*) "The Director of Chari . . . i . . . i——" (*Begins stammering*)

KOROBKIN Well, what are you stopping for?

DIRECTOR OF CHARITIES Why, his handwriting is rather hard to make out. However, one can see he's a good-for-nothing! 1120

KOROBKIN Let me have it. There, I think my eyes are better than yours! (*Tries to take letter*)

DIRECTOR OF CHARITIES (*Holding on to letter*) No, this place can be skipped— and it's much easier to read further on—

KOROBKIN Do permit me—I know all about it. 1125

DIRECTOR OF CHARITIES Well, as for reading it, I'll read it myself—really, it's all easy to read further on.

POSTMASTER No, you read everything! After all, everything up to now was read out loud.

ALL Give it up! Give up that letter! (*To* KOROBKIN) You read it! 1130

DIRECTOR Just a minute! (*Surrenders letter to* KOROBKIN) Here, permit me (*Covers part of letter with forefinger*)—read from here on. (*All surround him*)

POSTMASTER Read on, read on! Stuff and nonsense! Read the whole thing!

KOROBKIN (*Reading*) "The Director of Charities, Zemlyanika, is a perfect swine —in a skullcap——" 1135

DIRECTOR OF CHARITIES (*To the spectators*) That's supposed to be witty. A swine —in a skullcap. Why, whoever saw a swine in a skullcap?

KOROBKIN (*Going on with his reading*) "The Superintendent of Schools is saturated—but saturated!—with the fragrance of onions——"

SUPERINTENDENT OF SCHOOLS (*To spectators*) So help me, I've never so 1140 much as tasted onions!

JUDGE (*Aside*) Glory be, at least there isn't anything there about me!

KOROBKIN "The Judge——"

JUDGE (*Aside*) There it is! (*Aloud*) Ladies and gentlemen, I think the letter is much too long, and besides, what the devil is there to it—what's the 1145 of reading such rubbish?

SUPERINTENDENT OF SCHOOLS Don't stop!

POSTMASTER Don't stop. Keep on reading!

DIRECTOR OF CHARITIES Yes, you'd better keep on with the reading.

KOROBKIN (*Resumes*) "The Judge, Lyapkin-Tyapkin, is *mauvais ton** to the 1150 *n*th degree——" (*Pauses*) That must be French.

JUDGE Why, the devil knows what it means! Good thing if it means only "swindler"—but maybe it's even worse than that.

KOROBKIN "But on the whole they're a hospitable and kind-hearted lot. Good-bye, my dear friend Tryapichkin. I want to go into literature myself, 1155

1150 "Vulgar tone."

following your example. It's a bore, brother, to lead the life I do; after all, one wants some spiritual food; I perceive that one must really occupy himself with something or other of a lofty nature. Write to me in the Saratov Province—the Village of Podkatilovka." (*Turns letter over and reads address*) "To the Right Honourable Ivan Vassilievich Tryapichkin, Saint Peters- 1160 burg, Post Office Street, House Number Ninety-Seven, within the Courtyard. Third Floor, Turn Right."

LADY GUEST   What an unexpected reprimand!

MAYOR   There! When he set out to slit my throat he slit it from ear to ear! I'm killed, killed, killed entirely! I can't see a thing! All I can see before 1165 me are some swinish snouts instead of faces, and not another thing! Bring him back—bring him back! (*Waves his arm*)

POSTMASTER   How can you bring him back? As if on purpose, I ordered the station-master to give him the very best team of three horses, and on top of that the devil himself must have egged me on to give him an order 1170 for all the relays of horses ahead.

KOROBKIN'S WIFE   Well, this is an unparalleled mess, sure enough!

JUDGE   But, devil take it, gentlemen! He took three hundred from me as a loan.

DIRECTOR OF CHARITIES   And three hundred from me too.

POSTMASTER (*With a sigh*)   Oh, and three hundred from me as well.   1175

BOBCHINSKI   He took sixty-five from Peter Ivanovich and me—in bills, sir. Yes, sir!

JUDGE (*Spreading his hands in bewilderment*)   But how can this be, gentlemen? Really, now, how was it he took us in like that?

MAYOR (*Striking his forehead*)   But what about me? But what about me, now, 1180 old fool that I am? I've lost my wits through age, like an old ram! Thirty years of my life have I spent in serving the public; never a business man, never a contractor could take me in; I horn-swoggled swindlers who could show tricks to other swindlers; such cheats and knaves as were wise enough to cheat the whole world did I rope in; three governors have I hood- 1185 winked! But what do governors amount to! (*Deprecating gesture*) As if governors were even in the running—

ANNA   But this can't be, Tony darling; he's engaged to our Maria—

MAYOR (*Really stirred up*)   "Engaged!" He's engaged in a pig's eye! Don't go shoving that engagement at me! (*In a frenzy*) There, look—let all the 1190 world, let all of Christianity look—look, all of you, how the Mayor has been made a fool of! Call him a fool, call him a fool, the old, low-down villain! (*Shakes his fist in his own face*) Hey there, you with the thick nose! You took a squirt, a rag like that for a person of importance! There, he's eating up the road now, rolling along to the tinkling of his jingle bells! 1195 He'll spread this story through the whole world, nor will it be enough that you'll be a general laughing stock. . . . Some scribbler, some waster of good white paper will turn up, and he'll plunk you into a comedy—that's what hurts! He won't spare your rank, your title, and all the people will bare their teeth, grinning, and clapping their hands. (*Turning on the spectators*) What 1200 are you laughing at? You're laughing at your own selves! (*With a "What's-the-use!" gesture*) Eh, you! . . . (*Stamps his feet in frenzied malice*) I'd take all these wasters of good white paper and—— (*Roars*) oo-oo-oooooh! You scribblers, you damned liberals! Seed of the devil! I'd tie all of you in a knot, I'd grind you all into powder and shove you in the devil's hip pocket! 1205 And in his hat as well! (*Shakes his fist and grinds his boot-heel into the floor. After a brief silence*) I can't come to myself to this very minute. There, verily: Him whom God would chastise He first deprives of reason. Well, now, what was there about this snot-nose that looked like an Inspector General? Nary a thing! There, not even that much. (*Measures off the very tip of his* 1210 *little finger*) And suddenly they all set up a chorus: "The Inspector General! The Inspector General!" There now, who was the first to come out with the rumour that he was the Inspector General? Answer me!

DIRECTOR OF CHARITIES (*Spreading his hands*) If you were to kill me I couldn't explain how all this came about; I'm dazed and in a fog, it seems; the 1215 devil must have led me astray—

JUDGE Why, who do you think was the first to come out with that rumour? They're the ones! (*Pointing to* DOBCHINSKI *and* BOBCHINSKI) Those two fine fellows!

BOBCHINSKI So help me, so help me, it wasn't me; I never even thought any 1220 such thing—

DOBCHINSKI I didn't do a thing—not a single thing—

DIRECTOR OF CHARITIES Of course it was the two of you!

SUPERINTENDENT OF SCHOOLS Of course. They came running from the hotel as if they were mad: "He's arrived, he's arrived, and he won't lay out 1225 any money. . . ." You sure found a fine bird that time.

MAYOR Naturally, it had to be you two! You town gossips, you damned liars!

JUDGE May the devil take both of you with your Inspector General and your stories!

MAYOR All you do is snoop through the town and mix everybody up, you 1230 damned chatterboxes; you breed gossip, you bobtailed magpies, you!

JUDGE You confounded bunglers!

SUPERINTENDENT OF SCHOOLS Dunce caps!

DIRECTOR OF CHARITIES You potbellied toadstools! (*All surround* BOBCHINSKI *and* DOBCHINSKI) 1235

BOBCHINSKI Honest to God, it wasn't me—it was Peter Ivanovich—

DOBCHINSKI Oh no, Peter Ivanovich, for you were the first to—

BOBCHINSKI Oh no—so there! You were the first—

GENDARME (*Entering*) The official sent here in the Emperor's name from Petersburg demands your immediate presence. He is stopping at the 1240 hotel. (*All are thunderstruck by his words. An outcry of astonishment escapes all the ladies simultaneously; all the characters, suddenly shifting their positions, become petrified*)

Tableau

(*The* MAYOR *stands in the centre, looking like a post, with outspread arms and head thrown back. To his right are his* WIFE *and* DAUGHTER, *each strain-* 1245 *ing towards him with all her body. Behind them is the* POSTMASTER, *who has*

turned into a living question mark addressed to the spectators. Behind him is the SUPERINTENDENT OF SCHOOLS, *most guilelessly nonplussed. Behind him, near the very side of the proscenium, are three* LADY GUESTS, *leaning together with the most sarcastic expressions on their faces, meant for the* MAYOR *and still more for his* WIFE *and* DAUGHTER. *To the left of the* MAYOR *is the* DIRECTOR OF CHARITIES, *with his head somewhat cocked, as though he were hearkening to something. Behind him is the* JUDGE, *with his arms spread wide, squatting almost to the ground, and with his lips puckered as if to whistle, or to say,* "Oh, my sainted aunt! This is it, sure enough!" *Behind him is* KOROBKIN, *turning to the spectators with one eye narrowed and putting over a caustic insinuation concerning the* MAYOR. *Behind him, at the very side of the proscenium, are* DOBCHINSKI *and* BOBCHINSKI, *the arrested motion of their hands directed at each other, their mouths gaping and their eyes goggling at each other. The other* GUESTS *remain where they are, like so many pillars of salt. All the characters, thus petrified, retain their positions for almost a minute and a half.*
                    Slow curtain)

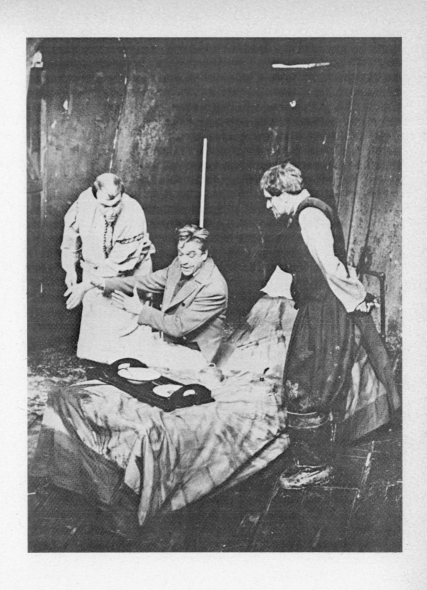

Scene from *The Inspector General*
as presented at London's Aldwych Theatre, 1966.
Photo Crawford Theatre Collection, Yale University

Ivan Turgenev

Ivan Turgenev (1818–1883) gave only ten years of his long and productive literary life to the theater, but in that time he succeeded both in developing the dramatic form in which most of the important drama in Russian was to be written and in providing one masterpiece of the type. After experimenting with comedies, now in the manner of Gogol, now in that of Alfred de Musset, he began moving in the direction of the tragic-comic studies of manners in THE PARASITE *and* THE SINGLE MAN; *with* A MONTH IN THE COUNTRY *he demonstrated the form's full range and power. Plagued by the censors, however, and finally imprisoned and exiled to his estate, he gave up playwriting shortly thereafter and devoted most of his remaining years to stories and novels, the most celebrated being* FATHERS AND SONS.

Chronology

1818   Born at Orel, Russia.
1828   His family moved to Moscow.
1834   Entered the University of Moscow, then the University of St. Petersburg, where he studied philology.
1837   Wrote a fantastic drama entitled *Steniya*.
1838–40   Studied in Berlin, where his "western" tastes were formed.
1840   Returned to Moscow.
1843   Published a narrative poem, *Parasha*.
1847   Began writing short stories, published in 1852 as *A Sportsman's Sketches*.

1848–49   Wrote the tragicomedies *The Parasite* and *The Single Man*.
1850   Wrote *A Month in the Country*.
1852   Was exiled to his country estate for his eulogy on Gogol.
1855   Published *Dmitri Rudin*, a novel.
1860   Published *On the Eve*.
1862   Published *Fathers and Sons*.
1863   Moved to Baden-Baden.
1867   Wrote *Smoke*.
1870   Wrote *A Lear of the Steppes*.
1877   Wrote *Virgin Soil*.
1880   Made his last visit to Russia.
1883   Died at Bourgival, near Paris.

Selected Bibliography

Dupuy, Ernest, *The Great Masters of Russian Literature in the Nineteenth Century*, trans. Nathan Haskell Dole, London, 1886.

Lloyd, J. A. T., *Two Russian Reformers: Ivan Turgenev, Leo Tolstoy*, London, 1910.

Magarshack, David, *Turgenev, A Life*, London, 1954.

Perry, Henry Ten Eyck, *Masters of Dramatic Comedy*, Cambridge, Mass., 1939.

Yarmolinsky, Avrahm, *Turgenev, The Man, His Art, His Age*, New York, 1926.

A MONTH IN THE COUNTRY

by Ivan Sergeyevich Turgenev

Translated by George Rapall Noyes

Characters

ARKÁDY SERGÉICH ISLÁYEV, *a rich landowner, thirty-six years old*
NATÁLYA PETRÓVNA (NATÁSHA), *his wife, twenty-nine years old*
KÓLYA, *their son, ten years old*
VERA (VÉROCHKA), *a protegée of the family, seventeen years old*
ANNA SEMÉNOVNA ISLÁYEV, *mother of* ISLÁYEV, *fifty-eight years old*
LIZAVÉTA BOGDÁNOVNA, *a companion, thirty-seven years old*
ADÁM IVÁNOVICH SCHAAF, *a German tutor, forty-five years old*
MIKHÁYLO ALEXÁNDROVICH RAKÍTIN, *a friend of the family, thirty years old*
ALEXÉY NIKOLÁYEVICH BELYÁYEV, *a student, teacher of* KÓLYA,
twenty-one years old
AFANÁSY IVÁNOVICH BOLSHINTSÓV, *a neighbor, forty-eight years old*
IGNÁTY ILYÍCH SHPIGÉLSKY, *a doctor, forty years old*
MATVÉY, *a servant, forty years old*
KÁTYA, *a maid, twenty years old*

The action takes place on ISLAYEV'S *estate, about 1840. There is a lapse of
one day between Acts I and II, II and III, and IV and V*

Act One

*A drawing-room. On the right a card table and door to the study. Center, a
a door to the hall. On the left, two windows and a round table. In the corners
of the room are couches. At the card table* ANNA SEMENOVNA, LIZAVETA
BOGDANOVNA, *and* SCHAAF *are playing preference. At the round table are
seated* NATALYA PETROVNA *and* RAKITIN. NATALYA *is embroidering on
canvas.* RAKITIN *has a book in his hands. The wall clock points to three*

SCHAAF   Hearts.

ANNA SEMENOVNA*   Once more! My dear sir, you will beat us all to nothing.

SCHAAF (*Phlegmatically*)   Eight on hearts.

ANNA SEMENOVNA (*To* LIZAVETA BOGDANOVNO)   What a man! There's no
playing with him. (LIZAVETA BOGDANOVNA *smiles*)   ₅

NATALYA PETROVNA (*To* RAKITIN)   Why have you stopped? Go on reading.

---

2 Pronounced Se-myŏ'-no-vna [trans. note].

RAKITIN (*Slowly raising his head*) "Monte Cristo se redressa haletant.* . . ." Natalya Petrovna, are you interested?

NATALYA PETROVNA Not a bit.

RAKITIN Why are we reading this, then? 10

NATALYA PETROVNA This is why. The other day a lady said to me, "Haven't you read Monte Cristo? You ought to read it; it is charming." At the time I made her no reply, but now I can tell her I have read it and did not find it charming at all.

RAKITIN Very well, if you have already convinced yourself. . . . 15

NATALYA PETROVNA Oh, how lazy you are!

RAKITIN I am ready to go on, certainly. (*He finds the place where he has stopped*) "Se redressa haletant, et . . ."

NATALYA PETROVNA (*Interrupting him*) Have you seen Arkady to-day?

RAKITIN I met him at the dam. Your men are repairing it. He was explaining 20 something to the workmen, and to make it clearer, he waded into the sand up to his knees.

NATALYA PETROVNA He takes hold of everything with too much enthusiasm —tries too hard. That's his failing. What do you think about it?

RAKITIN I agree with you. 25

NATALYA PETROVNA How tiresome! You always agree with me. Go on reading.

RAKITIN Ah, so you want me to quarrel with you. All right.

NATALYA PETROVNA I do! . . . I do! . . . I want you to have a will of your own. Read on, I tell you.

RAKITIN I obey. (*Applies himself to the book again*) 30

SCHAAF On hearts.

ANNA SEMENOVNA What! Once more? This is unbearable. (*To* NATALYA PETROVNA) Natasha! Natasha!

NATALYA PETROVNA What?

ANNA SEMENOVNA Just imagine! Schaaf has been beating us all to pieces. He 35 keeps saying seven or eight on hearts.

SCHAAF Zis time, seven once more.

ANNA SEMENOVNA Do you hear? This is awful.

NATALYA PETROVNA Yes. Awful. (*To* SCHAAF) Well, you can have them!

ANNA SEMENOVNA (*To* NATALYA PETROVNA) But where's Kolya? 40

NATALYA PETROVNA He's gone walking with the new teacher.

ANNA SEMENOVNA Ah, Lizaveta Bogdanovna, I call you.

RAKITIN (*To* NATALYA PETROVNA) With what teacher?

NATALYA PETROVNA Oh, yes. I forgot to tell you. While you were gone we hired a new teacher. 45

RAKITIN In place of Dufour?

NATALYA PETROVNA No. A Russian teacher. The princess will send us a Frenchman from Moscow.

RAKITIN What kind of a man is he—this Russian? Old?

NATALYA PETROVNA No. Young. However, we have taken him only for the 50 summer months.

---

7 "Monte Cristo stood up again, panting." They are reading Alexandre Dumas' novel *The Count of Monte Cristo* (1844).

RAKITIN Oh, a general tutor.

NATALYA PETROVNA Yes. That's what they call it, I believe. And, let me tell you, Rakitin, you like to observe people, to analyze them, to study their natures. . . .   55

RAKITIN Good gracious! Why do you . . . ?

NATALYA PETROVNA Yes, yes. . . . Observe him carefully. I like him. He's slender and well-built. He has a merry glance and a confident expression—you will see. To be sure, he is a little clumsy, and in your eyes, that's a drawback.   60

RAKITIN Natalya Petrovna, you are frightfully hard on me to-day.

NATALYA PETROVNA Joking aside, just observe him. It seems to me that he may turn out a splendid man. However Lord knows!

RAKITIN You arouse my curiosity.

NATALYA PETROVNA Really? (*Pensively*) Go on reading.   65

RAKITIN "Se redressa haletant, et . . ."

NATALYA PETROVNA (*Suddenly looking around*) Where is Vera? I haven't seen her since morning. (*With a smile to* RAKITIN) Drop that book! I see we shan't be able to read to-day. You'd better tell me some story or other.

RAKITIN Very well. What shall I tell you? You know I have spent some days   70 with the Krinitsyns. Just imagine! Our young people already are being bored.

NATALYA PETROVNA How did you manage to observe that?

RAKITIN Is it possible to conceal boredom? You can conceal anything else, but not boredom.

NATALYA PETROVNA (*With a glance at him*) Can you conceal everything else?   75

RAKITIN (*After a short silence*) I think so.

NATALYA PETROVNA (*Lowering her eyes*) So, what did you do at the Krinitsyns'?

RAKITIN Nothing at all. Being bored with friends is an awful thing. You feel at ease, you are not embarrassed, you like them, you have nothing to be vexed at, but still boredom torments you, and your heart is silly enough   80 to ache as if it were hungry.

NATALYA PETROVNA Probably you are often bored with friends.

RAKITIN As if you yourself did not know what it means to be with a person whom you love and of whom you are tired!

NATALYA PETROVNA (*Slowly*) Whom you love—that is a great word. You   85 speak somewhat mysteriously.

RAKITIN Mysteriously? Why mysteriously?

NATALYA PETROVNA Yes. That's your failing. Do you know, Rakitin, of course you are a very clever man, but . . . (*Stopping*) sometimes you and I converse as if we were weaving lace. . . . And have you watched people weaving   90 lace! They do it in stuffy rooms, without moving from the spot. Lace is a beautiful thing, but a swallow of fresh water on a hot day is far better.

RAKITIN Natalya Petrovna, to-day you—

NATALYA PETROVNA What?

RAKITIN To-day you are angry at me for some reason.   95

NATALYA PETROVNA Oh, you shrewd men! How little penetration you have even if you are shrewd! . . . No. I am not angry at you.

ANNA SEMENOVNA Oh, at last he's caught. He has to pay a fine. (*To* NATALYA

PETROVNA) Natasha, our villain has had to pay a fine.

SCHAAF (*Sourly*) Lissafet Bogdanovna is to blame. 100

LIZAVETA BOGDANOVNA (*Crossly*) Excuse me. How was I to know that Anna Semenovna had no hearts?

SCHAAF In ze future I vill not call Lissafet Bogdanovna.

ANNA SEMENOVNA (*To* SCHAAF) But how is she to blame?

SCHAAF (*Repeats in exactly the same voice*) In ze future I vill not call Lissafet 105 Bogdanovna.

LIZAVETA BOGDANOVNA What do I care? The idea!

RAKITIN The more I watch you, Natalya Petrovna, the more I find your face strange to-day.

NATALYA PETROVNA (*With a certain curiosity*) Really? 110

RAKITIN It's true I observe a definite change in you.

NATALYA PETROVNA In that case, will you be so kind—you know me—guess the nature of that change that has taken place in me. What is it?

RAKITIN Well, just wait a moment. . . .

(KOLYA *suddenly runs in noisily from the hall, straight to* ANNA SEMENOVNA) 115

KOLYA Grandma! Grandma! Just look what I have. (*He shows her a bow and arrows*) Just look!

ANNA SEMENOVNA Show them to me, my darling. Oh, what a splendid bow! Who made it for you?

KOLYA He did! He did! 120

(*He points at* BELYAYEV, *who has stopped at the door of the hall*)

ANNA SEMENOVNA Oh, how nicely it is made.

KOLYA I've shot from it at a tree, grandma, and I hit it twice. (*He jumps up and down*)

NATALYA PETROVNA Show it to me, Kolya. 125

KOLYA (*Runs to her and talks while* NATALYA PETROVNA *examines the bow*) Oh, maman, how splendidly Alexey Nikolayevich climbs trees! He's going to teach me how, and he's going to teach me to swim, too. He's going to teach me everything. (*He jumps up and down*)

NATALYA PETROVNA (*To* BELYAYEV) I'm very grateful to you for your 130 attention to Kolya—

KOLYA (*Interrupting her excitedly*) I'm so fond of him, maman—so very fond of him.

NATALYA PETROVNA (*Stroking* KOLYA *on the head*) My boy is a little bit pampered. Try to change him into a strong and vigorous lad. 135

(BELYAYEV *bows*)

KOLYA Alexey Nikolayevich, come on to the stable. We'll take some bread to Favorit.

BELYAYEV Come on.

ANNA SEMENOVNA (*To* KOLYA) Come here and kiss me first. 140

KOLYA (*Running away*) Later, grandma, later. (*Runs off into the hall;* BELYAYEV *follows him*)

ANNA SEMENOVNA (*Following* KOLYA *with her eyes*) What a charming child! (*To* SCHAAF *and* LIZAVETA BOGDANOVNA) Is he not?

LIZAVETA BOGDANOVNA Yes, indeed. 145

SCHAAF (*After a short silence*) I pass.

NATALYA PETROVNA (*With a certain animation*) Well, how did he strike you?

RAKITIN Who?

NATALYA PETROVNA (*After a short silence*) That—Russian teacher.

RAKITIN Oh, excuse me. I quite forgot. I was so occupied with the question 150 that you put to me. (NATALYA PETROVNA *looks at him with a hardly perceptible, mocking smile*) However, his face . . . is really . . . Yes, he has a nice face. I like him, only he seems very bashful.

NATALYA PETROVNA Yes.

RAKITIN (*Glancing at her*) But, nevertheless, I cannot make up my mind . . . 155

NATALYA PETROVNA What if you and I took him in hand, Rakitin. Do you wish to? Let us finish his education. This is a splendid chance for sober, sedate people like you and me! We are very sedate, aren't we?

RAKITIN This young man interests you. If he knew it—he would feel flattered.

NATALYA PETROVNA Oh, believe me, not at all! You can't judge of him 160 by what—people like us would do in his place. He's not at all like us, Rakitin. That's the trouble, my friend. We study ourselves with great diligence and then imagine that we know men.

RAKITIN Another man's soul is a dark forest. But why these hints? Why do you keep teasing me to-day?   165

NATALYA PETROVNA Whom should we tease if not our friends? And you are my friend—you know it. (*Presses his hand.* RAKITIN *smiles and his face brightens*) You are my old friend.

RAKITIN I'm only afraid that you may grow tired of that old friend.

NATALYA PETROVNA (*Laughing*) We grow tired only of good things.   170

RAKITIN Maybe. . . . Only that makes it no easier for them.

NATALYA PETROVNA Stop it. (*Lowering her voice*) As if you did not know . . . *ce que vous êtes pour moi.**

RAKITIN Natalya Petrovna, you are playing with me as a cat with a mouse. . . . But the mouse does not complain.   175

NATALYA PETROVNA Oh, poor little mouse!

ANNA SEMENOVNA Twenty kopeks* from you, Adam Ivanovich. . . . Aha!

SCHAAF In ze future I vill not call Lissafet Bogdanovna.

MATVEY (*Entering from the hall and announcing*) Ignaty Ilyich has arrived.

SHPIGELSKY (*Entering after him*) Doctors are not announced. (MATVEY *goes* 180 *out*) My most humble respects to the whole family. (*Goes to* ANNA SEMENOVNA *and kisses her hand*) Good day, madam. I trust you are winning?

ANNA SEMENOVNA Winning! I had hard work to come out even. . . . Thank the Lord for that! It's all owing to this villain. (*Points to* SCHAAF)

SHPIGELSKY (*To* SCHAAF) Adam Ivanovich, with ladies! That is not nice. . . . 185 I'm ashamed of you!

SCHAAF (*Muttering through his teeth*) Wiz ladies, wiz ladies. . . .

SHPIGELSKY (*Going up to the round table on the left*) Good day, Natalya Petrovna! Good day, Mikhaylo Alexandrovich!

173 "What you are for me."
177 A Russian coin of small value, 1/100th of a rouble.

NATALYA PETROVNA   Good day, doctor! How are you? 190
SHPIGELSKY   I like that question very much. . . . So *you* are well. How am I getting along? A respectable doctor is never ill. He just suddenly up and dies. . . . Ha! Ha!
NATALYA PETROVNA   Sit down. I am well, to be sure—but I'm not in good spirits. . . . And even that is ill health. 195
SHPIGELSKY   (*Sitting down beside* NATALYA PETROVNA)   Permit me to feel your pulse. (*He feels it*) Ah, those nerves, those nerves. . . . You take too little exercise, Natalya Petrovna. You laugh too little. . . . That's the trouble. Mikhaylo Alexandrovich, what are you looking at? Now, I can prescribe white drops. 200
NATALYA PETROVNA   I'm not averse to laughing. . . . (*With animation*) Now, doctor, you have a spiteful tongue. I'm honestly very fond of you for that quality and respect you for it. . . . Tell me something funny. Mikhaylo Alexandrovich insists upon talking seriously to-day.
SHPIGELSKY   (*Looking stealthily at* RAKITIN)   Evidently it is not only the 205 nerves that suffer, but you have a slight effusion of bile.
NATALYA PETROVNA   ⁻Oh, you are singing the same song! Observe as much as you wish, doctor, but not aloud. We all know that you are frightfully penetrating. . . . You are both very penetrating.
SHPIGELSKY   I agree. 210
NATALYA PETROVNA   Tell us something funny.
SHPIGELSKY   I agree. I never thought of expecting you all of a sudden to want me to tell a story. Let me take a pinch of snuff. (*He takes one*)
NATALYA PETROVNA   What preparations!
SHPIGELSKY   But, my dear madam, Natalya Petrovna, please consider there 215 are different sorts of funny stories. It depends on the person. In the case of your neighbor, Mr. Hlopushkin, you only have to raise one finger and he explodes into laughter and wheezes and weeps. . . . But you . . . Well, permit me. Do you know Platon Vasilyevich Verinitsyn?
NATALYA PETROVNA   I think I know him, or I have heard of him 220
SHPIGELSKY   He has an insane sister. In my opinion, either both of them are insane or both of them in their right mind, because there is absolutely no difference between brother and sister, but that is not the point. Fate always, fate always, fate, fate everywhere. Verinitsyn has a daughter, a sallow girl, you know, with pale eyes, a little red nose, and yellow lips—in a word, 225 a very amiable girl. She plays the piano and lisps, too. So everything is as it should be. She has two hundred serfs,* and her aunt has one hundred and fifty. Her aunt is still alive and will live a long time, as all insane people are long-lived. But still there is a remedy for every grief. She has made a will in favor of her niece. Only yesterday I, with my own hands, poured cold 230 water on her head, and I had absolutely no reason to do so, because there is utterly no possibility of curing her. Well, so then, Verinitsyn has a daughter —not the worst match in the world. He began to take her into society; suitors began to make their appearance. Among others, there was a certain Perekuzov, an anæmic young fellow, timid, but of excellent principles. 235

---

²²⁷ A landed proprietor's wealth was reckoned by the number of serfs he owned [trans. note].

So the father liked our Perekuzov, and the daughter liked him too. Then where was the hindrance, you say? Let them be married, and good luck to them! And really everything went finely. Mr. Verinitsyn, Platon Vasilyevich, was already beginning to tap Mr. Perekuzov on the stomach, this way, you know, and to pat him on the shoulder, when suddenly, from somewhere or other, an officer turned up—Ardalion Protobekasov. At the ball of the Marshal of the Nobility he saw Verinitsyn's daughter. He danced three polkas with her, and he said to her, probably rolling his eyes like this, "Oh, how unhappy I am!" And the young lady immediately fell for it. Then there were tears, sighs, and "ohs." She wouldn't look at Perekuzov, wouldn't talk to Perekuzov—she had spasms at the mere word "marriage." Good Lord my God, what a story! "Well," thinks Verinitsyn, "if it's Protobekasov, then Protobekasov it must be. It's lucky that he, too, is a man of property." They invite Protobekasov and say, "Do us the honor." Protobekasov does them the honor. Protobekasov arrives, hangs around, falls in love, finally offers his hand and heart. What do you think about it? Does the Verinitsyn girl immediately agree with joy? Not much! God forbid! Again tears, sighs, spasms! The father is clean stuck: "What's this anyway? What does she want?" And what do you think she answers him? "I don't know, dad," says she, "whether I love this man or the other one." "What's that?" "Honest to God, I don't know, and I'd better not marry either one, but just love him." Verinitsyn, of course, immediately had a fit, and the suitors, also, didn't know what was up, but she held her ground! Pray consider what miracles take place at these parts.

NATALYA PETROVNA I don't see anything surprising in this. . . . As if it were impossible to love two men at once!

RAKITIN Ah, you think . . .

NATALYA PETROVNA (*Slowly*) I think— However, I don't know. Maybe this proves only that you love neither one of them.

SHPIGELSKY (*Taking snuff and looking first at* NATALYA PETROVNA *and then at* RAKITIN) That's it. That's it.

NATALYA PETROVNA (*To* SHPIGELSKY *with animation*) Your story is very good, but nevertheless you didn't make me laugh.

SHPIGELSKY But, my dear madam, who could ever make you laugh now, if you please? You don't need that now.

NATALYA PETROVNA What do I need?

SHPIGELSKY (*With an affectedly submissive air*) The Lord only knows!

NATALYA PETROVNA Oh, how tiresome you are! No better than Rakitin!

SHPIGELSKY That is a great honor, if you please.

(NATALYA PETROVNA *makes an impatient movement*)

ANNA SEMENOVNA (*Rising from her place*) Well, at last! . . . (*Sighs*) I've sat still so long that my joints are stiff. (LIZAVETA BOGDANOVNA *and* SCHAAF *also rise*) O—oh!

NATALYA PETROVNA (*Rises and goes to them*) You must like sitting still for so long. (SHPIGELSKY *and* RAKITIN *rise*)

ANNA SEMENOVNA (*To* SCHAAF) You owe seventy kopeks, my dear sir. (SCHAAF *bows stiffly*) You can't give us orders all the time. (*To* NATALYA PETROVNA)

You seem to be pale to-day, Natasha. Are you well? Shpigelsky, is she well? . . .

SHPIGELSKY (*Who has been whispering with* RAKITIN) Oh, perfectly. 285

ANNA SEMENOVNA That's right. . . . But I'll go and rest a bit before dinner. I'm tired to death! Liza, come on. Oh, my joints, my joints! . . . (*She goes into the hall with* LIZAVETA BOGDANOVNA. NATALYA PETROVNA *accompanies her to the door.* SHPIGELSKY, RAKITIN, *and* SCHAAF *remain in the foreground*)

SHPIGELSKY (*To* SCHAAF, *offering his snuff box*) Well, Adam Ivanovich, *wie* 290 *befinden sie sik?* *

SCHAAF (*Taking snuff with dignity*) Very vell. And how are you?

SHPIGELSKY Thank you kindly. . . . So, so. (*To* RAKITIN *in a low voice*) Don't you really know what the matter is with Natalya Petrovna to-day?

RAKITIN I honestly don't know. 295

SHPIGELSKY Well, if *you* don't know . . . (*He turns aside and goes to meet* NATALYA PETROVNA, *who returns from the door*) I have a small bit of business with you, Natalya Petrovna.

NATALYA PETROVNA (*Going to the window*) Really? What?

SHPIGELSKY I need to speak with you alone. 300

NATALYA PETROVNA Really? You frighten me!

(RAKITIN *meanwhile has taken* SCHAAF'S *arm and is walking back and forth with him and is whispering something to him in German.* SCHAAF *laughs, and says in a low voice:* "Ja, ja, ja! Ja wohl, ja wohl! Sehr gut."*)

SHPIGELSKY (*Lowering his voice*) This matter really concerns others besides 305 yourself.

NATALYA PETROVNA (*Looking into the garden*) What do you mean?

SHPIGELSKY This is how the matter stands. One of my acquaintances asked me to find out . . . so to speak . . . your intentions with regard to your protégée . . . Vera Alexandrovna 310

NATALYA PETROVNA My intentions?

SHPIGELSKY That is, to speak frankly . . . my acquaintance—

NATALYA PETROVNA Is he making a proposal for her?

SHPIGELSKY Quite so.

NATALYA PETROVNA Are you joking? 315

SHPIGELSKY Not at all, madam.

NATALYA PETROVNA (*Laughing*) But pray consider, she is still a child. What a strange commission!

SHPIGELSKY Why strange, Natalya Petrovna? My acquaintance—

NATALYA PETROVNA You're a splendid man of business, Shpigelsky. And 320 who is your acquaintance?

SHPIGELSKY (*Smiling*) Permit me, permit me, you have not yet told me anything positive with regard to—

NATALYA PETROVNA Stop, doctor. Vera is still a child. You know that yourself, Mr. Diplomat. (*Turning around*) By the way, here she is. 325

(VERA *and* KOLYA *run in from the hall*)

KOLYA (*Running to* RAKITIN) Rakitin, tell 'em to give us some glue, some glue!

291 "How are you?"

304 "Yes, yes, yes! Yes, indeed, yes, indeed. Very good."

NATALYA PETROVNA (*To* VERA) Where do you come from? (*Patting her on the cheek*) How flushed you are!

VERA From the garden. . . . (SHPIGELSKY *bows to her*) How do you do, Ignaty 330
Ilyich?

RAKITIN (*To* KOLYA) What do you want glue for?

KOLYA I must have it! I must have it! . . . Alexey Nikolayevich is making a kite
for us. . . . Tell 'em! . . .

RAKITIN (*About to ring the bell*) Wait, right away. 335

SCHAAF *Erlauben Sie.** . . . Mr. Kolya hass not hat hiss lesson to-day. (*Takes*
KOLYA *by the hand*) *Kommen Sie!**

KOLYA (*In a melancholy tone*) *Morgen, Herr Schaaf, morgen.**

SCHAAF *"Morgen, Morgen, nur nicht heute, sagen alle faule Leute." Kommen Sie!**
(KOLYA *resists*) 340

NATALYA PETROVNA (*To* VERA) Who have you been walking with for so long?
I haven't seen you since morning.

VERA With Alexey Nikolayevich . . . with Kolya. . . .

NATALYA PETROVNA Ah. (*Turning*) Kolya, what does this mean?

KOLYA (*Lowering his voice*) Mr. Schaaf . . . Mamma dear. 345

RAKITIN (*To* NATALYA PETROVNA) They are making a kite outside, and in here
he's due for a lesson.

SCHAAF (*With a feeling of dignity*) *Gnädige Frau** . . .

NATALYA PETROVNA (*Sternly to* KOLYA) Kindly be obedient? You have had
enough fun to-day. Go with Mr. Schaaf. 350

SCHAAF (*Leading* KOLYA *into the hall*) *Es ist unerhört!**

KOLYA (*Whispering to* RAKITIN *as he leaves*) All the same, tell 'em to get the glue.
(RAKITIN *nods*)

SCHAAF (*Pulling at* KOLYA) *Kommen Sie, mein Herr.* . . . (*Goes out into the hall with
him,* RAKITIN *follows them*) 355

NATALYA PETROVNA (*To* VERA) Sit down. You must be tired.
(*She sits down herself*)

VERA (*Sitting down*) Not at all.

NATALYA PETROVNA (*With a smile to* SHPIGELSKY) Shpigelsky, look at her.
Isn't she tired? 360

SHPIGELSKY But that does Vera Alexandrovna good.

NATALYA PETROVNA I do not say . . . (*To* VERA) Well, what have you been
doing in the garden?

VERA Playing, running. At first we watched them building the dam, and then
Alexey Nikolayevich climbed a tree for a squirrel—way, way up, and he 365
began to shake the top of the tree. . . . We all felt very scared. . . . At last the
squirrel fell, and Trezor almost caught it, but it got away.

NATALYA PETROVNA (*Looking at* SHPIGELSKY *with a smile*) And then?

336 "Allow me."
337 "Come."
338 "Tomorrow, Herr Schaaf, tomorrow."
339 " 'Tomorrow, tomorrow, not today, say all the lazy people.' Come!"
348 "Kind madam."
351 "It's unheard of."

VERA And then Alexey Nikolayevich made a bow for Kolya, and so quickly! . . . And then he stole up to our cow in the meadow and all of a sudden 370 jumped on her back. . . . The cow was scared and began to run and kick, and he just laughed. (*She laughs herself*) And then Alexey Nikolayevich wanted to make a kite for us and so we came here.

NATALYA PETROVNA (*Patting her on the cheek*) You're a child, a child, a perfect child. Aren't you?—What do you think about it, Shpigelsky? 375

SHPIGELSKY (*Speaks slowly, watching* NATALYA PETROVNA) I agree with you.

NATALYA PETROVNA That's right.

SHPIGELSKY But this does no harm. . . . On the contrary. . . .

NATALYA PETROVNA Do you think so? (*To* VERA) Well, did you have a very good time? 380

VERA Yes. . . . Alexey Nikolayevich is so amusing.

NATALYA PETROVNA So that's it. (*After a short silence*) Vera, how old are you? (VERA *looks at her with a certain amazement*) You're a child, a child.

(RATIKIN *comes in from the hall*)

SHPIGELSKY (*Fussily*) Oh, I forgot. . . . Your coachman is ill . . . and I haven't 385 seen him yet.

NATALYA PETROVNA What's the matter with him?

SHPIGELSKY Fever. However, there's no great danger.

NATALYA PETROVNA (*Calling after him*) Are you dining with us, doctor?

SHPIGELSKY If you'll permit me. (*Goes out into the hall*) 390

NATALYA PETROVNA *Mon enfant, vous feriez bien de mettre une autre robe pour le diner.** . . . (VERA *rises*) Come to my room. (*Kisses her on the forehead*) A child! A child! (VERA *kisses her hand and goes into the study*)

RAKITIN (*In a low voice to* VERA, *winking*) I've sent everything necessary to Alexey Nikolayevich. 395

VERA (*Whispering*) Thank you, Mikhaylo Alexandrovich. (*Goes out*)

RAKITIN (*Approaching* NATALYA PETROVNA, *who stretches out her hand to him. He immediately seizes it*) At last we're alone. . . . Natalya Petrovna, tell me what is the matter with you?

NATALYA PETROVNA Nothing, Michel, nothing. And even if there was any- 400 thing, it is all over now. Sit down. (RAKITIN *sits down beside her*) This happens to everybody. Little clouds pass over the sky. Why are you looking at me in this way?

RAKITIN I'm looking at you. . . . I'm happy.

NATALYA PETROVNA (*Smiling in reply to him*) Open the window, Michel. 405 How fine it is in the garden. (RAKITIN *gets up and opens the window*) Greetings, wind! (*She laughs*) The wind seems to have been waiting for a chance to break in. (*She looks around*) How it has taken possession of the whole room! . . . You can't drive it out now.

RAKITIN Now you're as soft and quiet as an evening after a thunderstorm. 410

NATALYA PETROVNA (*Pensively repeating his last words*) "After a thunderstorm." . . .

RAKITIN (*Shaking his head*) One was gathering.

NATALYA PETROVNA Really? (*Looking at him after a short silence*) Let me tell you, Michel, I cannot imagine a kinder man than yourself. Honestly. (RAKITIN

392 "My child, you would do well to put on another dress for dinner."

tries to stop her) No, don't hinder me from expressing myself. You are 415 sympathetic, affectionate, faithful. You do not betray one. I am indebted to you in many ways.

RAKITIN Natalya Petrovna, why do you say this to me at this particular moment?

NATALYA PETROVNA I don't know. I feel gay. I'm taking a bit of relaxation. 420 Don't forbid me to chatter.

RAKITIN (*Pressing her hand*) You are kind as an angel.

NATALYA PETROVNA (*Laughing*) This morning you would not have said that! . . . But listen to me, Michel. You know me, you must excuse me. Our relations are so pure, so sincere, and yet they are not entirely natural.—You 425 and I have a right to look straight in the eyes, not only of Arkady, but of all the world. Yes, but .,. . (*Falls into meditation*) that is why I am sometimes troubled and depressed and cross. I am ready like a child to vent my vexation upon another person, especially upon you. . . . This preference does not make you angry? 430

RAKITIN (*With animation*) On the contrary. . . .

NATALYA PETROVNA Yes. Sometimes it's pleasant to torture a person whom you love . . . whom you love. You see that I, like Tatyana, can say, "Why dissemble?"*

RAKITIN Natalya Petrovna, you— 435

NATALYA PETROVNA (*Interrupting him*) Yes . . . I love you. But let me tell you, Rakitin, do you know that occasionally it seems strange to me. I love you, and that feeling is so clear, so peaceful. . . . It does not excite me . . . I am warmed by it, but . . . (*With animation*) You never have caused me to weep, and I apparently should— (*Interrupting herself*) What does this mean? 440

RAKITIN (*Somewhat sadly*) Such a question demands no answer.

NATALYA PETROVNA (*Pensively*) Yet you and I are old acquaintances.

RAKITIN Four years. Yes. We're old friends. . . .

NATALYA PETROVNA Friends. No, you are more than a friend to me.

RAKITIN Natalya Petrovna, do not touch on that question. I fear for my 445 happiness—that it may vanish under your hands.

NATALYA PETROVNA No . . . no . . . no! The whole thing is that you are too kind. You humor me too much. . . . You have spoiled me. . . . You are too kind. . . . Do you hear?

RAKITIN (*With a smile*) I hear. 450

NATALYA PETROVNA (*Looking at him*) I don't know how you . . . I wish no other happiness. . . . Many people might envy me. (*She stretches out both hands to him*) Is that not true?

RAKITIN I am in your power. . . . Do with me as you wish. (*From the hall is heard* ISLAYEV'S *voice:* "So you have sent for him.") 455

NATALYA PETROVNA (*Rising quickly*) It is he. I cannot see him now. . . . Goodby! (*She goes out into the study*)

RAKITIN (*Gazing after her*) What does this mean? Is it the beginning of the end, or absolutely the end? (*After a short silence*) Or the beginning? (ISLAYEV *comes in with a troubled air and takes off his hat*) 460

434 A reference to Pushkin's poem *Eugene Onegin* [trans. note].

ISLAYEV Good day, Michel!*

RAKITIN We've seen each other before to-day.

ISLAYEV Oh, excuse me! . . . I have been absorbed in business. (*Paces the room*)
It is queer. The Russian peasant is very clever, very quick to understand; I
respect the Russian peasant. . . . And yet sometimes you tell him some- 465
thing—tell him, explain, and explain. . . . Everything seems clear, but nothing
comes of it. The Russian peasant hasn't that . . . that . . .

RAKITIN Are you still bothering with the dam?

ISLAYEV That . . . so to speak . . . hasn't that love for his work. That's the point.
He hasn't a love for it. He won't let you explain your meaning fully— 470
"I understand, sir . . ." and yet he understood nothing at all. Look at a German—that's another story. The Russian has no patience.— With all that, I
respect him. . . . But where is Natasha. Don't you know?

RAKITIN She was here just now.

ISLAYEV And what time is it? It must be time for dinner. I've been on my 475
legs since morning. I've loads of work . . . and yet I haven't looked at the
building operations to-day. Time does pass so. It's simply terrific—you can't
get anywhere! (RAKITIN *smiles*) You're laughing at me, I see. . . . But what's
to be done, friend? Each to his own business. I'm a matter-of-fact man, born
to be a landlord and nothing more. There was a time when I had dreams 480
of something else, but I missed fire, friend. I burnt my fingers—like that!—
Why is it Belyayev doesn't come?

RAKITIN Who is Belyayev?

ISLAYEV Our new teacher, the Russian. He's a queer lad, but he'll get used to
things. He's not a stupid fellow. I asked him to-day to see how the build- 485
ing was getting on.

(BELYAYEV *comes in*)

Oh, here he is! Well, how about it? How are they getting along there? They
aren't doing a thing, I suppose. Are they?

BELYAYEV Yes. They are at work.   490

ISLAYEV Have they finished the second frame?

BELYAYEV They have begun on the third.

ISLAYEV And about the beams? Did you tell them?

BELYAYEV I did.

ISLAYEV Well, and what did they say?   495

BELYAYEV They say they never have done it in any other fashion.

ISLAYEV Hm! Is Ermil, the carpenter, there?

BELYAYEV Yes.

ISLAYEV Oh! . . . Well, thank you.

(NATALYA PETROVNA *comes in*)   500

Oh, good day, Natasha!

RAKITIN How is it that to-day you are bidding everybody good day twenty times
over?

ISLAYEV I tell you I got deep in business. Oh, by the way, I haven't shown you

---

461 In Russia friends greet each other and shake hands on their first meeting each day. It is a breach of
etiquette to repeat the salutation later [trans. note].

my new winnowing fan.* Come on, please; it's worth seeing. Just imagine! 505
It makes a hurricane, a regular hurricane. We'll have time before dinner. . . .
Want to?

RAKITIN All right.

ISLAYEV And Natasha—won't you come with us?

NATALYA PETROVNA The idea of my understanding anything about your 510
winnowing fans!—You two go on alone and see that you don't get delayed.

ISLAYEV (*Going out with* RAKITIN) We'll be back directly. (BELYAYEV *is about to
follow them*)

NATALYA PETROVNA (*To* BELYAYEV) Where are you going, Alexey Nikolayevich.   515

BELYAYEV I . . . I . . .

NATALYA PETROVNA However, if you wish to take a walk—

BELYAYEV No, I've been in the open air all the morning.

NATALYA PETROVNA Well, in that case, sit down here. . . . Sit down here. (*She
points to a chair*) You and I have not yet had a real conversation, Alexey 520
Nikolayevich; we've not yet got acquainted. (BELYAYEV *bows and sits down*)
And I want to get acquainted with you.

BELYAYEV I . . . that is very flattering to me.

NATALYA PETROVNA (*With a smile*) Now you are afraid of me again; I see that.
But wait! You will learn to know me and you will stop being afraid of me. 525
Tell me . . . tell me how old you are.

BELYAYEV Twenty-one, madam.

NATALYA PETROVNA Are your parents living?

BELYAYEV My mother is dead; my father is living.

NATALYA PETROVNA And did your mother pass away long ago?   530

BELYAYEV Yes, madam.

NATALYA PETROVNA But, do you remember her?

BELYAYEV Of course I remember her.

NATALYA PETROVNA And is your father living in Moscow?

BELYAYEV No, madam, in the country.   535

NATALYA PETROVNA Well, have you brothers and sisters?

BELYAYEV One sister.

NATALYA PETROVNA Do you love her very much?

BELYAYEV Yes, I do. She is much younger than I.

NATALYA PETROVNA And what's her name?   540

BELYAYEV Natalya.

NATALYA PETROVNA (*With animation*) Natalya? That's queer! My name is
Natalya also. (*She pauses*) And you love her very much?

BELYAYEV Yes, madam.

NATALYA PETROVNA Tell me, how do you find my Kolya?   545

BELYAYEV He's a very charming boy.

NATALYA PETROVNA Isn't he? And so affectionate! He's already become
attached to you.

BELYAYEV I try to do my best. . . . I am glad . . .

505 A machine used to expose grain to the air for the purposes of separating the grain from the chaff.

NATALYA PETROVNA Now you see, Alexey Nikolayevich, of course I should ₅₅₀ like to make a man of action out of him. I don't know whether I shall succeed in that, but at any rate I want him always to remember with pleasure the time of his childhood. Let him grow up at liberty—that is the main thing. I myself was educated otherwise, Alexey Nikolayevich. My father, although not an ill-tempered man, was irritable and stern. . . . Every one in the ₅₅₅ house, beginning with mamma, was afraid of him. My mother and I used to cross ourselves secretly every time we were summoned to him. Sometimes my father would undertake to caress me, but even in his embraces, I remember, I felt faint all over. My brother grew up, and perhaps you have heard of his rupture with father. . . . I shall never forget that awful day. . . . I remained ₅₆₀ my father's obedient daughter to the very end. . . . He called me his comfort, his Antigone*—he was blind during the last years of his life. But his most tender caresses could not efface from my mind the first impressions of my youth. . . . I was afraid of him, the blind old man, and in his presence I never felt myself free. . . . The traces of this timidity, of this long constraint, per- ₅₆₅ haps have not yet completely disappeared. . . . I know that at first glance I appear . . . what shall I call it? . . . cold, possibly. . . . But I notice that I am telling you of myself, instead of speaking to you of Kolya. I just want to say that I know of my own experience how good it is for a child to grow up at liberty. . . . Now I think that in your childhood you did not suffer from ₅₇₀ constraint.

BELYAYEV How can I tell you? . . . Of course, no one constrained me . . . no one paid any attention to me.

NATALYA PETROVNA (*Timidly*) But perhaps, your father—

BELYAYEV He had no interest in the matter. He was always riding round to ₅₇₅ our neighbors . . . on business. Or maybe not on business, but . . . He made his living through them, I may say, . . . through his services to them.

NATALYA PETROVNA Oh, and so no one attended to your education?

BELYAYEV To tell the truth, no one. However, probably you've noticed that already. I am only too conscious of my own defects. ₅₈₀

NATALYA PETROVNA Perhaps . . . but on the other hand— (*She stops and continues with a certain confusion*) Oh, by the way, was it you, Alexey Nikolayevich, who was singing in the garden yesterday?

BELYAYEV When?

NATALYA PETROVNA In the evening, near the pond. ₅₈₅

BELYAYEV Yes. (*Hastily*) I did not think . . . the pond is so far from here . . . I did not think that it could be heard here.

NATALYA PETROVNA And you seem to be excusing yourself? You have a very pleasant, sonorous voice, and you sing so well. Have you studied music?

BELYAYEV Not a bit. I sing by ear . . . only simple songs. ₅₉₀

NATALYA PETROVNA You sing them splendidly. I shall ask you sometime . . . not now . . . but when you and I get better acquainted, when we become intimate. You see, Alexey Nikolayevich, we shall certainly become intimate,

---

⁵⁶² The devoted daughter of Oedipus in Greek story.

shan't we? I feel confidence in you. My chatter may prove it. . . . (*She stretches out her hand to him in order that he may press it.* BELYAYEV *takes it inde-* 595 *cisively and has a certain perplexity in knowing what to do with that hand; he kisses it.* NATALYA PETROVNA *blushes and withdraws her hand. At that moment* SHPIGELSKY *enters from the hall, stops and takes a step backward.* NATALYA PETROVNA *rises quickly,* BELYAYEV *also*)

NATALYA PETROVNA (*In confusion*) Oh, is that you, doctor? Alexey Niko- 600 layevich and I are here. (*She stops*)

SHPIGELSKY (*In a loud, casual tone*) Just imagine, Natalya Petrovna, what things are going on in your household! I went into your servants' room and asked for your sick coachman. Lo and behold! My invalid was sitting at the table and consuming pancakes and onions full speed. After this you can quit 605 studying medicine and relying on disease as an innocent source of income!

NATALYA PETROVNA (*With a forced smile*) Oh, really . . . (BELYAYEV *is about to go*) Alexey Nikolayevich, I forgot to tell you. . . .

(VERA, *runs in from the hall*)

VERA Alexey Nikolayevich, Alexey Nikolayevich! (*She suddenly stops at the* 610 *sight of* NATALYA PETROVNA) ›

NATALYA PETROVNA (*With a certain surprise*) What's all this? What do you want?

VERA (*Blushing and lowering her eyes; points to* BELYAYEV) They're calling him.

NATALYA PETROVNA Who?   615

VERA Kolya. That is, Kolya asked me about the kite.

NATALYA PETROVNA Oh! (*In a low voice to* VERA) On n'entre pas comme cela dans une chambre. . . . Cela ne convient pas.* (*Turning to* SHPIGELSKY) Well, what time is it, doctor? Your watch is always right. . . . Is it time for dinner?

SHPIGELSKY Just a moment, please. (*Takes his watch from his pocket*) Now . . . 620 now . . . I may report, it's twenty minutes past four.

NATALYA PETROVNA So you see, it's time. (*Goes to the mirror and adjusts her hair; meanwhile* VERA *whispers something to* BELYAYEV. *They both laugh.* NATALYA PETROVNA *sees them in the mirror.* SHPIGELSKY *takes a sidelong glance at her*)   625

BELYAYEV (*Laughing softly*) Really?

VERA (*Nodding and also in a low voice*) Yes, yes, she just fell.

NATALYA PETROVNA (*With an affected indifference, turning to* VERA) What's that? Who fell?

VERA (*Confused*) No . . . Alexey Nikolayevich had made a swing, and then 630 nurse took it into her head—

NATALYA PETROVNA (*Without waiting for the end of the answer, to* SHPIGELSKY) Oh, by the way, Shpigelsky, come here. (*She leads him aside and again turns to* VERA) Did she hurt herself?

VERA Oh, no.   635

NATALYA PETROVNA That's good. And yet, Alexey Nikolayevich, you make a mistake to—

---

618 "One does not come into a room in that way. It's not fitting."

MATVEY (*Enters from the hall and announces*) Dinner is served.

NATALYA PETROVNA Oh, where is Arkady Sergeich? He and Mikhaylo Alexandrovich will be late again. 640

MATVEY They are already in the dining-room.

NATALYA PETROVNA And mamma?

MATVEY She is in the dining-room also.

NATALYA PETROVNA Oh, very well. Come on! (*Pointing to* BELYAYEV) Vera, *allez en avant avec monsieur.** 645

(MATVEY *goes out, followed by* BELYAYEV *and* VERA)

SHPIGELSKY (*To* NATALYA PETROVNA) Did you wish to say anything to me?

NATALYA PETROVNA Oh, yes! To be sure. . . . Now you see . . . I'll speak to you later about . . . about your proposal.

SHPIGELSKY In regard to . . . Vera Alexandrovna? 650

NATALYA PETROVNA Yes, I'll think it over. . . . I'll think it over.

(*Both go out into the hall*)

Act Two

A garden. On the right and left, under the trees, benches. Center a raspberry patch. KATYA *and* MATVEY *come in from the right.* KATYA *has a basket in her hands*

MATVEY Well, then, Katerina Vasilyevna. Will you please explain yourself? I earnestly beg you to. 5

KATYA Why really, Matvey Egorych . . .

MATVEY You know only too well, Katerina Vasilyevna, what my attitude is towards you. Of course, I am older than you. There is no dispute about that, but all the same I can still look out for myself. I am still in the very prime of life, and also, as you perfectly well know, I am of a gentle disposition, so 10 what more do you want?

KATYA Believe me, Matvey Egorych, I appreciate it very much. I am very grateful, Matvey Egorych. . . . But you see . . . I think I had better wait.

MATVEY But what shall we wait for, pray, Katerina Vasilyevna? Formerly, if you will permit me to remark, you did not talk in this way, and as for showing 15 you due respect, I think I may vouch for myself. You will receive such respect, Katerina Vasilyevna, that you could ask for nothing better. Besides that, I don't drink, and I have never heard any reproaches from the gentlefolk.

KATYA Really, Matvey Egorych, I don't know what to say to you. . . .

MATVEY Oh, Katerina Vasilyevna, a little while ago you began to be . . . 20

KATYA (*With a slight blush*) A little while ago? Why so?

MATVEY I really don't know. . . . Only before . . . before you behaved quite differently towards me.

KATYA (*Looking hastily off stage*) Look out! . . . The German is coming.

MATVEY (*With vexation*) Plague take him, the long-nosed donkey! . . . But 25 I'll have further conversation with you later. (*Goes out to the right.* KATYA *also is about to go into the raspberry patch*)

645 "Go on ahead with *monsieur.*"

(SCHAAF *comes in from the left with a fishing rod on his shoulder*)

SCHAAF (*Calling after* KATYA) Vere to, vere to, Caterin?

KATYA (*Stopping*) They told me to pick some raspberries, Adam Ivanovich. 30

SCHAAF Raspberriess? . . . Raspberriess are a pleasant fruit. You luf raspberriess?

KATYA Yes, I do.

SCHAAF Hee, hee! . . . I do . . . I do too. I luf every sing zat you luf. (*Seeing that she is about to leave*) Oh, Caterin, vait a bit.

KATYA No time. . . . The housekeeper will scold me. 35

SCHAAF Oh, zat's all right. Now I am going to . . . (*Pointing to his fishing rod*) I am going vat you say, you understart, fishing, zat is, catching fish. You like zem, fish?

KATYA Yes.

SCHAAF Eh, hee, hee! So do I. So do I. And let me tell you, Caterin. . . . In 40 German zere is a song (*Sings*) *Cathrinchen, Cathrinchen, wie lieb' ich dich so sehr!** Zat iss in Russian: Oh, Caterin, Caterin, you are pretty, I luf you.
(*Tries to embrace her with one arm*)

KATYA Stop! Stop! Aren't you ashamed! . . . And here comes the mistress!
(*Takes refuge in the raspberry patch*) 45

SCHAAF (*Assuming a stern air, in a low voice*) Das ist dumm. . . .**
(NATALYA PETROVNA *comes in from the right, arm in arm with* RAKITIN)

NATALYA PETROVNA (*To* SCHAAF) Oh, Adam Ivanovich, are you going fishing?

SCHAAF Yoost so!

NATALYA PETROVNA And where is Kolya? 50

SCHAAF Mit Lissavet Bogdanovna. . . . A lesson on ze piano. . . .

NATALYA PETROVNA Oh! (*Looking around*) Are you alone here?

SCHAAF Yes, ma'am.

NATALYA PETROVNA Haven't you seen Alexey Nikolayevich?

SCHAAF Not at all. 55

NATALYA PETROVNA (*After a pause*) Let's go on together, Adam Ivanovich, shan't we? We'll watch you fish.

SCHAAF I am very glat.

RAKITIN (*In a low voice to* NATALYA PETROVNA) What an idea!

NATALYA PETROVNA (*To* RAKITIN) Come on, come on, *beau ténébreaux.** 60
(*All three go out to the right*)

KATYA (*Cautiously putting her head out of the raspberry patch*) They have gone.
(*She comes out, pauses for a moment, and falls to thinking*) That German! . . .
(*Sighs, and again begins to pick raspberries, humming in a low voice*)
    The fire does not burn, the pitch does not boil 65
    But there boils and there burns my eager heart. . . .
Matvey Egorych was certainly right! (*Continues to hum*)
    But there boils and there burns my eager heart;
    And not for my father, not for my mother dear . . .
(*Stops singing and exclaims*) What huge raspberries! (*Continues to hum*) 70
    Not for my father, not for my mother dear . . .

---

42 "Dear Catherine, dear Catherine, I love you so much."
46 "That is stupid."
60 A hero wrapped in Byronic gloom.

How hot it is! Absolutely suffocating. (*Continues to hum*)
Not for my father, not for my mother dear:
It boils and it burns—
(*Suddenly she looks around, stops singing, and half hides herself behind a bush.* 75
BELYAYEV *and* VEROCHKA *come in from the left.* BELYAYEV *has a kite in his hands*)

BELYAYEV (*Walking past the raspberry patch, to* KATYA) Why do you stop, Katya?
(*He sings*)
But it boils and burns for a maiden fair. 80

KATYA (*Blushing*) That's not the way *we* sing it.

BELYAYEV Well, how do you? (KATYA *laughs and does not answer*) What are you doing, picking raspberries? Let me try some.

KATYA (*Giving him the basket*) Take 'em all.

BELYAYEV Why all of them? . . . Vera Alexandrovna, will you have some? 85
(*Both* VERA *and he take some from the basket*) Well, that's enough.
(*Tries to give back the basket to* KATYA)

KATYA (*Pushing away his hand*) Take 'em all, take 'em.

BELYAYEV No, thank you, Katya. (*He gives her back the basket*) Thank you.
(*To* VERA) Vera Alexandrovna, let's sit down on the bench. (*Pointing to the* 90
kite) We must tie on the tail. You'll help me. (*They both go and sit down on
the bench.* BELYAYEV *hands her the kite*) That's the way. Now look out, hold
it straight. (*He begins to tie on the tail*) What are you doing?

VERA Put that away! I can't see you.

BELYAYEV And what do you want to see me for? 95

VERA I mean, I want to see how you tie on the tail.

BELYAYEV Oh, well, stand still. (*He arranges the kite so that she can see him*)
Katya, why don't you sing? Go ahead.
(*In a moment* KATYA *begins to hum in a low voice*)

VERA Tell me, Alexey Nikolayevich, do you sometimes fly kites in Moscow 100
too?

BELYAYEV No time for kites in Moscow! Hold the cord! . . . That's the way. Do
you think we haven't anything else to do in Moscow?

VERA What do you do in Moscow?

BELYAYEV What do we do? We study and listen to the professors. 105

VERA What do they teach you?

BELYAYEV Everything.

VERA You must be a very good student. Best of all of them.

BELYAYEV No, not very good. Very far from the best! I'm lazy.

VERA Why are you lazy? 110

BELYAYEV Lord knows! I must have been born so.

VERA (*After a pause*) Well, have you some student friends in Moscow?

BELYAYEV Of course. Oh, that cord isn't strong enough.

VERA And do you love them?

BELYAYEV Certainly! . . . Don't you love your friends among the boys? 115

VERA Among the boys? I haven't any friends among them.

BELYAYEV I meant to say, your girl friends. .

VERA (*Slowly*)   Yes.

BELYAYEV   You have girl friends?

VERA   Yes, only—I don't know why—for some time I haven't been thinking 120 much about them. I haven't even answered Liza Moshnin and she so urged me in her last letter.

BELYAYEV   What do you mean by saying that you haven't any boy friends? . . . Where do I come in?

VERA (*With a smile*)   Oh, you . . . you are another story. (*After a pause*) Alexey 125 Nikolayevich!

BELYAYEV   What?

VERA   Do you write poetry?

BELYAYEV   No. Why do you ask?

VERA   No special reason. (*After a pause*) In our pension* one young lady wrote 130 verses.

BELYAYEV (*Pulling a knot with his teeth*)   Well, well, were they good ones?

VERA   I don't know. She used to read them to us and we wept.

BELYAYEV   Why did you weep?

VERA   For sorrow. We were so sorry for her!   135

BELYAYEV   Were you educated in Moscow?

VERA   Yes, at Mrs. Bolus's. Natalya Petrovna took me from there last year.

BELYAYEV   Do you love Natalya Petrovna?

VERA   Yes, she is so kind. I love her very much.

BELYAYEV (*With a grin*)   And you are afraid of her, I suppose?   140

VERA (*Also with a grin*)   A little bit.

BELYAYEV (*After a pause*)   And who put you in the pension?

VERA   Natalya Petrovna's mother, who is now dead. I grew up in her house. I am an orphan.

BELYAYEV (*Letting his hands fall*) You are an orphan? And you don't remem- 145 ber either your father or your mother?

VERA   No.

BELYAYEV   And my mother is dead, too. We are both of us orphans. What can we do about it? But anyhow we needn't be cast down.

VERA   They say that orphans make friends with each other very quickly.   150

BELYAYEV (*Looking into her eyes*)   Really, what do you think about it?

VERA (*Also looking into his eyes with a smile*)   I think they do.

BELYAYEV (*Laughing, and again applying himself to the kite*)   I should like to know how long I have been in these parts.

VERA   To-day is the twenty-eighth day.   155

BELYAYEV   What a memory you have! Well, here's the kite finished. Just see what a tail! We must go for Kolya.

KATYA (*Coming up to them with a basket*)   Will you have some more raspberries?

BELYAYEV   No, thank you, Katya. (KATYA *silently moves away*)

VERA   Kolya is with Lizaveta Bogdanovna.   160

BELYAYEV   They must like to keep a child indoors in such weather.

VERA   Lizaveta Bogdanovna would just be in our way.

---

130 A boarding-house.

BELYAYEV I am not talking about her.

VERA (*Hastily*) Kolya couldn't come with us without her. . . . By the way, she spoke of you in a very complimentary fashion yesterday. 165

BELYAYEV Really!

VERA You don't like her?

BELYAYEV Plague take her. Let her take snuff, and much good may it do her! . . . Why are you sighing?

VERA (*After a pause*) I don't know. How bright the sky is! 170

BELYAYEV Is that what makes you sigh? (*Silence*) Maybe you feel lonesome.

VERA Me, lonesome? No! I never know myself why I sigh. . . . I am not lonesome at all. On the contrary . . . (*After a pause*) . . . I don't know. I probably am not in perfect health. Yesterday I went upstairs for a book and all of a sudden—just imagine!—I sat down on a step and began to cry . . . God 175 knows why . . . and for a long time after tears kept coming into my eyes. What does that mean? And yet I feel very well.

BELYAYEV That is because you are growing. You are growing up. Such things happen. . . . That's true: yesterday evening your eyes looked swollen.

VERA Did you notice it? 180

BELYAYEV Certainly.

VERA You notice everything.

BELYAYEV Oh, no! . . . Not everything.

VERA (*Pensively*) Alexey Nikolayevich . . .

BELYAYEV What? 185

VERA (*After a pause*) What was it that I wanted to ask you any way? I've really forgotten what I wanted to ask.

BELYAYEV You are so absent-minded.

VERA No . . . but . . . oh, yes! Here's what I wanted to ask you. You were telling me you have a sister? 190

BELYAYEV Yes.

VERA Tell me, am I like her?

BELYAYEV Oh, no! You are a lot nicer than she.

VERA Impossible! Your sister . . . I should like to be in her place.

BELYAYEV What? You would like to be in our little house now? 195

VERA I didn't mean that. . . . Is your house a little one?

BELYAYEV Very little. . . . Not like this one here.

VERA But what's the use of so many rooms?

BELYAYEV What's the use of them? You'll find out in due time what the use of rooms is. 200

VERA In due time? . . . When?

BELYAYEV When you become a housewife yourself.

VERA (*Pensively*) Do you think so?

BELYAYEV You will see. (*After a pause*) Well then, shall we go for Kolya, Vera Alexandrovna? Shall we? 205

VERA Why don't you call me Verochka?*

BELYAYEV And can you really call me Alexey?

---

[206] An affectionate diminutive [trans. note].

VERA Why not? . . . (*With a sudden start*) Oh!

BELYAYEV What's the matter?

VERA (*In a low voice*) Natalya Petrovna is coming this way.   210

BELYAYEV (*Also in a low voice*) Where?

VERA (*Indicating with her head*) Along the path there with Mikhaylo Alexandrovich.

BELYAYEV (*Rising*) Let's go to Kolya. . . . He must have finished his lesson by this time.   215

VERA Come on! Otherwise I'm afraid she'll scold me. (*They both rise and go out quickly to the left.* KATYA *again hides in the raspberry patch*)
(NATALYA PETROVNA *and* RAKITIN *come in from the right*)

NATALYA PETROVNA (*Stopping*) I think that's Mr. Belyayev going out with Verochka.   220

RAKITIN Yes, it's they.

NATALYA PETROVNA They seem to be running away from us.

RAKITIN Perhaps.

NATALYA PETROVNA (*After a pause*) However, I don't think that Verochka ought . . . to be alone with a young man in the garden in this way. . . . Of   225
course she's a child but all the same it isn't proper. I'll tell her.

RAKITIN How old is she?

NATALYA PETROVNA Seventeen. She's already seventeen. . . . How warm it is to-day! I'm tired. Let's sit down. (*They both sit down on the bench where* VERA *and* BELYAYEV *have been sitting*) . . . Has Shpigelsky gone?   230

RAKITIN Yes.

NATALYA PETROVNA You made a mistake not to keep him. I don't know how that man got the idea of becoming a country doctor. . . . He's very amusing. He makes me laugh.

RAKITIN But I imagine that you are not in a laughing humor to-day.   235

NATALYA PETROVNA Why do you think so?

RAKITIN Just a fancy!

NATALYA PETROVNA Is it because to-day I dislike everything sentimental? Oh yes, I forewarn you: to-day absolutely nothing can touch my emotions. . . . But that doesn't keep me from laughing. . . . Besides, I needed to have a   240
talk with Shpigelsky.

RAKITIN May I inquire—what about?

NATALYA PETROVNA No, you may not. Anyhow, you know everything that I think . . . that I do. That's tiresome.

RAKITIN Excuse me! . . . I did not suppose . . .   245

NATALYA PETROVNA I should like to conceal at least some one little thing from you.

RAKITIN Good gracious. From your words I might infer that I knew everything. . . .

NATALYA PETROVNA (*Interrupting him*) And don't you?   250

RAKITIN You seem to enjoy laughing at me.

NATALYA PETROVNA So really don't you know everything that goes on within me? In that case I don't congratulate you. Impossible! A man observes me from morning till evening—

RAKITIN What's that? A reproach? 255

NATALYA PETROVNA A reproach? (*After a pause*) I now see clearly: you are not a man of penetration.

RAKITIN Perhaps not. . . . But since I observe you from morning till evening, permit me to make one remark to you. . . .

NATALYA PETROVNA In regard to me? Pray do so. 260

RAKITIN You won't be angry with me?

NATALYA PETROVNA Oh, no! I should like to be, but I shan't.

RAKITIN For some time, Natalya Petrovna, you have been in a sort of constantly irritated condition and this irritation of yours is involuntary, from within. You seem to be struggling with yourself, seem to be in perplexity. Before 265 my trip to the Krinitsyns' I did not observe this. It is of recent date with you. (NATALYA PETROVNA *draws figures on the ground with her parasol*) Sometimes you sigh so deeply . . . just as a weary, a very weary person sighs, a person who never has a chance to take a rest.

NATALYA PETROVNA What conclusion do you form from that, Mr. 270 Observer?

RAKITIN None at all. . . . But this disquiets me.

NATALYA PETROVNA Thank you humbly for your sympathy.

RAKITIN And besides—

NATALYA PETROVNA (*With a certain impatience*) Please let's change the sub- 275 ject. (*Silence*)

RAKITIN You don't intend to take a ride anywhere to-day?

NATALYA PETROVNA No.

RAKITIN Why not? The weather's fine.

NATALYA PETROVNA I'm too lazy. (*Silence*) Tell me. . . . You are acquainted 280 with Bolshintsov?

RAKITIN Our neighbor, Afanasy Ivanovich?

NATALYA PETROVNA Yes.

RAKITIN What a question! Only day before yesterday you and I were playing preference with him. 285

NATALYA PETROVNA What kind of a man is he, I should like to know.

RAKITIN Bolshintsov?

NATALYA PETROVNA Yes, yes, Bolshintsov.

RAKITIN Well, I must confess, I never expected this.

NATALYA PETROVNA (*With impatience*) What didn't you expect? 290

RAKITIN That you would ever ask me about Bolshintsov! He is a stupid, fat, heavy man, and yet one can't say anything bad about him.

NATALYA PETROVNA He is by no means so stupid and so heavy as you think.

RAKITIN Maybe. I confess I haven't studied that gentleman with any great attention. 295

NATALYA PETROVNA (*Ironically*) You haven't been observing *him?*

RAKITIN (*With a forced smile*) How did you get that idea?

NATALYA PETROVNA Just a fancy! (*Again a silence*)

RAKITIN Look, Natalya Petrovna, how beautiful that dark-green oak is against the dark-blue sky! It is all bathed in the sunbeams—and what vivid colors! 300

. . . How much indomitable life and force there is in it, especially when you compare it with that young birch. . . . The birch seems already to vanish in the radiance; its little leaves gleam with a sort of moist luster, as if they were melting, and yet the birch also is beautiful. . . .

NATALYA PETROVNA Let me tell you, Rakitin. I long ago noticed this trait in 305 you: You have a very keen sense for the so-called beauties of nature, and you speak of them very elegantly, very cleverly . . . so elegantly, so cleverly, that I imagine nature ought to be inexpressibly grateful to you for your aptly-turned expressions. You pay court to it as a perfumed marquis with red-heeled shoes does to a pretty peasant girl. . . . Only here's the trouble: it occasionally 310 seems to me that nature could not in the least understand or appreciate your acute observations, just as the peasant girl would not understand the elegant courtesies of the marquis. Nature is far simpler, even coarser, than you suppose, because, thank God, it is healthy. . . . Birches do not melt and do not faint away like nervous ladies. 315

RAKITIN *Quelle tirade!* * Nature is healthy. That is, in other words, I am a sickly creature.

NATALYA PETROVNA You are not the only sickly creature. Both you and I are by no means healthy.

RAKITIN Oh, I know very well that method of telling another person the 320 most unpleasant things in the most inoffensive fashion. . . . Instead of telling him straight to his face, for instance: "My boy, you are stupid," you merely have to remark to him with a good-natured smile, "You see, both of us are stupid."

NATALYA PETROVNA Are you taking offense? Stop! What nonsense! I only 325 meant that both of us . . . you don't like the word "sickly" . . . that both of us are old, very old.

RAKITIN Why old? That's not my opinion of myself.

NATALYA PETROVNA Well, anyway, listen to me. Here you and I are sitting now . . . perhaps on the very same bench on which a quarter of an hour 330 ago there were sitting . . . two genuinely young creatures.

RAKITIN Belyayev and Verochka? Of course they are younger than we are. . . . Between us and them there is a few years' difference, that is all. . . . But that doesn't make us old yet awhile.

NATALYA PETROVNA The difference between us is not in years alone. 335

RAKITIN Oh, I understand. You envy their . . . naïveté and freshness and innocence . . . in a word, their stupidity. . . .

NATALYA PETROVNA You think so? Ah! You think they are stupid? I see that you regard every one as stupid to-day. No, you don't understand me. And besides . . . stupid! Where's the harm in that? What's the use of intellect 340 when it isn't amusing? . . . There's nothing more wearisome than melancholy intellect.

RAKITIN Hm. . . . Why won't you say straight out, without beating around the bush, that I don't amuse you? That's what you really mean. . . . And why do you make intellect in general suffer for my sins? 345

316 "What a long fancy speech!"

NATALYA PETROVNA You take everything wrong. . . . (KATYA *comes out of the raspberry patch*) Well, have you picked the raspberries, Katya?

KATYA Yes, madam.

NATALYA PETROVNA Show them to me. . . . (KATYA *comes up to her*) Splendid raspberries! What a bright color! . . . But your cheeks are still brighter. ₃₅₀ (KATYA *smiles and lowers her eyes*) Well, go along. (KATYA *goes out*)

RAKITIN There is one more young creature to your taste.

NATALYA PETROVNA To be sure. (*She rises*)

RAKITIN Where are you going?

NATALYA PETROVNA In the first place I want to see what Verochka is doing. ₃₅₅ It's time for her to be going indoors. . . . And in the second place I must confess that I don't specially like our conversation. It would be better for a while to cut short our discussion of nature and youth.

RAKITIN Maybe you would like to have a walk alone?

NATALYA PETROVNA To tell the truth, I should. We'll soon see each other ₃₆₀ again. . . . All the same, we part friends, do we not? (*Extends her hand to him*)

RAKITIN Of course. (*Presses her hand*)

NATALYA PETROVNA *Au revoir.* (*She opens her parasol and goes out to the left*)

RAKITIN (*Walks for some time back and forth*) What's the matter with her? (*After a pause*) Just a caprice. Caprice? I've never before thought her capricious. ₃₆₅ On the contrary, I don't know a woman of more equable temper. What's the reason? . . . (*He paces back and forth again and suddenly stops*) Oh, how ridiculous people are who have only one thought in their head, one aim, one occupation in life! . . . Take me, for example. She told the truth: from morning till evening you observe trifles and so you become trifling yourself. . . . That's ₃₇₀ all true, but I can't live without her. In her presence I am more than happy. This feeling cannot be called mere happiness. I belong to her entirely. To part from her would be just as difficult for me, without any exaggeration, as to part with life itself. What's the matter with her? What is the meaning of that inner emotion, that involuntary bitterness of expression. Am I not beginning to ₃₇₅ bore her? Hm (*He sits down*) I have never deceived myself. I know very well in what way she loves me, but I hoped that this calm feeling would in the course of time . . . I hoped! Have I the right, may I dare to hope? I confess my position is ridiculous enough . . . almost contemptible. (*After a pause*) Well, what's the use of such words? She's an honorable woman and I am ₃₈₀ not a Lovelace.* (*With a bitter smile*) Unfortunately. (*Rising quickly*) Well, that's enough! I must get all this nonsense out of my head. (*Walking up and down*) What a splendid day this is! (*After a pause*) How cleverly she wounded me! . . . My "aptly-turned expressions"! . . . She is very, very shrewd, especially when she is out of spirits. And what a sudden adoration for sim- ₃₈₅ plicity and innocence! . . . That Russian teacher! . . . She often speaks to me of him. I confess I don't see anything special in him. He is simply a student like other students. Is it possible that she . . . ? Impossible! She is out of spirits. . . . She doesn't know herself what she wants, and so she scratches me. Even children beat their nurse. . . . What a happy comparison! But I don't want ₃₉₀

₃₈₁ Robert Lovelace, a rake in Samuel Richardson's novel *Clarissa* (1747–1748).

to hinder her. When this attack of uneasiness and disquiet is over she will be the first to laugh at that lanky fledgling, at that unspoiled youth. . . . Your explanation is not bad, Mikhaylo Alexandrovich, my friend. But is it correct? The Lord knows! We'll see later. It has often happened, my dear fellow, that after long debate with yourself, you have suddenly had to renounce all ₃₉₅ suppositions and surmises, fold your arms calmly and wait humbly to see what would happen. And meanwhile, confess that you are in a decidedly embarrassing and bitter position. . . . Such is your trade now. . . . (*Looking around*) But here he comes himself, our unspoiled youth. . . . He has arrived just in time . . . I haven't had a single conversation with him worth men- ₄₀₀ tioning. Let's see what sort of man he is.

(BELYAYEV *comes in from the left*)
Oh, Alexey Nikolayevich, have you been out walking in the fresh air?

BELYAYEV   Yes.

RAKITIN   That is to say, we must confess the air to-day isn't altogether fresh: ₄₀₅ it's frightfully hot. But here under these linden trees in the shade it's bearable enough. (*After a pause*) Have you seen Natalya Petrovna?

BELYAYEV   I just met her. . . . She and Vera Alexandrovna have gone into the house.

RAKITIN   But wasn't it Vera Alexandrovna that I saw here a half hour ago? ₄₁₀

BELYAYEV   Yes. . . . I was strolling with her.

RAKITIN   Ah! (*Takes his arm*) Well, how do you like life in the country?

BELYAYEV   I like the country. The only trouble is that the hunting here is poor.

RAKITIN   Are you a sportsman?

BELYAYEV   Yes. And you? ₄₁₅

RAKITIN   I? No, I must confess I am a poor shot. I am too lazy.

BELYAYEV   And I am lazy too . . . only not about walking.

RAKITIN   Oh! Are you lazy about reading?

BELYAYEV   No, I like to read. I am lazy about working for a long time at a stretch; I am especially lazy about applying myself continuously to one ₄₂₀ and the same subject.

RAKITIN (*Smiling*)   As for instance, conversing with the ladies?

BELYAYEV   Oh! You are laughing at me. . . . I am generally afraid of the ladies.

RAKITIN (*Slightly confused*)   Why did you think . . . ? Why should I make fun of you? ₄₂₅

BELYAYEV   Just a fancy. Where's the harm! (*After a pause*) Tell me, where can I get powder here?

RAKITIN   In the town, I think. They sell it there under the name of poppy seed. Do you need good powder?

BELYAYEV   No, musket powder will do. I don't want to shoot. I want to make ₄₃₀ some fireworks.

RAKITIN   What, do you know how?

BELYAYEV   I do. And I have already chosen a place on the other side of the pond. I've heard that next week will come the name day* of Natalya Petrovna, and so fireworks would be appropriate. ₄₃₅

⁴³⁴ The day in honor of the saint after whom a person is named. In many European countries "name days" are occasions like birthdays.

RAKITIN Natalya Petrovna will be much pleased at such an attention on your part. . . . She likes you, Alexey Nikolayevich, let me tell you.

BELYAYEV That is very flattering for me. . . . Oh, by the way, Mikhaylo Alexandrovich, I think you receive a magazine. Could you lend it to me?

RAKITIN Certainly, with pleasure. . . . It contains good poetry.   440

BELYAYEV I'm not fond of poetry.

RAKITIN Why not?

BELYAYEV I just am not. Humorous poetry seems to me forced; and besides, there is very little of it. . . . And sentimental verse . . . Somehow I don't believe in it.   445

RAKITIN Do you prefer stories?

BELYAYEV Yes. I like good stories. . . . But critical articles, those are what take hold of me.

RAKITIN Why so?

BELYAYEV A man of heart writes those.   450

RAKITIN And you yourself do not cultivate literature?

BELYAYEV Oh, no! What's the use of writing if God has given you no talent? It only makes people laugh. And besides, here is what is surprising; here is what you must explain to me, if you please: Sometimes a man seems clever, but when he takes up a pen you have to call the fire department. No,   455 what's the use of our writing? Lord help us to understand what other people write!

RAKITIN Let me tell you, Alexey Nikolayevich, not many young men have as much common sense as you have.

BELYAYEV Thank you humbly for the compliment. (*After a pause*) I have   460 selected a place for the fireworks the other side of the pond, because I know how to make Roman candles that burn on water.

RAKITIN That must be very beautiful. Excuse me, Alexey Nikolayevich . . . but permit me to ask you . . . do you know French?

BELYAYEV No. I translated a novel of Paul du Kock, *The Milkmaid of Mont-*   465 *fermel* *—maybe you have heard of it—for fifty rubles paper money, but I don't know a word of French. Just imagine, I translated *quatre-vingt dix** as four twenty ten! . . . Poverty, you know, forced me to. But I'm sorry. I should like to know French. I should like to read George Sand in French. But that pronunciation! How can you expect me to manage it? *An, on, in, un.* . . .   470 Isn't it awful?

RAKITIN Well, we can help that trouble.

BELYAYEV Permit me to inquire what time it is?

RAKITIN (*Looking at his watch*) Half past one.

BELYAYEV Why is it that Lizaveta Bogdanovna is keeping Kolya at the   475 piano for so long? . . . I think he must want awfully to have a run.

RAKITIN (*In a kind tone*) But yet people must study, Alexey Nikolayevich.

BELYAYEV (*With a sigh*) It's not for you to say that, Mikhaylo Alexandrovich, or for me to listen to it. . . . Of course not everybody should be as shiftless as I.

---

[466] Actually, Charles Paul de Kock (1794-1871), a French novelist and dramatist who, among many other works, wrote *The Milkmaid of Montfermeil* (1827).

[467] "Ninety."

RAKITIN Oh, stop!   480

BELYAYEV I know very well what I am talking about.

RAKITIN But, on the contrary, I know quite as well—I am convinced—that the
very quality which you regard as a defect in yourself, your lack of constraint,
your ease of manner, is what makes you liked by people.

BELYAYEV By whom, for example?   485

RAKITIN Well, by Natalya Petrovna, for instance.

BELYAYEV Natalya Petrovna? But I do not feel myself at ease with her, as you say.

RAKITIN Oh, really?

BELYAYEV And finally, if you please, Mikhaylo Alexandrovich, is not education
the matter of first importance for a man? It is easy for you to speak. . . . 490
I really don't understand you. . . . (*Suddenly stopping*) What's that? I thought
I heard a rail* call in the garden. (*Is about to leave*)

RAKITIN Perhaps. . . . But where are you going?

BELYAYEV For my gun.

(*He goes off to the left.* NATALYA PETROVNA *meets him. Seeing him, she smiles* 495
suddenly)

NATALYA PETROVNA Where are you going, Alexey Nikolayevich?

BELYAYEV I . . .

RAKITIN For his gun. . . . He heard a rail in the garden. . . .

NATALYA PETROVNA No, please don't shoot in the garden. . . . Let the poor 500
bird live. . . . Besides that, you may scare grandmother.

BELYAYEV I obey.

NATALYA PETROVNA (*Laughing*) Oh, Alexey Nikolayevich, aren't you ashamed?
"I obey." What an expression! . . . How can you speak that way? But wait,
Mikhaylo Alexandrovich and I will attend to your education. Yes, yes. . . . 505
We have already spoken of you several times. . . . We have a conspiracy
against you. I warn you. Will you permit me to attend to your education?

BELYAYEV Why . . . I . . .

NATALYA PETROVNA In the first place, don't be so bashful. That is not becoming to you at all. Yes, we will take charge of you. (*Pointing to* RAKITIN) 510
He and I are old people—and you are a young man. . . . Isn't that so? You'll
see how well everything turns out. You will attend to Kolya and I . . . and we
will attend to you.

BELYAYEV I shall be very grateful to you.

NATALYA PETROVNA That's right. What were you talking about here with 515
Mikhaylo Alexandrovich?

RAKITIN (*Smiling*) He was telling me how he translated a French book without
knowing a word of French.

NATALYA PETROVNA Well, then, we'll teach you French too. And by the way,
what have you done with your kite?   520

BELYAYEV I took it to my room. It seemed to me that you . . . did not like it.

NATALYA PETROVNA (*With a certain confusion*) How did you get that idea?
Because I said to Verochka . . . because I took Verochka into the house? No,
that . . . no, you made a mistake. (*With animation*) However, let me tell you:

---
492 A species of crane.

Kolya must have finished his lesson by this time. Let's go and get him and 525
Verochka and the kite, will you? And we'll all go to the meadow together.
Shall we?

BELYAYEV With pleasure, Natalya Petrovna.

NATALYA PETROVNA That's fine! Well, come on, come on! (*Stretches out her
hand to him*) Oh, take my hand! How clumsy you are! Come on, hurry up! 530
(*They go out quickly to the left*)

RAKITIN (*Gazing after them*) What animation . . . what gayety! I have never
seen such an expression on her face. And what a sudden change! (*After a
pause*) Souvent femme varie.* . . . But I . . . it is evident that to-day I don't suit
her. That's clear. (*After a pause*) Well, we'll see what comes next. (*Slowly*) 535
Is it possible that . . . ? (*Waves his hand*) Impossible! . . . But that smile, that
affable, soft, radiant expression! . . . Oh, Lord forbid that I should experience
the torments of jealousy, especially senseless jealousy! (*Looking around*) Bah,
bah, bah! . . . And what brought *them?*
(*From the left* SHPIGELSKY *and* BOLSHINTSOV *come in.* RAKITIN *goes to meet* 540
them)
How do you do, gentlemen. . . . I must confess, Shpigelsky, I didn't expect
you to-day. (*Shakes hands with them*)

SHPIGELSKY And I, myself . . . I myself had no such idea. . . . But you see, I
called on him (*Pointing to* BOLSHINTSOV) and he was already sitting in his 545
carriage, starting for this house. Well, I immediately turned right-about-face
and came back here.

RAKITIN Well, you are welcome.

BOLSHINTSOV I was really preparing to—

SHPIGELSKY (*Shutting him off*) The servants told us that the ladies and gentle- 550
men were in the garden. . . . At any rate, there was no one in the drawing-
room.

RAKITIN But didn't you meet Natalya Petrovna?

SHPIGELSKY When?

RAKITIN Why, just now.   555

SHPIGELSKY No, we didn't come straight from the house. Afanasy Ivanovich
wanted to see whether there were any mushrooms in the grove.

BOLSHINTSOV (*Perplexed*) I . . .

SHPIGELSKY Well, we know that you are a great lover of birch mushrooms. So
Natalya Petrovna has gone indoors. Well, then we may return.   560

BOLSHINTSOV Of course.

RAKITIN But she went indoors to call all of them to go for a walk. . . . I think
they were going to fly the kite.

SHPIGELSKY Oh, splendid. In such weather you must stroll about the country.

RAKITIN You can stay here. . . . I'll go and tell her that you've arrived.   565

SHPIGELSKY But why trouble yourself? . . . Pray don't, Mikhaylo Alexandrovich.

RAKITIN Oh, I need to go there anyway.

SHPIGELSKY Oh, well, in that case, we won't detain you. . . . Without ceremony,
you know. . . .

534 "Woman is often changeable."

RAKITIN Good-by for the moment, gentlemen. (*Goes out to the left*) 570

SHPIGELSKY Good-by. (*To* BOLSHINTSOV) Well, Afanasy Ivanovich?

BOLSHINTSOV (*Interrupting him*) How did you get that idea about mushrooms, Ignaty Ilyich? . . . I'm astonished. What mushrooms?

SHPIGELSKY I suppose I ought to have said that my friend Afanasy Ivanovich got scared, and didn't want to come the straight road, but begged to take 575 a bypath.

BOLSHINTSOV That's the truth. . . . But all the same, mushrooms! . . . I don't know. Maybe I'm mistaken. . . .

SHPIGELSKY You're certainly mistaken, my friend. Here's what you had better reflect on. You see, you and I have come here. We've done what you 580 wished. Look out that you don't make a fizzle of it!

BOLSHINTSOV But, Ignaty Ilyich, you . . . you told me that . . . That is, I should like to know positively what answer . . .

SHPIGELSKY My most respected Afanasy Ivanovich! From your village to this place is at least ten miles. Every half mile at least you have asked me the 585 same question three times over. . . . Isn't that enough for you? Now listen, I'll humor you just this last time. Here's what Natalya Petrovna told me: "I . . ."

BOLSHINTSOV (*Nodding*) Yes.

SHPIGELSKY (*With vexation*) "Yes" . . . well, why "Yes"? I haven't said any- 590 thing to you yet. . . . "I am little acquainted with Mr. Bolshintsov," she told me, "but he seems to me a good man. On the other hand, I have no intention of putting pressure on Verochka, and so let him come to see us, and if he wins—"

BOLSHINTSOV "Wins"? Did she say "wins"? 595

SHPIGELSKY "If he wins her regard, Anna Semenovna and I will not interpose objections."

BOLSHINTSOV "Will not interpose objections"? Is that what she said? "Will not interpose objections"?

SHPIGELSKY Oh, yes, yes, yes. What a queer man you are. "We will not 600 interpose objections to their happiness."

BOLSHINTSOV Hm.

SHPIGELSKY "To their happiness." Yes, but observe, Afanasy Ivanovich, what your problem is now. . . . Now you need to convince Vera Alexandrovna herself that a marriage with you will be happiness for her. You need to 605 win her regard.

BOLSHINTSOV (*Blinking*) Yes, yes. Win . . . To be sure, I agree with you.

SHPIGELSKY You insisted that I should bring you here to-day. . . . Well, let's see how you will get down to work.

BOLSHINTSOV Get down to work? Yes, yes, I must get down to work; I must 610 win her regard. Only here's the point, Ignaty Ilyich. . . . I must confess to you my single weakness, since you are my best friend. I desired, as you have said, to have you bring me here to-day.

SHPIGELSKY You didn't desire it. You demanded it. You demanded it insistently. 615

BOLSHINTSOV Well, let's suppose so. . . . I agree with you. But just see here.

At home I really . . . at home I was ready for everything, I think, but now timidity overcomes me.

SHPIGELSKY But why are you timid?

BOLSHINTSOV (*Looking at him in an embarrassed fashion*) The risk.   620

SHPIGELSKY Wha-at?

BOLSHINTSOV The risk. It's a great risk. Ignaty Ilyich, I must confess to you that . . .

SHPIGELSKY (*Interrupting him*) "As to your best friend." I know, I know. . . . Next?   625

BOLSHINTSOV Quite so. I agree with you. I must confess to you, Ignaty Ilyich, that I . . . that in general, I have had only slight contact with the female sex in general, so to speak. I confess to you openly, Ignaty Ilyich, that I simply cannot imagine what you can talk about with a person of the female sex, and besides that, all alone . . . especially with a girl.   630

SHPIGELSKY You surprise me! I don't know what you *can't* talk about with a person of the female sex, especially with a girl, and especially all alone.

BOLSHINTSOV Yes, but you . . . consider what a difference there is between you and me. Now, on this occasion, I should like to ask your help, Ignaty Ilyich. They say that in these matters it is the first step that counts. So couldn't   635 you tell me something to serve as an introduction to the conversation? Some little word. Something pleasant, in the nature of a remark, for instance—and then I'll go to meet them. After that, I'll manage it myself, somehow.

SHPIGELSKY I can't tell you any little word, Afanasy Ivanovich, because no word will be of any use to you. . . . But I can give you some advice, if you wish.   640

BOLSHINTSOV Be kind enough to do so, sir. . . . And as for my gratitude . . . You know . . .

SHPIGELSKY Stop, stop! Am I driving a bargain with you?

BOLSHINTSOV (*Lowering his voice*) You may rest easy about that team of three horses.   645

SHPIGELSKY Oh, do stop! Now you see, Afanasy Ivanovich. . . . Without any dispute, you are a splendid man in all respects . . . (BOLSHINTSOV *makes a slight bow*) a man of excellent qualities.

BOLSHINTSOV Oh, pray don't!

SHPIGELSKY And, besides, I believe you have three hundred serfs.   650

BOLSHINTSOV Three hundred and twenty.

SHPIGELSKY Not mortgaged.

BOLSHINTSOV I am not a single kopek in debt.

SHPIGELSKY Well, you see, I told you you were a most excellent man, and a suitor of the finest kind. Well then, you say yourself that you have asso-   655 ciated little with ladies. . . .

BOLSHINTSOV (*With a sigh*) Quite so. I might say, Ignaty Ilyich, that from my childhood I have avoided the female sex.

SHPIGELSKY (*With a sigh*) Well, there, you see. In a husband that's not a vice. Quite the contrary. But still in some cases—for instance, at the first con-   660 fession of love, it's indispensable to be able to say at least something. . . . Isn't that so?

BOLSHINTSOV I quite agree with you.

SHPIGELSKY And then, possibly Vera Alexandrovna may think that you don't feel well, and nothing more. Besides that, your figure, although it's pre- 665 sentable in every respect, is not of the sort, you know, that elicits instant admiration, and that's required nowadays.

BOLSHINTSOV (*With a sigh*) That's required nowadays.

SHPIGELSKY At least, the girls like it. Well, and then, your years! . . . In a word, you and I can't hope to succeed by our personal attractions. So you needn't 670 think about any pleasant remarks. That's a poor support. But you have another support which is far more firm and dependable. That's your personal qualities, my most excellent Afanasy Ivanovich, and your three hundred and twenty serfs. In your place, I should simply say to Vera Alexandrovna . . .

BOLSHINTSOV All alone? 675

SHPIGELSKY Oh, all alone, by all means.—"Vera Alexandrovna," (*By the movements of* BOLSHINTSOV'S *lips you can see that in a whisper he repeats every word after* SHPIGELSKY) "I love you, and I ask for your hand. I am a good, simple man, of gentle disposition, and far from poor. With me, you will be at complete liberty. I will try to suit you in every way, and pray make inquiries 680 about me. Pray devote a little more attention to me than you have previously, and give me what answer you choose, and when you choose. I am ready to wait, and shall even regard that as a pleasure."

BOLSHINTSOV (*Pronouncing aloud the last word*) "Pleasure." Yes, yes, yes. . . . I agree with you. Only here's the point, Ignaty Ilyich. I think that you were 685 pleased to employ the words, "of gentle disposition." So I am a man of gentle disposition?

SHPIGELSKY Well, aren't you a man of gentle disposition?

BOLSHINTSOV Ye-es. . . . But all the same, it seems to me . . . Will that be proper, Ignaty Ilyich? Wouldn't it be better to say, for instance . . . ? 690

SHPIGELSKY For instance?

BOLSHINTSOV For instance . . . for instance . . . (*After a pause*) However, it may do to say "of gentle disposition."

SHPIGELSKY Oh, Afanasy Ivanovich, listen to me. The more simply you express yourself, the fewer ornamentations you introduce into your speech, the 695 better things will go, believe me; and above all, don't insist, Afanasy Ivanovich, don't insist. Vera Alexandrovna is still very young. You may scare her. . . . Give her time to consider your proposal thoroughly. . . . And one more point! . . . I almost forgot. You see, you have permitted me to give you advice. . . . Sometimes it happens, my dear Afanasy Ivanovich, that you say "duin" 700 and "noo." Of course, why not? You can do it. But you know, the word "doing" and the word "new" are rather more usual. They are in better usage, so to speak. And then, I remember once in my presence you called a certain hospitable landowner a "bonzhiban." You remarked, "What a bonzhiban he is." It's a fine word, but unfortunately, it doesn't mean anything. You 705 know, I myself am not any too strong in the French dialect, but I know that much. Avoid eloquence, and I warrant your success. (*Looking around*) But here they are! They are all coming this way. (BOLSHINTSOV *is about to with-*

draw) Where are you going? For mushrooms again? (BOLSHINTSOV *smiles, blushes, and holds his ground*) The main thing is not to be timid! 710

BOLSHINTSOV (*Hastily*) But Vera Alexandrovna doesn't know anything about it yet.

SHPIGELSKY Of course not.

BOLSHINTSOV At any rate, I rely on you. (*Blows his nose*)
(*From the left there come in* NATALYA PETROVNA, VERA, BELYAYEV *with the* 715 *kite,* KOLYA, *and following them,* RAKITIN *and* LIZAVETA BOGDANOVNA.
NATALYA PETROVNA *is in high spirits*)

NATALYA PETROVNA (*To* BOLSHINTSOV *and* SHPIGELSKY) Oh, how do you do, gentlemen! How do you do, Shpigelsky! I didn't expect to see you to-day, but I'm always glad to see you. How do you do, Afanasy Ivanovich! 720
(BOLSHINTSOV *bows with a certain confusion*)

SHPIGELSKY (*To* NATALYA PETROVNA, *indicating* BOLSHINTSOV) You see, this gentleman insisted on bringing me here.

NATALYA PETROVNA (*Laughing*) I am much obliged to him. . . . But do you need to be forced to come to see us? 725

SHPIGELSKY Not at all. But . . . I left here only this morning. . . . Just think. . . .

NATALYA PETROVNA Oh, you have got mixed up, you have got mixed up, Mr. Diplomat!

SHPIGELSKY It is very pleasant for me, Natalya Petrovna, to see you in such a gay mood, if I observe correctly. 730

NATALYA PETROVNA And you think it necessary to remark on that? . . . But is that such a rare occurrence with me?

SHPIGELSKY Oh, no indeed. . . . But . . .

NATALYA PETROVNA M. *le diplomate,* you are getting more and more mixed up.

KOLYA (*Who has all this time been impatiently hovering about* BELYAYEV *and* 735 VERA) But, mamma, when are we going to fly the kite?

NATALYA PETROVNA Whenever you please. . . . Alexey Nikolayevich—and you, too, Verochka—let's go to the meadow. (*Turning to the rest of the group*) Gentlemen, I don't think that this will be very interesting for you. Lizaveta Bogdanovna, and you, too, Mr. Rakitin, I commend to you our good 740 friend, Afanasy Ivanovich.

RAKITIN But why do you think, Natalya Petrovna, that we shall not be interested?

NATALYA PETROVNA You are clever people. . . . This may seem to you a silly frolic. . . . However, as you wish. We won't hinder you from following 745 us. . . . (*To* BELYAYEV *and* VEROCHKA) Come on! (NATALYA PETROVNA, VERA, BELYAYEV *and* KOLYA *go out on the right*)

SHPIGELSKY (*Looking with a certain amazement at* RAKITIN. *To* BOLSHINTSOV) My good friend, Afanasy Ivanovich, offer your arm to Lizaveta Bogdanovna.

BOLSHINTSOV (*Hastily*) With great pleasure. . . . 750
(*Takes* LIZAVETA BOGDANOVNA'S *arm*)

SHPIGELSKY (*To* RAKITIN) And you and I will go together, if you will allow me, Mikhaylo Alexandrovich. (*Takes his arm*) You see how they are running down the path by the trees. Come on, let's see how they fly the kite, even if we are clever people. . . . Afanasy Ivanovich, won't you go in front? 755

BOLSHINTSOV (*To* LIZAVETA BOGDANOVNA, *as they walk off*) To-day . . . the weather . . . is . . . quite pleasant . . . one may say.

LIZAVETA BOGDANOVNA (*Coquettishly*) Oh, very!

SHPIGELSKY (*To* RAKITIN) But I need to talk over something with you, Mik- 760 haylo Alexandrovich. . . . (RAKITIN *suddenly laughs*) What are you laugh- ing at?

RAKITIN Oh . . . nothing! . . . It amuses me that we've fallen into the rear guard.

SHPIGELSKY The vanguard may very easily, you know, become the rear guard. . . . Everything depends on a change of direction. (*They all go off on the right*)

Act Three

The same setting as in Act One. From the hall door RAKITIN *and* SHPIGELSKY
come in

SHPIGELSKY Well, then, Mikhaylo Alexandrovich, help me out, if you please.

RAKITIN But how can I help you, Ignaty Ilyich?

SHPIGELSKY How? Just consider. Just understand my situation, Mikhaylo 5 Alexandrovich. I am really only a third party in this matter, of course. I may say that I acted merely from a desire to be of service. . . . My kind heart will be my ruin yet!

RAKITIN (*Laughing*) Well, your ruin is still a long way off.

SHPIGELSKY (*Also laughing*) Can't tell about that yet, but my position is cer- 10 tainly embarrassing. I brought Bolshintsov here according to Natalya Petrovna's desire, and I informed him of her answer, with her permission. And now, on one side, they look askance at me, as if I had done something silly, and on the other hand, Bolshintsov won't give me any rest. They avoid him, and won't talk to me. 15

RAKITIN Why did you want to take up this matter, Ignaty Ilyich? You see, just between ourselves, Bolshintsov is simply stupid.

SHPIGELSKY "Between ourselves," you say! What news you are giving me! How long is it since only clever people have been getting married? You can ruin the business of fools in everything else, but you ought not to do so in the 20 marrying line. You say, I took up this affair. . . . Not at all. This is how the matter came about. My friend asked me to put in a word for him. Well, should I have refused him? I am a kind man. I don't know how to refuse. I carried out my friend's commission, and they replied: "We thank you humbly. Don't trouble about the matter any more." I understood, and I didn't trouble 25 them any more. Then, all of a sudden, they made a proposal to me themselves, and urged me, so to speak. . . . I submitted, and now they are discontented with me. How am I to blame in this?

RAKITIN Who ever said that you were to blame? . . . I am surprised at just one thing: Why are you taking so much trouble? 30

SHPIGELSKY Why? . . . Why? The man won't give me any rest.

RAKITIN Oh, don't say that! . . .

SHPIGELSKY And, besides, he is my old, old friend.

RAKITIN (*With a distrustful smile*) Well, that's different.

SHPIGELSKY (*Also smiling*) However, I won't dissemble to you. . . . Nobody 35 can deceive *you*. Well, yes . . . he promised me. My side horse has gone lame, and so he promised me—

RAKITIN Another side horse?

SHPIGELSKY No, I must confess, a whole team of three.

RAKITIN You ought to have said that long ago! 40

SHPIGELSKY (*With animation*) But please don't think . . . I wouldn't have agreed on any consideration to mediate in such a matter—that is completely against my nature—(RAKITIN *smiles*) if I did not know Bolshintsov as the most honorable of men. . . . However, even now, I am anxious for only one thing: let them give me a decisive answer, yes or no. 45

RAKITIN Has the matter reached that point?

SHPIGELSKY How can you imagine that? . . . I am not talking about marriage, but about permission to make visits here. . . .

RAKITIN But who can forbid that?

SHPIGELSKY Forbid it, you say! Of course, for any other person. . . . But 50 Bolshintsov is a timid man, an innocent soul, straight from the Golden Age of Astræa.* He is almost like a baby sucking his thumb. . . . He has little self-confidence. He needs to be encouraged a bit. Besides that, his intentions are the most honorable.

RAKITIN And his horses are good? 55

SHPIGELSKY And his horses are good. (*Takes snuff and offers the snuff box to RAKITIN*) Will you have some?

RAKITIN No, I thank you.

SHPIGELSKY That's the way it is, Mikhaylo Alexandrovich. I don't want to deceive you, you see, and what's the use? The whole matter is as clear as a 60 bell. A man of honorable principles, and a man of property, of gentle disposition . . . if he suits, all right. If he doesn't suit, then tell him so.

RAKITIN All that's fine, I suppose, but how do I come in? I really don't see how *I* can help you.

SHPIGELSKY Oh, Mikhaylo Alexandrovich, don't I know that Natalya 65 Petrovna esteems you highly, and even sometimes takes your advice. . . . Really, Mikhaylo Alexandrovich, (*Putting his arm around him*) be my friend. Put in a word for me.

RAKITIN And do you think he is a good husband for Verochka?

SHPIGELSKY (*Assuming a serious air*) I am convinced of it. You don't believe 70 it. . . . Well, you'll see. In the marrying game, as you know yourself, the principal thing is a solid character, and there is nothing solider than Bolshintsov. (*Looking around*) But I think that here comes Natalya Petrovna herself. . . . My friend, my father, my benefactor! Two roans as side horses, and a dark brown for the center! Will you make efforts? 75

RAKITIN (*Smiling*) Well, all right, all right.

SHPIGELSKY See to it! I rely on you. (*Takes refuge in the hall*)

RAKITIN (*Gazing after him*) What an intriguer that doctor is! Vera . . . and Bolshintsov! . . . And yet why not? There are worse marriages than that. I'll

---

52 According to Greek legend, Astraea was the goddess of justice and the last of the gods to withdraw from earth after the Golden Age, that fabled time after the Creation when everything was peace and innocence.

fulfill his commission, and what follows is none of my affair. ⁸⁰

(*He turns around*)

(NATALYA PETROVNA *comes in from the study and stops when she sees him*)

NATALYA PETROVNA (*Indecisively*) Is that . . . you? . . . I thought you were in the garden.

RAKITIN You seem displeased. ⁸⁵

NATALYA PETROVNA (*Interrupting him*) Oh, don't say that! (*Coming to the front of the stage*) Are you alone here?

RAKITIN Shpigelsky has just left.

NATALYA PETROVNA (*Slightly frowning*) Oh, that district Talleyrand!* What was he saying to you? Is he still hanging around here? ⁹⁰

RAKITIN That district Talleyrand, as you call him, is evidently not in favor with you to-day. . . . But I think that yesterday . . .

NATALYA PETROVNA He is ridiculous. He is amusing, to be sure, but . . . but he doesn't mind his own business. . . . That's unpleasant. . . . And besides, with all his servility, he is very insolent and importunate. . . . He is a great cynic. ⁹⁵

RAKITIN (*Approaching her*) Yesterday you did not speak of him in any such tone.

NATALYA PETROVNA Possibly. (*With animation*) So what was he telling you?

RAKITIN He was telling me . . . about Bolshintsov.

NATALYA PETROVNA Oh? About that stupid man?

RAKITIN Yesterday you spoke differently of him, too. ¹⁰⁰

NATALYA PETROVNA (*With a forced smile*) Yesterday isn't to-day.

RAKITIN For most men. . . . But evidently my case is different.

NATALYA PETROVNA (*Lowering her eyes*) How so?

RAKITIN For me, to-day is the same as yesterday.

NATALYA PETROVNA (*Extending her hand to him*) I understand your re- ¹⁰⁵ proach, but you are mistaken. Yesterday, I should not have confessed that you had any cause to blame me. (RAKITIN *is about to stop her*) Do not reply to me. I know, and you know, what I mean. . . . And to-day I confess it. To-day I have thought over many things. . . . Believe me, Michel, whatever stupid thoughts may occupy me, whatever I may say, whatever I may do, I rely ¹¹⁰ on no one so much as on you. (*Lowering her voice*) I do not love . . . any one as I love you. . . . (*After a short pause*) Do you not believe me?

RAKITIN I believe you, but to-day you seem sad. . . . What's the matter with you?

NATALYA PETROVNA (*Not listening to him, continues*) Only, I have become ¹¹⁵ convinced of one thing, Rakitin. I cannot answer for myself on any occasion, and I can vouch for nothing. Often we do not understand our own past, and how can we answer for the future? You cannot put chains on the future.

RAKITIN That's true.

NATALYA PETROVNA (*After a long silence*) Listen, I want to be frank with ¹²⁰ you. Perhaps I shall slightly wound you . . . but I know that my reticence would wound you still more. I confess to you, Michel: that young student —that Belyayev—has produced a rather strong impression upon me.

RAKITIN (*In a low voice*) I knew it.

NATALYA PETROVNA Oh, you noticed it? Long ago? ¹²⁵

⁸⁹ French statesman and diplomat (1754–1838).

RAKITIN Only yesterday.

NATALYA PETROVNA Ah!

RAKITIN The day before yesterday, you remember, I was talking to you about the change that had occurred in you. . . . At that time I did not yet know to what to ascribe it. But yesterday, after our conversation . . . and out there in the meadow . . . if you could have seen yourself! I did not recognize you. You seemed to have become another woman. You laughed, you skipped, you frolicked like a little girl. Your eyes glittered, your cheeks glowed—and with what trustful curiosity, with what joyous attention you gazed at him, how you smiled! (*Glancing at her*) And even now your face lights up at the mere recollection. (*He turns away*)

NATALYA PETROVNA No, Rakitin, for the Lord's sake, do not turn away from me. . . . Listen: why exaggerate? This man has infected me with his youth —that's all. I myself was never young, Michel. Never from my childhood until now. . . . You know my whole life. . . . All this was so unwonted that it went to my head like wine, but I know it will pass away just as quickly as it came. . . . It's hardly worth speaking of. (*After a pause*) Only do not turn away from me. Do not withdraw your hand from me. . . . Help me!

RAKITIN (*In a low voice*) Help you! . . . A cruel word! (*Aloud*) You do not know, yourself, Natalya Petrovna, what is occurring within you. You are convinced that it is not worth talking of, and yet you ask for help. . . . Evidently you feel that you need it!

NATALYA PETROVNA That is . . . I . . . I appeal to you as a friend.

RAKITIN (*Bitterly*) Yes . . . I am ready to justify your confidence. . . . But permit me to collect myself a bit.

NATALYA PETROVNA Collect yourself? But are you threatened by any . . . unpleasantness? Has anything changed?

RAKITIN (*Bitterly*) Oh, no! Everything is as formerly.

NATALYA PETROVNA Well, what are you thinking of, Michel? It's impossible that you can suppose . . . ?

RAKITIN I don't suppose anything.

NATALYA PETROVNA It's impossible that you so despise me that—

RAKITIN Stop, for the Lord's sake. We had better talk about Bolshintsov. The doctor expects an answer with regard to Verochka, you know.

NATALYA PETROVNA (*Gloomily*) You are angry with me.

RAKITIN I? Oh, no! But I am sorry for you.

NATALYA PETROVNA Well, that is genuinely irritating. Michel, aren't you ashamed? (RAKITIN *is silent. She shrugs her shoulders and continues with irritation*) You say the doctor expects an answer? But who asked him to meddle?

RAKITIN He assured me that you did yourself.

NATALYA PETROVNA (*Interrupting him*) Perhaps, perhaps. . . . Although I think I said nothing positive to him. . . . Besides, I may change my intentions. And now—good Heavens!—what difference does it make? Shpigelsky interests himself in affairs of every sort, and in that trade he ought not to succeed every time.

RAKITIN He only desires to know what answer . . .

NATALYA PETROVNA What answer? . . . (*After a pause*) Michel, stop! Give me your hand. Why this indifferent glance, this cold courtesy? . . . How am I to blame? Just think, is all this my fault? I came to you in the hopes of getting some good advice. I did not hesitate a single moment. I did not 175 think of dissembling with you. And you . . . I see that I was wrong to be so open with you. . . . It would never have entered your head. You suspected nothing. You deceived me. And now, the Lord knows what you think.

RAKITIN I? The idea!

NATALYA PETROVNA Give me your hand. . . . (*He does not move. She continues* 180 *with a somewhat offended air*) Do you turn away from me for good and all? Look out, it will be so much the worse for you. However, I don't blame you. . . . (*Bitterly*) You are jealous!

RAKITIN I have no right to be jealous, Natalya Petrovna. . . . What an idea!

NATALYA PETROVNA (*After a pause*) As you wish. And as for Bolshintsov, 185 I have not yet spoken to Verochka.

RAKITIN I can send her to you directly.

NATALYA PETROVNA Why directly? . . . However, as you choose.

RAKITIN (*Going towards the door of the study*) Then will you have me send her?

NATALYA PETROVNA Michel, for the last time! . . . You have just told me 190 that you are sorry for me. . . . So, are you sorry for me? Is it possible that . . . ?

RAKITIN (*Coldly*) Shall I send her?

NATALYA PETROVNA (*With vexation*) Yes! (RAKITIN *goes into the study*. NATALYA PETROVNA *for some time remains motionless. She sits down, takes a book from the table, opens it, and drops it in her lap*) And that man! What does this mean? 195 He! . . . And he . . . And yet I relied on him. And Arkady? I didn't even remember him! (*Straightening up*) I see it's time to stop all this.

(VERA *comes in from the study*)

Yes, it's time.

VERA (*Timidly*) You asked for me, Natalya Petrovna? 200

NATALYA PETROVNA (*Looking around quickly*) Ah, Verochka! Yes, I asked for you.

VERA (*Coming up to her*) Are you well?

NATALYA PETROVNA Yes. Why do you ask?

VERA It seemed to me . . . 205

NATALYA PETROVNA No, I'm all right. I'm a little heated. . . . That's all. Sit down. (VERA *sits down*) Listen, Vera, you aren't busy with anything at present?

VERA No.

NATALYA PETROVNA I ask you because I need to talk with you . . . to talk seriously. Now, you see, my darling, hitherto you have seemed a mere 210 child, but now you are seventeen. You are clever. . . . It's time for you to be thinking of your future. You know I love you as a daughter. My house will always be your house. . . . But, all the same, in the eyes of other people, you are an orphan, you are not rich. In the course of time you may grow tired of living constantly with people not your own. Listen, should you like to 215 be a housewife, mistress of your own house?

VERA (*Slowly*) I don't understand you, Natalya Petrovna.

NATALYA PETROVNA (*After a pause*) I am asked for your hand. (VERA *with amazement looks at* NATALYA PETROVNA) You didn't expect that? I confess

that I myself find it rather strange. You are still so young. . . . I need not 220
tell you that I have no intention of putting pressure upon you. . . . In my
opinion, it is still early for you to marry. I only thought it my duty to inform
you. . . . (VERA *suddenly covers her face with her hands*) Vera, what does this
mean? You are weeping. (*Takes her by the hand*) You are trembling all over?
. . . Is it possible that you are afraid of me, Vera? 225

VERA (*In a choking voice*) I am in your power, Natalya Petrovna.

NATALYA PETROVNA (*Removing* VERA'S *hands from her face*) Vera, aren't you
ashamed to weep? Aren't you ashamed to say that you are in my power?
Who do you take me for? I am speaking to you as to a daughter, and you
. . . (VERA *kisses her hands*) So? Are you in my power? Then please laugh 230
right off. . . . I command you to. . . . (VERA *smiles through her tears*) That's
the way. (NATALYA PETROVNA *embraces her with one arm, and draws her to her*)
Vera, my child, behave toward me as you would toward your mother, or,
no, rather imagine that I am your older sister. And now, let's talk together
about all these marvelous things. . . . Will you? 235

VERA I am ready.

NATALYA PETROVNA Well, then, listen. . . . Move up nearer. That's the way.
In the first place, since you are my sister, let's suppose that I need not assure
you that you are here at home. Such eyes are always at home. Therefore, it
ought not to enter your head that you can be a burden to anybody in the 240
world, and that they want to get rid of you. . . . Do you hear? But now, one
fine day your sister comes to you and says, "Just imagine, Vera, they are
making proposals for you." Well, what will you reply to that? That you
are still very young, that you don't even think of marriage?

VERA Yes, madam. 245

NATALYA PETROVNA Don't say, "Yes, madam." Do sisters say, "Yes, madam"
to each other?

VERA (*Smiles*) Well, yes.

NATALYA PETROVNA Your sister agrees with you. They refuse the suitor and
the matter is over. But if the suitor is a good man with property, if he is 250
ready to wait, if he merely asks permission to see you occasionally in the
hope that in time you will like him . . .

VERA And who is this suitor?

NATALYA PETROVNA Oh, you are curious. You don't guess?

VERA No. 255

NATALYA PETROVNA You have seen him to-day. (VERA *blushes all over*) To be
sure, he isn't very handsome, and not very young. . . . Bolshintsov.

VERA Afanasy Ivanovich?

NATALYA PETROVNA Yes, Afanasy Ivanovich.

VERA (*Looks for some time at* NATALYA PETROVNA. *She suddenly begins to laugh* 260
and then stops) You aren't joking?

NATALYA PETROVNA (*Smiling*) No. . . . But I see that Bolshintsov has no further
business here. If you had wept at his name, he might still have hopes, but
you laugh. There's only one thing left for him, to go home, and the Lord
help him! 265

VERA Excuse me. . . . But I really never expected . . . At his age, do men still marry?

NATALYA PETROVNA What do you think? How old is he? He isn't fifty yet. He is in the very prime of life.

VERA Perhaps . . . but he has such a queer face.   270

NATALYA PETROVNA Well, we won't speak of him any more. He is dead and buried. . . . Let him stay so! However, this much is plain. A girl of your age cannot like a man such as Bolshintsov. . . . All of you want to marry for love, and not from interested motives. Is that not true?

VERA But, Natalya Petrovna . . . did you not yourself marry Arkady Sergeich 275 for love?

NATALYA PETROVNA (*After a pause*) Of course I married him for love. (*After another pause, and clasping* VERA'S *hands*) But Vera . . . I just called you a little girl . . . but little girls are right. (VERA *lowers her eyes*) Well, then, the matter is decided. Bolshintsov is dismissed. I must confess I myself should not 280 greatly enjoy seeing his puffy old countenance alongside your fresh little face, although, after all, he is a very good man. So you see now how wrong it was of you to be afraid of me. How quickly everything was settled! . . . (*With a reproach*) Really, you have behaved with me as if I were your benefactress! You know how I hate that word.   285

VERA (*Embracing her*) Pardon me, Natalya Petrovna.

NATALYA PETROVNA That's right! You are really not afraid of me?

VERA No, I love you. I am not afraid of you.

NATALYA PETROVNA Well, thank you. So now we are great friends, and hide nothing from each other. Well, what if I were to ask you: "Verochka, 290 whisper to me: Do you refuse, then, to marry Bolshintsov merely because he is very much older than you, and not at all good-looking?"

VERA Well, isn't that enough, Natalya Petrovna?

NATALYA PETROVNA I don't dispute it, but isn't there any other reason?

VERA I don't know him at all.   295

NATALYA PETROVNA Quite true, but you do not answer my question.

VERA There is no other reason.

NATALYA PETROVNA Really? In that case, I should advise you to reflect a bit more. I know that it is hard to fall in love with Bolshintsov . . . but I repeat to you, he is a good man. Now, if you had fallen in love with some other 300 man . . . well, then matters would be different. But your heart is still silent, is it not?

VERA (*Timidly*) What?

NATALYA PETROVNA You do not yet love any one?

VERA I love you . . . and Kolya. I also love Anna Semenovna.   305

NATALYA PETROVNA No, I am not talking about that kind of love; you don't understand me. . . . For instance, of the various young men whom you may have met in our house, or when visiting, is it possible that you do not care for a single one?

VERA No, I like several of them, but . . .   310

NATALYA PETROVNA For instance, I noticed that at the evening party at the

Krinitsyns', you danced three times with that tall officer. . . . What's his name?

VERA With an officer?

NATALYA PETROVNA Yes, he has a large mustache. . 315

VERA Oh, that man? No, I don't care for him.

NATALYA PETROVNA Well, how about Shalansky?

VERA Shalansky is a good man, but he . . . I think he has no use for me.

NATALYA PETROVNA Why so?

VERA He . . . He seems to think more of Liza Velsky. 320

NATALYA PETROVNA (*Glancing at her*) . . . Ah, you noticed that? (*After a pause*) Well, Rakitin?

VERA I am very fond of Mikhaylo Alexandrovich. . . .

NATALYA PETROVNA Yes, as a brother. Well, how about Belyayev?

VERA (*Blushing*) Alexey Nikolayevich? I like Alexey Nikolayevich. 325

NATALYA PETROVNA (*Observing* VERA) Yes, he is a good man, only he is so shy with every one.

VERA (*Artlessly*) No . . . he is not shy with me.

NATALYA PETROVNA Ah!

VERA He talks with me. Perhaps the reason why you think that, is that he 330 . . . he is afraid of you. He has not yet learned to know you.

NATALYA PETROVNA But how do you know that he is afraid of me?

VERA He told me so.

NATALYA PETROVNA Ah, he told you so? . . . So he is franker with you than with other people? 335

VERA I don't know how he behaves towards others, but with me . . . perhaps because we are both orphans. . . . And besides, in his eyes, I am a child.

NATALYA PETROVNA You think so? I also like him very much. Probably he has a very kind heart.

VERA Oh, awfully kind! If you only knew! . . . Everybody in the house likes 340 him. He is so friendly. He talks to everybody. He is ready to help everybody. Day before yesterday he carried a poor old woman in his arms from the road to the hospital. . . . Once he picked a flower for me from such a steep ravine that I just shut my eyes for fear he might fall and hurt himself, but he's so very active! You yourself, yesterday, in the meadow, could see how active 345 he was.

NATALYA PETROVNA Yes, that is true.

VERA Do you remember when he was running after the kite, what a broad ditch he jumped across? But that was nothing for him.

NATALYA PETROVNA And, really, did he pick a flower for you from a dan- 350 gerous place? Evidently he loves you.

VERA (*After a pause*) And he is always gay, always in good spirits.

NATALYA PETROVNA Well, that seems strange! Why in my presence is he—?

VERA (*Interrupting her*) But I tell you that he doesn't know you. Just wait, I'll tell him. I'll tell him that he needn't be afraid of you—isn't that true?— 355 that you are so kind. . . .

NATALYA PETROVNA (*With a forced laugh*) Thanks.

VERA Wait, you'll see. . . . And he takes my advice, in spite of my being younger than he.

NATALYA PETROVNA I didn't know that you and he were such friends. . . . 360 But look out, Vera; be cautious. Of course he is a splendid young man . . . but you know at your age . . . this isn't proper. People may gossip. I reminded you of this yesterday—do you remember?—in the garden. (VERA *lowers her eyes*) On the other hand, I do not wish to hinder your inclinations. I have too much confidence in you and in him. . . . But all the same, do not be 365 angry with me, my darling, for my straitlaced ways. This is what old people like me are for—to bore young people with advice. With advice and instruction. However, I am wrong in saying all this. It is true, is it not, you like him—and nothing more?

VERA (*Timidly raising her eyes*) He . . . 370

NATALYA PETROVNA Now you are looking at me again as you did before. Is that the way to look at a sister? Listen, Verochka, bend down to me. . . . (*Caressing her*) Well, if your sister, your real sister, were to ask you in a whisper, "Verochka, do you really love no one, are you sure?" What should you answer her? (VERA *looks in perplexity at* NATALYA PETROVNA) These 375 eyes wish to tell me something. . . . (VERA *suddenly presses her face against the bosom of* NATALYA PETROVNA. NATALYA PETROVNA *turns pale, and after a pause continues*) Do you love him? Tell me, do you love him?

VERA (*Not raising her head*) Oh, I don't know myself what is the matter with me. 380

NATALYA PETROVNA Poor little girl! You are in love. (VERA *presses still closer to the bosom of* NATALYA PETROVNA) You are in love. . . . And he, what about him, Vera?

VERA (*Still not raising her head*) Why do you ask me? . . . I don't know. . . . Maybe. . . . I don't know. . . . I don't know. . . . (NATALYA PETROVNA 385 *trembles and remains motionless.* VERA *raises her head and suddenly notices a change on* NATALYA PETROVNA'S *face*) Natalya Petrovna, what is the matter with you?

NATALYA PETROVNA (*Coming to herself*) Nothing is the matter with me. Why do you ask? Nothing at all. 390

VERA You are so pale, Natalya Petrovna. . . . What is the matter with you? Permit me, I'll ring. (*She rises*)

NATALYA PETROVNA No, no, don't ring. . . . It's nothing. . . . It will pass. There, it's past, already.

VERA Permit me at least to call somebody. 395

NATALYA PETROVNA No indeed. I . . . I . . . want to be left alone. Leave me. Do you hear? We'll have a talk later. Go away.

VERA You are not angry with me, Natalya Petrovna?

NATALYA PETROVNA I? What for? Not at all. On the contrary, I am grateful to you for your confidence. . . . Only leave me, please, now. 400

(VERA *tries to take her hand, but* NATALYA PETROVNA *turns away, as if she did not notice* VERA'S *movement*)

VERA (*With tears in her eyes*) Natalya Petrovna!

NATALYA PETROVNA Leave me, I beg of you. (VERA *slowly goes off to the study.*
NATALYA PETROVNA *remains alone for some time, motionless*) Now everything 405
is clear to me. . . . These children love each other. (*She stops and passes her
hand over her face*) Well, so much the better. God grant them happiness!
(*Laughing*) And I . . . I might have thought . . . (*She stops again*) She blurted
it out very quickly. . . . I confess I never suspected. . . . I confess this news
overwhelmed me. . . . But just wait. It isn't all over yet. Good Heavens, 410
what am I saying? What is the matter with me? I don't recognize myself.
What have I come to? (*After a pause*) What am I doing? I am trying to
marry a poor little girl . . . to an old man! . . . I send the doctor as a messenger. . . . He guesses what is up and hints at it. . . . Arkady . . . Rakitin . . .
and I . . . (*She trembles and suddenly raises her head*) But what does this 415
mean, really? Am I jealous of Vera? Am I . . . am I in love with him? (*After
a pause*) And do you still doubt it? You are in love, unhappy woman! How
this happened, I do not know. It is as if I had been given poison. . . . Suddenly
all is crushed, shattered, swept away. . . . He is afraid of me. . . . Everybody
is afraid of me. What does he care for me? . . . What use has he for such 420
a creature as I? He is young, and she is young. And I? (*Bitterly*) How can
he appreciate me? They are both stupid, as Rakitin says. Oh, how I hate
that clever man! And Arkady, my kind, trustful Arkady! My God! My God!
This will kill me! (*Rises*) Really, it seems to me that I am going mad. Why
exaggerate? Well, yes, I am overwhelmed. . . . This is a new thing to me. 425
This is the first time that I . . . Yes, the first time! I am in love now for the
first time! (*She sits down again*) He must go away. Yes, and Rakitin, too.
It's time for me to come to my senses. I have permitted myself to take one
step, and see what has happened. Here's what I have come to. And what
is it that I like in him? (*Meditates*) So here it is, that frightful emotion. 430
. . . Arkady! Yes, I will run to his embrace. I will implore him to forgive
me, to defend me, to save me—he . . . and no one else. All other men are
strangers to me, and must remain strangers. . . . But, is it possible . . . is it
possible there is no other means? That little girl, she is only a child. She
may have been mistaken. This is all childishness, after all. . . . Why did 435
I . . . ? I will have an explanation with him myself. I will ask him . . . (*With
a reproach*) Ah, ha? Do you still have hope? Do you still desire to have hope?
And what do I hope for! Good God, do not let me despise myself!
(*She leans her head on her hands*)
(RAKITIN *comes in from the study, pale and agitated*)   440
RAKITIN (*Going up to* NATALYA PETROVNA) Natalya Petrovna! . . . (*She does not
move. To himself*) What can have happened between her and Vera? (*Aloud*)
Natalya Petrovna!
NATALYA PETROVNA (*Raising her head*) You, is it? Ah, you.
RAKITIN Vera Alexandrovna told me that you were not well. I . . .   445
NATALYA PETROVNA (*Turning aside*) I am well. . . . How did she get that idea?
RAKITIN No, Natalya Petrovna, you are not well. Just look at yourself.
NATALYA PETROVNA Well, maybe. . . . But what's that to you? What do you
want? Why did you come here?
RAKITIN (*In a voice full of feeling*) I'll tell you why I came here. I came here 450

to beg your forgiveness. A half-hour ago I was unspeakably stupid and harsh to you. . . . Forgive me! You see, Natalya Petrovna, however modest may be the desires and . . . and the hopes of a man, it is hard for him not to lose control of himself for a moment, when they suddenly spring up within him; but I now have come to myself. I understand my position, and my fault, 455 and I wish for only one thing, your forgiveness. (*He sits down quietly beside her*) Look at me. . . . Pray do not turn away from me. Before you is your former Rakitin, your friend, a man who demands nothing but the permission to serve as a support, to use your own words. . . . Do not deprive me of your confidence—let me serve you—and forget that once on a time I . . . 460 Forget everything that may have offended you.

NATALYA PETROVNA (*Who has been looking fixedly at the floor all this time*) Yes, yes. (*Stopping*) Oh, pardon me, Rakitin! I did not hear anything of what you were saying to me.

RAKITIN (*Sadly*) I was saying . . . I was begging your forgiveness, Natalya 465 Petrovna. I was asking you whether you would permit me to remain your friend.

NATALYA PETROVNA (*Slowly turning toward him, and putting both her hands on his shoulders*) Tell me, Rakitin, what is the matter with me?

RAKITIN (*After a pause*) You are in love.   470

NATALYA PETROVNA (*Slowly repeating after him*) I am in love. . . . But this is madness, Rakitin. This is impossible. Can it happen so suddenly? You say I am in love. (*She becomes silent*)

RAKITIN Yes, you are in love, poor woman. . . . Do not deceive yourself.

NATALYA PETROVNA (*Without looking at him*) What is there left for me to 475 do now?

RAKITIN I am ready to tell you, Natalya Petrovna, if you will promise me—

NATALYA PETROVNA (*Interrupting him, and still not looking at him*) You know that that little girl, Vera, loves him. . . . They are in love with each other.

RAKITIN In that case, there is one further reason—   480

NATALYA PETROVNA (*Again interrupting him*) I long ago suspected this, but just now she confessed the whole story to me . . . just now.

RAKITIN (*In a low voice, as if to himself*) Poor woman!

NATALYA PETROVNA (*Passing her hand over her face*) Well, at all events . . . it is time for me to come to my senses. I think you wish to say something 485 to me. . . . Advise me, for God's sake, Rakitin, what I should do.

RAKITIN I am ready to advise you, Natalya Petrovna, but under one condition.

NATALYA PETROVNA Tell me what it is.

RAKITIN Promise me that you will not suspect my intensions. Tell me that you believe in my disinterested desire to aid you. And you must aid me 490 also. Your confidence will give me strength. Otherwise, you had better permit me to be silent.

NATALYA PETROVNA Speak. Speak.

RAKITIN You do not doubt me!

NATALYA PETROVNA Speak.   495

RAKITIN Well, then, listen. He must go away. (NATALIA PETROVNA *looks at him in silence*) Yes, he must go away. I will not speak to you of your husband . . .

of your duty. From me these words . . . would be out of place. . . . But these children love each other. You yourself told me that just now. Then imagine yourself now as standing between them. . . . You will perish! 500

NATALYA PETROVNA He must go away. . . . (*After a pause*) And you? You will remain?

RAKITIN (*Confused*) I? . . . I? . . . (*After a pause*) I too must go away. For your peace, for your happiness, for the happiness of Verochka, both he . . . and I . . . we both must go away forever. 505

NATALYA PETROVNA Rakitin . . . I have sunk so low that I . . . I was almost ready to marry that poor little girl, an orphan, entrusted to me by my mother . . . to marry her to a stupid, ridiculous old man! . . . I did not have the courage, Rakitin; the words died on my lips when she laughed, in reply to my proposal. . . . But I made a conspiracy with that doctor. I permitted 510 him to smile in a knowing way. I endured those smiles, those courtesies of his, his hints. . . . Oh, I feel that I am on the edge of an abyss! Save me!

RAKITIN Natalya Petrovna, you see that I was right. . . . (*She is silent. He hastily continues*) He must go away. . . . We must both go away. . . . There is no other salvation. 515

NATALYA PETROVNA (*Wearily*) But what shall I live for after that?

RAKITIN Good heavens! Has it come to this? . . . Natalya Petrovna, you will recover, believe me. . . . This will all pass off. How can you ask what you will live for?

NATALYA PETROVNA Yes, yes, what shall I live for when every one is desert- 520 ing me?

RAKITIN But . . . your family . . . (NATALYA PETROVNA *lowers her eyes*) Listen. If you wish, after his departure I can remain for a few days more . . . in order to . . .

NATALYA PETROVNA (*Gloomily*) Ah! I understand you. You count on habit, 525 on our former friendship. . . . You hope that I shall come to my senses, that I shall return to you, do you not? I understand you.

RAKITIN (*Blushing*) Natalya Petrovna! Why do you insult me?

NATALYA PETROVNA (*Bitterly*) I understand you. . . . But you deceive yourself.

RAKITIN What? After your promises? After what I have done for you, for 530 you alone, for your happiness, and finally, for your position in the world?

NATALYA PETROVNA Ah, is it long since you have taken such care of it? Why have you never spoken to me of that subject before?

RAKITIN (*Rising*) Natalya Petrovna, I shall leave here to-day—at once. And you will never see me again. (*Is about to go*) 535

NATALYA PETROVNA (*Stretching out her hands to him*) Michel, forgive me. I do not know myself what I am saying. . . . You see what a position I am in. Forgive me!

RAKITIN (*Quickly returning to her and taking her hands*) Natalya Petrovna! . . .

NATALYA PETROVNA Ah, Michel, I cannot tell you what torment I suffer! 540 (*Leans on his shoulder and presses her handkerchief to her eyes*) Help me! Without you I shall perish!

(*At this moment the door of the hall opens, and* ISLAYEV *and* ANNA
SEMENOVNA *come in*)

ISLAYEV (*In a loud voice*) I have also been of the opinion . . . ₅₄₅
(*He stops in amazement at the sight of* RAKITIN *and* NATALYA PETROVNA.
NATALYA PETROVNA *looks around and quickly walks out into the study.*
RAKITIN *does not stir, but is extremely abashed*)

ISLAYEV (*To* RAKITIN) What does this mean? What sort of scene is this?

RAKITIN Oh! . . . Nothing. . . . This . . . ₅₅₀

ISLAYEV Is Natalya Petrovna ill?

RAKITIN No. . . . But . . .

ISLAYEV But why should she run out so suddenly? What were you talking about together? She seemed to be weeping. . . . You were comforting her. . . . What does this mean? ₅₅₅

RAKITIN Nothing at all.

ANNA SEMENOVNA Let me ask you why this is nothing at all, Mikhaylo Alexandrovich? (*After a pause*) I'll go and see. (*Is about to go into the study*)

RAKITIN (*Stopping her*) No, you had better leave her in peace, now; I beg of you. ₅₆₀

ISLAYEV But what does all this mean? Tell me, pray!

RAKITIN Nothing, I swear to you. Listen, I promise you both that I will explain everything this very day. I give you my word. But just now, please, if you have confidence in me, do not ask me anything, and do not trouble Natalya Petrovna. ₅₆₅

ISLAYEV All right. . . . Only this is surprising. This is not like Natasha. This is something unusual.

ANNA SEMENOVNA Above all, what could make Natasha weep, and why did she go out? . . . Are we strangers?

RAKITIN What are you saying? How can you!— But listen: I must confess, ₅₇₀ we had not finished our conversation. . . . I must ask you . . . both of you . . . to leave us alone for a little while.

ISLAYEV Well, well! So you had a secret?

RAKITIN A secret. . . . But you will learn it.

ISLAYEV (*After meditation*) Come on, mamma! . . . Let's leave them. Let them ₅₇₅ finish their mysterious conversation.

ANNA SEMENOVNA But . . .

ISLAYEV Come on, come on! You have heard him promise to explain everything.

RAKITIN You may rest at peace. ₅₈₀

ISLAYEV (*Coldly*) Oh, I am perfectly at peace! (*To* ANNA SEMENOVNA) Come on.
(*They both go out*)

RAKITIN (*Gazing after them and going quickly to the door of the study*) Natalya Petrovna! . . . Natalya Petrovna! . . . Come out, I beg of you!

NATALYA PETROVNA (*Coming out of the study. She is very pale*) What did they ₅₈₅ say?

RAKITIN Nothing. Calm yourself. . . . They were really a trifle surprised. Your husband thought that you were not well. He noticed your agitation. . . . (NATALYA PETROVNA *sits down*) I told him . . . I asked him not to disturb you . . . to leave us alone. ₅₉₀

NATALYA PETROVNA And he agreed?

RAKITIN Yes. I must confess that I had to promise him that I would explain everything to-morrow. . . . Why did you go out?

NATALYA PETROVNA (*Bitterly*) Why! . . . But what will you tell him?

RAKITIN I . . . I will think up something. . . . That's not the question now. 595 . . . We must take advantage of this postponement. You see, this cannot continue in the same way. . . . You are not in a condition to bear such agitations. . . . They are unworthy of you. . . . I, myself . . . But that is not what we were speaking of. Only be firm, and I will attend to the matter. Listen. You agree with me? 600

NATALYA PETROVNA In what?

RAKITIN As to the necessity . . . of our departure? Do you agree? In that case there is no use delaying. If you will permit me, I will talk things over immediately myself with Belyayev. . . . He is a gentleman. He will understand.

NATALYA PETROVNA You wish to talk things over with him? You? . . . But 605 what can you say to him?

RAKITIN (*Confused*) I . . .

NATALYA PETROVNA (*After a pause*) Listen, Rakitin. Don't you think that we both seem out of our senses? . . . I was frightened. I frightened you. And perhaps the whole thing is just nonsense. 610

RAKITIN What?

NATALYA PETROVNA Honestly, what are you and I doing? A while ago, as I think of it, everything was so calm, so peaceful in this house . . . and all of a sudden, what has happened? On my word, we've all gone mad. Really, we've played the fool long enough! . . . Now we'll begin to live as we 615 used to. . . . And you will have no need to explain things to Arkady. I myself will tell him of our misdeeds, and he and I will laugh at them together. I do not need a mediator between my husband and myself.

RAKITIN Natalya Petrovna, now you *are* frightening me. You are smiling, but you are pale as death. . . . Do at least remember what you were telling me 620 a quarter of an hour ago.

NATALYA PETROVNA There's a lot to remember! However, I see how the matter stands. . . . You yourself raised this storm . . . in order at least not to drown alone.

RAKITIN Again! Again suspicion, again reproach, Natalya Petrovna! . . . The 625 Lord help you! . . . But you are tormenting me. Or do you repent your frankness?

NATALYA PETROVNA I repent nothing.

RAKITIN Then how shall I understand you?

NATALYA PETROVNA (*With animation*) Rakitin, if you say even a word to 630 Belyayev about me, or as coming from me, I shall never forgive you.

RAKITIN Oh, so that's it! . . . Be at peace, Natalya Petrovna, I not only shall say nothing to Mr. Belyayev, but I shall not even say good-by to him when I leave here. I have no intention of forcing my services on people.

NATALYA PETROVNA (*With some confusion*) But perhaps you think that I have 635 changed my opinion with regard to . . . his departure?

RAKITIN I don't think anything at all.

NATALYA PETROVNA On the contrary, I am so convinced of the necessity of his departure, as you term it, that I, myself, have decided to dismiss him. (*After a pause*) Yes, I will dismiss him myself. 640

RAKITIN You?

NATALYA PETROVNA Yes, I, and immediately. I beg you to send him to me.

RAKITIN What? Right away?

NATALYA PETROVNA Right away. I beg you to do so, Rakitin. You see, I am now calm. Besides, I am now at liberty. I must take advantage of this. 645 . . . I shall be very grateful to you. I will cross-examine him.

RAKITIN But may I remark that he won't tell you anything! He himself confessed to me that he felt embarrassed in your presence.

NATALYA PETROVNA (*Suspiciously*) Ah, you have already spoken with him about me? (RAKITIN *shrugs his shoulders*) Well, excuse me, excuse me, Michel, 650 but send him to me. You will see that I shall dismiss him, and everything will be over. Everything will pass by and be forgotten like a bad dream. Please send him to me. It is absolutely necessary for me to have a final talk with him. You will be content with me. Please!

RAKITIN (*Who all the time has kept his eyes fixed upon her: coldly and sadly*) Very 655 well, your desires shall be fulfilled. (*He goes to the door of the hall*)

NATALYA PETROVNA (*Calls after him*) Thank you, Michel.

RAKITIN (*Turning around*) Oh, don't thank me, at any rate! (*He quickly goes out into the hall*)

NATALYA PETROVNA (*Alone, after a pause*) He is a gentleman. . . . But is it 660 possible that I ever loved him? (*Rising*) He is right: the teacher must leave. But how shall I dismiss him? I only wish to know whether he really likes that little girl. Perhaps that is all nonsense. How could I have become so agitated? . . . What is the use of all these bursts of emotion? Well, now there is no help for it! I want to know what he will say to me. But he must leave 665 . . . without fail . . . without fail. . . . Perhaps he will refuse to answer me, seeing that he is afraid of me. . . . Well, so much the better. I have no need to converse much with him. . . . (*Puts her hand to her forehead*) But my head aches. Shan't I postpone it until to-morrow? That would be better. To-day I keep thinking that I am being observed. . . . What have I come to! No, 670 it is better to finish it up all at once. . . . One more final effort and I am free! . . . Oh, yes! . . . I thirst for freedom and peace.
(BELYAYEV *comes in from the hall*)
It is he. . . .

BELYAYEV (*Going up to her*) Natalya Petrovna, Mikhaylo Alexandrovich told 675 me that you desired to see me.

NATALYA PETROVNA (*With a certain effort*) Quite so. . . . I need to have . . . an explanation with you.

BELYAYEV An explanation?

NATALYA PETROVNA (*Without looking at him*) Yes, an explanation. (*After 680 a pause*) Permit me to tell you, Alexey Nikolayevich, that I . . . that I am dissatisfied with you.

BELYAYEV May I inquire the reason?

NATALYA PETROVNA Listen to me. . . . I . . . I really don't know how to begin. . . . At all events I must forewarn you that my displeasure does not proceed 685 from any neglect of duty . . . on your part. . . . On the contrary, I have liked your conduct with Kolya.

BELYAYEV But what can be the reason?

NATALYA PETROVNA (*Glancing at him*) You have no cause for alarm. Your fault is not of any great importance. You are young, and probably have 690 never lived in another person's house. You could not foresee . . .

BELYAYEV But, Natalya Petrovna . . .

NATALYA PETROVNA You wish to know what the trouble is? I understand your impatience. Well, I must inform you that Verochka . . . (*With a glance at him*) Verochka has confessed everything to me. 695

BELYAYEV (*Amazed*) Vera Alexandrovna? What could Vera Alexandrovna confess to you? And how do I come in?

NATALYA PETROVNA Don't you really know what she could confess? Don't you guess?

BELYAYEV I? Not a bit. 700

NATALYA PETROVNA In that case, pardon me. If you really don't guess—I must ask your forgiveness. I really thought . . . I was mistaken. But permit me to remark to you . . . I don't believe you. I understand what makes you speak in that way. . . . I greatly respect your modesty.

BELYAYEV I absolutely do not understand you, Natalya Petrovna. 705

NATALYA PETROVNA Really? Is it possible that you think that you can make me believe that you have not noticed the affection of that child Verochka for you?

BELYAYEV The affection of Vera Alexandrovna for me? I don't even know what to reply to you. . . . Good gracious, I think I have always behaved with 710 Vera Alexandrovna as—

NATALYA PETROVNA As with every one else, I suppose? (*After a slight pause*) However it may be, whether you really do not know it, or whether you are pretending you do not know, here's the point: that little girl is in love with you. She herself has confessed it to me. Well, now I ask you as an honor- 715 able man what you intend to do.

BELYAYEV (*Amazed*) What I intend to do?

NATALYA PETROVNA (*Folding her arms*) Yes.

BELYAYEV All this is so unexpected, Natalya Petrovna.

NATALYA PETROVNA (*After a pause*) Alexey Nikolayevich, I see . . . I haven't 720 taken hold of this affair correctly. You don't understand me. You think I am angry with you, and I . . . and I . . . am just a little excited. . . . And this is very natural. Calm yourself. Let us sit down. (*They both sit down*) I will be frank with you, Alexey Nikolayevich. And on your side, pray show a little less reserve toward me. Honestly, you are wrong in holding aloof 725 from me. Vera loves you. . . . Of course you are not to blame for that. I am ready to suppose that you are not to blame for that. . . . But you see, Alexey Nikolayevich, she is an orphan, my protégée. . . . I am responsible for her, for her future, for her happiness. She is still young, and I am convinced that the feeling you have inspired in her may soon vanish. . . . At her years, 730 love doesn't last for long. But you understand that it was my duty to forewarn you. And, moreover, it is always dangerous to play with fire . . . and

I don't doubt that you, since you now know her affection for you, will alter your behavior toward her, will avoid meetings and walks in the garden. . . . Is not that the case? I may rely upon you, I am sure. . . . With another man 735 I should have been afraid of so direct an explanation.

BELYAYEV Natalya Petrovna, believe me, I am able to appreciate—

NATALYA PETROVNA I tell you that I have confidence in you. . . . Besides, this will all remain a secret between us two.

BELYAYEV I confess to you, Natalya Petrovna, all that you have told me 740 seems to me so strange. . . . Of course I do not dare to disbelieve you, but—

NATALYA PETROVNA Listen, Alexey Nikolayevich, all that I have just now told you I . . . I have said on the supposition that on your side there is nothing . . . (*Interrupting herself*) Because in any other case . . . Of course, I am still little acquainted with you, but I already know you well enough to see no 745 reason for opposing your intentions. You are not rich . . . but you are young. You have a future, and when two people love each other . . . I repeat to you, I regarded it as my duty to forewarn you, as an honorable man, with regard to the consequences of your acquaintance with Vera. But if you . . .

BELYAYEV (*With perplexity*) I really don't know what you mean, Natalya 750 Petrovna.

NATALYA PETROVNA (*Hastily*) Oh, believe me, I do not require a confession from you. Even without it . . . I shall understand from your conduct how the matter stands. (*With a glance at him*) However, I must tell you that Vera thought that on your side you were not entirely indifferent to her. 755

BELYAYEV (*After a pause. Rising*) Natalya Petrovna, I see that I cannot remain in your house.

NATALYA PETROVNA (*Flashing up*) I think that you might have waited for me to discharge you myself. (*She rises*)

BELYAYEV You have been frank with me. . . . Permit me also to be frank 760 with you. I do not love Vera Alexandrovna. At least, I do not love her in the way you suppose.

NATALYA PETROVNA But have I . . . ? (*She stops*)

BELYAYEV And if Vera Alexandrovna has come to like me; if it appears to her that I, too, as you say, am not indifferent to her, I do not wish to deceive 765 her. I will tell the whole story to her herself, the whole truth. But after such an explanation, you will understand yourself, Natalya Petrovna, it will be hard for me to remain here. My position would be too embarrassing. I will not tell you how hard it is for me to leave your house, but there is nothing else for me to do. I shall always remember you with gratitude. . . . Permit 770 me to withdraw. . . . I shall have the honor of bidding you farewell later.

NATALYA PETROVNA (*With feigned indifference*) As you wish . . . but I confess I did not expect this. . . . This was not at all the reason why I wished to have an explanation with you. . . . I only wished to forewarn you. . . . Vera is still a child. . . . Perhaps I have attached too much importance to all this. 775 I see no necessity for your departure. However, as you wish.

BELYAYEV Really, Natalya Petrovna . . . it is impossible for me to remain here longer.

NATALYA PETROVNA Evidently it is very easy for you to bid us farewell!

BELYAYEV No, Natalya Petrovna, it is not easy.

NATALYA PETROVNA I am not accustomed to retain persons against their will . . . but I confess this is very unpleasant to me.

BELYAYEV (*With a certain indecision*) Natalya Petrovna . . . I should not like to cause you the least unpleasantness. . . . I will remain.

NATALYA PETROVNA (*Suspiciously*) Ah! . . . (*After a pause*) I did not expect 785 that you would change your decision so quickly. . . . I am grateful to you, but . . . permit me to think. Perhaps you are right. Perhaps it is really necessary for you to leave. I will think it over and inform you. . . . You will permit me to leave you in uncertainty until this evening?

BELYAYEV I am ready to wait as long as you please. (*He bows and is about* 790 *to leave*)

NATALYA PETROVNA You promise me . . .

BELYAYEV (*Stopping*) What?

NATALYA PETROVNA I think that you wish to have an explanation with Vera. I do not know whether that will be proper. However, I will inform you 795 of my decision. I begin to think that it is really necessary for you to leave. Good-by for the present. (BELYAYEV *bows for a second time and goes out into the hall*)

NATALYA PETROVNA (*Gazes after him*) I am calm. He does not love her. . . . (*Pacing up and down the room*) So instead of dismissing him, I was the one 800 to retain him? He remains here. . . . But what shall I tell Rakitin? What have I done? (*After a pause*) And what right did I have to publish abroad the love of that poor little girl? . . . How could I? I myself enticed a confession from her . . . a half-confession, and then I behaved so pitilessly, so harshly! (*Covers her face with her hands*) Perhaps he was beginning to love her. 805 What right did I have to trample that budding flower? . . . But after all, did I trample it? Perhaps he deceived me. . . . And I wished to deceive him! . . . Oh, no! He has too much fineness for that. . . . He is not like me! And why was I in such a hurry? Why did I blurt it all out at once? (*Sighing*) What didn't I do? If I could have foreseen! . . . How cunning I was! What lies 810 I told him! . . . And he! How boldly and freely he spoke! . . . I bowed before him. . . . That is a man! I never knew him before. . . . He must leave. . . . If he remains . . . I feel I shall come to such a pass that I shall lose all self-respect. . . . He must leave or I am lost! I will write him before he has a chance to see Vera. He must leave! (*She goes out quickly into the study*) 815

Act Four

A large, empty hall. The walls are bare. The floor is of uneven stones. Six brick columns, whitewashed, and in poor repair, support the ceiling, three on each side. On the left are two open windows and a door into the garden. On the right is a door to a corridor which leads to the main house. In the center is an iron door, which leads to the storehouse. Near the first column at the right is a green 5 *garden bench. In one corner are several spades, watering pots, and flower pots. It is evening. The red beams of the sun fall on the floor through the windows.*

KATYA (*Entering from a door on the right, goes quickly to the window, and for some time looks into the garden*) No, he is not to be seen. And they told me that he had gone to the hothouse. So, he cannot have come out from there yet. 10 I'll wait till he passes by. He must come by that path. (*She sighs and leans against the window*) They say that he is going away. (*Sighs again*) How can we live without him? . . . Poor young lady! How she begged me! . . . Well, why shouldn't I be of service to her? Let her have a talk with him for the last time! How warm it is to-day! And I think the rain is beginning to 15 patter. (*Again looks out of the window and suddenly moves back*) But aren't they coming here? . . . They certainly are. Oh, Heavens!

(*She starts to run away, but before she can reach the door of the corridor, there enter from the garden* SHPIGELSKY *and* LIZAVETA BOGDANOVNA. KATYA *hides behind the column*) 20

SHPIGELSKY (*Brushing off his hat*) We may wait here till the shower is over. It will pass soon.

LIZAVETA BOGDANOVNA I suppose so.

SHPIGELSKY (*Looking around*) What kind of structure is this? Is it a storehouse?

LIZAVETA BOGDANOVNA (*Pointing to the iron door*) No, the storehouse is 25 there. They call this a hall. The father of Arkady Sergeich built it when he returned from abroad.

SHPIGELSKY Oh, I see what this means. This is Venice, pray observe! (*Sitting down on the bench*) Let's sit here. (LIZAVETA BOGDANOVNA *sits down*) And you must agree, Lizaveta Bogdanovna, that that shower came at the wrong 30 moment. It interrupted our interview at the most delicate point.

LIZAVETA BOGDANOVNA (*Lowering her eyes*) Ignaty Ilyich . . .

SHPIGELSKY But no one can hinder us from renewing our conversation. . . . By the way, you say that Anna Semenovna is out of sorts to-day?

LIZAVETA BOGDANOVNA Yes, she is. She even had dinner in her own room. 35

SHPIGELSKY Well, well! What a misfortune! I declare!

LIZAVETA BOGDANOVNA This morning she found Natalya Petrovna in tears . . . with Mikhaylo Alexandrovich. . . . He, of course, is a friend of the family, but all the same . . . However, Mikhaylo Alexandrovich promised to explain everything. 40

SHPIGELSKY Ah! Well, she is quite wrong in being agitated. Mikhaylo Alexandrovich, in my opinion, was never a dangerous man, and now he is less so than ever.

LIZAVETA BOGDANOVNA Why so?

SHPIGELSKY Well, you see, he talks too cleverly. Some people are subject to 45
a rash, but these clever men are subject to too much wagging of the tongue.
In the future, Lizaveta Bogdanovna, don't be afraid of people who talk a lot.
They aren't dangerous. But those who are generally silent, and have a dash
of madness, and a lot of temperament, and broad craniums—those people
are dangerous.   50

LIZAVETA BOGDANOVNA (*After a pause*) Tell me, is Natalya Petrovna really ill?

SHPIGELSKY Just as ill as you and I.

LIZAVETA BOGDANOVNA She didn't eat anything at dinner.

SHPIGELSKY Other things than illness take away the appetite.

LIZAVETA BOGDANOVNA Did you dine with Bolshintsov?   55

SHPIGELSKY Yes, I did. . . . I went to call on him. And I came back solely on
your account, I swear.

LIZAVETA BOGDANOVNA Oh, stop! Let me tell you, Ignaty Ilyich, Natalya
Petrovna is angry at you for some reason. . . . At table she expressed herself
about you in no flattering terms.   60

SHPIGELSKY Really? Evidently fine ladies don't like it when men like me have
keen eyes. You must act according to their wishes and help them—and
pretend into the bargain that you don't understand them. That's their kind!
But we'll see later. And Rakitin, I suppose, is hanging his head, too?

LIZAVETA BOGDANOVNA Yes. To-day he seems to be a little bit off his 65
balance.

SHPIGELSKY Hm! And Vera Alexandrovna? And Belyayev?

LIZAVETA BOGDANOVNA Every one. Absolutely every one is out of sorts. I really
can't think what's the matter with all of them to-day.

SHPIGELSKY If you know too much, you will grow old too soon, Lizaveta 70
Bogdanovna. Well, anyway, deuce take 'em! Let's talk about our own affair.
The shower, you see, hasn't stopped yet. . . . Will you?

LIZAVETA BOGDANOVNA (*Lowering her eyes affectedly*) What are you asking me,
Ignaty Ilyich?

SHPIGELSKY Oh, Lizaveta Bogdanovna, let me inquire of you: Why do you 75
want to be so affected and lower your eyes all of a sudden in this fashion?
You and I are not young people any longer! These ceremonies, these tender-
nesses, these sighs—all such things are unbecoming to us. Let's speak calmly
and to the point, as befits people of our years. And so here's the question:
We like each other . . . at least I presume that you like me. . . .   80

LIZAVETA BOGDANOVNA (*With slight affectation*) Ignaty Ilyich, really. . . .

SHPIGELSKY Well, yes, yes, all right. For you, as a woman, it's proper, I suppose
. . . in a way . . . (*With a gesture*) to beat about the bush like this, so to speak.
Well, then, we like each other, and in other regards we are also well suited.
Of course I must admit that I myself am not of high birth. But then, you 85
also are not of gentle origin. I am not a rich man, otherwise I should . . .
(*Grins*) But I have a fair practice, my patients don't all die, and you, according
to your own account, have fifteen thousand in cash. That's all not so bad,
you see. Besides, I imagine that you are tired of an eternal existence as a
governess. And the perpetual fussing with an old woman, and playing 90

preference with her, and humoring her—that also cannot be gay. On my side, I am not exactly bored with a bachelor life, but I am getting old. My cooks are plundering me. And so, all these circumstances harmonize with each other. But here's where the difficulty comes in, Lizaveta Bogdanovna. We don't know each other at all: that is, to be more exact, you don't know 95 me. . . . I do know you. Your character is well known to me. I don't say that you have no defects. Since you are an old maid, you have soured a bit, but there's no harm in that. For a good man, a wife is like soft wax, but I desire that you, too, should be acquainted with me before our marriage, otherwise maybe you'll begin to complain of me later. I don't want to 100 deceive you.

LIZAVETA BOGDANOVNA (*With dignity*) But it seems to me, Ignaty Ilyich, that I also have had a chance to observe your character.

SHPIGELSKY You? Oh, stop it! . . . That's not a woman's business. For instance, I warrant, you think that I'm a man of gay disposition, a jolly fellow, 105 don't you?

LIZAVETA BOGDANOVNA You have always seemed to me a very genial man.

SHPIGELSKY That's the point. You see how easy it is to make a mistake. Because I play the fool to other people, tell them funny stories, and pay court to them, you immediately assumed that I was really a jolly fellow. If I had 110 no need for them, those strangers, I wouldn't even look at them. . . . And even so, whenever I can—without any great danger, you know—I hold those very people up to ridicule. . . . However, I don't deceive myself. I know that some people, who need my services at every step, and who are bored when I am gone, nevertheless think they have the right to despise me. But I give 115 them as good as I get. Now take Natalya Petrovna, for instance. . . . You think that I don't see through her? (*Taking her off*) "My dear doctor, I really am very fond of you. . . . You have such a sharp tongue. . . ." Hee, hee! Coo, dovey, coo! Oh, those fine ladies! They smile at you, and they screw up their eyes this way—and condescending contempt is written on their 120 faces. . . . They scorn men like me, but what can you do about it! I understand why she is giving a poor report of me to-day. Really, these fine ladies are a surprising lot of people! Because they wash themselves every day with cologne, and speak with a certain carelessness, as if they were dropping words —"You can pick 'em up," they tell you—they imagine that you can't 125 catch 'em by the tail. Well, can't you, though! They are just such mortals as all the rest of us sinners.

LIZAVETA BOGDANOVNA Ignaty Ilyich, you surprise me.

SHPIGELSKY I knew I should surprise you. You see I'm not a jolly man at all, possibly not even a very kind man. . . . But I do not wish to pass in your 130 eyes for something that I have never been. However much I show off before the gentlefolk, no one ever saw me a buffoon, and no one ever slapped my face. I may say that they are even a bit afraid of me. They know that I bite. Once, three years ago, a certain gentleman, a country squire, was foolish enough at table to stick a radish into my hair. What do you think hap- 135 pened? Immediately—without getting excited, you know—in the most courteous fashion, I challenged him to a duel. My squire almost got paralysis with terror. My host made him apologize. The effect was startling. . . . I must confess I knew in advance that he wouldn't fight. So you see, Lizaveta Bogdanovna, I have a huge amount of self-esteem—but so it is. I have 140 also no great talent, and I had only a helter-skelter education. I am a poor doctor. I have no need of dissembling to you, and if you ever fall ill here, it is not I who will treat you. If I had talent and education, I should hurry off to the capital. But for the inhabitants of these parts, of course, no better doctor is necessary. As for my personal character, I must forewarn you, 145 Lizaveta Bogdanovna: at home I am glum, silent and exacting. I do not get angry when people humor me and show respect to me. I like to have them note my habits and give me tasty food, but all the same I am not jealous and not stingy, and in my absence you can do anything you choose. Any romantic love between us you need not expect. But nevertheless, I imagine 150 you will find it possible to live under one roof with me, so long as you humor me and don't weep in my presence—I can't stand that! And I don't pick quarrels. There's my whole confession. Well, what will you say now?

LIZAVETA BOGDANOVNA   What can I say to you, Ignaty Ilyich? . . . If you have not purposely blackened yourself—   155

SHPIGELSKY   But how did I blacken myself? Do not forget that another man in my place would calmly have kept quiet about his own defects, seeing that you had noticed nothing. But after the marriage is over—after the marriage it's too late. But I am too proud for that. (LIZAVETA BOGDANOVNA glances at him) Yes, yes, too proud. . . . Why won't you look at me? 160 I have no intention of deceiving my future wife and lying to her, not for a hundred thousand, to say nothing of fifteen. But I will bow down humbly to a stranger for the sake of a sack of flour. Such is my character. . . . To a stranger I grin and I think within me: "What a blockhead, my boy, to be caught with such a bait!" But with you I say what I think. That is, if you 165 will permit me, I do not tell you everything that I think, but at any rate, I don't deceive you. I must seem to you a great freak, to be sure. But just wait, sometime I will tell you the story of my life. You will be surprised that I am still so well preserved. I don't think that in your childhood you ate off of gold plates. But nevertheless, my darling, you can't understand 170 what genuine hardpan poverty is like. . . . However, I will tell you all this at some other time. Now, then, you had better think over what I have had the honor to report to you. . . . Think over this little matter well by yourself, and then give me your decision. So far as I have been able to observe, you are a woman of good judgment. You . . . By the way, how old are you?   175

LIZAVETA BOGDANOVNA   I . . . I . . . am thirty.

SHPIGELSKY (Calmly)   That's not true. You are all of forty.

LIZAVETA BOGDANOVNA (Flushing up)   Not forty at all, but thirty-six.

SHPIGELSKY   That's more than thirty, anyway. Well, you must lose this habit, Lizaveta Bogdanovna . . . the more so as a married woman is by no means 180 old at thirty-six. You also make a mistake in taking snuff. (Rising) But I think the shower has stopped.

LIZAVETA BOGDANOVNA (*Also rising*) Yes, it has.

SHPIGELSKY So you will give me the answer in a few days?

LIZAVETA BOGDANOVNA I will tell you my decision to-morrow. 185

SHPIGELSKY Well, I like that. . . . That's sensible. So sensible! Good for you, Lizaveta Bogdanovna. Well, give me your hand. Let's go in the house.

LIZAVETA BOGDANOVNA (*Giving him her hand*) Come on!

SHPIGELSKY And, by the way, I haven't kissed it. . . . And that's obligatory, I think. . . . Let this be done at all hazards! (*Kisses her hand.* LIZAVETA 190 BOGDANOVNA *blushes*) There now! (*He goes towards the garden door*)

LIZAVETA BOGDANOVNA (*Stopping*) So you think, Ignaty Ilyich, that Mikhaylo Alexandrovich is really not a dangerous man?

SHPIGELSKY That's what I think.

LIZAVETA BOGDANOVNA Let me tell you, Ignaty Ilyich, it seems to me that 195 Natalya Petrovna for some time . . . It seems to me that Mr. Belyayev . . . She is paying attention to him, isn't she? And Verochka, what do you think about her? Wasn't that the reason that to-day—

SHPIGELSKY (*Interrupting her*) I forgot to tell you one thing, Lizaveta Bogdanovna: I myself am awfully curious, but I can't stand curious women. 200 Let me explain. In my opinion, a wife should be curious and observant—that is really useful for her husband—but only with outsiders. You understand me? With outsiders. However, if you insist on knowing my opinion about Natalya Petrovna, Vera Alexandrovna, Mr. Belyayev, and in general, the inhabitants of this house, just listen while I sing you a song. I have a wretched voice, 205 but don't expect too much.

LIZAVETA BOGDANOVNA (*With surprise*) A song!

SHPIGELSKY Listen, first stanza! (*Sings first verse*)
Grandma had a little goat, gray goat;
Grandma had a little goat, gray goat: 210
  Hey hey! ha ha! a little goat!
  Hey hey! ha ha! a little goat!
Second stanza! (*Sings*)
Goatie wished to roam the woods, the woods;
Goatie wished to roam the woods, the woods: 215
  Hey hey! ha ha! to roam the woods!
  Hey hey! ha ha! to roam the woods!

LIZAVETA BOGDANOVNA But I really don't understand.

SHPIGELSKY Listen! Third stanza! (*Sings*)
Great gray wolves ate up the goat, the goat; 220
Great gray wolves ate up the goat, the goat: (*Cutting a caper*)
  Hey hey! ha ha! ate up the goat!
  Hey hey! ha ha! ate up the goat!
And now, let's come on. By the way, I must have a talk with Natalya Petrovna. I don't think she'll bite me. If I'm not mistaken, I'm still necessary 225 to her. Come on! (*They go out into the garden*)

KATYA (*Cautiously emerging from behind the column*) I thought they'd never go! How spiteful that doctor is! . . . He talked and talked, how he talked! And how he does sing! I'm afraid that meanwhile Alexey Nikolayevich may have returned to the house . . . and they needed to come to this very spot! (*Goes* 230 *to the window*) So Lizaveta Bogdanovna will be a doctor's wife. . . . (*Laughing*) What a woman! . . . Well, I don't envy her. . . . (*Looking out of the window*) The grass looks as if it had been washed. . . . What a lovely fragrance! . . . It's from the cherry tree. Ah, so here he comes! (*After waiting a moment*) Alexey Nikolayevich! . . . Alexey Nikolayevich! 235

BELYAYEV (*Off stage*) Who is calling me? Oh, is that you, Katya? (*Comes up to the window*) What do you want?

KATYA Come in here. . . . I want to tell you something.

BELYAYEV Oh, all right. (*He goes away from the window and in a moment comes in at the door*) Here I am. 240

KATYA You didn't get wet in the shower?

BELYAYEV No. . . . I was sitting in the hothouse with Potap. . . . Is he your uncle or something of the sort?

KATYA Yes, he's my uncle.

BELYAYEV How pretty you are to-day! (KATYA *smiles and lowers her eyes. He* 245 *takes a peach out of his pocket*) Will you have it?

KATYA (*Declining*) Thank you kindly. . . . Eat it yourself.

BELYAYEV But did I decline when you brought me some raspberries yesterday? Take it. I picked it for you. . . . Honest.

KATYA Well, thank you. (*Takes the peach*) 250

BELYAYEV That's right. Well then, what did you want to tell me?

KATYA The young lady . . . Vera Alexandrovna . . . asked me. . . . She wants to see you.

BELYAYEV Oh! Well, I'll go to her directly.

KATYA No. She is coming here herself. She wants to have a talk with you. 255

BELYAYEV (*With marked amazement*) She wants to come here?

KATYA Yes, here. Here, you know. . . . Nobody comes here. Here you won't be interrupted. (*Sighing*) She loves you very much, Alexey Nikolayevich. . . . She is so kind. Now I'll go for her, shall I? And you'll wait here?

BELYAYEV Of course, of course. 260

KATYA Right away. (*She goes off and stops*) Alexey Nikolayevich, is it true, as they say, that you are leaving us?

BELYAYEV I? No. . . . Who told you that?

KATYA Then you are not leaving? Well, thank Heaven! (*With confusion*) I'll return directly. (*She goes out by the door leading to the house*) 265

BELYAYEV (*Remains motionless for some time*) What marvels! Marvels are certainly happening to me. I confess I never expected this. . . . Vera loves me. . . . Natalya Petrovna knows it. . . . Vera herself confessed everything to her. . . . Marvels! Vera is such a dear, kind child. But . . . but what does this note mean, for instance? (*Takes out of his pocket a small bit of paper*) From Natalya 270 Petrovna . . . written in pencil: "Do not go away. Do not decide on anything until I have discussed matters with you." What does she want to talk over with me? (*After a pause*) What stupid thoughts come into my head! I confess all this disturbs me extremely. If any one had told me a month ago that I . . .

I . . . I can't recover my senses after that conversation with Natalya 275
Petrovna. Why is my heart beating so fast? Now it's Vera that wants to see
me. What shall I tell her! At any rate, I will find out what the matter is. . . .
Perhaps Natalya Petrovna is angry with me. . . . But why? (*He looks at the note
again*) All this is strange, very strange.
(*The door quietly opens. He quickly hides the note.* VERA *and* KATYA *appear* 280
on the threshold. He goes up to them. VERA *is very pale. She does not raise her*
eyes and does not move from the spot)

KATYA Don't be afraid, young lady, go up to him. I'll stand guard. . . . Don't be
afraid. (*To* BELYAYEV) Oh, Alexey Nikolayevich! (*She closes the window, goes*
into the garden, and shuts the door behind her) 285

BELYAYEV Vera Alexandrovna, you wanted to see me. Come here. Sit down here.
(*He takes her arm and leads her to the bench.* VERA *sits down*) That's the way.
(*Looking at her with surprise*) Have you been crying?

VERA (*Without raising her eyes*) That's nothing. I've come to ask your forgiveness,
Alexey Nikolayevich. 290

BELYAYEV What for?

VERA I heard that you had . . . an unpleasant explanation with Natalya Petrovna.
. . . You are going away. . . . You have been discharged.

BELYAYEV Who told you that?

VERA Natalya Petrovna herself. . . . I met her after your explanation with her. 295
. . . She told me that you yourself did not care to stay with us longer. But I
think that she discharged you.

BELYAYEV Tell me, do the people in the house know it?

VERA No . . . only Katya. . . . I had to tell her. . . . I wanted to speak with you
and to ask your forgiveness. But please just imagine how hard this must 300
be for me. I am the cause of it all, Alexey Nikolayevich; I am the only one
to blame.

BELYAYEV You, Vera Alexandrovna?

VERA I didn't expect it at all. . . . Natalya Petrovna . . . However, I excuse her.
And you must excuse me. . . . This morning I was a stupid child, but 305
now . . . (*She stops*)

BELYAYEV There is nothing decided yet, Vera Alexandrovna. . . . Maybe I shall
stay.

VERA (*Sadly*) You say that nothing is decided, Alexey Nikolayevich. . . . No,
everything is decided; everything is ended. You see how you are behaving 310
to me now. But do you remember—only yesterday in the garden. . . . (*After*
a pause) Ah, I see, Natalya Petrovna has told you everything.

BELYAYEV (*Confused*) Vera Alexandrovna . . .

VERA She has told you everything; I can see that. . . . She wanted to catch me,
and I was just silly enough to throw myself into her net. . . . But she 315
betrayed herself too. . . . Anyhow, I am not a child any longer. (*Lowering her*
voice) Oh, no!

BELYAYEV What do you mean?

VERA (*Glancing at him*) Alexey Nikolayevich, do you really want to leave us
yourself? 320

BELYAYEV Yes.

VERA Why? (BELYAYEV *is silent*) You do not answer me?

BELYAYEV Vera Alexandrovna, you were not mistaken. Natalya Petrovna did tell me everything.

VERA (*In a weak voice*) What, for instance? 325

BELYAYEV Vera Alexandrovna, it is really impossible . . . for me. . . . You understand me.

VERA Perhaps she told you that I was in love with you?

BELYAYEV (*Indecisively*) Yes.

VERA (*Quickly*) But that's not true. 330

BELYAYEV (*Taken aback*) What?

VERA (*Covering her face with her hands and whispering through her fingers in a choked voice*) At any rate, I didn't tell her that. I don't remember. (*Raising her head*) Oh, how cruelly she acted towards me! And you . . . Is that why you wanted to leave? 335

BELYAYEV Vera Alexandrovna, consider yourself. . . .

VERA (*Glancing at him*) He doesn't love me! (*Again covers her face*)

BELYAYEV (*Sitting down near her and taking her hands*) Give me your hand. . . . Listen, there must be no misunderstanding between us. I love you as a sister. I love you because I cannot help loving you. Pardon me if I . . . Never in 340 my life have I been in such a position. . . . I don't want to hurt your feelings. . . . I will not dissemble to you. I know that you have come to like me, that you have come to love me. . . . But judge for yourself what the result of this may be. I am only twenty years old, and I haven't a penny. Please do not be angry with me. I really do not know what to say to you. 345

VERA (*Removing her hands from her face and looking at him*) As if I had demanded anything! Good heavens! But why do you act so cruelly, so mercilessly?

(*She stops*)

BELYAYEV I did not wish to grieve you, Vera Alexandrovna.

VERA I do not blame you, Alexey Nikolayevich. How are you to blame? I am 350 the only one to blame. . . . That is why I am punished. I do not blame even her. I know that she is a good woman, but she could not restrain herself. . . . She lost her self-control.

BELYAYEV (*With perplexity*) Lost her self-control?

VERA (*Turning to him*) Natalya Petrovna is in love with you, Belyayev. 355

BELYAYEV What?

VERA She is in love with you.

BELYAYEV What are you saying?

VERA I know what I am saying. To-day has aged me. . . . I am no longer a child, believe me. She took upon herself to be jealous . . . of me! (*With a bitter* 360 *smile*) How do you like that?

BELYAYEV But that is impossible!

VERA Impossible! . . . But why did she suddenly form the idea of marrying me to that gentleman, what's his name, Bolshintsov? Why did she send the doctor to me? Why did she herself try to persuade me? Oh, I know what I am 365 saying! If you could have seen, Belyayev, how her face changed when I told her! . . . Oh, you cannot imagine how cunningly, how craftily, she extorted this confession from me. . . . Yes, she loves you. That is only too clear.

BELYAYEV You are mistaken, Vera Alexandrovna, I assure you.

VERA No, I am not mistaken. Believe me, I am not mistaken. If she does not 370 love you, why did she torture me so? What have I done to her? (*Bitterly*) Jealousy excuses everything! But what is the use of talking! . . . Even now, why does she dismiss you? . . . She thinks that you . . . that you and I . . . Oh, she may be at ease! You may remain here! (*She covers her face with her hands*)

BELYAYEV She has not yet discharged me, Vera Alexandrovna. . . . I have 375 already told you that nothing is yet decided.

VERA (*Suddenly raising her head and looking at him*) Really?

BELYAYEV Yes. . . . But why are you looking at me in this way?

VERA (*As if to herself*) Ah, I understand. . . . Yes, yes. . . . She . . . she herself still has hopes. 380

(*The door to the corridor opens suddenly and on the threshold appears* NATALYA PETROVNA. *She stops at the sight of* VERA *and* BELYAYEV)

BELYAYEV What are you saying?

VERA Yes, everything is clear to me now. . . . She has come to herself. She understands that I am not dangerous to her. And really, what do I amount to? 385 I am a stupid girl, and she—!

BELYAYEV How can you think, Vera Alexandrovna . . . ?

VERA And anyway, who knows? Perhaps she is right. . . . Perhaps you do love her.

BELYAYEV I? 390

VERA (*Rising*) Yes, you. Why do you blush?

BELYAYEV I, Vera Alexandrovna?

VERA Do you love her? Can you fall in love with her? . . . You do not answer my question.

BELYAYEV But consider: what do you wish me to reply to you? You are so 395 excited, Vera Alexandrovna. . . . Calm yourself, for Heaven's sake!

VERA (*Turning away from him*) You behave towards me as if I were a child. . . . You do not even think me worth a serious answer. . . . You simply want to get rid of me. . . . You are comforting me! (*She is about to leave, but suddenly stops at the sight of* NATALYA PETROVNA) Natalya Petrovna! 400

(BELYAYEV *looks around quickly*)

NATALYA PETROVNA (*Making a few steps forward*) Yes, it is I. (*She speaks with a certain effort*) I have come for you, Verochka.

VERA (*Slowly and coldly*) Why did you think of coming to this place of all others? So you have been looking for me? 405

NATALYA PETROVNA Yes, I have been looking for you. You are indiscreet, Verochka. . . . I have already cautioned you several times. . . . And you, Alexey Nikolayevich, you have forgotten your promise. . . . You have deceived me.

VERA Oh, do stop, Natalya Petrovna; do please stop! (NATALYA PETROVNA *looks at her with amazement*) You needn't talk to me as you would to a child 410 any longer (*Lowering her voice*) I am a woman from this day forward. . . . I am just as much a woman as you.

NATALYA PETROVNA (*In confusion*) Vera!

VERA (*Almost in a whisper*) He did not deceive you. . . . It was not he who sought for this interview with me. He is not in love with me, you know that. You 415 have no occasion to be jealous.

NATALYA PETROVNA (*With rising amazement*) Vera!

VERA Believe me! . . . Do not be crafty any more. These crafty devices are of no further use to you now. . . . I see through them now. Believe me that I do. Natalya Petrovna, I am no longer your protégée whom you watch over 420 (*With irony*) as an elder sister. . . . (*Moving towards her*) I am your rival.

NATALYA PETROVNA Vera, you forget yourself.

VERA Perhaps. . . . But who has brought me to this pass? I do not understand myself how I dare to speak to you in this way. . . . Perhaps I am speaking thus because I no longer have any hopes, because you have been good enough 425 to trample me in the dust. . . . And you succeeded in doing so . . . completely. But listen to me: I do not intend to dissemble with you, if you do not with me. . . . Be sure of that. I have told him everything. (*Indicating* BELYAYEV)

NATALYA PETROVNA What could you tell him?

VERA What? (*With irony*) Why, everything that I have been able to observe. 430 You hoped to learn everything from me without giving yourself away. You made a mistake, Natalya Petrovna. You were too confident of your own strength.

NATALYA PETROVNA Vera, Vera, recollect yourself.

VERA (*In a whisper and coming still nearer to her*) Tell me that I made a mis- 435 take. . . . Tell me that you do not love him. . . . He has told me that he does not love me! (NATALYA PETROVNA *is silent with amazement.* VERA *remains immovable for some time, and suddenly puts her hand to her brow*) Natalya Petrovna, forgive me! . . . I . . . do not know myself . . . what is the matter with me. Pardon me; be indulgent to me. (*She bursts into tears and quickly goes out by* 440 *the corridor door. A pause*)

BELYAYEV (*Going up to* NATALYA PETROVNA) I may assure you, Natalya Petrovna . . .

NATALYA PETROVNA (*Looking fixedly at the floor and stretching out her hand towards him*) Stop, Alexey Nikolayevich. Really . . . Vera is right . . . It is time 445 . . . it is time for me to stop dissembling. I have done her wrong and done you wrong. You have the right to despise me. (BELYAYEV *makes an involuntary movement*) I have lowered myself in my own eyes. I have left only one means of again winning your regard: frankness, complete frankness, whatever may be the consequences. Besides that, I now see you for the last time, and 450 now speak to you for the last time. I love you. (*She gazes fixedly at him*)

BELYAYEV You, Natalya Petrovna!

NATALYA PETROVNA Yes, I. I love you. Vera was not deceived and did not deceive you. I fell in love with you the very first day of your arrival, but I recognized this myself only yesterday. I do not intend to justify my con- 455 duct. . . . It was unworthy of me . . . but at least you now can understand, can excuse me. Yes, I was jealous of Vera. Yes, in my thoughts I married her to Bolshintsov in order to remove her from myself and from you. Yes, I took advantage of my greater age, of my position in society, to find out her secret and—of course I didn't expect this—I betrayed myself. I love you, Belya- 460 yev, but be sure of this, only pride forces this confession from me. . . . The farce that I have played up till now has at last disgusted me. You cannot remain here. . . . However, after what I have just told you, it will doubtless be very embarrassing for you in my presence, and you yourself will wish to withdraw from here as quickly as may be. I am convinced of that. This con- 465 viction has given me boldness. I confess I did not wish you to carry away a bad memory of me. Now you know everything. . . . Perhaps I have hindered you. Perhaps if all this had not happened, you would have fallen in love with Verochka. . . . I have only one excuse, Alexey Nikolayevich. . . . All this was beyond my power. (*She becomes silent. She says all this in a rather even and* 470 *calm voice, without looking at* BELYAYEV. *He is silent. She continues with a certain agitation, still without looking at him*) You do not answer me? . . . However, I understand that. You have nothing to tell me. The position of a man who does not love but who receives a declaration of love is altogether too difficult. I thank you for your silence. Believe me: when I told you . . . that I loved 475 you . . . I was not dissembling . . . as I had been before. I did not count on anything. On the contrary, I wished finally to throw off the mask, to which, I may assure you, I was not accustomed. . . . And finally, why should I coquette and dissemble any longer when all is known? Why should I play the hypocrite any more when there is no one to deceive? All is ended between us. I will 480 not detain you any longer. You may leave here without saying a word to me, without even bidding me farewell. I shall not even regard that as a discourtesy. On the contrary, I shall be grateful to you. There are occasions in which delicacy is out of place . . . worse than rudeness. Evidently it was not fated for us to understand each other. Farewell! No, it was not fated for us to under- 485 stand each other . . . but at least I hope that now, in your eyes, I have ceased to be an oppressive, secretive, and cunning creature. . . . Farewell forever! (BELYAYEV *in agitation tries to say something, but cannot*) You are not leaving?

BELYAYEV (*Bowing, is about to leave, but after a short struggle with himself returns*) No, I cannot leave. (NATALYA PETROVNA *for the first time looks at him*) I 490 cannot leave in this way! . . . Listen, Natalya Petrovna, you have just told me . . . you do not desire me to carry away an unfavorable memory of you, and for my part I do not wish you to remember me as a man who . . . Good Heavens! I do not know how to express myself! . . . Natalya Petrovna, excuse me. . . . I do not know how to speak with ladies. . . . Up till now I have known . . . 495 women of an altogether different sort. You say that we are not fated to understand each other, but consider: could I, a simple, almost uneducated boy—could I even think of any intimacy with you? Remember who you are and who I am! Remember: could I even think . . . ? With your education. . . . But why do I speak of education? . . . Look at me. . . . This old coat and 500 your fragrant garments! . . . Consider! Yes, I was afraid of you, and I am afraid of you now! . . . Without any exaggeration I looked upon you as a higher being . . . and at the same time . . . you, you tell me that you love me. You, Natalya Petrovna, love me! . . . I feel my heart beating within me as it has

never beat in my life. It beats not from amazement only. It is not my self 505
conceit that is flattered. . . . Why so! . . . It is not a question of self-conceit
now . . . but I . . . I cannot leave in this way, if you will permit me to say so!

NATALYA PETROVNA (*After a pause, as if to herself*) What have I done?

BELYAYEV Natalya Petrovna, believe me, please, for God's sake! . . .

NATALYA PETROVNA (*In a changed voice*) Alexey Nikolayevich, if I did not 510
know you as a gentleman, as a man to whom falsehood is impossible, I should
think the Lord knows what. Perhaps I should repent my own frankness. But
I believe you. I do not wish to hide my feelings from you. I thank you for
what you have just now told me. Now I know why we have not become intimate. . . . And so it was not my own personality, it was nothing in me that 515
repelled you. . . . It was only my position. . . . (*Stopping*) All this makes
things better, of course. . . . And now it will be easier for me to part with you
. . . farewell! (*She is about to leave*)

BELYAYEV (*After a pause*) I know, Natalya Petrovna, that I cannot stay here. . . .
But I cannot make you understand all that is going on within me. You 520
love me! . . . It is terrible for me even to pronounce those words! . . . All this is
so new to me. . . . It seems to me that I see you, hear you, for the first time.
But I feel one thing. It is indispensable for me to go away. . . . I feel that I
cannot be responsible for anything that may happen.

NATALYA PETROVNA (*In a feeble voice*) Yes, Belyayev, you must go away. . . . 525
Now, after this explanation, you must go away. . . . But is it really possible,
notwithstanding all that I have done? . . . Oh, believe me, if I had suspected
even distantly all that you have told me, that confession would have died
within me. . . . I merely wished to put an end to all the misunderstandings.
I wished to repent, to punish myself. I wished once for all to snap the last 530
thread. If I could have imagined—! (*She covers her face with her hands*)

BELYAYEV I believe you, Natalya Petrovna, I believe you. But I myself, a quarter
of an hour ago . . . did I imagine? . . . Only to-day, during the time of our last
meeting before dinner, did I feel for the first time something unusual, something unwonted, as if some one's hand were gripping my heart; and I felt 535
such ardent warmth in my bosom. . . . Really, formerly I held myself aloof
from you, as it were, I even seemed to dislike you, but when you told me
to-day that Vera Alexandrovna thought . . . (*He pauses*)

NATALYA PETROVNA (*With an involuntary smile of happiness on her lips*) Enough,
enough, Belyayev. We must not think of that. We must not forget that we 540
are speaking to each other for the last time . . . that you leave to-morrow.

BELYAYEV Oh, yes! I shall leave to-morrow. I may still leave now. . . . All this
will pass. . . . You see, I do not wish to exaggerate. . . . I am going. . . . And
then as God wills! I shall carry away with me one memory; I shall remember
eternally that you loved me. . . . But how is it that I never knew you be- 545
fore? . . . Here you are looking at me now. . . . Is it possible that I ever tried to
avoid your glance? . . . Is it possible that I ever felt timidity in your presence?

NATALYA PETROVNA (*With a smile*) You just now told me that you were afraid
of me.

BELYAYEV I? (*After a pause*) To be sure. . . . I am surprised at myself. . . . Do 550
I—I speak so boldly to you? I do not recognize myself.

NATALYA PETROVNA   And you are not deceiving yourself?

BELYAYEV   In what?

NATALYA PETROVNA   In thinking that you love me? (*With a shudder*) Oh, Heavens, what am I doing? Listen, Belyayev. . . . Come to my aid. . . . No 555 woman ever found herself in such a position before. I have no more strength, truly. . . . Perhaps it is better thus. Everything has been cut off at one blow. But we, at least, have come to understand each other. . . . Give me your hand —and farewell forever!

BELYAYEV (*Taking her hand*)   Natalya Petrovna . . . I do not know what to 560 say to you in farewell. . . . My heart is so full. . . . God grant you . . . ! (*He stops and presses her hand to his lips*) Farewell!
   (*He is about to leave by the door into the garden*)

NATALYA PETROVNA (*Gazing after him*)   Belyayev!

BELYAYEV (*Turning around*)   Natalya Petrovna!

NATALYA PETROVNA (*After a considerable pause, in a weak voice*)   Remain!   565

BELYAYEV   What?

NATALYA PETROVNA   Remain! And let God pass judgment on us!
   (*She buries her head in her hands*)

BELYAYEV (*Quickly approaching her and stretching out his hands to her*)   Natalya 570 Petrovna!
   (*At that moment the door into the garden opens and* RAKITIN *appears on the threshold. He looks at them both for some time and suddenly approaches them*)

RAKITIN (*In a loud voice*)   They are looking for you everywhere, Natalya Petrovna. (NATALYA PETROVNA *and* BELYAYEV *glance around*)   575

NATALYA PETROVNA (*Removing her hands from her face and seeming to come to herself*) Ah, is that you? Who is looking for me? (BELYAYEV, *confused, bows to* NATALYA PETROVNA *and is about to leave*) Are you going, Alexey Nikolayevich? . . . Don't forget, you know— (*He bows to her a second time and goes out into the garden!*

RAKITIN   Arkady is looking for you. . . . I confess I didn't expect to find you 580 here. . . . But as I was passing by . . .

NATALYA PETROVNA (*With a smile*)   You heard our voices. . . . I met Alexey Nikolayevich here . . . and I had a long explanation with him. . . . To-day is evidently a day of explanations, but now we can go to the house. (*She is about to leave by the corridor door*)   585

RAKITIN (*With some agitation*)   May I inquire . . . what decision? . . .

NATALYA PETROVNA (*Pretending to be surprised*)   What decision? . . . I don't understand you.

RAKITIN (*After a long silence, in a gloomy voice*)   In that case I understand everything.   590

NATALYA PETROVNA   Well, so it is. . . . Again mysterious hints! Well, yes, I have had an explanation with him, and now everything is straightened out again. . . . Those were trifles, exaggerations. . . . Everything that you and I have been speaking of is all childishness. We must forget it now.

RAKITIN   I am not cross-examining you, Natalya Petrovna.   595

NATALYA PETROVNA (*Forcing herself to speak casually*)   What was it I wanted to tell you? . . . I don't remember. It's all the same. Come on. All that is over now. . . . It's all past.

RAKITIN (*Looking at her fixedly*) Oh, it's all over. And how vexed you are with yourself now, most likely . . . because of your frankness to-day! 600

NATALYA PETROVNA (*Turning away from him*) Rakitin. . . . (*He again glances at her. She evidently does not know what to say*) You haven't spoken with Arkady yet?

RAKITIN By no means. . . . I haven't yet managed to prepare myself. . . . You understand that I need to make up something. 605

NATALYA PETROVNA How unbearable this is! What do they want of me? They follow after me at every step. Really, Rakitin, I feel ashamed to see you.

RAKITIN Oh, don't be disturbed, Natalya Petrovna. . . . Why should you be? This is all in the natural course of things. But one can see that Mr. Belyayev is still a novice! And why was he so confused? Why did he run away? . . . 610 However, in the course of time . . . (*In a low, hurried voice*) you will both learn how to dissemble. (*Aloud*) Come on.

(NATALYA PETROVNA *is about to come up to him, but stops. At that moment the voice of* ISLAYEV *is heard just outside the garden door:* "He came this way, you say?" *After these words,* ISLAYEV *and* SHPIGELSKY *come in*) 615

ISLAYEV To be sure, there he is.—Bah, bah, bah! And Natalya Petrovna is here too! (*Coming up to her*) What's this? A continuation of to-day's explanation?— Evidently it's an important subject.

RAKITIN I met Natalya Petrovna here.

ISLAYEV Met her? (*Looking around*) What a frequented place, to be sure! 620

NATALYA PETROVNA But you came here yourself.

ISLAYEV I came here because . . . (*He stops*)

NATALYA PETROVNA You were looking for me?

ISLAYEV (*After a pause*) Yes, I was looking for you. Would you not like to come back to the house? Tea is ready. It will be dark soon. 625

NATALYA PETROVNA (*Taking his hand*) Come on, then.

ISLAYEV (*Looking around*) And we can make this hall into two good rooms for the gardeners—or another servant's room—what do you think about it, Shpigelsky?

SHPIGELSKY Of course. 630

ISLAYEV Come on through the garden, Natasha. (*He goes out by the door into the garden. During the course of all this scene, he has not once glanced at* RAKITIN. *On the threshold he half turns around*) Well, folks, come on and have tea. (*He goes out with* NATALYA PETROVNA)

SHPIGELSKY (*To* RAKITIN) Well, Mikhaylo Alexandrovich, come on! . . . 635 Give me your hand. . . . Evidently fate has cast us into the rear guard.

RAKITIN (*Testily*) Oh, Mr. Doctor, permit me to tell you, I am decidedly sick of you.

SHPIGELSKY (*With affected good humor*) But I am sick of myself, Mikhaylo Alexandrovich, if you did but know it! (RAKITIN *smiles involuntarily*) Come 640 on, come on. (*They both go out by the door into the garden*)

Act Five

The scene is the same as in Acts One and Three. Morning. ISLAYEV *is sitting at
his desk looking over papers. He rises suddenly*

ISLAYEV No, I absolutely can't work to-day. It's as if a nail were run through my
head. (*Pacing the room*) I must confess I didn't expect this. I didn't expect that
I should be disturbed . . . as I am now. . . . What shall I do then? . . . That's 5
the problem. (*Falls to thinking and suddenly calls*) Matvey!

MATVEY (*Coming in*) What will you have, sir?

ISLAYEV Call my overseer . . . and tell the diggers to wait for me at the dam. . . .
Go along!

MATVEY Yes, sir. (*Goes out*) 10

ISLAYEV (*Going to the table again. Running through his papers*) Yes, that's the
problem.

ANNA SEMENOVNA (*Coming in and approaching* ISLAYEV) Arkasha!

ISLAYEV Oh, is that you, mamma? How are you feeling?

ANNA SEMENOVNA (*Sitting down on the couch*) I am well, thank Heaven! 15
(*Sighing*) I'm well. (*Sighing still louder*) Thank Heaven! (*Seeing that* ISLAYEV
does not listen to her, she gives a very vigorous sigh, with a slight groan)

ISLAYEV You are sighing. . . . What's the matter with you?

ANNA SEMENOVNA (*Again sighing, but this time more gently*) Oh, Arkasha, as if
you didn't know what I am sighing about. 20

ISLAYEV What do you mean?

ANNA SEMENOVNA (*After a pause*) I am your mother, Arkasha. Of course you
are already a grown man, and a man of sense. But all the same, I am your
mother. That is a great word, "mother"!

ISLAYEV Oh, please explain yourself! 25

ANNA SEMENOVNA You know what I am hinting at, my dear. Your wife
Natasha . . . Of course, she is a splendid woman—and her conduct up till now
has been most exemplary . . . but she is still so young, Arkasha! And youth . . .

ISLAYEV I understand what you mean. . . . It seems to you that her relations with
Rakitin— 30

ANNA SEMENOVNA God forbid! I wasn't thinking of that at all.

ISLAYEV You didn't let me finish my speech. . . . It seems to you that her relations with Rakitin . . . are not quite . . . plain. . . . Those mysterious conver-
sations, those tears—all that seems to you strange.

ANNA SEMENOVNA Well, Arkasha, did he finally tell you what those conver- 35
sations of theirs were about? . . . He hasn't told me anything.

ISLAYEV I haven't cross-examined him, and he evidently is in no great hurry to
gratify my curiosity.

ANNA SEMENOVNA So what do you intend to do now?

ISLAYEV I, mamma? Nothing at all. 40

ANNA SEMENOVNA Nothing?

ISLAYEV Certainly. Nothing.

ANNA SEMENOVNA (*Rising*) I confess that I am surprised. Of course you are the
master in your own house, and you know better than I what's good and what's
bad. However, consider what consequences . . . 45

ISLAYEV   Really, mamma, you are quite wrong in being disturbed.

ANNA SEMENOVNA   My dear, I am a mother. . . . But, however, as you think best. (*After a pause*) I came to see you, I must confess, with the intention of offering my services as mediator.

ISLAYEV (*With animation*)   No. In this matter, I must ask you not to trouble 50 yourself, mamma. . . . Please oblige me!

ANNA SEMENOVNA   As you wish, Arkasha; as you wish. I won't say a word more. I have forewarned you, I have done my duty. But now—my lips are sealed.

(*A short silence*)

ISLAYEV   You aren't going anywhere to-day?   55

ANNA SEMENOVNA   But I merely felt obliged to forewarn you. You are too trustful, my dear boy. You judge every one by yourself! Believe me, true friends are very rare in these times!

ISLAYEV (*With impatience*)   Mamma! . . .

ANNA SEMENOVNA   Well, I am silent, I am silent! And why should an old 60 woman like me mix in? I suppose I have outlived my wits! And I was brought up on other principles and I tried to teach them to you. . . . Well, well, attend to your business. I won't hinder you. . . . I am going. (*She goes to the door and stops*) Well, then? . . . Well, as you wish, as you wish. (*She goes out*)

ISLAYEV (*Gazing after her*)   Why is it that people who really love you like to 65 put each and every one of their fingers in your wound? And yet they are convinced that this makes it easier for you—that's what's amusing! However, I don't blame mother. Her intentions, I know, are of the best, and how can she help giving advice? But that is not the point. . . . (*Sitting down*) How shall I act? (*After reflecting, he rises*) Ah, the simplest way is the best! Diplomatic 70 finesse doesn't suit me. . . . I am the first to get entangled in it. (*He rings the bell.* MATVEY *comes in*) Is Mikhaylo Alexandrovich in the house? Do you know?

MATVEY   He is. I just saw him in the billiard room.

ISLAYEV   Ah! Then ask him to come to see me.   75

MATVEY   Very well, sir. (*He goes out*)

ISLAYEV (*Walking back and forth*)   I am not used to such perplexities. . . . I hope they won't be often repeated. . . . Although I am of a strong build, I couldn't stand this for long. (*Putting his hand to his breast*) Ah! . . .

(RAKITIN *comes in from the hall in some confusion*)   80

RAKITIN   Did you call me?

ISLAYEV   Yes. . . . (*After a pause*) Michel, you owe me something.

RAKITIN   I?

ISLAYEV   Certainly. Have you forgotten your promise about . . . Natasha's tears . . . and in general? . . . You remember how mother and I found you. . . . 85 You told me then that there was a secret between Natasha and yourself that you wished to explain to me.

RAKITIN   Did I say "secret"?

ISLAYEV   Yes.

RAKITIN   But what secret can there be between us? We were just talking. 90

ISLAYEV   What about? And why was she weeping?

RAKITIN   You know, Arkady . . . moments occur in the life of a woman . . . even the happiest . . .

ISLAYEV   Wait a bit, Rakitin. You can't act this way—I can't see you in such a position. . . . Your confusion is more embarrassing for me than for yourself. 95 (*Taking him by the hand*) You see, you and I are old friends. . . . You have known me from childhood. . . . I am unable to dissemble. . . . And you have always been frank with me. Give me permission to ask you one question. . . . I give you my word of honor that I will not doubt the sincerity of your answer. You are in love with my wife, aren't you? (RAKITIN *glances at* 100 ISLAYEV) You understand me? You love her . . . well, in a word, you love my wife with the sort of love that is hard to confess to a husband?

RAKITIN   (*After a pause. In a horse voice*)   Yes. I love your wife with that sort of love.

ISLAYEV   (*Also after a pause*)   Thank you for your frankness, Michel. You are a 105 gentleman. Well, anyway, what shall we do now? Sit down and let's consider this matter together. (RAKITIN *sits down.* ISLAYEV *paces the room*) I know Natasha. I know her value. But I also know my own value. I am not your equal, Michel . . . don't interrupt me, please! . . . I am not your equal. You're more clever. You're a finer man. In a word, a more pleasing person than I. 110 I am a simple fellow. Natasha loves me, I think, but she has eyes. . . . Well, in a word, she must like you. And so here's what I'll tell you further. I have long remarked your mutual regard for each other. . . . But I have also been confident of you both—and so far nothing has come to light. . . . Oh, I don't know how to speak of it! (*He stops*) But after the scene yesterday, after your 115 second meeting in the evening, what can I think? If it were only I who had found you! But witnesses were involved in the case; mamma, and that rascal Shpigelsky. . . . Well, what have you to say, Michel?

RAKITIN   You are quite right, Arkady.

ISLAYEV   That's not the question. . . . But what's to be done? I must tell you, 120 Michel, that though I am a simple man, I have this much sense: I know that it isn't a good thing to embitter another man's life, and there are cases when it is sinful to insist on one's own rights. I didn't read that in books, my friend. . . . Conscience tells me so. If I must give you freedom . . . well, then I'll do so. Only we must think this over. It's too important.   125

RAKITIN   (*Rising*)   I have thought it over already.

ISLAYEV   Well?

RAKITIN   I must be leaving. . . . I am going away.

ISLAYEV   (*After a pause*)   Do you think so? . . . To leave us for good and all?

RAKITIN   Yes.   130

ISLAYEV   (*Again beginning to pace the room*)   What . . . what is this you propose! But perhaps you are right. It will be hard for us without you. . . . Lord knows, perhaps this won't lead to the desired end. . . . But you can see things better; you can judge best. I think that you have the right idea. You are dangerous to me, my boy. (*With a mournful smile*) Yes . . . you are dangerous to me. 135 So what I have just said . . . in regard to freedom—but really, I could not live after that! For me to exist without Natasha . . . (*He waves his hand*) And one thing further, my boy. For some time, especially during these last few days, I have noticed a great change in her. She has given indications of a certain deep, constant agitation, which alarms me. Is not that true? I am not mistaken, am !? 140

RAKITIN (*Bitterly*) Oh, no! You are not mistaken.

ISLAYEV Well, there, you see! And so you are going away?

RAKITIN Yes.

ISLAYEV Hm. And how suddenly this load was shaken off! And really, did 145 you need to be so confused when mother and I found you?

MATVEY (*Coming in*) The overseer has come.

ISLAYEV Let him wait. (MATVEY *goes out*) Michel, you aren't going to leave us for long, are you? All this is nonsense, my boy!

RAKITIN I really don't know.... I think . . . for a long time. 150

ISLAYEV Well, you don't take me for an Othello,* do you? Really, since the world was made, I don't think any such conversation has ever taken place between two friends! I cannot part with you in this way.

RAKITIN (*Pressing his hand*) You will inform me when it is possible for me to return. 155

ISLAYEV But we have no one to replace you here! Certainly not Bolshintsov!

RAKITIN There are other people here.

ISLAYEV Who? Krinitsyn? That dandy? Belyayev is of course a good fellow . . . but he is as far below you as he is below the stars of heaven.

RAKITIN (*Caustically*) You think so? You don't know him, Arkady. . . . You 160 just pay attention to him. . . . I advise you to. . . . Do you hear? He is a very . . . very remarkable fellow!

ISLAYEV Bah! You and Natasha were always going to attend to his education. (*Glancing at the door*) Ah, here he comes himself, I think. . . . (*Hastily*) And so, my dear fellow, this is decided, you are leaving us . . . for a short time 165 . . . in a day or two. . . . There is no need of haste. We must prepare Natasha. . . . I'll calm mother down. . . . And God grant you happiness! You have moved a stone from my heart. . . . Embrace me, my dear fellow. (*He hastily embraces him, and turns towards* BELYAYEV, *who has just come in*) Ah, is that you? Well . . . well . . . how are you? 170

BELYAYEV First rate, Arkady Sergeich.

ISLAYEV Well, where's Kolya?

BELYAYEV He is with Mr. Schaaf.

ISLAYEV Ah, fine! (*Taking his hat*) Well, gentlemen, good-by. I haven't made my daily rounds to-day. I haven't been either at the dam or at the new 175 building. . . . Why, I haven't even looked over my papers. (*Tucks them under his arm*) Good-by for the moment! Matvey, Matvey, come on with me!

(*He goes out.* RAKITIN *remains in the foreground, buried in thought*)

BELYAYEV (*Coming up to* RAKITIN) How do you feel to-day, Mikhaylo Alexandrovich? 180

RAKITIN Thank you. As usual. And how are you?

BELYAYEV I am well.

RAKITIN That's evident!

[151] A jealous husband driven to murder.

BELYAYEV Why so?

RAKITIN Why, just . . . by your face. . . . Ah, so you've put on a new frock 185 coat to-day. . . . And what's this I see? A flower in your buttonhole? (BELYA-YEV, *blushing, pulls it out*) But why should you, why should you, pray? . . . It looks very nice. (*After a pause*) By the way, Alexey Nikolayevich, if you need anything . . . I am going to town to-morrow.

BELYAYEV To-morrow? 190

RAKITIN Yes . . . and from there, perhaps, to Moscow.

BELYAYEV (*With surprise*) To Moscow? But I think you told me only yesterday that you intended to stay here about a month.

RAKITIN Yes . . . but business . . . circumstances have occurred.

BELYAYEV And are you leaving for a long time? 195

RAKITIN I don't know. . . . Maybe for a long time.

BELYAYEV Permit me to inquire: Does Natalya Petrovna know of your intention?

RAKITIN No. Why do you ask me about her in particular?

BELYAYEV Why? (*With some confusion*) No special reason. 200

RAKITIN (*After a pause, and looking round*) Alexey Nikolayevich, I think that there is no one in the room except ourselves. Isn't it strange that we are playing a comedy to each other, eh? What do you think about it?

BELYAYEV I don't understand you, Mikhaylo Alexandrovich.

RAKITIN Really? You actually don't understand why I am going away? 205

BELYAYEV No.

RAKITIN That's queer. . . . However, I am ready to believe you. Possibly you really don't know the reason. . . . Do you want me to tell you why I am leaving?

BELYAYEV Pray do. 210

RAKITIN You see, Alexey Nikolayevich—by the way, I rely on your discretion— you found me with Arkady Sergeich just now. . . . He and I had a rather important conversation, and in consequence of that very conversation I have decided to go away. Do you know why? I am telling you all this because I regard you as a gentleman. . . . He fancies that I . . . that I am in love with 215 Natalya Petrovna. What do you think of that, eh? Isn't it really rather a strange idea? But I am thankful to him that he didn't begin to dissemble and keep watch of us, but that he addressed himself to me frankly and directly. Well now, tell me what should you have done in my place? Of course, his suspicions have no foundation, but they cause him anxiety. . . . For the 220 peace of his friends, a gentleman should know how . . . sometimes, to sacrifice . . . his own pleasure. And that is the reason I am going away. . . . I am convinced that you will approve my decision; will you not? Is it not true that you . . . that you would have acted in just the same way in my place? You, too, would have gone away? 225

BELYAYEV (*After a pause*) Perhaps.

RAKITIN I am very glad to hear that. . . . Of course, I don't dispute that in my intention of withdrawing there is a comic side; it is as if I regarded myself as a dangerous person. But you see, Alexey Nikolayevich, the honor of a woman is such an important matter. . . . And besides—of course I don't say this in 230 reference to Natalya Petrovna—but I have known women who were pure and innocent in heart, genuine children in their intellect, who in consequence of that very purity and innocence were more likely than any others to give way to a sudden infatuation. . . . And then, who knows? An excess of caution does no harm in such cases, so much the more that— By the way, Alexey Nikolayevich, perhaps you still have the notion that love is the highest good on earth.

BELYAYEV (*Coldly*)   I have not experienced that emotion, but I think that to be loved by a woman whom you love must be a great happiness.

RAKITIN   God grant that you long preserve such a pleasant conviction! In my opinion, Alexey Nikolayevich, every love, whether it be happy or unhappy, is a genuine misery when you give yourself up to it entirely. . . . Just wait! You will perhaps find out in the future how those tender little hands know how to torture, with what caressing persistency they tear your heart to bits. . . . Just wait! You will find out how much burning hatred lies hidden under the most ardent love! You will remember me when, as a sick man thirsts for health, you thirst for peace, for the most nonsensical, the most commonplace peace; when you envy every man who is free and has no cares. . . . Just wait! You will learn what it means to belong to a skirt, what it means to be enslaved, to be infected, and how shameful and tormenting is that slavery! . . . You will learn, finally, what trifles are purchased at so high a price. . . . But why am I saying all this to you? You will not believe me now. The thing is that your approval is very pleasant to me. Yes, yes. In such cases, one should be cautious.

BELYAYEV (*Who all this time has gazed fixedly at* RAKITIN)   Thank you for the lesson, Mikhaylo Alexandrovich, although I did not need it.

RAKITIN (*Taking his hand*)   Excuse me, please. I had no intention . . . I am not in a position to give lessons to any man whatsoever. . . . I merely got started talking.

BELYAYEV (*With slight irony*)   Without any reason?

RAKITIN (*Slightly confused*)   That's just it: without any special reason. I merely wished . . . Up to this time, Alexey Nikolayevich, you have had no opportunity of studying women. Women are a very peculiar kind of people.

BELYAYEV   Of whom are you speaking?

RAKITIN   Well, of no one in particular.

BELYAYEV   Of all women in general, I suppose?

RAKITIN (*With a forced smile*)   Yes, maybe. I really don't know for what reason I have fallen into this instructive tone, but permit me, in saying farewell, to give you one piece of good advice. (*Stopping and waving his hand*) Oh, but anyhow, who am I to give advice! Pray excuse my chatter.

BELYAYEV   On the contrary, on the contrary.

RAKITIN   Well then, so you don't need anything from town?

BELYAYEV   No, I thank you. But I am sorry that you are going away.

RAKITIN   I thank you humbly. . . . Pray believe that I, also . . .

(*From the door of the study come out* NATALYA PETROVNA *and* VERA. VERA *is very sad and pale*)

I have been very glad to make your acquaintance. (*He again presses his hand*)

NATALYA PETROVNA (*Gazes at both for some time, and goes up to them*) How do you do, gentlemen!

RAKITIN (*Turning around quickly*) How do you do, Natalya Petrovna! . . . 280 How do you do, Vera Alexandrovna! . . .

(BELYAYEV *bows slightly to* NATALYA PETROVNA *and* VERA. *He is confused*)

NATALYA PETROVNA (*To* RAKITIN) What in the world are you up to?

RAKITIN Oh, nothing.

NATALYA PETROVNA Vera and I have been strolling in the garden. It's so 285 nice out of doors to-day. . . . The lindens have such a sweet fragrance. We strolled all the time under the lindens. . . . It's pleasant in the shade to listen to the humming of the bees over your head. . . . (*Timidly to* BELYAYEV) We hoped to meet you there. (BELYAYEV *is silent*)

RAKITIN (*To* NATALYA PETROVNA) Ah, so you are interested in the beauties 290 of nature to-day. . . . (*After a pause*) Alexey Nikolayevich could not go into the garden. . . . He has put on his new frock coat to-day.

BELYAYEV (*With a slight flash of temper*) Of course: it's naturally the only frock coat I have, and in the garden I might tear it. Is that what you mean?

RAKITIN (*Reddening*) Oh, no! . . . I didn't mean that at all. (VERA *goes silently* 295 *to the couch on the right, sits down, and takes up some work.* NATALYA PETROVNA *smiles in a constrained fashion to* BELYAYEV. *There is a short and rather oppressive silence.* RAKITIN *continues with biting carelessness*) Oh, yes, I forgot to tell you, Natalya Petrovna, that I am going away to-day.

NATALYA PETROVNA (*With some agitation*) You are going away? Where to? 300

RAKITIN To town. . . . On business.

NATALYA PETROVNA I hope not for long.

RAKITIN As business demands.

NATALYA PETROVNA Be sure to come back soon. (*To* BELYAYEV, *without looking at him*) Alexey Nikolayevich, were those your drawings that Kolya was 305 showing me? Were they your work?

BELYAYEV Yes . . . I . . . trifles.

NATALYA PETROVNA On the contrary, they are very charming. You have talent.

RAKITIN I see that you are discovering new excellences every day in Mr. Belyayev. 310

NATALYA PETROVNA (*Coldly*) Possibly. . . . So much the better for him. (*To* BELYAYEV) Probably you have still other drawings. You will show them to me? (BELYAYEV *bows*)

RAKITIN (*Who all this time seems to be on pins and needles*) However, I recollect that it is time for me to be packing. . . . Good-by for the moment. 315

(*He goes to the door of the hall*)

NATALYA PETROVNA (*Calling after him*) But you will come back to say good-by to us?

RAKITIN Of course.

BELYAYEV (*After hesitating slightly*) Wait, Mikhaylo Alexandrovich, I'll go 320 with you. I want to say a couple of words to you.

RAKITIN Ah! (*They both go out into the hall.* NATALYA PETROVNA *remains in the middle of the stage. After waiting a short time she sits down at the left*)

NATALYA PETROVNA (*After a short pause*) Vera!

VERA (*Without raising her head*) What do you wish? 325

NATALYA PETROVNA For the Lord's sake, Vera, don't act so with me! . . . For the Lord's sake, Vera . . . Verochka! . . . (VERA *says nothing.* NATALYA PETROVNA *rises, crosses the stage, and quietly kneels before her.* VERA *tries to raise her, turns away, and hides her face*)

NATALYA PETROVNA (*Speaks, still kneeling*) Vera, forgive me. Don't cry, 330 Vera. I have done you wrong. I am to blame. Is it possible that you cannot forgive me?

VERA (*Through her tears*) Please get up, please do!

NATALYA PETROVNA I shall not get up, Vera, until you forgive me. It is hard for you . . . but consider . . . is it easier for me? . . . Consider, Vera! . . . 335 You know everything. . . . Between us there is only this difference, that you have done me no wrong at all and I . . .

VERA (*Bitterly*) Only that difference! No, Natalya Petrovna, between us there is another difference. . . . To-day you are so soft, so kind, so caressing. . . .

NATALYA PETROVNA (*Interrupting her*) Because I feel my own guilt. 340

VERA Really? Only for that reason?

NATALYA PETROVNA (*Rising and sitting down beside her*) But what other reason can there be?

VERA Natalya Petrovna, do not torture me any more. Do not question me.

NATALYA PETROVNA (*With a sigh*) Vera, I see that you cannot forgive me. 345

VERA To-day you are so good and so soft because you feel that you are loved.

NATALYA PETROVNA (*Confused*) Vera?

VERA (*Turning towards her*) Well, isn't that the truth?

NATALYA PETROVNA (*Sadly*) Believe me, both of us are equally unfortunate.

VERA He loves you! 350

NATALYA PETROVNA Vera, why should we desire to torture each other? It is time for both of us to come to our senses. Remember in what a position I am, in what a position we both are. Remember that our secret and the wrong that I have done you are already known to two persons here. . . . (*Stopping*) Vera, instead of tormenting each other by suspicions and 355 reproaches, would it not be better for both of us to think how to find a way out from this hard position . . . how to save ourselves! Do you think that I can bear these agitations, these anxieties? Have you forgotten who I am? But you are not listening to me.

VERA (*Pensively gazing at the floor*) He loves you. . . . 360

NATALYA PETROVNA He is going away, Vera.

VERA (*Turning around*) Oh, let me alone! . . .

(NATALYA PETROVNA *looks at her with indecision. At that moment the voice of* ISLAYEV *is heard in the study:* "Natasha! Oh, Natasha! Where are you?")

NATALYA PETROVNA (*Rising quickly and going to the door of the study*) I am 365 here. What do you wish?

VOICE OF ISLAYEV Come here, I want to tell you something.

NATALYA PETROVNA Right away.

(*She returns to* VERA *and extends her hand to her.* VERA *does not move.* NATALYA PETROVNA *sighs and goes out into the study*) 370

VERA (*Alone, after a pause*) He loves her! . . . And I must remain in her house! . . . Oh, that is too much.

(*She covers her face with her hands, and remains motionless. From the door leading into the hall peers the head of* SHPIGELSKY. *He cautiously looks around and comes up on tiptoe to* VERA, *who does not notice him*) 375

SHPIGELSKY (*After standing in front of her with arms folded and with a biting smile on his countenance*) Vera Alexandrovna! . . . Oh, Vera Alexandrovna!

VERA (*Raising her head*) Who is that? Is it you, doctor?

SHPIGELSKY Well, my young lady, are you not feeling well?

VERA No, I'm all right. 380

SHPIGELSKY Let me feel your pulse. (*Feels her pulse*) Hm! Why so fast? Oh, my young lady, my young lady! . . . You are not listening to me. . . . But I think that I sincerely wish you happiness.

VERA (*Looking at him with decision*) Ignaty Ilyich!

SHPIGELSKY (*Quickly*) I am listening, Vera Alexandrovna. . . . What an 385 expression there is on your face: good gracious! . . . I am listening.

VERA That Mr. . . . Bolshintsov, your acquaintance—is he really a good man?

SHPIGELSKY My friend Bolshintsov? A most excellent, a most honorable man . . . the mold and pattern of virtue!

VERA He isn't bad-tempered? 390

SHPIGELSKY The kindest sort of man. He isn't really a man, he is just soft dough. All you have to do is to take him and knead him. You couldn't find another man as kind as he in all the world, by daylight, with a candle. He's a dove and not a man.

VERA Do you vouch for him? 395

SHPIGELSKY (*Putting one hand on his heart and raising the other on high*) As I would for myself!

VERA In that case, you may tell him . . . that I am ready to marry him.

SHPIGELSKY (*With joyous amazement*) Well, really?

VERA Only, as quickly as possible—do you hear?—As quickly as possible. 400

SHPIGELSKY To-morrow, if you wish. . . . By all means! Good for you, Vera Alexandrovna! Splendid girl! I'll gallop away for him right off, and won't I make him happy! . . . What an unexpected turn things have taken! He is fairly infatuated with you, Vera Alexandrovna.

VERA (*Impatiently*) I am not inquiring of you about that, Ignaty Ilyich. 405

SHPIGELSKY As you choose, Vera Alexandrovna, as you choose. Only you'll be happy with him; you'll thank me, you'll see. . . . (VERA *again makes an impatient move*) Well, I am silent. I am silent. . . . So I may tell him?

VERA You may, you may.

SHPIGELSKY Very good. Then I'll set out right off. Good-by for a while. 410 (*Listening*) By the way, some one's coming in here. (*He goes into the study, and on the threshold makes a grimace of amazement for his own benefit*) Good-by for the moment. (*He goes out*)

VERA (*Gazing after him*) Anything in the world rather than remain here! . . . (*She rises*) Yes, I have decided. I will not remain in this house, not under 415 any consideration. I can't endure her gentle look, her smiles; I can't see how her whole being seems refreshed, how she revels in her own happiness. . . . For she is happy, however she may pretend to be sad and melancholy. . . . Her caresses are more than I can stand. . . .

(BELYAYEV *appears from the hall door. He looks around and goes up to* VERA) 420

BELYAYEV (*In a low voice*) Vera Alexandrovna, are you alone?

VERA (*Looks around, shudders, and after a short pause utters the word*) Yes.

BELYAYEV I am glad you are alone. . . . Otherwise I should not have come here. I have come to bid you farewell, Vera Alexandrovna.

VERA Farewell? 425

BELYAYEV Yes, I am going away.

VERA You are going away? You, too, are going away?

BELYAYEV Yes. . . . I, too. (*With intense internal agitation*) You see, Vera Alexandrovna, it is impossible for me to remain here. My presence has already been the cause of many troubles here. Besides the fact that, without myself 430 knowing how, I have disturbed your peace of mind, and the peace of mind of Natalya Petrovna, I have also broken up old ties of friendship. Thanks to me, Mr. Rakitin is leaving here, and you have quarreled with your benefactress. . . . It is time to put a stop to all this. After my departure I hope that all will calm down again and return to its former quiet routine. . . . 435 Turning the heads of rich ladies and young girls is not my line. . . . You will forget me, and perhaps in time you will be surprised how all this could have happened. . . . Even now it surprises me. . . . I do not wish to deceive you, Vera Alexandrovna: I am afraid, I am alarmed at the thought of staying here. . . . I cannot be responsible for anything. . . . You know I am not accus- 440 tomed to such things as this. I feel embarrassed. . . . It seems to me that every one is looking at me. . . . And finally, it will be impossible for me . . . now . . . with both of you. . . .

VERA Oh, don't be anxious about me! I shan't remain here long.

BELYAYEV Why so? 445

VERA That's my secret, but I shan't hinder you. You may be sure of that.

BELYAYEV Well, then, you see, how can I help departing? Judge for yourself. I seem to have brought the plague into this house; every one is fleeing from here. . . . Is it not better for me alone to disappear while there is still time? I had a long conversation with Mr. Rakitin just now. . . . You can't 450 imagine how much bitterness there was in his words. . . . And he was right in making fun of my new frock coat. . . . He was right. Yes, I must depart. Believe me, Vera Alexandrovna, I can hardly wait for the moment when I shall be rushing along the highway in a carriage. . . . I am suffocating here; I want fresh air. I am exhausted; I have a sense of bitterness, and at the 455 same time, of relief, just like a man who is setting out on a long sea voyage. He is loath to part with his friends, he feels oppressed; and at the same time, the sea ripples so merrily, the wind blows so freshly in his face, that the blood involuntarily leaps in his veins, however heavy his heart may be. . . . Yes, I am going away without fail. I shall return to Moscow to my com- 460 panions. I shall set to work.

VERA So you love her, Alexey Nikolayevich. You love her, and yet you are going away.

BELYAYEV Oh, don't, Vera Alexandrovna! Why do you say that? Do you not see that all is ended? It flashed up and went out like a spark. Let us part 465 friends. It is time. I have come to myself. I wish you health and happiness. Sometime we shall see each other again. . . . I shall never forget you, Vera Alexandrovna. . . . I have become very fond of you, believe me! . . . (*He presses her hand, and hastily adds*) Give this note to Natalya Petrovna from me.

VERA (*Looking at him in confusion*) A note? 470

BELYAYEV Yes. . . . I cannot bid her farewell.

VERA But are you going off right away?

BELYAYEV Right away. . . . I have told no one about this . . . with the exception of Mikhaylo Alexandrovich. He approves my decision. From here I shall go immediately on foot to Petróvskoye. In Petróvskoye I shall wait for 475 Mikhaylo Alexandrovich, and together we shall go to town. From town I shall write. They will send me my things. You see, everything has been arranged. . . . By the way, you may read that note. There are only two words in it.

VERA (*Taking the note from him*) And are you really going away? 480

BELYAYEV Yes, yes. . . . Give her this note and tell her— No, don't tell her anything. What's the use? (*Listening*) They are coming here. Good-by. . . . (*He rushes to the door, stops for a moment on the threshold, then runs out.*

VERA *remains with the note in her hand*)

(NATALYA PETROVNA *comes in*) 485

NATALYA PETROVNA (*Going up to* VERA) Verochka! (*Looking at her and stopping*) What is the matter with you? (VERA *silently extends the note to her*) A note? From whom?

VERA (*In a hoarse voice*) Read it.

NATALYA PETROVNA You alarm me. (*She reads the note to herself, suddenly 490 presses both hands to her face, and falls into the chair*)

(*A long pause*)

VERA (*Approaching her*) Natalya Petrovna!

NATALYA PETROVNA (*Not removing her hands from her face*) He is going away! . . . He did not even wish to say good-by to me! . . . Oh, to you he at least 495 said good-by!

VERA (*Sadly*) He did not love me.

NATALYA PETROVNA (*Removing her hands and raising*) But he has no right to go away in such fashion. . . . I wish . . . He can't do it. . . . Who permitted him to break off so stupidly? . . . This amounts to contempt. . . . I . . . How 500 does he know that I should never have decided . . . ? (*She drops into a chair*) My God, my God!

VERA Natalya Petrovna, you yourself told me just now that he must leave. . . . Recollect!

NATALYA PETROVNA You are happy now. . . . He is going away. . . . Now 505 you and I are in the same position. . . . (*Her voice breaks*)

VERA You just said to me, Natalya Petrovna . . . These are your own words: "Instead of torturing each other, would it not be better for both of us to think how to escape from this position, how to save ourselves?" . . . Now we are saved. 510

NATALYA PETROVNA (*Turning away from her, almost with hatred*) Ah!

VERA I understand you, Natalya Petrovna. . . . Do not be disturbed. . . . I shall not longer hamper you by my presence. It is impossible for us to live together.

NATALYA PETROVNA (*Starting to extend her hand to her, and dropping it on her knees*) Why do you say that, Verochka? . . . Is it possible that you, too, wish to leave me? Yes, you are right. We are saved now. All is ended. . . . Everything is again quite normal.

VERA (*Coldly*) Don't be disturbed, Natalya Petrovna.

(VERA *gazes at her sadly.* ISLAYEV *comes out of the study*)

ISLAYEV (*After looking for some time at* NATALYA PETROVNA, *in a low voice to* VERA) Does she know that he is going away?

VERA (*Perplexed*) Yes. She knows.

ISLAYEV (*To himself*) But why is he leaving so soon? (*Aloud*) Natasha! (*He takes her hand. She raises her head*) It is I, Natasha. (*She strives to smile*) You are not well, my darling? I should advise you to lie down . . . really.

NATALYA PETROVNA I am perfectly well, Arkady. . . . This is nothing at all.

ISLAYEV But you are pale. . . . Really, listen to me. . . . Take a bit of rest.

NATALYA PETROVNA Oh, very well. (*She tries to rise, but cannot*)

ISLAYEV (*Helping her*) There, you see! (*She leans on his arm*) Do you want me to see you to your room?

NATALYA PETROVNA Oh, I am not yet so weak as that! Come on, Vera! (*She goes towards the study.* RAKITIN *comes in from the hall.* NATALYA PETROVNA *stops*)

RAKITIN I have come, Natalya Petrovna—

ISLAYEV (*Interrupting him*) Ah, Michel, come here! (*Leading him aside. In a low voice, with vexation*) Why did you tell her everything right away? You know I asked you not to, I think! What was the use of hurrying? . . . I found her here in such agitation.

RAKITIN (*With amazement*) I don't understand you.

ISLAYEV You have told Natasha that you are going away.

RAKITIN Then you suppose that this was what caused her agitation?

ISLAYEV Shh!— She is looking at us. (*Aloud*) Aren't you going to your room, Natasha?

NATALYA PETROVNA Yes. . . . I am going.

RAKITIN Good-by, Natalya Petrovna! (NATALYA PETROVNA *takes hold of the door knob and makes no reply*)

ISLAYEV (*Putting his hand on* RAKITIN's *shoulder*) Natasha does not know that this is one of the best men. . . .

NATALYA PETROVNA (*With a sudden burst of emotion*) Yes, I know he is a splendid man. All of you are splendid men . . . all of you . . . all of you . . . and yet— (*She suddenly covers her face with her hands, pushes the door with her knee, and quickly goes out.* VERA *follows her.* ISLAYEV *sits down silently at the table and rests his head on his hands*)

RAKITIN (*After looking at him for some time, shrugging his shoulders with a bitter smile: to himself*) What a position I am in! Splendid, I must say! Really, it is quite refreshing. And what a farewell after four years of love! It's fine, very fine; serves the chatterbox right. But, thank God, it's all for the best. It was time to stop these morbid, these feverish relations. (*Aloud to* ISLAYEV) Well, Arkady, good-by!

ISLAYEV (*Raising his head. He has tears in his eyes*) Good-by, my friend—but 560 this . . . isn't very easy. I didn't expect this, friend. It was like a thunderstorm on a clear day. Well, things will come out all right. And all the same, thank you, thank you! You are a true friend!

RAKITIN (*To himself*) This is too much. (*Abruptly*) Good-by.
(*He is about to go into the hall.* SHPIGELSKY *comes running in and meets him*) 565

SHPIGELSKY What's this? They told me that Natalya Petrovna was not feeling well.

ISLAYEV (*Rising*) Who told you?

SHPIGELSKY The girl . . . the chambermaid.

ISLAYEV No, it's of no importance, doctor. I think you'd better not trouble 570 Natasha now.

SHPIGELSKY Very well! (*To* RAKITIN) They say that you are going to town.

RAKITIN Yes, on business.

SHPIGELSKY Oh, on business!
(*At that moment there burst in together from the hall* ANNA SEMENOVNA, 575 LIZAVETA BOGDANOVNA, KOLYA, *and* SCHAAF)

ANNA SEMENOVNA What's this? What's all this? What's the matter with Natasha?

KOLYA What's the matter with mamma? What's the matter with her?

ISLAYEV Nothing is the matter with her. . . . I saw her a moment ago. 580 What's the matter with you?

ANNA SEMENOVNA But really, Arkasha, we've been told that Natasha was not feeling well.

ISLAYEV And you were quite wrong in believing it.

ANNA SEMENOVNA Why are you getting so excited, Askasha? Our sympathy 585 is perfectly natural.

ISLAYEV Of course! . . . Of course!

RAKITIN However, it is time for me to be going.

ANNA SEMENOVNA Are you leaving?

RAKITIN Yes, I am leaving.   590

ANNA SEMENOVNA (*To herself*) Ah! Well, now I understand.

KOLYA (*To* ISLAYEV) Papa.

ISLAYEV What do you want?

KOLYA Why has Alexey Nikolayevich gone off?

ISLAYEV Gone off where?   595

KOLYA I don't know. . . . He kissed me, put on his cap, and walked off. . . . And now it's the time for our Russian lesson.

ISLAYEV Probably he will come back right away. . . . However, we can send for him.

RAKITIN (*In a low voice*) Don't send for him, Arkady; he won't come back. 600
(ANNA SEMENOVNA *tries to hear what is being said.* SHPIGELSKY *whispers with* LIZAVETA BOGDANOVNA)

ISLAYEV What does this mean?

RAKITIN He is leaving also.

ISLAYEV Leaving? Where is he going?

RAKITIN To Moscow.

ISLAYEV What? To Moscow? Well, are all of you going crazy to-day?

RAKITIN (*In a still lower voice*) Between us two . . . Verochka fell in love with him. . . . Well, as an honorable man, he decided to withdraw. (ISLAYEV, *spreading out his hands, drops into a chair*) Why . . . you understand now. 610

ISLAYEV I? I don't understand anything. My head is in a whirl. This is all beyond anybody's understanding. Everybody is flying away helter-skelter, like partridges, and all because they are honorable men. . . . And all this, all of a sudden, on one and the same day.

ANNA SEMENOVNA (*Coming up to him from one side*) But what's this? Mr. 615 Belyayev, you say . . .

ISLAYEV (*Shouting nervously*) That's all right, mother, that's all right! Mr. Schaaf, will you please take care of Kolya now instead of Mr. Belyayev. Will you kindly take him away!

SCHAAF Very well. (*Takes* KOLYA *by the hand*) 620

KOLYA But, papa—

ISLAYEV (*Shouting*) Go away, go away! (SCHAAF *leads* KOLYA *away*) I'll see you off, Rakitin. . . . I'll order my horse saddled, and I'll wait for you at the dam. . . . And you, mamma, for the present, for God's sake, don't trouble Natasha —nor you either, doctor! . . . Matvey, Matvey (*He goes out hastily.* ANNA 625 SEMENOVNA *sits down with an air of grief and dignity.* LIZAVETA BOGDAN-OVNA *takes her stand behind her.* ANNA SEMENOVNA *raises her eyes to Heaven as if desirous of withdrawing from everything that is happening around her*)

SHPIGELSKY (*Stealthily and craftily to* RAKITIN) Well, Mikhaylo Alexandrovich, won't you permit me to take you to the highway with my new team of 630 three?

RAKITIN Ah! . . . Have you already got your horses?

SHPIGELSKY (*Modestly*) I have had a talk with Vera Alexandrovna. . . . Then you will permit me?

RAKITIN Very well! (*He bows to* ANNA SEMENOVNA) Anna Semenovna, I have 635 the honor. . . .

ANNA SEMENOVNA (*As majestically as ever, without rising*) Good-by, Mikhaylo Alexandrovich. . . . I wish you a happy journey.

RAKITIN Thank you humbly. Good-by, Lizaveta Bogdanovna.

(*He bows to her, and she curtsies in reply. He goes out into the hall*) 640

SHPIGELSKY (*Taking* ANNA SEMENOVNA'S *hand in order to kiss it*) Good-by, madam.

ANNA SEMENOVNA (*With less majesty, but still sternly*) Ah, are you too going away, doctor?

SHPIGELSKY Yes. . . . My patients, you know, need . . . And besides, you see 645 my presence is not required here. (*While bowing, he winks craftily to* LIZAVETA BOGDANOVNA, *who answers him with a smile*) Good-by.

(*He runs out after* RAKITIN)

(ANNA SEMENOVNA *lets him go out, and folding her arms, slowly turns to* LIZAVETA BOGDANOVNA) 650

ANNA SEMENOVNA   What do you think of all this, my dear? Eh?

LIZAVETA BOGDANOVNA (*Sighing*)   I really don't know what to tell you, Anna Semenovna.

ANNA SEMENOVNA   Have you heard? Belyayev also is leaving.

LIZAVETA BOGDANOVNA (*Sighing once more*)   Oh, Anna Semenovna, perhaps 655 I, too, shall not be staying here for very long. . . . I am going away too.

(ANNA SEMENOVNA *looks at her with inexpressible amazement.* LIZAVETA BOGDANOVNA *stands before her without raising her eyes*)

0   1   2   3   4   5   6   7   8   9   0